UN

Understanding POETRY

Third Edition

BY

CLEANTH BROOKS, 1906- ed.

Yale University

ROBERT PENN WARREN

Holt, Rinehart and Winston

New York · Chicago · San Francisco

Toronto

Library of Congress Catalog Card Number: 60-10578
ISBN 0-03-007495-9
Printed in the United States of America
345 065 1918171615

COPYRIGHT ACKNOWLEDGMENTS

Brandt & Brandt
for E. E. Cummings, "Portrait" and "the season 'tis, my lovely lambs" from *Collected Poems,* published by Harcourt, Brace & Company, Inc. Copyright 1926 by Horace Liveright.

Chatto and Windus
for Canadian rights for Richard Eberhart, "The Fury of Aerial Bombardment" from *Burr Oaks* and "The Groundhog" from *Reading the Spirit.*
for an extract from *Vulgarity in Literature* by Aldous Huxley, by permission of Chatto and Windus and the author.

The Clarendon Press, Oxford, England
for Robert Bridges, "Low Barometer" from *New Verse* and "Nightingales" from *The Shorter Poems by Robert Bridges* (1931). By permission of The Clarendon Press, Oxford.

The Cresset Press Ltd
for Ruth Pitter, "Rainy Summer" from *The Bridge* by Ruth Pitter.

Dell Publishing Co., Inc.
for Elizabeth Drew, *Poetry: A Modern Guide to Its Understanding and Enjoyment,* pp. 75-76, 123. Copyright 1959 by Elizabeth Drew.

J. M. Dent & Sons Ltd
for rights, exclusive of U.S., for Dylan Thomas, "A Refusal to Mourn the Death, by Fire, of a Child in London" from *The Collected Poems of Dylan Thomas,* copyright 1952, 1953.

The Dial Press, Inc.
for Randall Jarrell, "The Death of the Ball Turret Gunner" and "Losses." Reprinted from *Little Friend, Little Friend* by Randall Jarrell by permission of The Dial Press, Inc. Copyright 1945 by The Dial Press, Inc.

Doubleday & Company, Inc.
for Joyce Kilmer, "Trees" from *Trees and Other Poems* by Joyce Kilmer, copyright 1914 by Doubleday, Doran & Co., Inc.
for Rudyard Kipling, "Danny Deever" from *Departmental Ditties and Ballads and Barrack Room Ballads.* Reprinted by permission of Mrs. George Bambridge and Doubleday & Company, Inc.
for Theodore Roethke, "I Knew a Woman" from *Words for the Wind,* copyright 1954 by Theodore Roethke. For "The Visitant" from *The Waking,* copyright 1950 by Theodore Roethke. Reprinted by permission of Doubleday & Company, Inc.

Faber and Faber Limited
for Canadian rights for W. H. Auden, "As I Walked Out One Evening," "Doom Is Dark," "In Memory of W. B. Yeats," "Lay Your Sleeping Head,

My Love," and "O Where Are You Going?" from *Collected Poems* of W. H. Auden.

for Canadian rights for T. S. Eliot, "Journey of the Magi," "The Love Song of J. Alfred Prufrock," "Preludes," and "The Waste Land" from *Collected Poems* of T. S. Eliot.

for Canadian rights for William Empson, "Just a Smack at Auden" from *The Gathering Storm.*

for English rights for Marianne Moore, "A Grave," from *Collected Poems* of Marianne Moore.

for English rights for Ezra Pound, "Hugh Selwyn Mauberley, I–V" from *Personae* by Ezra Pound.

Funk & Wagnalls Company

for Léonie Adams, "Grapes Making" from *Poems: A Selection* by Léonie Adams. Reprinted by permission of the publishers, Funk & Wagnalls, N. Y.

Robert Graves

for Robert Graves, "To Juan at the Winter Solstice" from *Collected Poems* published by Doubleday & Company, Inc. and Cassell & Co. Ltd., © 1955 by Robert Graves.

Robert Graves and Laura Riding

for a passage from Robert Graves and Laura Riding, *A Pamphlet Against Anthologies,* published by A. P. Watt & Son and used with permission of the authors.

Thom Gunn

for Thom Gunn, "On the Move" from *The Sense of Movement,* published by The University of Chicago Press. Copyright 1959.

Harcourt, Brace and Company, Inc.

for E. E. Cummings, "My Father Moved through Dooms of Love," copyright 1940 by E. E. Cummings. Reprinted from *Poems 1923–1954* by E. E. Cummings by permission of Harcourt, Brace and Company, Inc.

for T. S. Eliot, "Journey of the Magi," "The Love Song of J. Alfred Prufrock," "Preludes," "The Waste Land," and *Notes on* "The Waste Land" from *Collected Poems 1909–1935* by T. S. Eliot, copyright 1936 by Harcourt, Brace and Company.

for William Empson, "Just a Smack at Auden" from *Collected Poems,* copyright 1935, 1940, 1949 by William Empson. Reprinted by permission of Harcourt, Brace and Company, Inc.

for Robert Lowell, "As a Plane Tree by the Water" and "The Quaker Graveyard in Nantucket" from *Lord Weary's Castle,* copyright 1944, 1946 by Robert Lowell. Reprinted by permission of Harcourt, Brace and Company, Inc.

for Karl Shapiro, "The Leg" from *V-Letter and Other Poems* by Karl Shapiro. Reprinted by permission of Harcourt, Brace and Company, Inc.

Holt, Rinehart and Winston, Inc.

for Walter de la Mare, "Voices" from *Collected Poems, 1901–1918,* by Walter de la Mare. Copyright, 1920, by Henry Holt and Company, Inc. Copyright, 1948, by Walter de la Mare. For "The Miracle" from *Collected Poems* by Walter de la Mare. Copyright, 1940, by Walter de la Mare. Used by permission of Henry Holt and Company, Inc.

for Robert Frost, "After Apple-Picking," "Birches," "Come In," "Desert Places," "Dust of Snow," "Mowing," "Out, Out," "Stopping by Woods on a

Snowy Evening," and "Two Tramps in Mud Time" from *Complete Poems of Robert Frost, 1949* by Robert Frost. Copyright, 1916, 1923, 1949, by Henry Holt and Company, Inc. Copyright, 1936, 1942, 1943, by Robert Frost.

for A. E. Housman, "Epitaph on an Army of Mercenaries" and "Hell Gate" from *Last Poems* by A. E. Housman, copyright, 1922, by Henry Holt and Company, Inc., copyright, 1950, by Barclay's Bank of London. Used by permission of Henry Holt and Company, Inc. For "1887," "Farewell to Barn and Stack and Tree," "I Hoed and Trenched and Weeded," "The Immortal Part," and "To an Athlete Dying Young" from *A Shropshire Lad* by A. E. Housman. Reprinted by permission of Henry Holt and Company, Inc.

for a passage from *Poems for Study* by Leonard Unger and William Van O'Connor, published by Rinehart & Company, Inc.

Houghton Mifflin Company

for John Betjeman, "The Cottage Hospital" from *Collected Poems.*

for Elizabeth Bishop, "Little Exercise" from *Poems: North and South.*

for Hilda Doolittle, "Heat" and "Pear Tree" from *Sea Garden,* published in 1916.

for Archibald MacLeish, "Frescoes for Mr. Rockefeller's City" from *Poems, 1924–1933;* copyright 1924, 1926, 1928, 1932, 1933, by Archibald MacLeish.

Randall Jarrell

for Randall Jarrell, "The Woman at the Washington Zoo." By permission of the author.

Alfred A. Knopf, Inc.

for William Meredith, "The Open Sea" from *The Open Sea* by William Meredith, by permission of Alfred A. Knopf, Inc. Copyright 1953, 1957 by William Meredith.

for John Crowe Ransom, "Bells for John Whiteside's Daughter" and "Winter Remembered" from *Selected Poems* by John Crowe Ransom, by permission of Alfred A. Knopf, Inc. Copyright 1924, 1927, 1945, by Alfred A. Knopf, Inc.

for W. D. Snodgrass, "Ten Days Leave" from *Heart's Needle* by W. D. Snodgrass, by permission of Alfred A. Knopf, Inc. Copyright 1956, 1959 by William Snodgrass.

for Wallace Stevens, "Peter Quince at the Clavier" from *Harmonium* by Wallace Stevens, by permission of Alfred A. Knopf, Inc. Copyright 1923, 1941, by Alfred A. Knopf, Inc.

Estate of the late Frieda Lawrence

for rights other than U. S. and Canadian for D. H. Lawrence, "Bavarian Gentians" from *The Complete Poems of D. H. Lawrence,* published in England by William Heinemann Ltd.

Little, Brown and Company

for Emily Dickinson, "After Great Pain a Formal Feeling Comes," "Because I Could Not Stop for Death," and "The Soul Selects" from *The Poems of Emily Dickinson,* Centenary Edition, edited by Martha Dickinson Bianchi and Alfred Leete Hampson. Reprinted by permission of Little, Brown & Co.

for Ogden Nash, "Kind of an Ode to Duty," from *The Face Is Familiar,* copyright 1938, by Ogden Nash, by permission of Little, Brown & Co.

Liveright Publishing Corporation

for Hart Crane, "At Melville's Tomb," "Praise for an Urn," "Voyages,

II," and "Voyages, VI" from *The Collected Poems of Hart Crane* by Hart Crane, published by Liveright Publishing Corp., New York. Copyright 1933, Liveright, Inc.

Longmans, Green & Co., Inc.
for a passage from F. W. Bateson, *English Poetry: A Critical Introduction,* copyright 1950.

Macmillan & Co., Ltd., London
for Canadian rights for Thomas Hardy, "Channel Firing," "The Going," "In Tenebris, I," "The Man He Killed," and "Wessex Heights," from *Collected Poems* of Thomas Hardy. By permission of the Trustees of the Hardy Estate and Macmillan & Co., Ltd., publishers.
for Canadian rights for James Stephens, "The Goat Paths" and "The Main-Deep" from *Collected Poems of James Stephens.* By permission of the author and Macmillan & Co., Ltd., publishers.

The Macmillan Company
for Thomas Hardy, "Channel Firing," "The Going," "In Tenebris, I," "The Man He Killed," and "Wessex Heights" from Thomas Hardy *Collected Poems.* Copyright 1925 by The Macmillan Company and used with their permission.
for Marianne Moore, "In Distrust of Merits" from Marianne Moore *Nevertheless.* Copyright 1944 by Marianne Moore and used with the permission of The Macmillan Company. For "The Grave" from *Collected Poems.*
for Edwin Arlington Robinson, "Mr. Flood's Party" from Edwin Arlington Robinson *Avon's Harvest.* Copyright 1921, 1949, by Edwin Arlington Robinson and used with the permission of The Macmillan Company.
for James Stephens, "The Goat Paths" from James Stephens *Songs from Clay.* Copyright 1915, 1943, by The Macmillan Company, and used with their permission. And for "The Main-Deep" from *Poetry Recital* by James Stephens. Copyright 1925 by The Macmillan Company and used with their permission.
for William Butler Yeats, "After Long Silence" from William Butler Yeats *Winding Stair.* Copyright 1933 by The Macmillan Company and used with their permission. For "Among School Children," "Sailing to Byzantium," and "Two Songs from a Play," from William Butler Yeats *The Tower.* Copyright 1928 by The Macmillan Company and used with their permission. For "A Deep-Sworn Vow" and "Upon a Dying Lady" from William Butler Yeats *Wild Swans at Coole.* Copyright 1917 by Margaret C. Anderson, 1919, 1946 by The Macmillan Company and used with their permission. And for "The Second Coming" from William Butler Yeats *Michael Robartes and Dancer.* Copyright 1924 by The Macmillan Company and used with their permission. Passage from *A Vision.* Copyright 1938 by W. B. Yeats and used with the permission of The Macmillan Company.

The Marvell Press
for Philip Larkin, "Church Going," reprinted from *The Less Deceived* by permission of The Marvell Press, Hessle, Yorkshire, England.

John Murray
for Canadian and world rights other than U. S. for John Betjeman, "The Cottage Hospital" from *Collected Poems.*

New Directions
for Ezra Pound, "Envoi (1919)" and "Hugh Selwyn Mauberley I–V" from *Personae,* copyright 1926 by Ezra Pound For lines from "Canto LXXXI"

from *The Cantos,* copyright 1948 by Ezra Pound; and for "In a Station in the Metro." Reprinted by permission of New Directions.

for Delmore Schwartz, "The Heavy Bear Who Goes with Me" from *In Dreams Begin Responsibilities,* copyright 1938 by New Directions and reprinted with their permission.

for Dylan Thomas, "The Force That through the Green Fuse" and "A Refusal to Mourn the Death, by Fire, of a Child in London" from *The Collected Poems of Dylan Thomas,* copyright 1952, 1953 by Dylan Thomas. Reprinted by permission of New Directions.

for Vernon Watkins, "The Heron" from *The Death Bell.* All rights reserved. Reprinted by permission of New Directions.

for William Carlos Williams, "Poem" from *The Complete Collected Poems of William Carlos Williams,* copyright 1938 by New Directions. For "Red Wheelbarrow" from *The Collected Earlier Poems of William Carlos Williams,* copyright 1938, 1951 by William Carlos Williams. Reprinted by permission of New Directions.

for Yvor Winters, "A Summer Commentary" from *The Giant Weapon,* copyright 1943 by New Directions and reprinted with their permission.

The New Yorker

for Richard Wilbur, "Two Voices in a Meadow" from *The New Yorker,* August 17, 1957. Copyright © 1957 The New Yorker Magazine, Inc. Oxford University Press, Inc., New York

for Richard Eberhart, "The Fury of Aerial Bombardment" from *Burr Oaks* by Richard Eberhart, and for "The Groundhog" from *Reading the Spirit* by Richard Eberhart. Reprinted by permission of Oxford University Press, Inc.

for Gerard Manley Hopkins, "Binsey Poplars" from *Poems of Gerard Manley Hopkins.* Third edition edited by W. H. Gardner. Copyright 1948 by Oxford University Press, Inc. Reprinted by permission.

Poetry: A Magazine of Verse

for extracts from the correspondence of Harriet Monroe and Hart Crane.

Ezra Pound

for world rights exclusive of U. S. and Canadian for Ezra Pound, "Hugh Selwyn Mauberley, I–V" from *Personae,* published by Faber & Faber. For a passage from *Gaudier-Brzeska,* copyright 1935 by Ezra Pound.

PMLA and the authors

for a passage from William K. Wimsatt, Jr., and Monroe C. Beardsley, "The Concept of Meter" in *PMLA,* December 1959, p. 598.

Random House, Inc.

for W. H. Auden, "As I Walked Out One Evening" from *Another Time* by W. H. Auden. Copyright, 1940, by W. H. Auden. Reprinted by permission of Random House, Inc. For "Doom Is Dark." Reprinted by permission of Random House, Inc. For "In Memory of W. B. Yeats," "Lay Your Sleeping Head, My Love," and "O Where Are You Going?" from *Collected Poetry of W. H. Auden.* Copyright, 1945, by W. H. Auden. Reprinted by permission of Random House, Inc.

for Robert Graves, "Rocky Acres." Reprinted by permission of Random House, Inc.

for Robinson Jeffers, "Shine, Perishing Republic" from *Roan Stallion* by Robinson Jeffers. Copyright, 1925, by Boni & Liveright; copyright, 1935, by Modern Library. Reprinted by permission of Random House, Inc.

Russell & Volkening, Inc.
for world rights exclusive of U. S. and British Empire for Theodore Roethke, "I Knew a Woman" and "The Visitant."

Charles Scribner's Sons
for John Peale Bishop, "The Return" and "Twelfth Night." Reprinted from *The Collected Poems of John Peale Bishop;* copyright 1917 by Sherman, French & Company, 1922 by John Peale Bishop, 1948 by Charles Scribner's Sons; used by permission of the publishers, Charles Scribner's Sons.
for Donald Davidson, "Lee in the Mountains," copyright 1926 by the Poetry Society of South Carolina, 1938 by Donald Davidson; from *Lee in the Mountains and Other Poems* (1949) by Donald Davidson. Reprinted by permission of the publishers, Charles Scribner's Sons.
for Edwin Arlington Robinson, "Luke Havergal." Reprinted from *The Children of the Night* by Edwin Arlington Robinson; published by Charles Scribner's Sons.
for Allen Tate, "The Last Days of Alice" and "Ode to the Confederate Dead." Reprinted from *Poems 1922–1947* by Allen Tate; copyright 1932, 1948, by Charles Scribner's Sons; used by permission of the publishers, Charles Scribner's Sons.

Martin Secker & Warburg Ltd
for British rights for Theodore Roethke, "I Knew a Woman" from *Words for the Wind,* copyright 1954 by Theodore Roethke, and "The Visitant" from *The Waking,* copyright 1950 by Theodore Roethke.

Karl Shapiro
for permission, with *The Nation,* to reprint "The Minute."

Simon and Schuster, Inc.
for Max Eastman, *Heroes I Have Known,* p. 177. Reprinted from *Heroes I Have Known* by permission of Simon and Schuster, publishers. Copyright, 1942, by Max Eastman.

Dame Edith Sitwell
for a passage from "Dylan Thomas" from *The Atlantic Monthly,* vol. 193, February, 1954.

William Sloane Associates, Inc.
for a passage from Richard Chase, *Emily Dickinson,* pp. 249–251. Copyright 1951 by William Sloane Associates, Inc.

The Society of Authors, London
for Canadian rights for A. E. Housman, "1887," "Epitaph on an Army of Mercenaries," "Farewell to Barn and Stack and Tree," "Hell Gate," "I Hoed and Trenched and Weeded," "The Immortal Part," and "To an Athlete Dying Young." By permission of the Society of Authors as the Literary Representative of the Trustees of the Estate of the late A. E. Housman, with reference to Jonathan Cape, Ltd., and Henry Holt and Company as British and United States publishers of A. E. Housman *Collected Poems.*

Alan Swallow, Publisher
for a passage from Allen Tate, *Collected Essays,* copyright 1959, published by Alan Swallow.

Helen (Mrs. Edward) Thomas
for permission to include Edward Thomas, "The Gallows," "The Owl," and "When First I Came Here."

The Viking Press, Inc.
for Donald Hall, "Christmas Eve in Whitneyville, 1955" from *The Dark Houses* by Donald Hall. Copyright © 1958 by Donald Hall. Reprinted by permission of The Viking Press, Inc. and the authors.
for D. H. Lawrence, "Piano" from *The Portable D. H. Lawrence.* Copyright 1929 by Jonathan Cape and Harrison Smith, Inc. For "Bavarian Gentians" from *Last Poems* by D. H. Lawrence. Copyright 1933 by Frieda Lawrence. Reprinted by permission of The Viking Press, Inc.

A. P. Watt & Son
for Canadian rights for Robert Graves, "Rocky Acres" from *Collected Poems 1914–47,* with the permission of Mr. Graves and Cassell and Company.
for world rights exclusive of U. S. for Rudyard Kipling, "Danny Deever."
for Canadian rights for William Butler Yeats, "After Long Silence," "Among School Children," "A Deep-Sworn Vow," "Sailing to Byzantium," "The Second Coming," "Two Songs from a Play," and "Upon a Dying Lady." By permission of A. P. Watt & Son together with The Macmillan Company of Canada and Mrs. W. B. Yeats.

Wesleyan University Press
for James Wright, "At the Slackening of the Tide." Copyright © 1959 by James Wright. Reprinted from *Saint Judas,* by James Wright, by permission of Wesleyan University Press, publisher.
for Donald Justice, "Counting the Mad." Copyright © 1957 by Donald Justice. Reprinted from *The Summer Anniversaries,* by Donald Justice, by permission of Wesleyan University Press.

Yale University Press
for a passage from Florence Marsh, *Wordsworth's Imagery,* pp. 55–56. Copyright 1952.

To William A. Read

Preface

Poetry gives us knowledge. It is a knowledge of ourselves in relation to the world of experience, and to that world considered, not statistically, but in terms of human purposes and values. Experience considered in terms of human purpose and values is dramatic—dramatic in that it is concrete, in that it involves a process, and in that it embodies the human effort to arrive—through conflict—at meaning. We know that to conceive of poetry as knowledge is not the only possible way of conceiving it. It is, however, our basic assumption, clung to for many years, and it would be disingenuous not to state it as the assumption behind this book.

Because poetry—like all the arts—involves this kind of experiential knowledge, we miss the value of poetry if we think of its characteristic knowledge as consisting of "messages," statements, snippets of doctrine. The knowledge that poetry yields is available to us only if we submit ourselves to the massive, and subtle, impact of the poem as a whole. We have access to this special kind of knowledge only by participating in the drama of the poem, apprehending the form of the poem. What in this context do we mean by form? To create a form is to find a way to contemplate, and perhaps to comprehend, our human urgencies. Form is the recognition of fate made joyful, because made comprehensible.

Because the special knowledge that poetry gives reaches us only through form, we believe that the study of poetry should be inductive and concrete. We believe that one should observe as carefully as possible the elements of poetry—the human events, the images, the rhythms, the statements; and then that he should surrender as fully as possible to the impact of the whole, recognizing that the whole is greater than, and different from, the parts.

Form, of course, does not exist in a vacuum. It is not an abstraction. In thinking of form we should keep in mind the following matters that relate to its context:

1. Poems are written by human beings and the form of a poem is an individual's attempt to deal with a specific problem, poetic and personal.

2. Poems come out of a historical moment, and since they are written in language, the form is tied to a whole cultural context.

3. Poems are read by human beings, which means that the reader, unlike a robot, must be able to recognize the dramatic implications of the form. In earlier editions of this book we assumed, perhaps too confidently, that these provisos were clearly implicit in our thinking. If, in this revision, we spell them out, that can do no harm.

An attempt to realize more fully the foregoing principles has governed the present revision of *Understanding Poetry*. Specifically, our revision can be described under the following heads:

1. We have rewritten and greatly expanded the introductions to the several sections. Though not abandoning the inductive method, we have come to feel that the student needs a little more theoretical grounding before getting into the interpretation of individual poems.

2. We have dropped a number of the discussions printed in the previous edition. We have rewritten and tried to sharpen those discussions that we have retained.

3. We have added several new discussions. These bear upon poems that we consider specially significant or pedagogically useful.

4. We have elaborately overhauled and greatly expanded the exercises, recognizing that the kind of questions put to the student on individual poems is perhaps the most important part of the teaching process. Through these revised exercises, we feel that we have done much to coordinate various topics and to give the book a unified progression.

5. We have provided a better representation of certain periods of English and American poetry.

6. We have dropped two appendices ("Ambiguity, Added Dimension, and Submerged Metaphor" and "The Poem Viewed in Wider Perspective") and absorbed much of their material into the exercises and discussions.

7. We have revised and added new material to the section "How Poems Come About: Intention and Meaning."

8. Section VII, "Poems for Study," has become a rather full anthology of modern poetry. Though not intended to provide a systematic survey, the poems are not selected at random, but have been chosen with the idea of illustrating various methods and topics in planned but unlabeled clusters, an arrangement that makes for ready comparisons and contrasts on the basis of theme or style.

C.B.
R.P.W.

January 24, 1960

Contents

[Asterisks indicate poems that are analyzed]

Introduction

I. Narrative Poems

II. Descriptive Poems

III. Metrics

IV. Tone

V. Imagery

VI. Theme: Statement and Idea

VII. Poems for Study

Introduction

Wordsworth called the poet a man speaking to men. Poetry is a form of speech, written or spoken. To the person who is not well acquainted with poetry, the differences between poetic speech and other forms may seem to be more important than the similarities, but these differences should not be allowed to obscure the fundamental resemblances, for only by an understanding of the resemblances can one appreciate the meaning of the differences. In poetry, as in all other discourse, one person is saying something to another person. But what is that "something"? We usually identify it with information. As practical people going about our affairs, we ask directions, read road signs, order a dinner from a menu, study football scores or stock-market reports. It is altogether natural, therefore, that we should tend to think the important and central matter in all discourse to be information. But, after all, we may do well to ask how much of the discourse of an average man in any given day is primarily concerned with information for the sake of information. After he has transacted his business, obeyed his road signs, ordered and eaten his dinner, and read the stock-market reports, he might be surprised to reflect on the number of nonpractical functions speech had fulfilled for him that day. He had told the office boy a joke; he had commented on the weather to the traffic officer, who could observe the weather as well as he; he had told an old friend that he was glad to see him again; he had chatted with his wife on some subject on which there was already full knowledge and agreement.

Even when he had been at lunch with some business associates, with whom the talk ran on informational topics, the trend in the stock market, for instance, he had not intended to use the information for buying or selling. The interest in the conversation had not been finally practical. This practical man might discover that a large part of the business of discourse had been concerned not with matters which are ordinarily thought of as really "practical," but with his relations to other people—that is, with such elusive matters as feelings and attitudes.

Moreover, even when a man is using speech for the purpose of conveying information, it may prove surprising to see how little of such discourse is pure information, and how difficult it is to make speech deal only with pure and exact information. Almost always a speaker conveys not only the pure information but an attitude toward and a feeling about that information. For example, let us consider the case of a motorist who stops a man driving a hay wagon to ask about the condition of the road ahead. The man on the wagon says, "It's a tolerable good road, you won't have no trouble on it." The motorist drives on, encouraged. But after a mile or so, having experienced a few substantial jolts, he hails another motorist and asks the same question. This man says, "It's a devil of a road, it'll jerk your teeth out." Both the man on the hay wagon and the man in the second automobile think that they are telling the truth. Both intend to be helpful and to give exact information. And both feel that they know the road. But each man's language reflects his own experience with the road. For the man on the hay wagon the road *was* tolerably good, but for the second motorist, anxious to make time on his trip, the road was devilishly bad.

If this seems to be a fairly obvious example of confusion about information in ordinary speech, let us consider an example in which a trained scholar is trying to make an exact statement.

> For sentimental pacifism is, after all, but a return to the method of the jungle. It is in the jungle that emotionalism alone determines conduct, and wherever that is true no

> other than the law of the jungle is possible. For the emotion of hate is sure sooner or later to follow on the emotion of love, and then there is a spring for the throat. It is altogether obvious that the only quality which really distinguishes man from the brutes is his reason.*

The author of this statement is Robert Andrews Millikan, the internationally famous physicist and winner of the Nobel Prize. He is making a plea for the scientific attitude in political and international affairs, but when one inspects this statement carefully one finds that it is not "scientific." Some of the propositions asserted cannot be proved by Mr. Millikan, or by anyone else, in the same way that one can prove certain formulae of physics in the laboratory. The comparisons concerning the jungle and the leap of one infuriated beast at the throat of another represent the sort of comparison one finds in poetry; for the comparisons are not based on scientific analogy—the resemblance is prompted by the emotional attitude of the speaker and is calculated to incite a corresponding attitude in the reader. But the coloring of the general statement—that is, the bringing in of an implied interpretation of the statement—extends beyond the mere use of a "poetic" comparison. In the first sentence, for example, the word *pacifism* is qualified by the word *sentimental.* Presumably it is a particular sort of pacifism here defined to which Mr. Millikan's objections apply; but does the adjective *sentimental* really set off a "bad kind of pacifism" from a good kind? Could the reader determine from Mr. Millikan's statement whether or not he would consider the pacifism of Jesus Christ, the Prince of Peace, a sentimental or a nonsentimental sort? Since the only kind of pacifism that Mr. Millikan sets over against his sentimental pacifism is a scientific pacifism operating through an organization of sociologists and economists, one might conceivably assume that Jesus Christ would fall into the former classification. Or, to state the matter otherwise: is the basic argument for peace to be found in the fact that war is unprofitable or is horrible, or in the belief that it is wrong to kill one's fellow man? As a matter of fact, the adjective *sentimental* is, on logical grounds, a bogus qualification: its real function is

* "Science and Modern Life," *The Atlantic Monthly,* April, 1928.

to set up an attitude in the reader that will forbid his inspection of the basis of the statement.

Whether or not the general statement is logically sound, Mr. Millikan has not stated it with scientific precision; in Mr. Millikan's defense it may be said that *the proposition is one that cannot be stated with scientific precision by anyone.* Mr. Millikan, a scientist trying to state the virtues of a scientific method in human relationships, is forced to resort to devices which we associate with poetry. We should never find him coloring a mathematical formula by referring to a "sentimental figure four," or describing a well-known chemical reaction by saying that two ferocious atoms of hydrogen spring at the throat of one defenseless atom of oxygen.

LIMITATIONS OF SCIENTIFIC STATEMENT

The advantages of a scientific statement are not to be had without the limitations of a scientific statement also. The primary advantage of the scientific statement is that of absolute precision. But we must remember that such precision is possible only in relation to certain materials and can be gained only by using terms in special and previously defined senses. The scientist carefully cuts away from his technical terms all associations, emotional colorings, and implications of attitude and judgment. Science tends, indeed, toward the condition of mathematics, and the really exact scientific statements can be expressed in mathematical formulae. The chemist describes water as H_2O—two atoms of hydrogen and one atom of oxygen. The formula, H_2O, differs tremendously from even the common word *water,* for the word *water,* neutral as it seems in connotation, still may possess all sorts of different associations—drinking, bathing, boating, the pull of the moon to create tides, the liquid from which the goddess Aphrodite rose, or, as Keats put it,

> The moving waters at their priestlike task
> Of pure ablution round earth's human shores.

As with the liquid itself, so with the word: the scientist needs a distilled product.

The language of science represents an extreme degree of specialization of language in the direction of a certain kind of precision. It is unnecessary, of course, to point out that in this specialization tremendous advantages inhere, and that the man of the twentieth century is rightly proud of this achievement. But it is more often necessary to point out that scientific precision can be brought to bear only on certain kinds of materials. *Literature in general—poetry in particular—also represents a specialization of language for the purpose of precision;* but it aims at treating kinds of materials different from those of science.

We have already seen that science has to forego, because of its method, matters of attitude and interpretation; or that, when it does not forego them, it is so much the less science.* For better or worse, certain kinds of communication are not amenable to scientific statement. To return to the question raised at the beginning of this discussion, what is the "something" which is conveyed by speech? We have already seen that it is not exclusively information in the ordinary sense, and even less exclusively information in the scientific sense. The speech of that ordinary citizen in an ordinary day conveys many things, attitudes, feelings, and interpretations, that fall outside of these restrictions. These things, though they fill a large part of the speech of that ordinary citizen, are never stated very clearly or precisely by him. The specialization of speech which we find in poetry aims at clarity and precision of statement in these matters.

The "something" of most ordinary communication involves feelings, and these feelings are an essential and integral part of the meaning to be conveyed. Usually, a hearer unconsciously bases much of his definition of such pieces of communication, not on the words themselves, but on the gestures, tone of voice, and facial expression of the speaker, and on what he knows about the speaker. For instance, everyone understands how

* We have in mind a typically "pure" science such as modern physics, but we are quite aware of the fact that other sciences have to deal with other kinds of subject matter, a situation that has consequences for their appropriate methods and tests of validity. Our concern here is only to make the contrast between science and poetry as sharply distinct as possible: we are not at all interested in raising the vexed question of whether certain studies of society are "true" sciences.

difficult it is to deal with a delicate personal matter in a letter, for the letter has nothing but words—that is, symbols written on paper and divorced from the tone of the voice, gestures, and facial expression. Poetry, however, undertakes, by its special use of words, to make this "massive" kind of communication.

MATERIALS OF POETRY

By the very nature of the human being, the ordinary citizen in the ordinary day speaks much of what we might call incipient poetry—he attempts to communicate attitudes, feelings, and interpretations, including ideas. And poetry in this sense is not confined to the speech of the ordinary citizen. It appears also in editorials, sermons, political speeches, advertisements, and magazine articles—even if it is usually not recognized as poetry. For instance, the same reader who would regard as mere poetry the Biblical statement

> All they that take the sword shall perish by the sword,

might well regard Mr. Millikan's paragraph on pacifism as a sober and verifiable scientific pronouncement.

Let us now suppose that this person reads an avowed poem:

The Man He Killed

Thomas Hardy [1840–1928]

Had he and I but met
By some old ancient inn,
We should have sat us down to wet
Right many a nipperkin!

But ranged as infantry,
And staring face to face,
I shot at him as he at me,
And killed him in his place.

I shot him dead because—
Because he was my foe,
Just so: my foe of course he was;
That's clear enough; although

He thought he'd 'list, perhaps,
Off-hand like—just as I—
Was out of work—had sold his traps—
No other reason why.

Yes; quaint and curious war is!
You shoot a fellow down
You'd treat if met where any bar is,
Or help to half-a-crown.

He might dismiss this as mere literature, failing to see that Mr. Millikan's paragraph is "mere literature" also—and of course infinitely poorer literature.

Mr. Millikan might or might not have been aware that he was using some of the methods of poetry to color the attitude of his readers and bring them to his own point of view; but any writer of advertising copy is perfectly aware of the fact that he is trying to persuade his readers to adopt a certain attitude. Writers of advertising copy, anxious to sell a product, are not content to rest on a statement of fact, whether such a statement is verifiable or not. They will attempt to associate the attitude toward a certain product with an attitude toward beautiful women, little children, or gray-haired mothers; they will appeal to snobbishness, vanity, patriotism, religion, and morality. In addition to these appeals to the consumer's most basic and powerful feelings, the advertiser often attempts to imply a scientific validity for his claims—a validity which may, or may not, be justified by the product—by pictures of white-robed surgeons and research experts, statements of abstruse scientific formulae, hints of recent discoveries, coy references to the research laboratories of the plant involved, and very frequent use of the phrase "science tells us." Even the man who is quite certain that he cares nothing for "literature" will find that he constantly has to deal with literary appeals and methods while living in the hardheaded, scientific, and practical twentieth century.

POETRY AS A SPECIALIZATION OF ORDINARY SPEECH

It is important to remember that poetry is not a thing separate from ordinary life and that the matters with which poetry deals are matters with which the ordinary person is concerned. More will have to be said about the special characteristics of formal poetry—characteristics which set it off from this "stuff of poetry" appearing in ordinary life; but it is highly important to see that both the impulse and methods of poetry are rooted very deep in human experience, and that formal poetry itself represents, not a distinction from, but a specialization of, thoroughly universal habits of human thinking and feeling.

CONFUSION BETWEEN SCIENTIFIC AND POETIC COMMUNICATION

People are constantly confusing the two sorts of communication. This confusion that causes people to judge formal poetry as if it were science is the source of most of the misunderstandings of poetry and of literature in general. It is highly necessary, if one is to understand poetry, to take up some of the ways in which it is typically misread.

1. "MESSAGE-HUNTING"

"Message-hunting"—the business of looking only for the statement of an idea which the reader thinks he can apply profitably in his own conduct—is one of the most ordinary forms of this general confusion. Here is a poem by Longfellow that has been greatly admired by many people who read poetry in this fashion:

A Psalm of Life

WHAT THE HEART OF THE YOUNG MAN SAID TO THE PSALMIST

Henry Wadsworth Longfellow [1807–1882]

Tell me not, in mournful numbers,
   Life is but an empty dream!—
For the soul is dead that slumbers,
   And things are not what they seem.

Life is real! Life is earnest!
   And the grave is not its goal;

Dust thou art, to dust returnest,
  Was not spoken of the soul.

Not enjoyment, and not sorrow,
  Is our destined end or way;
But to act, that each tomorrow
  Find us farther than today.

Art is long, and Time is fleeting,
  And our hearts, though stout and brave,
Still, like muffled drums, are beating
  Funeral marches to the grave.

In the world's broad field of battle,
  In the bivouac of Life,
Be not like dumb, driven cattle!
  Be a hero in the strife!

Trust no Future, howe'er pleasant!
  Let the dead Past bury its dead!
Act,—act in the living Present!
  Heart within, and God o'erhead!

Lives of great men all remind us
  We can make our lives sublime,
And, departing, leave behind us
  Footprints on the sands of time;

Footprints, that perhaps another,
  Sailing o'er life's solemn main,
A forlorn and shipwrecked brother,
  Seeing, shall take heart again.

Let us, then, be up and doing,
  With a heart for any fate;
Still achieving, still pursuing,
  Learn to labor and to wait.

This poem seems to give a great deal of good advice. It tells the reader not to waste his time but to be up and doing; not to be discouraged by failures but to have a heart for any fate; not to judge life by temporary standards but to look to eternal reward. There are probably few people who would quarrel with the moral value of these statements. But granting that the advice is good advice, we can still ask whether or not the poem is a good poem. If the advice is what the poem has to offer us, then we can ask why a short prose statement of this good advice is not as good as, or even better than, the poem itself. But even the people who say they like the poem because of its "message" will usually prefer the poem to a plain prose statement. If such people would prefer the poem to the prose summary, they would probably also prefer it to certain other versions of the poetic statement. For instance, let us alter one of the stanzas of the poem, taking care in the alteration, however, to preserve the idea. An alteration of the seventh stanza might run

Lives of all sorts of great men remind us
  That we ourselves can make our lives sublime,
And when we die we can leave behind us
  Noble recollections printed on the sands of time.

The fact that any admirer of the poem would unhesitatingly choose the first version proves that "something" aside from the mere value of the idea is involved in the choice.

The fact that we have just an idea is in itself not enough to make a poem, even when the idea may be a worthy one. But another type of misreading may result from the fact that the reader does not happen to agree with an idea expressed in a poem. We may illustrate this distinction by a specific case: is an admirer of Longfellow's poem, even one who says that his admiration is based on the worth of the idea, disqualified from admiring the following poem?

Expostulation and Reply

William Wordsworth [*1770–1850*]

"Why, William, on that old gray stone,
  Thus for the length of half a day,
Why, William, sit you thus alone,
  And dream your time away?"

"Where are your books?—that light bequeathed
  To beings else forlorn and blind!

Up! up! and drink the spirit breathed
From dead men to their kind.

"You look round on your Mother Earth,
As if she for no purpose bore you;
As if you were her first-born birth,
And none had lived before you."

One morning thus, by Esthwaite lake,
When life was sweet, I knew not why,
To me my good friend Matthew spake,
And thus I made reply:

"The eye—it cannot choose but see;
We cannot bid the ear be still;
Our bodies feel, where'er they be,
Against or with our will.

"Nor less I deem that there are Powers
Which of themselves our minds impress;
That we can feed this mind of ours
In a wise passiveness.

"Think you, 'mid all this mighty sum
Of things forever speaking,
That nothing of itself will come,
But we must still be seeking?

"—Then ask not wherefore, here, alone,
Conversing as I may,
I sit upon this old gray stone,
And dream my time away."

This poem seems to give the advice that one should neglect the "light bequeathed" by the great men of the past in favor of what one can learn only for himself; that one should not fritter away his time by being "up and doing" or by being a "hero in the strife"; and that one should learn in contemplation to cultivate that "wise passiveness" by which, only, one comes into harmony with the great powers of the universe. If the admirer of Longfellow's poem means literally what he says when he praises the poem for the "message," then he is absolutely disqualified from enjoying this poem, for its "message" is diametrically opposed to that of "The Psalm of Life." Of course, many people who describe their appreciation of poems in terms of the "messages" do not mean literally what they say; they are simply groping for some ground to justify the fact that they like poetry at all. Since they are accustomed to think of all communication as concerned with practical information, they try to put their liking on some "practical" or "scientific" basis.

As a matter of fact, the place of ideas in poetry and their relation to the goodness of a poem cannot be treated in such an over-simplified manner. We know, for example, that devout Protestants can accept the poetry of the Catholic poet Dante, or that Catholics can accept the poetry of the Protestant poet John Milton. The fact that the Protestant reader who holds his religious beliefs seriously may still accept the poetry of Dante does not mean that the reader regards poetry as merely trivial and unserious. This whole matter is one that cannot be dismissed in a few sentences, but requires for a satisfactory understanding the analysis of many special poems. It will suffice to say here that the "message-hunting" method of reading poetry breaks down even in the simplest cases.

2. "PURE REALIZATION"

Many readers and critics of poetry, realizing the insufficiency of the "message-hunting" approach to poetry, have adopted a view that poetry does not deal with any ideas or truths at all, but is an "expression of pure emotion," or "deals with emotion." This view is sometimes put in other terms, as when one critic says that a poem is the expression of "a moment of pure realization of being"—that is, it attempts merely to bring vividly to the reader some scene or sensation.

When a critic trying to point out the distinguishing marks of poetry says that poetry expresses an emotion or that poetry deals with emotion, exactly what does he mean? Does he mean that a poem about grief, for instance, would "express" the grief a poet might feel, or have felt, in the same way as a burst of tears would express such an emotion? Or does he mean that the reading of a poem about grief would provoke in the reader an emotion of grief in the same way as would a personal bereavement? Quite obviously, the answer to both questions is "No." Certainly, the writing of a poem would be no substitute for the relief of a burst of tears; nor would the response to the reading of a poem be as intense as the experience of a real bereavement. On the mere ground of emotional intensity the poem does not compete with the real experience. The justification of poetry as "pure realization," like its justification on the basis of "message-hunting," breaks down even in simple cases, for the pure realization of an experience is the experience at the moment it occurs. For instance, the taste or the smell of a real apple is always more intense than any poem describing the taste or smell of an apple. The following passage from "Ode to a Nightingale," by John Keats has sometimes been praised as a moment of "pure realization":

> O for a draught of vintage! that hath been
>   Cooled a long age in the deep-delvèd earth,
> Tasting of Flora and the country-green,
>   Dance, and Provençal song, and sunburnt mirth!
> O for a beaker full of the warm South,
>   Full of the true, the blushful Hippocrene,
>   With beaded bubbles winking at the brim,
>   And purple-stainèd mouth. . . .

The stanza is obviously not a substitute for an actual glass of wine: not only does it fail to give the intensity of the sensation of actual wine-drinking but it gives an effect thoroughly different in kind from the experience of drinking a glass of wine. If there is a "pure realization" of anything it is of the poet's thinking about the wine as a thing which represents to him a certain kind of life—a warm, mirthful, carefree, healthy, pagan kind of life, which in the total context of the poem stands in contrast to his own troubled and fretful existence (see "Ode to a Nightingale" and analysis, pp. 426–31). As a matter of fact, when we inspect the passage we discover it is not so much a pictorial description of a beaker of wine, or a description of the sensation of drinking wine, as it is a cluster of associations with the wine—associations which suggest the kind of life we have mentioned. The poet is not saying, actually, that he is thirsty for a drink of wine but that he wants a certain kind of life, the qualities of which he implies.

To conceive of poetry as the "expression of emotion" or as "pure realization" is an attempt to get away from "message-hunting." But in Keats's poem the experience which is "realized" is far different from any mere sensation or emotional reaction. The experience, as we have seen, really involves an interpretation by the poet.

3. "BEAUTIFUL STATEMENT OF SOME HIGH TRUTH"

There is another confused conception of poetry arising from the attempt to combine in a mechanical fashion the two false approaches which have just been discussed. This conception is variously stated. For instance, it may be expressed in a definition of poetry as "fine sentiments in fine language." Or as the "beautiful statement of some high truth." Whatever the precise manner of description may be, the basic idea may be stated as follows: poetry is a "truth" with "decorations," which may either be pleasant in themselves or dispose the reader to accept the truth.

Most often victims of this general misconception have treated poetry as a kind of "sugar-coated pill." They have justified the characteristics of poetry—rhythmical language, figures of speech, stories and dramatic situations, and so on—as a kind of bait that leads the reader to expose himself to the influence of the "truth" contained in a poem. They value these characteristics only in so far as the characteristics lead to the acceptance of the "truth." The final value of a poem for such people would depend on the value of the "truth" contained—which leads us back to the mistake of the "message hunters," which we examined with reference to Longfellow's poem.

But even if the person who regards poetry as "fine sentiments in fine language" says that he values the language as much as he values the sentiments, or "truth," he is still using a mistaken approach to poetry. For he is apparently committed to saying that the language, quite apart from its relation to some central idea or "truth," is valuable. He seems to be saying that certain words, or certain objects suggested by the words, are in themselves "poetic." He would be forced to consider a poem as simply a bundle of melodious word-combinations and pretty pictures. He would probably be embarrassed if we asked him what held these things together in any given poem, making it a *poem* rather than simply a collection of pleasing items. And he would probably be further embarrassed if we asked him to show us by what standard he would call a particular combination of sounds or a particular set of pictures poetically fine. If he should say that he took as a standard for poetical fitness the fact that any item—let us say, for instance, a rose—was pleasing in real life, he would be making a dangerous confusion. It is certainly true that in real life various combinations of word sounds and various objects and scenes, such as the rose, the moon, the ruins of a mediaeval tower, a maiden standing on a balcony, etc., are pleasing. But poetry does not consist merely in the use of objects of this sort or in the use of agreeable word combinations. Nor does the mere presence of these things make poetry. But the falsity of this conception can quickly be demonstrated by turning to great poetry from Shakespeare or Milton where we find material that in real life would be disagreeable or mean used for poetic effect. The image of a man grunting and sweating under a burden too heavy for him is not a poetic thing if judged by the above standard, but we will find it used in a passage of great poetry that is universally admired. In Hamlet's most famous speech we find these lines:

> For who would bear the whips and scorns of time,
> The oppressor's wrong, the proud man's contumely,
> The pangs of despised love, the law's delay,
> The insolence of office, and the spurns
> That patient merit of the unworthy takes,
> When he himself might his quietus make
> With a bare bodkin? who would fardels bear,
> To grunt and sweat under a weary life,
> But that the dread of something after death
> The undiscovered country from whose bourn
> No traveler returns, puzzles the will. . . .

In fact, none of the things used in this passage would be thought of as being pleasing in itself in actual life. The passage does not give us a set of agreeable pictures that would be considered "poetic." Indeed, the more we examine good poetry the more absurd will appear the common notion that certain objects or situations or even ideas are in themselves poetic. *The poetic effect depends not on the things themselves but on the kind of use the poet makes of them.*

ORGANIC NATURE OF POETRY

We have seen, then, that a poem is not to be thought of as merely a bundle of things which are "poetic" in themselves. Nor is it to be thought of, as the "message hunters" would seem to have it, as a kind of box, decorated or not, in which a "truth" or a "fine sentiment" is hidden.

Certainly it is not to be thought of as a group of *mechanically* combined elements—meter, rhyme, figurative language, idea, and so on—put together to make a poem as bricks are put together to make a wall. The relationship among the elements in a poem is what is all important; it is not a mechanical relationship but one which is far more intimate and fundamental. If we must compare a poem to the make-up of some physical object it ought not to be to a wall but to something organic like a plant.

We may investigate this general principle by looking at some particular examples. The following lines could scarcely be called melodious. Indeed, they may be thought to have a sibilant, hissing quality rather than that of melody.

> If it were done when 'tis done, then 'twere well
> It were done quickly: if the assassination
> Could trammel up the consequence, and catch,
> With his surcease, success, that but this blow
> Might be the be-all and the end-all here,
> But here, upon this bank and shoal of time,
> We'd jump the life to come.

This is the speech of Macbeth at the moment when he is debating the murder of Duncan; innumerable critics and readers have considered the passage to be great poetry. We are not to consider that the passage is great poetry *in spite* of its lack of ordinary melodious effects; but rather we are to see that the broken rhythms and the tendency to harshness of sound are essential to the communication that Shakespeare wished. For instance, the piling up of the *s* sounds in the second, third, and fourth lines help give an impression of desperate haste and breathless excitement. The lines give the impression of a conspiratorial whisper. The rhythm and sound effects of the passage, then, are poetic in the only sense which we have seen to be legitimate: they are poetic because they contribute to the total significance of the passage.

Or we may approach the general problem in another way. Here are two lines by Robert Burns which have been greatly admired by the poet William Butler Yeats:

> The white moon is setting behind the white wave,
> And Time is setting with me, O!

Let us suppose that the lines had been written as follows:

> The white moon is setting behind the white wave,
> And Time, O! is setting with me.

Literally considered, the two versions would seem to say exactly the same thing: they describe a scene and give an exclamation provoked by it. If one will, however, read the two versions carefully with an ear for the rhythm he will discover that the transposition of the word *O* has made a great difference in the movement.

But this difference is not finally important *merely* because the first version may be in itself more melodious than the second. The movement of the first version is superior primarily because it contributes to the total effect, or to what we might call the total interpretation, of the scene. The placing of the cry at the emphatic position of a line-end implies that the speaker had scarcely realized the full force of his own statement until he had made it. The lingering rhythm caused by the position of the exclamation at the end of the second line coincides with the fact that the poet sees in the natural scene a representation of the pathos of the passing of Time and of his own life. By placing the exclamation anywhere else we impair this relationship between the rhythm and the other elements involved—the image of the moonset and the poet's statement about the passing of Time. Yeats has summarized the general effect of the passage and the relationship of the parts as follows:

> Take from them [the lines] the whiteness of the moon and of the waves, whose relation to the setting of Time is too

subtle for the intellect, and you take from them their beauty. But, when all are together, moon and wave and whiteness and setting Time and the last melancholy cry, they evoke an emotion which cannot be evoked by any other arrangement of colors and sounds and forms.*

The remarks by Yeats here apply, as we can see, to the elements of the scene itself as well as to the rhythm. He is not praising the lines merely because the scene of the white moon setting behind the white wave gives in itself a pretty picture. As a matter of fact, a white moon may not appear as beautiful as a golden moon, but if we rewrite the lines with a golden moon we have lost something from them:

The gold moon is setting behind the gold wave,
  And Time is setting for me, O!

The "something" that has been lost obviously depends on the relationship of the color to the other elements in the general effect. The whiteness of the moon and the wave in connection with the idea of "setting" and then more specifically in connection with the idea of the irrevocable passage of Time, suggests, even though unconsciously to most readers, a connection with the paleness of something waning or dying. The connection is not a logical connection, as Yeats intimates when he says the "relation . . . is too subtle for the intellect," but it is nonetheless a powerful one. All of this merely means that Yeats is saying that the beauty—by which he means the total poetic effect—of the lines depends on the relationship of the parts to each other.

This last point may be amply proved, as we have already hinted in discussing the passage from *Hamlet,* by considering a passage of great poetry in which the pictures used, unlike that in the lines from Burns, would be considered in ordinary life as positively ugly or at least neutral.

Time hath, my lord, a wallet at his back,
Wherein he puts alms for oblivion,
A great-sized monster of ingratitudes:
Those scraps are good deeds past; which are devoured

* From W. B. Yeats, "The Symbolism of Poetry," *Essays,* p. 191. Copyright, 1912, 1918, and used with the permission of The Macmillan Co.

As fast as they are made, forgot as soon
As done: perseverance, dear my lord,
Keeps honor bright: to have done, is to hang
Quite out of fashion, like a rusty mail
In monumental mockery. . . .

(From *Troilus and Cressida*)

This is a speech which Shakespeare puts into the mouth of a character, Ulysses, who is trying to persuade Achilles to take part again in the war against the Trojans and not to rest on the reputation for valor he has already made. The pictures given here are definitely unattractive: a beggar putting alms in his sack, a monster, scraps of food, a rusty suit of armor. The poetic effect of the passage, then, cannot depend on the intrinsic prettiness of any of the objects mentioned. If we speak of the beauty of the passage, as Yeats speaks of the beauty of the lines from Burns, we must mean the relation of the objects to each other and to the idea of the passage.

Let us try to see what these relationships are. Ulysses is saying that a reputation for good deeds is quickly forgotten. Good deeds are like alms given to an ungrateful beggar, or are like scraps of food which the beggar forgets as soon as he has satisfied his appetite. The picture is poetically good because it accurately indicates the *attitude* which Ulysses wishes Achilles to take toward his past achievements. If Ulysses had merely given Achilles the general statement that the public forgets good deeds, he could not have stirred the feelings which Achilles, the hero and aristocrat, must have felt toward beggars and broken scraps of food. He plays on this contempt and disgust. The images of the first five lines, as we have seen, are closely bound together to define a certain attitude. Then, after a general statement that perseverance is necessary to keep honor bright, the image of the coat of mail is introduced: a man who bases his claim to honor merely on a deed done in the past is like a suit of mail that, although it is hung up as a trophy of some great event, simply rusts. It is important to see that this is not a mere repetition of the general point made about perseverance, but that it also develops and adds to the idea, for it carries with it a special urgency to immediate action. There is not only the application, as it were, of the general idea in a concrete image that can be seen as a picture, but also an application appropriate to the special situation, the need for Achilles to arm and return to the battle.

DRAMATIC ASPECT OF POETRY

It may be objected that most of the examples given above are drawn from plays and do not represent poetry as we more ordinarily find it. But the principle illustrated by these examples applies to all other poetry. It applies because all poetry, including even short lyrics or descriptive pieces (p. 78), involves a dramatic organization. This is clear when we reflect that every poem implies a speaker of the poem, either the poet writing in his own person or someone into whose mouth the poem is put, and that the poem represents the reaction of such a person to a situation, a scene, or an idea. In this sense every poem can be—and in fact must be—regarded as a little drama.

WHAT GOOD IS POETRY?

But even if one understands the principles by which poetry is to be read, one may still ask, "What good is poetry?" The value of science we all know. But we have attempted in the preceding pages to show how different the organization of poetry is from that of science, and how different are their objectives. It is only fair to admit that what makes science valuable cannot be held to make poetry valuable also. Science gives us a certain kind of description of the world—a description which is within its own terms verifiable—and gives us a basis for more effective practical achievement. Science is, as Bertrand Russell has called it, "power-knowledge."

> But scientific thought is . . . essentially power-thought—the sort of thought, that is to say, whose purpose, conscious or unconscious, is to give power to its possessor. Now power is a causal concept, and to obtain power over any given material one need only understand the causal laws to which it is subject. This is an essentially abstract matter, and the more irrelevant details we can omit from our purview, the more powerful our thoughts will become. The same sort of thing can be illustrated in the eco-

nomic sphere. The cultivator, who knows every corner of his farm, has a concrete knowledge of wheat, and makes very little money; the railway which carries his wheat views it in a slightly more abstract way, and makes rather more money; the stock exchange manipulator, who knows it only in its purely abstract aspect of something which may go up or down, is, in his way, as remote from concrete reality as the physicist, and he, of all those concerned in the economic sphere, makes the most money and has the most power. So it is with science, though the power which the man of science seeks is more remote and impersonal than that which is sought on the stock exchange.*

But we have seen, and can see in real life every day, how much of our experience eludes the statements science can make; and how merely practical statements or statements that approximate a scientific form satisfy only a part of our interests. One does not have to look farther than the fact that this wide domain of human interests exists to find a justification for poetry. Most people are thoroughly satisfied to admit the value of any activity which satisfies a basic and healthy human interest. It may be well, however, to take a few moments to remind the reader that this interest exists, and to make plain that it is this interest which poetry seeks to satisfy.

We have already seen how often talk that is apparently practical really attempts to satisfy a non-practical interest. It is easy to point out many other aspects of our experience that testify to the fact that people—even people who think that they care nothing for poetry—really have interests which are the same as those satisfied by poetry. Very few people indeed depend for the satisfaction of these interests merely on their routine activities. Instead, they listen to speeches, go to church, view television programs, read magazine stories or the gossip columns of newspapers. Such people do not see any relation between these activities and poetry, but poetry does concern the same impulses and the same interests. Why and how good poetry, and good literature in general, give a fuller satisfaction to these impulses and interests is a matter which can best be stated in connection with concrete examples before us, and the attempt in this book to state this matter will be gradually

* *The Scientific Outlook,* New York, W. W. Norton & Co., 1931, p. 86.

developed by the study of examples. But the fundamental points, namely, that poetry has a basis in common human interests, that the poet is a man speaking to men, and that every poem is, at center, a little drama, must not be forgotten at the beginning of any attempt to study poetry.

The question of the value of poetry, then, is to be answered by saying that it springs from a basic human impulse and fulfills a basic human interest. To answer the question finally, and not provisionally, one would have to answer the question as to the value of those common impulses and interests. But that is a question which lies outside of the present concern. As we enter into a study of poetry it is only necessary to see that poetry is not an isolated and eccentric thing, but springs from the most fundamental interests which human beings have.

I

Narrative Poems

FOREWORD

We have said that the "stuff of poetry" is not something separate from the ordinary business of living, but itself inheres in that business. We hear some one say that a farm boy has suffered a fatal accident while cutting wood with a buzz-saw; or we read in the newspaper that a woman has shot her sweetheart; or we remember that there was once an outlaw from Missouri named Jesse James who was killed by treachery. This sort of thing, even though it may not at first strike us as beautiful, instructive, or elevating, appeals to the interest people have in other people. That interest, as we have indicated, is not scientific or practical but is simply the general interest we feel in people as human beings. Even though the account of a painful accident or a sordid murder seems almost as far removed as possible from poetry, it arouses the kind of interest which poetry attempts to satisfy, and, as we have already said, comprises the "stuff of poetry." In the case of the three incidents mentioned—the death of a farm boy, the murder of the sweetheart, and the betrayal of the outlaw—the "stuff of poetry" has actually been turned into poems. That is, the "human interest" has been put into a *form* (*Glossary*) that preserves it, even after the accidental and temporary curiosity has been satisfied.

The phrase, "put into a form that preserves it," can be misleading, if we are prone to think of poetic form as a kind of container, a kind of box, in which the stuff of poetry has been packed. Form is much more than that. The form does more than "contain" the poetic stuff: it organizes it; it shapes it; it defines its meaning. Much of our subsequent discussion will have to do with what form is and what it does.

"Out, Out—"

Robert Frost [1874–1963]

The buzz-saw snarled and rattled in the yard
And made dust and dropped stove-length sticks of wood,
Sweet-scented stuff when the breeze drew across it.
And from there those that lifted eyes could count
Five mountain ranges one behind the other
Under the sunset far into Vermont.
And the saw snarled and rattled, snarled and rattled,
As it ran light, or had to bear a load.
And nothing happened: day was all but done.
Call it a day, I wish they might have said
To please the boy by giving him the half hour
That a boy counts so much when saved from work.
His sister stood beside them in her apron
To tell them "Supper." At the word, the saw,
As if to prove saws knew what supper meant,
Leaped out at the boy's hand, or seemed to leap—
He must have given the hand. However it was,
Neither refused the meeting. But the hand!
The boy's first outcry was a rueful laugh,
As he swung toward them holding up the hand
Half in appeal, but half as if to keep
The life from spilling. Then the boy saw all—
Since he was old enough to know, big boy
Doing a man's work, though a child at heart—
He saw all spoiled. "Don't let him cut my hand off—
The doctor, when he comes. Don't let him, sister!"
So. But the hand was gone already.
The doctor put him in the dark of ether.

He lay and puffed his lips out with his breath.
And then—the watcher at his pulse took fright.
No one believed. They listened at his heart.
Little—less—nothing!—and that ended it.
No more to build on there. And they, since they
Were not the one dead, turned to their affairs.

Frankie and Johnny

Anonymous

Frankie and Johnny were lovers, O, how that couple could love.
Swore to be true to each other, true as the stars above.
He was her man, but he done her wrong.

Frankie she was his woman, everybody knows.
She spent one hundred dollars for a suit of Johnny's clothes.
He was her man, but he done her wrong.

Frankie and Johnny went walking, Johnny in his bran' new suit,
"O good Lawd," says Frankie, "but don't my Johnny look cute?"
He was her man, but he done her wrong.

Frankie went down to Memphis; she went on the evening train.
She paid one hundred dollars for Johnny a watch and chain.
He was her man, but he done her wrong.

Frankie went down to the corner, to buy a glass of beer;
She says to the fat bartender, "Has my loving man been here?
He was my man, but he done me wrong."

"Ain't going to tell you no story, ain't going to tell you no lie,
I seen your man 'bout an hour ago with a girl named Alice Fry.
If he's your man, he's doing you wrong."

Frankie went back to the hotel, she didn't go there for fun,
Under her long red kimono she toted a forty-four gun.
He was her man, but he done her wrong.

Frankie threw back her kimono; took out the old forty-four;
There was her lovin' Johnny a-lovin' up Alice Fry;
He was her man, but he done her wrong.

Frankie threw back her kimono; took out the old forty-four;
Roota-toot-toot, three times she shot, right through that hotel door.
She shot her man, 'cause he done her wrong.

Johnny grabbed off his Stetson. "O good Lawd, Frankie, don't shoot."
But Frankie put her finger on the trigger, and the gun went roota-toot-toot.
He was her man, but she shot him down.

"Roll me over easy, roll me over slow,
Roll me over easy, boys, 'cause my wounds are hurting me so,
I was her man, but I done her wrong."

With the first shot Johnny staggered; with the second shot he fell;
When the third bullet hit him, there was a new man's face in hell.
He was her man, but he done her wrong.

Frankie heard a rumbling away down under the ground.
Maybe it was Johnny where she had shot him down.
He was her man, and she done him wrong.

"Oh, bring on your rubber-tired hearses, bring on your rubber-tired hacks,
They're takin' my Johnny to the buryin' groun' but they'll never bring him back.
He was my man, but he done me wrong."

The judge he said to the jury, "It's plain as plain can be.
This woman shot her man, so it's murder in the second degree.
He was her man, though he done her wrong."

Now it wasn't murder in the second degree, it wasn't murder in the third.
Frankie simply dropped her man, like a hunter drops a bird.
He was her man, but he done her wrong.

"Oh, put me in that dungeon. Oh, put me in that cell.
Put me where the northeast wind blows from the southeast corner of hell.
I shot my man 'cause he done me wrong."

Frankie walked up to the scaffold, as calm as a girl could be,
She turned her eyes to heaven and said, "Good Lord, I'm coming to thee.
He was my man, and I done him wrong."

Jesse James

Anonymous

It was on a Wednesday night, the moon was shining bright,
They robbed the Danville train.
And the people they did say, for many miles away,
'Twas the outlaws Frank and Jesse James.

Jesse had a wife to mourn him all her life,
The children they are brave.
'Twas a dirty little coward shot Mister Howard,
And laid Jesse James in his grave.

Jesse was a man was a friend to the poor,
He never left a friend in pain.
And with his brother Frank he robbed the Chicago bank
And then held up the Glendale train.

It was Robert Ford, the dirty little coward,
I wonder how he does feel,
For he ate of Jesse's bread and he slept in Jesse's bed,
Then he laid Jesse James in his grave.

It was his brother Frank that robbed the Gallatin bank,
And carried the money from the town.
It was in this very place that they had a little race,
For they shot Captain Sheets to the ground.

They went to the crossing not very far from there,
And there they did the same;
And the agent on his knees he delivered up the keys
To the outlaws Frank and Jesse James.

It was on a Saturday night, Jesse was at home
Talking to his family brave,
When the thief and the coward, little Robert Ford,
Laid Jesse James in his grave.

How people held their breath when they heard of Jesse's death,
  And wondered how he ever came to die.
'Twas one of the gang, dirty Robert Ford,
  That shot Jesse James on the sly.

Jesse went to rest with his hand on his breast;
  He died with a smile on his face.
He was born one day in the county of Clay,
  And came from a solitary race.

The first of these poems was written by Robert Frost, a professional poet, who felt in the fatal accident to an obscure farm boy the pathos and horror of the unreasonable and unpredictable end that at any moment may come to life. We do not know who composed the other two poems, but certainly not professional poets. Apparently some ordinary person felt so strongly the force of an incident, the murder of Johnny or the betrayal of Jesse James, that he tried to express it in a song that would convey his own reactions to the event. And the songs did succeed in conveying something of the reactions of the unknown composers, for they have been passed down from mouth to mouth, probably being constantly altered in the process. Poems like "Frankie and Johnny" or "Jesse James," narratives to be sung that spring from unknown sources and are transmitted by word of mouth, and that may experience alteration in this process, are usually called *ballads* (*Glossary*).

The most ordinary way by which we express the interest we as human beings have in other human beings is by telling or attending to stories. Since poetry derives from this basic human interest we expect to find, and do find, many poems in which the element of story is large. As a matter of fact, the three poems we have just read, and all the poems in the first section of this book, give enough of the explicit action of a story to appeal to the usual curiosity we feel about how any situation will turn out. But this is not the only appeal the poems make to us, just as it is not the only appeal any good piece of fiction makes. We are interested not merely in getting the information about the conclusion, but in following the process by which the conclusion is reached. As a matter of fact, we do not even want all the details of the process, but just enough to make us experience the central feeling and grasp the central meaning of the events. But this is not all: we like a poem, not because it gives us satisfaction of our curiosity or because it gives us an idea we can "carry away with us," as people sometimes put it, but because the poem itself is an experience.

We can illustrate by a comparison with a football game. If a person listens to a radio report of a game, he may really have more accurate information about it than if he were present. And when the game is over, he will know the exact score. But if he has his choice he will probably take the trouble, and spend the money, to go to the game itself. He does this because the game is a richer experience. The score and the statistics of the game come to him, if he watches it, not as bare facts, but in terms of action.

This general principle is clear if we remember that the mere fact, as a fact, that a woman in the slums shot her sweetheart Johnny is of little interest to us. If we enjoy hearing "Frankie and Johnny" sung, we do so because of something more than the statistical importance of the subject. Furthermore, we do not enjoy it merely because it satisfies our curiosity about the outcome; for we enjoy the song for an indefinite length of time after we know the conclusion. It is obvious, then, that if we like it at all, we like it because of its particular nature as an experience—just as we like the football game.

The story element in a poem, then, whether it is prominent as in "Frankie and Johnny" or relatively unimportant as in "Out, Out," is only one of many elements which work together to give the total experience of the poem. We already know what some of these other elements are: rhythm, figurative language, and so on. But in these poems, where the story element is prominent, we may proceed best by studying the way in which this one element is treated in specific cases to give the effect we call poetry.

Johnie Armstrong

Anonymous

There dwelt a man in faire Westmerland,
  Johnie Armstrong men did him call,
He had neither lands nor rents coming in,
  Yet he kept eight score men in his hall.

He had horse and harness for them all,
  Goodly steeds were all milke-white;
O the golden bands an about their necks,
  And their weapons, they were all alike.

Newes then was brought unto the king
  That there was sick[1] a won as hee,
That livèd lyke a bold out-law,
  And robbèd all the north country.

The king he writt an a letter then,
  A letter which was large and long;
He signed it with his owne hand;
  And he promised to doe him no wrong.

When this letter came Johnie untill,[2]
  His heart it was as blythe as birds on the tree:
"Never was I sent for before any king,
  My father, my grandfather, nor none but mee.

"And if wee goe the king before,
  I would we went most orderly;
Every man of you shall have his scarlet cloak,
  Lacèd with silver laces three.

"Every won of you shall have his velvett coat,
  Lacèd with sillver lace so white;
O the golden bands an about your necks,
  Black hatts, white feathers, all alyke."

By the morrow morninge at ten of the clock,
  Towards Edenburough gon was hee,
And with him all his eight score men;
  Good Lord, it was a goodly sight for to see!

When Johnie came befower[3] the king,
  He fell downe on his knee;
"O pardon, my soveraine leige," he said,
  "O pardon my eight score men and mee!"

"Thou shalt have no pardon, thou traytor strong,
  For thy eight score men nor thee;
For tomorrow morning by ten of the clock,
  Both thou and them shall hang on the gallow-tree."

[1] such [2] unto [3] before

But Johnie looke'd over his left shoulder,
Good Lord, what a grevious look looked hee!
Saying, "Asking grace of a graceles face—
Why there is none for you nor me."

But Johnie had a bright sword by his side,
And it was made of the mettle so free,
That had not the king stept his foot aside,
He had smitten his head from his faire boddé.

Saying, "Fight on, my merry men all,
And see that none of you be taine;
For rather then men shall say we were hange'd,
Let them report how we were slaine."

Then, God wott, faire Eddenburrough rose,
And so besett poore Johnie rounde,
That fowerscore and tenn of Johnie's best men
Lay gasping all upon the ground.

Then like a mad man Johnie laide about,
And like a mad man then fought hee,
Untill a falce Scot came Johnie behinde,
And runn him through the faire boddee.

Saying, "Fight on, my merry men all,
And see that none of you be taine;
For I will stand by and bleed but awhile,
And then will I come and fight againe."

Newes then was brought to young Johnie Armstrong,
As he stood by his nurse's knee,
Who vowed if ere he live'd for to be a man,
On the treacherous Scots revengd hee'd be.

This poem treats the same kind of story as that treated by "Jesse James." In both cases there is the brave outlaw who is killed by treachery. In neither case do we know who composed the ballad, but both poems must have grown out of a fairly simple and illiterate society. In the case of this ballad, it was the society of the border peasantry in the sixteenth century; in the case of "Jesse James" the ballad appeared in a frontier society in America. But the differences in time and in place do not conceal the fundamental likeness between the two ballads and, even, between the characters of the two heroes. The fact that human nature is very much the same at all times and places, makes it possible for us to read such poems with sympathy and understanding. In both cases, that of the outlaw Johnie Armstrong and the outlaw Jesse James, some one—we do not know who—was struck by the pathos of courage betrayed and was impelled to express his feeling by putting the incident that stirred him into a poem—or more accurately, into the song-poem which we call a ballad. In so far as the unknown composer did this successfully we can now grasp the meaning which the incident had for him.

The incident of Johnie Armstrong, like that of Jesse James, derives from historical fact. Johnie Armstrong was an outlaw lord of the Scottish border country, who was lured into the power of the Scottish king, James V—treacherously, according to the ballad—and was killed with his men. It is a simple story of violent action, such a story as might be expected to appeal strongly to the kind of people among whom the ballad arose.

The basic facts as given in the summary above are not in themselves interesting to us. The event described, for instance, is of no historical importance. But when the event appears to us in the form of the poem it immediately gains an interest. Perhaps we can do something toward defining the process that gives this added interest.

First, we may look at the way the story of Johnie Armstrong is organized, a way characteristic of most ballads. The action is not presented in a straight narrative. The first two stanzas give us an identification of the hero, the *exposition* (*Glossary*), as one would say about ordinary fiction. The next two stanzas give a bit of narrative, but from that point on the action is handled by a succession of little scenes, presented much as in a play. There is the scene of Johnie Armstrong's reception of the letter, of the appearance of his company as it rides toward court, of the betrayal and the fight, and of the little son's vow of vengeance. The method, further, is dramatic in that much of the action is presented through dialogue and not indirectly by description. The characters speak up for themselves, and so we know them directly. By this selection of key scenes and by the emphasis on dialogue the reader or hearer gets an impression of speed and excitement and of nearness to the action.

In the second place, although the reader gets an impression of nearness, the story is not greatly elaborated. In a short story on the same subject one would expect a certain amount of description and detail that is absent in the poem. The only extended piece of description in the poem is that dealing with the appearance of the retainers of Armstrong as they get ready to go to court. But we can observe that this is not straight description. It is put in the mouth of Johnie Armstrong as he orders his men to make ready. And it serves a twofold purpose in the poem in addition to its value as a piece of *atmosphere* (*Glossary*) and setting. It indicates the joy the outlaw feels at the honor the king has done him, and it gives an *ironical* (*Glossary*) contrast to the betrayal that is to follow.

In ordinary prose fiction one would expect a certain amount of analysis and description of the thoughts and feelings of characters. But in this ballad there is very little of such material. For instance, only one line describes the feeling of a character:

> His heart it was as blythe as birds on the tree.

But at the climax of the situation, when Johnie Armstrong suddenly discovers that he has been betrayed, we are not told what he felt; we are given a glimpse of the way he looked, and so seize more imaginatively and directly on the meaning of the scene:

> But Johnie looke'd over his left shoulder,
>   Good Lord, what a grevious look looked hee!
> Saying, "Asking grace of a graceles face—
>   Why there is none for you nor me."

The ballad is moving as quickly as possible to its point, selecting such details as will most stimulate the imagination. With the sight of the betrayed outlaw's sudden glance over his shoulder (and notice how, to emphasize the scene and help us visualize it, the ballad specifies which shoulder), we can know as much about his reaction to the situation as a great deal of description would give us, and we know it in a way that makes us feel that our own imagination is participating in the poem.

This is a detail that by the power of suggestion makes us see the whole picture and feel the effect.

The aim of this kind of treatment is to make as vivid and as *concrete* (*Glossary*) an effect as possible, in contrast to the general and purely factual summary of the event which we gave above. For instance, we are not told that the king is treacherous, and we are told nothing of his intentions. What we learn, we learn from the behavior of the king himself. We are never told that Johnie Armstrong is a proud and courageous man who feels an obligation to his followers, but we learn it from his own conduct and from what he says: when he discovers the king's treachery, he thinks of his men as well as of himself; and there is a sort of exaltation rather than despair in his admonition to all of them to die fighting rather than be taken. "Let them report how we were slaine," he says. We are given a picture of Johnie Armstrong's character in action instead of a description of it. We know what his code is, even though it is not mentioned in the poem. It is a rather primitive one, a code of crude courage, and probably a very inadequate one for us, for he was a border outlaw living four hundred years ago, but he dies true to it. There is no moral given in the poem, no general statement of an idea, but an idea is suggested through the action itself: out of disaster may be produced a spiritual value that makes even disaster seem unimportant. All of these things are in the poem, but they are there by suggestion and implication of the action; we know them without being told, for we can discover them for ourselves.

What the poem does, in short, is to take some bare facts and treat them so that they have both an emotional and an intellectual interpretation. The sympathetic reader, or hearer, of the ballad might not analyze that interpretation but the effect would be there. He would react to the pathos of the betrayal of a strong, brave man, to the exaltation at Johnie Armstrong's courage and desire for an honorable death, to the ironical contrast between Johnie Armstrong's expectation as he goes to the court and his reception there, to the selection of imaginative detail, and to the suspense and speed of movement of the story. He might not analyze any of these items separately and might not try to understand the part they play in the poem; he might merely experience a certain pleasure in the poem, and simply attribute it, if asked, to the genius of the composer or composers. The genius is there, of course, but one's pleasure is enlarged by the attempt to understand as fully as possible the process by which that genius makes itself felt.

Sir Patrick Spence

Anonymous

The king sits in Dumferling toune,
  Drinking the blude-reid wine:
"O whar will I get guid sailor,
  To sail this schip of mine?"

Up and spak an eldern knicht,
  Sat at the kings richt kne:
"Sir Patrick Spence is the best sailor,
  That sails upon the se."

The king has written a braid[1] letter,
  And signd it wi his hand,
And sent it to Sir Patrick Spence,
  Was walking on the sand.

The first line that Sir Patrick red,
  A loud lauch lauchèd[2] he;
The next line that Sir Patrick red,
  The teir blinded his ee.[3]

"O wha is this has don this deid,
  This ill deid don to me,
To send me out this time o' the yeir,
  To sail upon the se!

"Mak hast, mak haste, my mirry men all
  Our guid schip sails the morne:"
"O say na sae, my master deir,
  For I feir a deadlie storme.

"Late, late yestreen I saw the new moone,
  Wi the auld[4] moone in hir arme,

[1] broad [2] laughed [3] eye [4] old

And I feir, I feir, my deir master,
  That we will cum to harme."

O our Scots nobles wer richt laith [1]
  To weet their cork-heild schoone; [2]
Bot lang owre [3] a' the play wer playd,
  Thair hats they swam aboone.

O lang, lang may their ladies sit,
  Wi thair fans into their hand,
Or eir they se Sir Patrick Spence
  Cum sailing to the land.

O lang, lang may the ladies stand,
  Wi thair gold kems [4] in their hair
Waiting for thar ain deir lords,
  For they'll se thame na mair.

Haf owre,[5] haf owre to Aberdour,
  It's fiftie fadom deip,
And thair lies guid Sir Patrick Spence,
  Wi the Scots lords at his feit.

EXERCISE

1. The poem begins with a scene at the royal court. Does the rest of the poem break up into scenes? What are they?

2. Discuss the use of concrete details such as "blude-reid wine," "richt kne," "cork-heild schoone," and so on.

3. What are the ironical contrasts?

4. Though the shipwreck would seem to be the climax of the poem, the poem actually omits all direct description of the shipwreck. Why? Does your answer to this question point to what the poem is "about"?

5. On p. 34 we observed that Johnie Armstrong lives by a code, and dies by his code. Does Sir Patrick live by a similar code?

6. What is the relation between the scene in the last stanza and that in the first? Can it be said that this relation leads us to the main idea of the poem?

[1] loath [2] shoes [3] ere
[4] combs [5] over

The Wife of Usher's Well

Anonymous

There lived a wife at Usher's Well,
  And a wealthy wife was she;
She had three stout and stalwart sons,
  And sent them oer the sea.

They hadna been a week from her,
  A week but barely ane,
Whan word came to the carline [1] wife
  That her three sons were gane.

They hadna been a week from her,
  A week but barely three,
Whan word came to the carlin wife
  That her sons she'd never see.

"I wish the wind may never cease,
  Nor fashes [2] in the flood,
Till my three sons come hame to me,
  In earthly flesh and blood."

It fell about the Martinmass,
  When nights are lang and mirk,
The carlin wife's three sons came hame,
  And their hats were o the birk.[3]

It neither grew in syke [4] nor ditch,
  Nor yet in ony sheugh; [5]
But at the gates o Paradise,
  That birk grew fair eneugh.

"Blow up the fire, my maidens,
  Bring water from the well;
For a' [6] my house shall feast this night,
  Since my three sons are well."

And she has made to them a bed,
  She's made it large and wide,

[1] peasant
[2] troubles
[3] birch
[4] trench
[5] furrow
[6] all

And she's taen her mantle her about,
  Sat down at the bed-side.

Up then crew the red, red cock,
  And up and crew the gray;
The eldest to the youngest said,
  " 'T is time we were away."

The cock he hadna crawd but once,
  And clappd his wings at a',
When the youngest to the eldest said,
  "Brother, we must awa.

"The cock doth craw, the day doth daw,
  The channerin [1] worm doth chide;
Gin we be mist out o our place,
  A sair pain we maun bide.

"Fare ye weel, my mother dear!
  Fareweel to barn and byre! [2]
And fare ye weel, the bonny lass
  That kindles my mother's fire!"

This poem, too, is a ballad. A woman loses her three sons at sea, and in her grief, expresses the wish that she may see them again in flesh and blood. The three sons return to the woman one night, but since they are only ghosts, they have to leave again before dawn. The poem uses many more words to give this simple narrative than the two-sentence paraphrase which we have just given. Indeed, if we judge the poem's excellence in terms of the conciseness and the clearness with which it states the facts which it undertakes to give, then the prose paraphrase is much superior. The difficulty which besets many people in reading poetry resides to a great extent in the fact that many people mistake the *concern* of poetry. Plainly in this poem, as we noticed in "Johnie Armstrong," the facts are *in themselves* unimportant. Furthermore, from one point of view, they are much less important than in "Johnie Armstrong," for here they are not even historically true.

With what is this poem concerned? And, judged in the light of that concern, in what ways is the poem superior to the

[1] devouring [2] cattle-shed

prose paraphrase? If one considers the poem carefully, he notices that the poem, like so many ballads, breaks up into a number of little pictures, and that some of the detail (otherwise irrelevant) becomes justified when we realize that it has been employed to make the scenes vivid for us. The poem is not content merely to state certain things *abstractly* (*Glossary*): we must see the pictures. For example, consider the pictures given us in the seventh and eighth stanzas. The seventh conveys some sense of the bustling excitement with which the woman puts her maids to work when her sons unexpectedly arrive; the eighth conveys with a great deal of intensity the joy with which the mother receives her long-lost sons. She is anxious to make them comfortable; she has prepared the beds carefully for them. But she cannot tear herself away from them, even to let them go to sleep, and having thrown a shawl around her shoulders to keep warm as she sits up late in the chill night air, lingers for a little while by their beds. The poem does not *tell* us of her joy and relief at seeing them home again; it conveys a sense of this to us by showing the mother's joyful activity. In preferring the concrete form of statement to the abstract, "The Wife of Usher's Well" is typical of poetry in general. Consider also the last four stanzas. The poet might have merely stated that the sons regretted having to leave their home and having to go back to the grave. He wishes to do more than communicate the idea, however: he wishes us to share in their feeling of dread as well as to know that they had such a feeling. Which is the better means of doing this: to say, they dreaded leaving "very much," or "a great deal," or "bitterly," —use whatever adverb you will; or to describe the scene itself? The latter method, the concrete method, is very properly the one chosen.

The crowing of the cocks announcing day is described, and the brief conversation between the brothers is given. Notice that the poem does not use words of great intensity in giving the conversation, but *understatement* (*Glossary*). The eldest brother merely says, " 'T is time we were away"; the youngest brother, "Brother, we must awa." There is no shrieking of terror. And yet in this case the brief understatement conveys perhaps more of a feeling of horror and grief than exaggerated outcries would have conveyed. We can readily see why this use of understatement is particularly effective here. The poet has refrained throughout from making comments on the situation or from hinting to us what we ought to feel. The poem is *objective* (*Glossary*); the poet stands aside, and lets the poem do its work on us in its own way.

Notice too that this poem, like the previous ones considered, makes use of suggestion. People prefer suggestion to explicit statement in these matters—if for no other reason than that the person who feels the suggestion participates fully and immediately—he feels that he has made a discovery for himself, which is quite another thing than having some one tell him what he ought to feel. Moreover, suggestion is rich in that the reader's own imagination, aroused, goes on to enrich the whole subject with feeling. We have an excellent example of this power in the last stanza. After the dialogue between the brothers to the effect that they must go back to the grave, the youngest brother says,

"Fare ye weel, my mother dear!
Fareweel to barn and byre!
And fare ye weel, the bonny lass
That kindles my mother's fire!"

Was the youngest brother in love with the bonny lass before his death? We have received no earlier hint that he was. Perhaps he has been. But it is not necessary for an appreciation of the poem to read this interpretation into the passage. The stanza gives us all we need to have if we see the bonny lass as representing the warm, beautiful life of flesh and blood which the dead men have lost and which they now must leave. If the girl does stand for this, then one may perhaps find the reason for the effect which the last line gives—

"That kindles my mother's fire!"

The description in its effect on us is not merely an identification of the girl; the association of the girl with the fire makes us think of her particularly in her contrast with the cold and desolate grave to which the dead brothers must return.*

* In order to accept this interpretation of the effect of the last stanza on the reader it is not necessary to assume that the effect was consciously planned by the poet. For a reference to the problem of the degree of self-consciousness in a poet's artistry, see pp. 320–23, 520–31.

One may raise the question at this point as to whether the average reader will feel that the line means this. Is the average reader expected to be able to make this interpretation? The answer must be, no; most readers do not make this interpretation consciously; and it is not necessary for them to make it consciously in order to enjoy the poem. Many of the details of poetry affect us *unconsciously*. We cannot explain just how the effect was made. But if we are to enjoy poetry to its fullest we must be alert and sensitive to such details as this. In "The Wife of Usher's Well," the suggestiveness of the images works rather simply. In some poems, especially those in Section V and Section VI, the suggestions made by the images may have a much more complicated relationship to the general intention of the poem.

One more point about this poem may be worth making. The *structure* (*Glossary*) of the poem is based on an appeal to the reader's feelings. It is not merely logical or chronological. The poem takes advantage of a reader's natural curiosity. It employs suspense. (Though the end is foreshadowed when we are told where the birch grew which adorns the dead men's hats, we are not told that they are dead—only that the wife was told that she would never see them. The solution is held up to the end.) Furthermore, the poem builds to a climax. That climax lies in the contrast between the horrors of the grave and the warmth and friendliness of life. The channering worm is contrasted with the bonny lass in the last two stanzas, and the final crowing of the cock has been so prepared for that we feel it as a gruesome summons—we feel it as the dead men feel it. Moreover, the effectiveness is increased by an ironic contrast in the crowing itself. The scene is a farm scene. The atmosphere of warmth and life has been developed in terms of the farmhouse setting. But the crowing of the birds, which have an integral part in this friendly setting—the crowing which is only one of the friendly noises associated with the boys' home—itself becomes the signal for departure from this comfortable and human world to the monstrous world to which the dead men must return.

Farewell to Barn and Stack and Tree

A. E. Housman [*1859–1936*]

"Farewell to barn and stack and tree,
  Farewell to Severn shore.
Terence, look your last at me,
  For I come home no more.

"The sun burns on the half-mown hill,
  By now the blood is dried;
And Maurice amongst the hay lies still
  And my knife is in his side.

"My mother thinks us long away;
  'Tis time the field were mown.
She had two sons at rising day,
  To-night she'll be alone.

"And here's a bloody hand to shake,
  And oh, man, here's good-bye;
We'll sweat no more on scythe and rake,
  My bloody hands and I.

"I wish you strength to bring you pride,
  And a love to keep you clean,
And I wish you luck, come Lammastide,
  At racing on the green.

"Long for me the rick will wait,
  And long will wait the fold,
And long will stand the empty plate,
  And dinner will be cold."

EXERCISE

1. It seems obvious that the poet here is modeling his work on the folk-ballad, several examples of which the student has just been reading. Has the poet managed to secure some of the qualities of the ballad, such as starkness, concreteness, and direct presentation? How does his poem differ from the folk ballads that you have read?

2. Do we need to know more about the motive for the quar-

rel between the brothers? Why has the poet left out any account of it? On what is the poem focused?

3. Are the last two lines flat and anticlimactic? Can you justify the poem's ending on the presentation of this detail?

The Three Ravens

Anonymous

There were three ravens sat on a tree,
  Downe a downe, hay downe, hay downe
There were three ravens sat on a tree,
  With a downe
There were three ravens sat on a tree,
They were as blacke as they might be.
  With a downe derrie, derrie, derrie,
    downe, downe.

The one of them said to his mate,
"Where shall we our breakfast take?"

"Downe in yonder greene field,
There lies a knight slain under his shield.

"His hounds they lie downe at his feete,
So well they can their master keepe.

"His haukes they flie so eagerly,
There's no fowle dare him come nie."

Downe there comes a fallow doe,
As great with yong as she might goe.

She lift up his bloudy hed,
And kist his wounds that were so red.

She got him up upon her backe,
And carried him to earthen lake.[1]

She buried him before the prime,
She was dead herselfe ere even-song time.

God send every gentleman,
Such haukes, such hounds, and such a leman.[2]

[1] pit

[2] loved one: wife or sweetheart

The story implied * by this ballad may be stated as follows: A knight has been killed, but his hounds guard the body, and his hawks, waiting by their master, keep away the crows that would prey upon it. The knight's leman comes and with her own hands buries him, and then dies herself. But we know nothing more about the "story" as such. We do not know how the knight was killed, or why, or by whom. We simply have the scene by the body, and as elements of the scene, the picture of the ravens gathered in the tree, the picture of the knight with the hounds at his feet and his hawks flying above him. The only thing that happens is the coming of the woman and her death. The poet is not so much interested, then, in giving the reader the consecutive facts of the story as he is in creating a certain feeling about the scene.

What is the feeling which the poet is interested in giving the reader? What does he want the poem to mean to us? We can best answer these questions by examining the manner in which the poet has used the elements of the poem.

As we can quickly see, the details are chosen, not haphazardly, but for a particular effect. The hounds on guard are a type of loyalty, and so also are the vigilant hawks. And these two references prepare for the mention of the third and most important of those who are loyal to the dead knight, the woman herself. She is the *climactic* (*Glossary*) example of loyalty.

Why, then, does the poet mention the ravens? They have no affection for the dead man whatsoever; they consider him only as so much food. The answer is that they form an effective contrast to what follows. They represent the cruelly impersonal background against which the various acts of loyalty are described. There is an ironic shock in passing from the ravens to the hounds, for we pass from a consideration of the knight as so much carrion to a consideration of him as master and friend, in death master and friend still.

We may observe the cunning with which the poem presents

* Fullness of presentation of a narrative is, of course, a relative matter. One could argue that the story in "Sir Patrick Spence" is also largely "implied"—not fully presented. Even so, this poem, and most of the poems that are to follow in this section, tend to be, in a special sense, implied narratives.

this material. The poet does not depend on the kind of general statement which we have given in our prose paraphrase. The material is arranged so that we feel the effect intended without the direct statement. The mere fact that the poet allows the ravens themselves to describe the scene accomplishes two things that would otherwise be impossible. First, what would otherwise be flat description of a scene becomes dramatic action. The reader comes more directly to the central fact of the poem. Second, the ironic contrast is more pointed when the ravens themselves, examples of mere brute appetite, comment on the hawk and the hounds, examples of a fidelity that reaches beyond such appetite. Thus, the material is arranged in such a manner that a comment on the meaning of the situation is unnecessary: we grasp it immediately, even when we do not take the trouble to put it in the form of a general statement.

After the poet has set the scene directly and dramatically, the development of the action is given in terms of narrative. We are told how the "doe" comes down to the dead knight. But why is the leman of the dead knight called a doe? * The poet gains again a sort of dramatic shock by characterizing the woman as a deer. But we see that the characterization is "right," after all. The shyness and timidity of the deer provides a fitting description for the gentleness of the woman. But the characterization does not merely give us meaning in the sense of information about the situation; by appealing to our attitude toward the timidity and shyness of the doe, it creates our attitude toward the woman herself.

The line

As great with yong as she might goe

emphasizes further the pathos of the situation and the strength of the fidelity that brings the "doe" to the scene. It tells us that her action in burying her lover was most difficult, and helps account for her death. It has another effect. She is evidently great with the knight's child. The love has been consummated, and her grief is therefore all the more poignant.

* For origin of this comparison see L. C. Wimberly: *Folklore in English and Scottish Ballads,* Chicago, The University of Chicago Press, 1928, p. 55.

In the body of the poem are given the various examples of loyalty in action. The poet himself refrains from any comment until the last stanza:

God send every gentleman,
Such haukes, such hounds, and such a leman.

But notice the form the comment takes. It does not insist on the loyalty. It does not exaggerate. It is, indeed, an understatement. But as such it employs a contrast which is more emphatic than fulsome praise would be. The form of the statement implies that there are few enough knights who have such hawks and hounds and such a lover. This implication is a clue to what might be called the *theme* (*Glossary*) of the poem. We may state the theme more largely somewhat as follows. The poem, taken as a whole, makes a contrast between two ways of looking at life. The ravens represent one way, the hawks, hounds, and "doe" the other. One view regards life in a purely materialistic way; the other finds an importance in life beyond mere material circumstance. The same theme appears in "Johnie Armstrong." Even though he knows he is going to be killed, he feels that the way in which he meets death is important. He says to his men,

Let them report how we were slaine.

And a similar theme is found in "Sir Patrick Spence."

The statement of the theme of a poem must not be taken as equivalent to the poem itself. It is not to be taken as a "message." But the definition of the theme of a poem may help us to a fuller understanding of the entire poem, if we are careful never to think of it as a little moral comment or platitude which the poem has been written in order to give. We may put the matter in this way: the theme does not give the poem its force; the poem gives the theme its force.

Lord Randal

Anonymous

"O where hae ye been, Lord Randal, my son?
O where hae ye been, my handsome young man?"
"I hae been to the wild wood; mother, make my bed soon,
For I'm weary wi hunting, and fain wald lie down."

"Where gat ye your dinner, Lord Randal, my son?
Where gat ye your dinner, my handsome young man?"
"I din'd wi my true-love; mother, make my bed soon,
For I'm weary wi hunting, and fain wald lie down."

"What gat ye to your dinner, Lord Randal, my son?
What gat ye to your dinner, my handsome young man?"
"I gat eels boiled in broo; [1] mother, make my bed soon,
For I'm weary wi hunting, and fain wald lie down."

"What became of your bloodhounds, Lord Randal, my son?
What became of your bloodhounds, my handsome young man?"
"O they swelld and they died; mother, make my bed soon,
For I'm weary wi hunting, and fain wald lie down."

"O I fear ye are poisond, Lord Randal, my son!
O I fear ye are poisond, my handsome young man!"
"O yes! I am poisond; mother, make my bed soon,
For I'm sick at the heart, and I fain wald lie down."

This ballad shows some devices that are not found in "Johnie Armstrong," for instance, but are characteristic of many folk ballads—dialogue, as the only vehicle for narration, and repetition. The poem does not give a consecutive narrative, as does "Johnie Armstrong," but merely takes a single dramatic moment in an action and presents that in five questions and answers that are framed in the repetition. That is, the movement is defined by a series of leaps and pauses.

The action proper is suppressed, or only hinted at. But the treatment is extremely effective, moving, as it does, with increasing suspense from a simple question and apparently innocent answer in the first stanza to the tragic discovery in the last. In each stanza the refrain serves to focus this growing intensity, for with its recurrence the reader begins to realize that more and more is implied, until he discovers in the end that, not healthy weariness from the hunt, but death makes the young man fain to lie down.

The treatment is not the treatment of narrative. A more rigid selectivity than would apply in direct narrative has been brought to bear on the material. Just such details are used as will be essential and will suggest the rest of the story. The

1 broth

reader is not provided with the kind of information on which a newspaper account or even an ordinary piece of fiction would thrive. We know nothing about the relation between Lord Randal and his true-love except the fact that she poisoned him. The motivation is entirely lacking. Nor do we know anything about the relation between the mother and her son's true-love, although by reason of the mother's quick suspicion we may venture the surmise that the relation was not one of untroubled confidence, perhaps one of mutual jealousy. Just enough information is given to stimulate the imagination, to give the reader a sudden glimpse into the depth of the tragic and ironical situation in the lives of these three people. This sudden glimpse, if the details are properly chosen, may be more effective in provoking the emotional response of the reader than a careful elaboration of facts that might satisfy the full curiosity. Poetry frequently employs this kind of suggestiveness rather than a method of detailed analysis.

A further word might be said about the use of repetition here. We have said that the repetition frames the questions and answers on which the movement of the action depends. In Section III we shall discuss the function of meter, rhyme, and stanza—that is, the effect of rhythmical patterns. It is enough for our purpose here to notice the effect of a regular pattern in the form of the questions and answers—that is, the use of repetition and refrain. Repetition and refrain are devices a poet may use to bring the material of a poem under control. The repetition and refrain, like meter, rhyme, and stanza, help give the poem a form.

Perhaps it cannot finally be said why we are affected as we are by artistic and other forms. For the present, it is enough that the reader should be aware of the part certain things like meter or repetition, things he may have regarded merely as mechanical decorations, are playing in his total response. In this poem, the repetition, for instance, serves as a kind of binder for each stanza, the fixed item to which the new material is tied each time. But it serves a further purpose, as well. The request to make the bed soon because he is weary with hunting begins to affect us with a secondary and symbolic meaning which is gradually developed: he is going to die, he is weary of life not merely because of his sickness from the poison but because his own true-love has betrayed him, life has disappointed him and he returns to his mother as when a child. All of this becomes involved in the repetition as the poem progresses, yet not explicitly; here again suggestiveness plays an important part. The poem does not state all that it has to say.

One may notice, in addition, the effect of the change from strict repetition in the last stanza of the poem. Instead of

> For I'm weary wi hunting, and fain wald lie down

there appears

> For I'm sick at the heart, and I fain wald lie down.

The reader has come to expect the strict repetition, and when this variation comes, it comes with an effect of emphasis and climax. This is an example of expressive *variation* (*Note on Versification*) from a form that has been established. A reader should, in studying a poem, watch for variations of metrical and other patterns and should try to determine whether such variations are truly expressive and not arbitrary or accidental.

EXERCISE

1. What is the meaning of the phrase "sick at the heart" in the last line?
2. Can you state the theme of this poem?

Danny Deever

Rudyard Kipling [*1865–1936*]

"What are the bugles blowin' for?" said Files-on-Parade.
"To turn you out, to turn you out," the Color-Sergeant said.
"What makes you look so white, so white?" said Files-on-Parade.
"I'm dreadin' what I've got to watch," the Color-Sergeant said.
  For they're hangin' Danny Deever, you can hear the Dead March play,
  The Regiment's in 'ollow square—they're hangin' him today;
  They've taken of his buttons off an' cut his stripes away,
  An' they're hangin' Danny Deever in the mornin'.

"What makes the rear-rank breathe so 'ard?" said Files-on-Parade.
"It's bitter cold, it's bitter cold," the Color-Sergeant said.
"What makes that front-rank man fall down?" said Files-on-Parade.
"A touch o' sun, a touch o' sun," the Color-Sergeant said.
They are hangin' Danny Deever, they are marchin' of 'im round,
They 'ave 'alted Danny Deever by 'is coffin on the ground;
An' 'e'll swing in 'arf a minute for a sneakin' shootin' hound—
O they're hangin' Danny Deever in the mornin'!

" 'Is cot was right-'and cot to mine," said Files-on-Parade.
" 'E's sleepin' out an' far to-night," the Color-Sergeant said.
"I've drunk 'is beer a score o' times," said Files-on-Parade.
" 'E's drinkin' bitter beer alone," the Color-Sergeant said.
They are hangin' Danny Deever, you must mark 'im to 'is place,
For 'e shot a comrade sleepin'—you must look 'im in the face;
Nine 'undred of 'is county an' the Regiment's disgrace,
While they're hangin' Danny Deever in the mornin'.

"What's that so black agin the sun?" said Files-on-Parade.
"It's Danny fightin' 'ard for life," the Color-Sergeant said.
"What's that that whimpers over'ead?" said Files-on-Parade.
"It's Danny's soul that's passin' now," the Color-Sergeant said.
For they're done with Danny Deever, you can 'ear the quickstep play,
The Regiment's in column, an' they're marchin' us away;
Ho! the young recruits are shakin', an' they'll want their beer to-day,
After hangin' Danny Deever in the mornin'!

EXERCISE

1. This modern poem uses many of the devices we have observed in the traditional ballads. List them. What is the most important difference between the method of this poem and that of "Lord Randal"?

2. Do you think that "Danny Deever" would be more effective if the treatment were confined to dialogue? What are your arguments?

3. What facts do we have about Danny Deever? His relation to his comrades? Their attitude toward him? His crime? A possible justification for the crime? What attitude does the poet expect us to take toward the event? Is there any relation between the dearth of actual information and the attitude the poet expects us to take?

4. In the second stanza, the Color-Sergeant says, first, that it is bitter cold, then that a man in the front rank has collapsed from a touch of the sun. Does this make sense?

5. Would you be satisfied if the name of the main character were Jackson Smithers. If not, why not? If so, why?

6. Get a good feeling for the rhythm of the poem. Do you see any relation between this rhythm and the subject matter and feeling of the poem?

Proud Maisie

Sir Walter Scott [*1771–1832*]

Proud Maisie is in the wood,
  Walking so early;
Sweet Robin sits on the bush,
  Singing so rarely.

"Tell me, thou bonny bird,
  When shall I marry me?"
"When six braw [1] gentlemen,
  Kirkward shall carry ye."

"Who makes the bridal bed,
  Birdie, say truly?"—
"The gray-headed sexton
  That delves the grave duly.

"The glow-worm o'er grave and stone
  Shall light thee steady;
The owl from the steeple sing,
  'Welcome, proud lady.' "

1 brave

EXERCISE

1. This poem evidently derives from the folk ballad. What are some of the specific ways in which it resembles the folk ballad?

2. The story is evidently a fantastic one: birds cannot speak, for example. But does the fairy-tale quality of the first stanza prevent the poem's becoming a thoroughly serious one?

3. Note that *carry* in line 8 may be used in the archaic sense of "escort," and does not necessarily mean "lift up and transport." Which interpretation does Maisie make (see line 9)?

4. Note that the funeral is consistently compared to a marriage, the six pall bearers becoming groomsmen, and so on. What effect is gained by this device?

5. How heavily are we to weight the word "proud"? Is the rebuke given to Maisie's pride harsh and bitter? What is the robin's attitude toward Maisie and her hopes? Jeering? Mocking? Playful? Or what? In trying to answer this question, read the last stanza very carefully.

Hell Gate

A. E. Housman [*1859–1936*]

Onward led the road again
Through the sad uncolored plain
Under twilight brooding dim,
And along the utmost rim
Wall and rampart risen to sight
Cast a shadow not of night,
And beyond them seemed to glow
Bonfires lighted long ago.
And my dark conductor broke
Silence at my side and spoke,
Saying, "You conjecture well:
Yonder is the gate of hell."

Ill as yet the eye could see
The eternal masonry,
But beneath it on the dark

To and fro there stirred a spark.
And again the somber guide
Knew my question and replied:
"At hell gate the damned in turn
Pace for sentinel and burn."

Dully at the leaden sky
Staring, and with idle eye
Measuring the listless plain,
I began to think again.
Many things I thought of then,
Battle, and the loves of men,
Cities entered, oceans crossed,
Knowledge gained and virtue lost,
Cureless folly done and said,
And the lovely way that led
To the slimepit and the mire
And the everlasting fire.
And against a smolder dun
And a dawn without a sun
Did the nearing bastion loom,
And across the gate of gloom
Still one saw the sentry go,
Trim and burning, to and fro,
One for women to admire
In his finery of fire.
Something, as I watched him pace,
Minded me of time and place,
Soldiers of another corps
And a sentry known before.

Ever darker hell on high
Reared its strength upon the sky,
And our footfall on the track
Fetched the daunting echo back.
But the soldier pacing still
The insuperable sill,
Nursing his tormented pride,
Turned his head to neither side,
Sunk into himself apart
And the hell-fire of his heart.
But against our entering in
From the drawbridge Death and Sin
Rose to render key and sword

To their father and their lord.
And the portress foul to see
Lifted up her eyes on me
Smiling, and I made reply:
"Met again, my lass," said I.
Then the sentry turned his head,
Looked, and knew me, and was Ned.

Once he looked, and halted straight,
Set his back against the gate,
Caught his musket to his chin,
While the hive of hell within
Sent abroad a seething hum
As of towns whose king is come
Leading conquest home from far
And the captives of his war,
And the car of triumph waits,
And they open wide the gates.
But across the entry barred
Straddled the revolted guard,
Weaponed and accoutred well
From the arsenals of hell;
And beside him, sick and white,
Sin to left and Death to right
Turned a countenance of fear
On the flaming mutineer.
Over us the darkness bowed,
And the anger in the cloud
Clenched the lightning for the stroke;
But the traitor musket spoke.

And the hollowness of hell
Sounded as its master fell,
And the mourning echo rolled
Ruin through his kingdom old.
Tyranny and terror flown
Left a pair of friends alone,
And beneath the nether sky
All that stirred was he and I.

Silent, nothing found to say,
We began the backward way;
And the ebbing luster died
From the soldier at my side,

As in all his spruce attire
Failed the everlasting fire.
Midmost of the homeward track
Once we listened, and looked back;
But the city, dusk, and mute,
Slept, and there was no pursuit.

This poem, like "The Wife of Usher's Well" and "The Three Ravens," presents a fantastic situation. In the two earlier poems, we saw that the fantastic situation (the return of the drowned sons to their mother's house, the conversation of the crows) embodies some idea and some feeling about ordinary life. Inwardly, the poems are not fantastic; they are relevant to our human concerns.

What is such relevance in "Hell Gate"?

In reading the poem we shall start with the most simple and obvious fact—always a good principle. Here that fact is that the damned man serving as sentinel at hell gate is able, as soon as he sees his friend's plight, to strike down Satan and free them both. That is the simple, central fact, and we can readily get a clue to a general idea, the theme: Man is saved by his loyalty to friends, his fidelity to, and concern for, others—to use the imagery of the poem, by his soldierly code.

But we may ask further: Saved from what?

We feel immediately that we are not dealing with salvation in the Christian sense. True, there are elements here that remind us of that—hell itself, the "dark conductor," and the figures of Death and Sin drawn from Milton's Christian epic *Paradise Lost*. Housman, no doubt, wants us to be reminded of the Christian version of salvation, but, we shall find, he wants to remind us as a way of ironically emphasizing the difference between his notion of salvation and the Christian one.

Certainly, if we try to force the Christian idea on the present poem, we create more difficulties than we avoid. If Ned, for instance, is taken as a kind of Christ figure, since he is the one who "saves," then we have to ask how Christ saves. But on this point the parallel between Christ and Ned breaks down. We cannot, then, depend on merely individual, and incidental, similarities with the Christian version, such as the idea of hell, the fact of salvation, the presence of Death and

Sin. Always, as a general principle in making an interpretation, we must look for an over-all coherence. If the poem is coherent, if it makes sense, then our reading must be applicable to the details of the poem. If there are lags and confusions, like that about Ned taken as a Christ figure, then we should modify our reading or discard it and try again.

A poem may, of course, be incoherent. The world is full of bad poems, incoherent poems, but it is always a good idea to assume a poem innocent until it is proved guilty. We can prove a poem guilty only by assuming its innocence—that is, by trying to find a coherent reading for it and failing in the attempt. Poetic coherence may be, we must recognize, a very complicated thing, and we cannot pause now for a definition. A definition is not, in any case, what we want. We want a general, lively sense of poetic coherence, knowing that it will be modified, however slightly, from poem to poem, and all of our study of poetry will be directed toward getting that.

To return to our particular poem, we have asked what the friends are saved from. From "hell," certainly. But what is this hell? Let us go back to the beginning of the poem, as the "I," the narrator, is being led toward hell gate.

The first word to raise a question is *again,* in the first line. The word tells us that we are in the middle of a process—a long, dreary, monotonous process. How do we know that it is dreary and monotonous? Because the road leads across a plain (a plain is level, unbroken) which is sad and uncolored. Damnation, then, is not being presented by reference to a sudden dramatic act; however it may have begun, it is presented as monotonous and dull, so dull that the glow of the fire of final torment comes as a point of interest in the sad plain, a kind of relief from the ennui and monotony.

By now another question must have obtruded itself. The "dark conductor" does not seem to be a victor dragging his captive along. In fact, the narrator scarcely seems to be a captive at all. He and the conductor seem, rather, to be old and perhaps mutually boring companions on a dull journey—companions intimate enough after their long association for the conductor to read the narrator's mind and answer his unspoken questions. Why, we ask ourselves, does the damned narrator proceed without protest or struggle? And, as the conductor, explaining the spark seen yonder, says that the damned themselves act as sentinels for hell, we are aware of the same question in another form: Why are the damned trustworthy sentinels, ready to guard their own hell? Why don't they run away?

We can assume this as the next unspoken question in the narrator's mind, for the statement from the conductor provokes the narrator to review his own life—the process that had led to damnation. And here, again, the monotony, the dreariness, the ennui is the striking thing. The eye of the narrator is "idle"—even the sight of the flames of his prospective torment cannot stir him to deep concern. The plain is "listless." The narrator recalls how life had begun in action and excitement and pleasure—the life of the soldier being the image used in the poem—but all the "lovely ways" have led only to the filth and degradation, "the slimepit and the mire," and now to the ennui in which he wanders toward the "everlasting fire."

We have said that the glow on the horizon has become a point of interest, even of relief, in the dim dullness of the plain, and now as the narrator reviews his life and approaches nearer hell gate, he sees the damned sentry as the point of interest, the one vital thing. The sentry is gallant, handsome, soldierly—

> One for women to admire
> In his finery of fire.

"Finery of fire"—so his damnation becomes him, makes him interesting. And that is a way of saying that the torment offers some value, as it were. Is it implied that the damned man really chooses torment as a relief from the ennui and monotony of the plain? Perhaps that is part of the answer. But we have the full answer very quickly: The sentinel is "sunk" —the implications of the word are significant—"into the hell-fire of his heart." If the hell is within, there is no place to run away to. The only thing left is to pace in his "finery of fire" and fulfill with tormented but soldierly pride his role of sentry.

That is all for the damned sentry to do until there is something to provoke him out of himself. Man can be saved from the final torment of self-absorbed isolation only by acting to save some one else. In terms of the poem, it is an old friend who is saved, friendship here with the notion of the soldier's code and *esprit de corps*. So now, back at the theme of the poem, we may ask another question: Does Housman mean to limit such an act to an old fellow-in-arms? Or in a broader sense, to a friend? Or is it possible to catch, not as an allusion but as a logical extension of the idea of the poem, an echo of the Biblical answer to the question as to who is one's neighbor? If so, the "corps," then, becomes the human race, and it is the exercise of human sympathy that gives salvation.

This is the theme of the poem—or it is one way to state it, for a theme may be stated in many ways. But in this statement have we exhausted the meaning of the poem? No, for we must remember that all the details of a poem—in this case the description of the plain, the narrator's review of his own damnation, the military imagery with all that that implies, the very rhythm, the brisk rhyming—contribute to our idea of the poet's general feeling about life, its tragic possibilities, the chances of disillusion, the need for stoic discipline.

EXERCISE

1. Let us approach the matter in another way. Why doesn't the poem end with lines 93–94? Tyranny and terror have left the friends alone:

> And beneath the nether sky
> All that stirred was he and I.

This would leave completed the theme as stated above. With the last section, however, some strange features emerge. The friends have nothing to say. We may take this as a sign of exhaustion, of deep feeling, or of friendship that has understanding beyond the need for words. But is there some ambiguity here? Some sense that they can no longer communicate, that once past the crisis each runs the risk of falling back into self-absorption and isolation? With this in mind as a possibility, look at the phrase "ebbing luster died." The luster that had made Ned remarkable is to be associated with his "damnation" —with the fire of his torment—and its disappearance is now described in words that carry a sense of loss and deprivation—*ebbing, died*. In the next line the "finery of fire" which had distinguished Ned begins to fail, and the word *fail,* like *ebbing* and *died,* imports into the poem the ironical sense of a loss at the very moment of victory and release.

What do you make of this?

2. From line 70 to line 86 the style is more "grand" than in other parts of the poem. What do you think was the poet's intention in this?

3. In line 91 we find that tyranny and terror are flown as a result of Ned's act. Tyranny and terror are the attributes of Satan in the scheme of the poem's story. But in terms of the poet's meaning, what is their origin?

4. The following words may move you to comment:

daunting in line 48
flaming in line 82
clenched in line 85

5. Look up the word *stoic*—both as a common adjective, which you will find in the dictionary, and as the name of a system of philosophy, which you will find described in some reference work. How well does the word (which we have used above) fit Housman?

Ulysses

Alfred, Lord Tennyson [*1809–1892*]

It little profits that an idle king,
By this still hearth, among these barren crags,
Matched with an agèd wife, I mete and dole
Unequal laws unto a savage race,
That hoard, and sleep, and feed, and know not me.
I cannot rest from travel: I will drink
Life to the lees: all times I have enjoyed
Greatly, have suffered greatly, both with those
That loved me, and alone; on shore, and when
Through scudding drifts the rainy Hyades
Vext the dim sea: I am become a name;
For always roaming with a hungry heart
Much have I seen and known; cities of men
And manners, climates, councils, governments,

Myself not least, but honored of them all;
And drunk delight of battle with my peers,
Far on the ringing plains of windy Troy.
I am a part of all that I have met;
Yet all experience is an arch wherethro'
Gleams that untraveled world, whose margin fades
For ever and for ever when I move.
How dull it is to pause, to make an end,
To rust unburnished, not to shine in use!
As though to breathe were life. Life piled on life
Were all too little, and of one to me
Little remains: but every hour is saved
From that eternal silence, something more,
A bringer of new things; and vile it were
For some three suns to store and hoard myself,
And this gray spirit yearning in desire
To follow knowledge like a sinking star,
Beyond the utmost bound of human thought.

This is my son, mine own Telemachus,
To whom I leave the scepter and the isle–
Well-loved of me, discerning to fulfill
This labor, by slow prudence to make mild
A rugged people, and through soft degrees
Subdue them to the useful and the good.
Most blameless is he, centered in the sphere
Of common duties, decent not to fail
In offices of tenderness, and pay
Meet adoration to my household gods,
When I am gone. He works his work, I mine.

There lies the port; the vessel puffs her sail:
There gloom the dark broad seas. My mariners,
Souls that have toiled, and wrought, and thought with me–
That ever with a frolic welcome took
The thunder and the sunshine, and opposed
Free hearts, free foreheads–you and I are old;
Old age hath yet his honor and his toil.
Death closes all: but something ere the end,
Some work of noble note, may yet be done,
Not unbecoming men that strove with Gods.
The lights begin to twinkle from the rocks;
The long day wanes: the slow moon climbs: the deep
Moans round with many voices. Come, my friends,

'T is not too late to seek a newer world.
Push off, and sitting well in order smite
The sounding furrows; for my purpose holds
To sail beyond the sunset, and the baths
Of all the western stars, until I die.
It may be that the gulfs will wash us down:
It may be we shall touch the Happy Isles,
And see the great Achilles, whom we knew.
Though much is taken, much abides; and though
We are not now that strength which in old days
Moved earth and heaven, that which we are, we are;
One equal temper of heroic hearts,
Made weak by time and fate, but strong in will
To strive, to seek, to find, and not to yield.

EXERCISE

1. Ulysses, the hero of Homer's *Odyssey,* has returned home from the siege of Troy after ten years of wandering and adventure. (Consult the library for a full account. See also a translation of Canto XXVI of the *Inferno,* by Dante.) He is here picturing the prospect of his old age. The poet uses this situation to dramatize what general attitude and feeling?

2. Why does Ulysses say that his people "know not me"? How is he different from them?

3. Does Ulysses patronize his wife ("an agèd wife")? Does he patronize his son Telemachus? If you feel that he does not, try to indicate, by reference to the text, why you feel that he does not.

4. The poem falls into two parts, the part up to line 43, and the part after. In the first part the king is reflecting on his past, describing his present situation, distinguishing himself from his subjects and family, and justifying his attitude. By and large, this part deals with generalizations. What images do you find that the imagination can fix on? Are they effective? Does the first line of the second section seem to indicate a difference from the first? If so, what difference, or differences?

5. Can you locate any line, or lines, in the second section in which the rhythm seems especially expressive?

6. What do you feel about the last three lines of the poem? Do they add anything to the poem? Do they "feel" right for

the character of Ulysses as you have known him from the rest of the poem? Are they over-assertive, bombastic? Or are they addressed to the mariners, and adapted to that purpose—a heartening harangue?

7. What distinguishes Ulysses' yearning for travel from mere wanderlust—from mere distaste for responsibility and hunger for new sensations? The answer to this question leads to the theme of the poem. Can you state it? Go back into the poem and assemble the items that bear, directly or indirectly, on the theme.

Badger

John Clare [*1793–1864*]

When midnight comes a host of boys and men
Go out and track the badger to his den,
And put a sack within the hole, and lie
Till the old grunting badger passes by.
He comes and hears—they let the strongest loose.
The old fox hears the noise and drops the goose.
The poacher shoots and hurries from the cry,
And the old hare half wounded buzzes by.
They get a forked stick to bear him down
And clap the dogs and take him to the town,
And bait him all the day with many dogs,
And laugh and shout and fright the scampering hogs.
He runs along and bites at all he meets:
They shout and hollo down the noisy streets.

He turns about to face the loud uproar
And drives the rebels to their very door.
The frequent stone is hurled where'er they go;
When badgers fight, then every one's a foe.
The dogs are clapt and urged to joint the fray;
The badger turns and drives them all away.
Though scarcely half as big, demure and small,
He fights with dogs for hours and beats them all.
The heavy mastiff, savage in the fray,
Lies down and licks his feet and turns away.
The bulldog knows his match and waxes cold,
The badger grins and never leaves his hold.

He drives the crowd and follows at their heels
And bites them through—the drunkard swears and reels.

The frighted women take the boys away,
The blackguard laughs and hurries on the fray.
He tries to reach the woods, an awkward race,
But sticks and cudgels quickly stop the chase.
He turns agen and drives the noisy crowd
And beats the many dogs in noises loud.
He drives away and beats them every one,
And then they loose them all and set them on.
He falls as dead and kicked by boys and men,
Then starts and grins and drives the crowd agen;
Till kicked and torn and beaten out he lies
And leaves his hold and cackles, groans, and dies.

EXERCISE

1. This poem presents a scene from the life of an English village. What human types appear? Do we need more for the purpose of the poem?

2. Much of the rhythm of the poem seems awkward and halting. How does this affect you?

3. The word *demure* in line 21 seems to carry a meaning slightly different from our ordinary sense. Look it up in the Oxford English Dictionary.

4. What is the poem about? What is the poet's attitude toward the badger? Toward the villagers?

5. Look up the author in some reference work. Do the facts of his life give you any better understanding of the poem?

Meeting at Night

Robert Browning [*1812–1889*]

The gray sea and the long black land:
And the yellow half-moon large and low;
And the startled little waves that leap
In fiery ringlets from their sleep,
As I gain the cove with pushing prow,
And quench its speed in the slushy sand.

Then a mile of warm sea-scented beach;
Three fields to cross till a farm appears;
A tap at the pane, the quick sharp scratch
And blue spurt of a lighted match,
And a voice less loud, thro' its joys and fears,
Than the two hearts beating each to each!

Parting at Morning

Robert Browning [*1812–1889*]

Round the cape of a sudden came the sea,
And the sun looked over the mountain's rim:
And straight was a path of gold for him,
And the need of a world of men for me.

EXERCISE

1. How much story do we have in these two little poems? Do we need more?

2. If the human details of the story are so carefully withheld, why does the poet give so fully, in "Meeting at Night," the physical details of the approach—the "fiery ringlets," the "slushy sand," the number of fields, the scratch of the match? Wouldn't we expect to find the emphasis reversed? Or would we?

3. The occasion in the poem is a romantic one—the night meeting of two lovers. Why does the poet select, by and large, such matter-of-fact details to fill out his poem? Why do we not find the scent of blossoms, the song of the nightingale, the soft caress of the night breeze?

4. Consider the *image* (*Glossary*) in the first two lines of "Parting at Morning." How can the sea suddenly come round the cape? Literally? If not literally, how does the observer get that impression? What position of the observer might make such an impression possible? If the image is, at first glance, puzzling, why would the poet use it at all? And why would he start his poem with it?

5. Do you make sense of the last two lines of "Parting at Morning"?

The Demon Lover

Anonymous

"O where have you been, my long, long love,
This long seven years and mair?"
"O I'm come to seek my former vows
Ye granted me before."

"O hold your tongue of your former vows,
For they will breed sad strife;
O hold your tongue of your former vows,
For I am become a wife."

He turned him right and round about,
And the tear blinded his ee:
"I wad never hae trodden on Irish ground,
If it had not been for thee.

"I might hae had a king's daughter,
Far, far beyond the sea;
I might have had a king's daughter,
Had it not been for love o thee."

"If ye might have had a king's daughter,
Yer sel ye had to blame;
Ye might have had taken the king's daughter,
For ye kend[1] that I was nane.[2]

"If I was to leave my husband dear,
And my two babes also,
O what have you to take me to,
If with you I should go?"

"I hae seven ships upon the sea—
The eighth brought me to land—
With four-and-twenty bold mariners,
And music on every hand."

She has taken up her two little babes,
Kissd them baith[3] cheek and chin:

[1] knew [2] none [3] both

"O fair ye weel, my ain[1] two babes,
  For I'll never see you again."

She set her foot upon the ship,
  No mariners could she behold;
But the sails were o the taffetie,
  And the masts o the beaten gold.

She had not sailed a league, a league,
  A league but barely three,
When dismal grew his countenance,
  And drumlie[2] grew his ee.

They had not sailed a league, a league,
  A league but barely three,
Until she espied his cloven foot,
  And she wept right bitterlie.

"O hold your tongue of your weeping," says he,
  "Of your weeping now let me be;
I will shew you how the lilies grow
  On the banks of Italy."

"O what hills are yon, yon pleasant hills,
  That the sun shines sweetly on?"
"O yon are the hills of heaven," he said,
  "Where you will never win."

"O whaten a mountain is yon," she said,
  "All so dreary wi frost and snow?"
"O yon is the mountain of hell," he cried,
  "Where you and I will go."

He strack the tap-mast wi his hand,
  The fore-mast wi his knee,
And he brake that gallant ship in twain,
  And sank her in the sea.

EXERCISE

1. What finally motivates the woman to yield to the lover's entreaties?

[1] own   [2] dark

2. What is the implication of the fact that the ship's sails are taffeta and the masts, gold? Is the ship too good to be true?

3. When the woman spies the "cloven foot"—the devils, for all their power to disguise themselves, are not permitted to conceal one mark of their deviltry—she knows that her supposed lover is a demon. How justify, then, the keeping up of the pretense until line 55? Is the portrayal of the woman and the demon from 43 to 55 aceptable? Is the psychology sound?

4. What actually happens in the last stanza? Read carefully, noting the details of the action, and describe the picture that emerges. What, physically, has happened to the lover?

In the version of this ballad printed by Sir Walter Scott in his *Minstrelsy of the Scottish Border,* two stanzas (made up by Scott's friend William Laidlaw) are made to precede the last stanza. The first of these reads as follows:

> And aye when she turn'd her round about,
>   Aye taller he seem'd to be;
> Until that the tops o' that gallant ship
>   Nae taller were than he.

This stanza "explains" what happens in the last stanza; but is the explanation needed? Does its inclusion strengthen or enfeeble the effect of the last stanza?

5. Can you think why this poem is put so far toward the end of this section and not earlier with the other traditional ballads?

La Belle Dame sans Merci

John Keats [*1795–1821*]

O what can ail thee, knight at arms,
  Alone and palely loitering?
The sedge has withered from the lake
  And no birds sing!

O what can ail thee, knight at arms,
  So haggard and so woe-begone?
The squirrel's granary is full,
  And the harvest's done.

I see a lily on thy brow,
  With anguish moist and fever dew;
And on thy cheeks a fading rose
  Fast withereth too.—

I met a lady in the meads,
  Full beautiful, a faery's child;
Her hair was long, her foot was light,
  And her eyes were wild.

I made a garland for her head,
  And bracelets, too, and fragrant zone;
She looked at me as she did love,
  And made sweet moan.

I set her on my pacing steed,
  And nothing else, saw all day long;
For sidelong would she bend, and sing
  A faery's song.

She found me roots of relish sweet,
  And honey wild, and manna dew;
And sure in language strange she said,
  "I love thee true."

She took me to her elfin grot,
  And there she wept and sighed full sore;
And there I shut her wild, wild eyes
  With kisses four.

And there she lullèd me asleep,
  And there I dreamed, ah woe betide!
The latest dream I ever dreamt,
  On the cold hillside.

I saw pale kings, and princes too,
  Pale warriors, death-pale were they all,
Who cried, "La Belle Dame sans Merci
  Thee hath in thrall!"

I saw their starved lips in the gloam
  With horrid warning gaped wide—
And I awoke and found me here,
  On the cold hill's side.

And this is why I sojourn here,
  Alone and palely loitering;
Though the sedge is withered from the lake,
  And no birds sing.

EXERCISE

1. This poem, like "Farewell to Barn and Stack and Tree," "Danny Deever," and "Proud Maisie," clearly owes much to the method of the traditional ballad. What features does it seem to derive from the ballad?

2. "La Belle Dame sans Merci" is, of course, a modern poem by an extremely accomplished poet using the pretense of ballad simplicity. Suppose you came on this poem without knowing its authorship or anything about it. Could you fix on any features which might make you think it was not a true ballad? Language, for instance? Or rhythm? Or the attitude of the narrator? Or method of developing the narrative?

3. Keats, clearly, was not trying to imitate a ballad merely as a kind of trick. Can you imagine why he should have followed the ballad method so closely?

4. Who is the knight? Who is La Belle Dame? If you can answer these two questions, you can state the theme of the poem.

5. In a letter to his brother, Keats makes some remarks about the lines

And there I shut her wild, wild eyes
  With kisses four.

He writes: "Why four kisses—you will say—why four, because I wish to restrain the headlong impetuosity of my Muse—she would fain have said 'score' without hurting the rhyme—but we must temper the imagination as the Critics say with Judgment. I was obliged to choose an even number that both eyes might have fair play, and to speak truly I think two a piece quite sufficient. Suppose I had said seven there would have been three and a half a piece, a very awkward affair, and well got out of on my side." Later when Keats revised the poem—we have printed the first version, which nearly everyone feels is the better of the two—the lines in question became

And there I shut her wild sad eyes
So kiss'd to sleep.

Is the revision an improvement? If you prefer the first version, can you, Keats's banter aside, justify the phrase "kisses four"?

Battle of the Bonhomme Richard *and the* Serapis

Walt Whitman [*1819–1892*]

I

Would you hear of an old-time sea-fight?
Would you learn who won by the light of the moon and stars?
List to the yarn, as my grandmother's father the sailor told
  it to me.

Our foe was no skulk in his ship I tell you, (said he,)
His was the surly English pluck, and there is no tougher
  or truer, and never was, and never will be;
Along the lower'd eve he came horribly raking us.

We closed with him, the yards entangled, the cannon touch'd,
My captain lash'd fast with his own hands.

We had receiv'd some eighteen pound shots under the water,
On our lower-gun-deck two large pieces had burst at the first
  fire, killing all around and blowing up overhead.

Fighting at sun-down, fighting at dark,
Ten o'clock at night, the full moon well up, our leaks on the
  gain, and five feet of water reported,
The master-at-arms loosing the prisoners confined in the after-
  hold to give them a chance for themselves.

The transit to and from the magazine is now stopt by the
  sentinels,
They see so many strange faces they do not know whom to
  trust.

Our frigate takes fire,
The other asks if we demand quarter?
If our colors are struck and the fighting done?

Now I laugh content for I hear the voice of my little captain,
We have not struck, he composedly cries, *we have just begun our part of the fighting.*

Only three guns are in use,
One is directed by the captain himself against the enemy's main-mast,
Two well serv'd with grape and canister silence his musketry and clear his decks.

The tops alone second the fire of this little battery, especially the main-top,
They hold out bravely during the whole of the action.

Not a moment's cease,
The leaks gain fast on the pumps, the fire eats toward the powder-magazine.

One of the pumps has been shot away, it is generally thought we are sinking.

Serene stands the little captain,
He is not hurried, his voice is neither high nor low,
His eyes give more light to us than our battle-lanterns.

Toward twelve there in the beams of the moon they surrender to us.

II

Stretch'd and still lies the midnight,
Two great hulls motionless on the breast of the darkness,
Our vessel riddled and slowly sinking, preparations to pass to the one we have conquer'd,
The captain on the quarter-deck coldly giving his orders through a countenance white as a sheet,
Near by the corpse of the child that serv'd in the cabin,
The dead face of an old salt with long white hair and carefully curl'd whiskers,
The flames spite of all that can be done flickering aloft and below,
The husky voices of the two or three officers yet fit for duty,
Formless stacks of bodies and bodies by themselves, dabs of flesh upon the masts and spars,
Cut of cordage, dangle of rigging, slight shock of the soothe of waves,

Black and impassive guns, litter of powder-parcels, strong scent,
A few large stars overhead, silent and mournful shining,
Delicate sniffs of sea-breeze, smells of sedgy grass and fields by the shore, death-messages given in charge to survivors,
The hiss of the surgeon's knife, the gnawing teeth of his saw,
Wheeze, cluck, swash of falling blood, short wild scream, and long, dull tapering groan,
These so, these irretrievable.

(From "Song of Myself," sections 35 and 36)

EXERCISE

1. Here is a very vivid and thrilling account of John Paul Jones's most famous victory. The poem does celebrate the "little captain," but is that the main intention of the poem? To answer this we may think of the context in which the action is set. To begin, let us ask what Whitman intends by his second line:

Would you learn who won by the light of the moon and stars?

Certainly the fact that the battle lasted for hours, into the night, is implied by the line. But is that all? If so, why do we return to the night scene in line 32, at the end of Part I, and again in line 45, where there are other effective details, the "shock of the soothe of the waves," and the "smells of sedgy grass and fields by the shore"? If a mere celebration of Jones's courage were all intended, what would, in fact, be the use of most of Part II?

But is this to imply that Whitman means to underrate the courage of captain and crew, and to deplore the event? Is it not, rather, that he intends to put the courage into a special context? What are the elements of this context? What added dimension do you feel from the context? What we are now trying to do is to work toward the main idea—the theme—of the poem. How would you state it?

2. If we have some notion of the theme of the poem—and as a corollary, the main effect the poet is trying to give—we can begin to think of what principle governs his selection of

detail. The action, historically speaking, was very complicated. Whitman has ignored most of it. Why? *

It may be said that Part I deals with the main outlines of the battle, the stages in the action. What keeps this from being a mere summary? Rhythm? Flashes of dramatic action? Shrewdly observed detail and image? Sharp *simile* or *metaphor* (*Glossary*)? A progression toward a climax? (What, by the way, is the climax of Part I?)

The action is narrated in fits and starts; we are made to leap from one thing to another more athletically, we may say, than in ordinary prose narrative. Does it make for greater imaginative involvement? Let us look at one striking example of such a leap, the break in continuity between line 5 and line 6. Lines 4 and 5 describe "the surly English pluck" of the enemy. Then, suddenly, comes the line

> Along the lower'd eve he came horribly raking us.

What is the effect of this leap? Can you find similar effects elsewhere in Part I, especially toward the end? See also Exercise 4 of "The Demon Lover."

3. We have said that Part I deals with the main outline of the action. What is the concern of Part II? In the massing of the images—the details of the scene—do you find any startling transitions that correspond in effect to the leaps in action in Part I?

4. Go back over the whole poem and point out the words, phrases, and images that seem especially effective—things like the word *cluck* in line 49, or the old salt's curled whiskers in line 39. (What associations, for example, are imported into the poem by the word *cluck?* Does the shock here make for vividness?)

5. Let us investigate some details.

(a) Why, in line 19, does the narrator say "my little captain" instead of "our" or "the"? What is the effect of the word

* For a fascinating historical account of the engagement, see Samuel Eliot Morison, *John Paul Jones* (Boston, Atlantic-Little, Brown, 1959). If that account is read in connection with Whitman's poem, we have a clear example of the difference in obligation and intention between a historical and a poetic treatment.

little here? Jones was very small, but is the word merely factual?

(b) What is the significance of the word *stretch'd* in line 33? Of the word *breast* in line 34?

(c) Why does Whitman use the word *conquer'd* and not *captur'd* in line 35?

(d) Why is the phrase "through a countenance white as a sheet," better than "with a countenance white as a sheet"?

(e) In line 43, in the phrase "slight shock of the soothe of the waves," what do you make of the apparent contradiction between *shock* and *soothe*? In fact, if it is a calm sea, why use the word *shock* at all? Or do the waves now give a shock that ordinarily would pass unobserved? Let us notice that the word *soothe* is used here as a noun. What does this distortion do for us? And does the word *soothe* here carry more meaning than the factual description? If so, to what other elements—details and interpretations—would you link it?

(f) Do you find any principle of progression in feeling and/or idea in the passage from line 45 to the end? If so, try to define it.

Epitaph on an Army of Mercenaries

A. E. Housman [1859–1936]

These, in the day when heaven was falling,
  The hour when earth's foundations fled,
Followed their mercenary calling
  And took their wages and are dead.

Their shoulders held the sky suspended;
  They stood, and earth's foundations stay;
What God abandoned, these defended,
  And saved the sum of things for pay.

EXERCISE

1. These "mercenaries" are not named, nor is the battle in which they fell. Has the poet given enough information about

them to allow you to identify them? What sort of people are they?

2. Their motives are not ostensibly patriotic or religious or idealistic. If they are "mercenaries," they fight for pay. But can a man be hired to die? What are their real motives for holding firm?

3. It has been maintained that the poet had in mind an actual group of soldiers in a particular war (the British professional soldiers in World War I). Even so, could it be argued that this poem has a more general reference—that it makes a penetrating comment upon courage and honor as they are actually met with in human beings? Is the poet contrasting a religious and a naturalistic view of the world—and dramatizing the values to be found in the latter?

AFTERWORD

In the section just completed we have been considering poems in which the narrative element is relatively prominent. In opening this section, we decided to use our interest in narrative as a device for leading into the study of poetry, because narrative presents the most obvious form which our interest in the stuff of literature takes. As we pointed out there, however, and as the analyses of various poems have indicated, narrative is only one element among several which the poet may use to gain his effect. The poet is not content with the narrative as such, even in poems which make a direct and prominent use of narrative. He is primarily interested in provoking a certain reaction toward the narrative. He wants to present the material of the narrative so that the reader will have a certain feeling toward it and will grasp a certain interpretation of it.

But this is also true of the writers of novels or short stories in prose, for such writers, like the poet, are more than reporters giving us a bare statement of facts and events. Indeed, it is not easy, except in regard to the use of verse, to make an absolute distinction between poetry and prose fiction, but it is possible on the basis of the poems we have already analyzed to state a difference in the following terms. Poetry *tends* toward *concentration* (*Glossary*). A poem treating, let us say, the story of Johnie Armstrong is a great deal shorter than a piece of prose fiction on the same subject would be. In general, it may be said that the writer of prose fiction tries to convince his reader by the accumulation of detail, and that the poet tries to convince his reader by the sharpness of selected detail. The distinction, as we have suggested, is not absolute, but the discussions that have already been studied will provide instances of the use which poetry makes of details. The poet tries to make a direct appeal to the imagination. The sort of suggestiveness which we have already remarked in several poems is an example of this. This method may be described as a short cut to the effect desired, as compared with the more roundabout method which prose fiction is forced to use. In the poems that follow we shall discover other methods whereby the poet can condense his material far more than the writer of prose fiction is able to do.

The effect of this condensation in poetry is a sense of greater *intensity* (*Glossary*) than is usually found in prose fiction. If poetry employs fewer details than prose fiction, then it stands to reason that to gain a comparable result the details must (1) be more effective in themselves than those in prose fiction—that is, they must be very carefully selected—and/or (2) they must be so arranged that they will have the greatest effect on the reader. The arrangement or form of a poem, then, is a most important matter and is directly connected with the concentration and intensity of poetry. In the analyses previously presented we have touched on certain aspects of the form of various poems, for the form of a poem must obviously differ from case to case according to the effect given. It is enough at this point, however, if we see that the form of poetry in general as contrasted with the form of prose fiction is more closely organized. For instance, in poetry the rhythms are controlled more strictly, usually being modified by the pattern of accentuation called meter. In Section III we shall discuss this matter at length, but for the present it is only necessary to be aware of the contribution meter makes to the concentration and intensity of poetry.

II

Descriptive Poems

FOREWORD

The poems of this section give us the more or less vivid and recognizable impression of some natural scene or natural object—a register, rendered as accurately as the poet could manage, of the impression he himself had received through his senses, or had imagined. A lively sense of the perceptible world with its sights, sounds, smells, is fundamental to poetry. Poetry puts us back in touch with the freshness of things—it restores our originally unprejudiced life of the senses. We may even go so far as to say that poetry starts there.

But it does not stop there. A human being, with his hopes and fears, thoughts and feelings, is in the midst of that perceptible world, and poetry is, finally, about him, and his situation. So, just as we have found that narrative poems do not merely give the facts of a story about others, but refer to our own lives and values, we shall find here that the descriptions involve our human concerns.

Let us dwell on this notion by pointing out that the image evoked by the words is not the same as the object in nature.

To begin with, the difference between the object in nature

and the image a poem puts into our imagination is not merely that the image is thinner and paler. The actual object out in the actual world is surrounded by a multitude of other objects and stands in a multitude of relations to other objects. When, however, the poet selects an object for his attention, it is suddenly jerked, as it were, out of the ordinary natural context and held up in isolation for us to stare at. As soon as it is thus set into focus—put under the light of our imagination—it looks different. It looks more interesting. It looks more important. The image reminds us, of course, of the object in nature, but we begin to feel, even though vaguely, that it carries some weight that the object had not borne.

For another thing, since we know that the image represents an object jerked out of its natural context by a human being, the poet, we are not alone with the image as we are alone with an object in nature. The poet stands between us and nature, no matter how unobtrusive he may try to be. The mere fact of the selecting of the image is a human act, and being human, it is significant to us. The image stirs us to feel that it carries some weight, not only because it is put into focus and therefore attracts the imagination, but also because it has been put into focus by a human being.

So always, in the back of our minds, we have the lurking question: *Why did the poet select this and not something else?*

That question is part of the human event in, and behind, every poem.

Pippa's Song

Robert Browning [*1812–1889*]

The year's at the spring,
And day's at the morn;
Morning's at seven;
The hillside's dew-pearled;
The lark's on the wing;
The snail's on the thorn:
God's in His Heaven—
All's right with the world!

(From *Pippa Passes*)

Some times the poet does not leave us alone to brood on and interpret as best we may the imagery of his poem. He himself may answer quite clearly the question in the back of our minds. In the foregoing poem (a song sung by a little Italian peasant girl in Browning's play *Pippa Passes*) the poet says that it is spring and that it is early morning, and then gives three images characteristically associated with the time of year and day. The poem might have ended here, and would have made an effect on us. But Browning adds his interpretation.*

His interpretation does no violence to the effect the poem might have made on us without the addition. In fact, if his interpretation did do violence to our previous feeling about the poem, we should say that the poem was incoherent, that it didn't hang together, that it was bad. As things stand, Browning's addition is, of course, consistent with the feeling of a fine spring morning when it seems that nothing can ever again go wrong; the addition merely makes the effect of the images more specific and forthright. All it does is to change our sense of the drift, the "feel" of the images, the mood created by them, into a general statement about the world.

This leads us to a most important consideration. In poetry (as in life) we make a very great error if we think of mood and thought as absolutely distinguished. A mood implies a certain attitude toward the world, and may shade over imperceptibly into thought, into general statement, into whole systems of philosophy. So, too, a general statement, or a system of philosophy, implies a certain drift of feeling. The ideas and imagery of a poem (it being the imagery by which mood is in large part determined) are intimately and organically related—just as ideas and mood are in our ordinary process of living.

EXERCISE

1. The first two of Browning's images are, in themselves, agreeable. Directly out of nature they bring, we may say, a

* We do not mean to imply that the poem would necessarily have been better without the addition. And certainly, since here we regard the poem merely as an isolated lyric, this is no place to discuss the dramatic considerations that might be adduced to justify the tag.

"plus" value into the poem. But this is not true of the snail. It brings in a "minus" value—or at best a neutral element. We scarcely think of snails as being "poetic."

Let us make a revision:

The bloom's on the thorn.

Do we now have a better poem? If so, why so? If not, why not?

2. At least one commentator finds the images in this poem, including the snail, too obviously agreeable, and leading too readily to the general conclusion. As he puts it, "Six pretty, co-ordinate images are marched, like six little lambs to the slaughter, to a colon and a powerful text—namely, that God's in his heaven, and so on." * How do you feel about this? Does the commentator ask, by implication, too much of a very brief lyric?

Written in March

William Wordsworth [1770–1850]

The cock is crowing,
The stream is flowing,
The small birds twitter,
The lake doth glitter,
The green field sleeps in the sun;
The oldest and youngest
Are at work with the strongest;
The cattle are grazing,
Their heads never raising:
There are forty feeding like one!

Like an army defeated
The snow hath retreated,
And now doth fare ill
On the top of the bare hill;
The plowboy is whooping—anon—anon:
There's joy in the mountains;
There's life in the fountains;
Small clouds are sailing,
Blue sky prevailing;
The rain is over and gone!

* John Crowe Ransom: *The World's Body,* New York, Charles Scribner's Sons, 1938, p. 121.

EXERCISE

1. Here is another poem celebrating the joy and energy of spring. In presenting its theme it is somewhat less specific than the song from *Pippa Passes.* How would you state the theme? How, if at all, does the theme differ from that of Browning's poem?

2. What images here strike you as fresh and effective? Why?

3. Does the word *whoop* surprise you?

4. The last line is an echo from the Bible.* What effect on the poem does this allusion have for you? How does this allusion strike you in relation to the word *whoop?*

5. Read the poem aloud several times, trying to surrender to its natural rhythm. Do you feel that the movement is suitable for the poem? Do you find any places where the poet breaks the general movement? Do you think these places irritating—and the result of bad craftsmanship? Or do you find them interesting, and perhaps effective? Argue your case.

Two Voices in a Meadow

Richard Wilbur [1921–]

1. *A Milkweed*

Anonymous as cherubs
Over the crib of God,
White seeds are floating
Out of my burst pod.
What power had I
Before I learned to yield?
Shatter me, great wind:
I shall possess the field.

2. *A Stone*

As casual as cow-dung
Under the crib of God,
I lie where chance would have me,
Up to the ears in sod.
Why should I move? To move

* Song of Solomon 2:11, "For, lo, the winter is past, the rain is over and gone."

Befits a light desire.
The sill of Heaven would founder,
Did such as I aspire.

EXERCISE

1. In each of these poems a common natural object—the bursting pod of the milkweed, the stone—is used as the image for a human attitude. What does the attitude in "A Milkweed" have in common with that in "A Stone"? The first poem deals with lightness, the second with heaviness. How does this contrast relate to what the poems have in common? Does the contrast affirm what the poems have in common, or does it cancel it out? Are the poems better taken individually, or together?

2. What is the "crib of God"? Why "cherubs" in one poem and "cow-dung" in the other, in connection with the crib? Does the contrast in the two sets of associations shock you?

3. Look at the line "I shall possess the field." It literally means, of course, that the seed of the milkweed will take root all over the field. But is there a metaphor hidden in the statement, a metaphor suggested by the phraseology?

4. It is clear what the metaphor is in the line "Up to the ears in sod." The stone is compared to a human being. But what kind of human being do you sense here? And how do you feel about the human being? How does the human being—or rather the stone—feel about himself? How serious, or how humorous, is the effect of the comparison?

The Main-Deep

James Stephens [*1882–1950*]

The long, rolling,
Steady-pouring,
Deep-trenchèd
Green billow:

The wide-topped,
Unbroken,
Green-glacid,
Slow-sliding,

Cold-flushing,
On—on—on—
Chill-rushing,
Hush-hushing,

Hush—hushing. . .

In the poems by Browning and Wordsworth we are aware of the presence of the poet between us and the natural scene described; in other words, we know what he wants the scene to mean to us. But with "The Main-Deep" we turn to a poem that seems purely objective, a poem in which there is no explicit indication of what the poet wants the scene to embody. How, then, are we to answer that question with which we began, the question always in the back of our minds? What makes the poet give us this scene in this particular way?

We may begin by reminding ourselves of the difference between the image in a poem and the object in nature. This poem does not attempt to provide us with a substitute for a trip to the seashore. If providing such a substitute were the purpose of the poem, then the poem would have very slight justification for being, for it can provide only a very inferior substitute for the real object in nature. The interest and pleasure one takes in the poem is of a different kind from the interest and pleasure one would take in the real object in nature. This can easily be proved if a reader studies his reaction to a poetic treatment of an object that in real nature would be unpleasant to look at. A pair of bloody hands would, in reality, be a disgusting rather than a pleasant sight. Let us take a passage from Shakespeare's *Macbeth,* however, that treats such a sight. Macbeth has just killed the king, Duncan, and is shocked at the sight of the blood on his hands:

> What hands are here! Ha! they pluck out mine eyes.
> Will all great Neptune's ocean wash this blood
> Clean from my hand? No, this my hand will rather
> The multitudinous seas incarnadine,
> Making the green one red.

The passage does not disgust us. Rather, it stirs our imagina tion so that we really grasp Macbeth's own feeling that noth ing in the world can remove the guilt from him. The blood has become an expression of a psychological fact.

But one might argue that a poem like "The Main-Deep" is different, because the passage from *Macbeth* comes in a play which provides us with a situation giving a basis for the interpretation of the expressive quality of the passage. This is, to a certain extent, true. We know nothing about the situation of "The Main-Deep" except that a human being, the poet, is looking at the sea. We know nothing about the circumstances leading up to the event and nothing about the spectator except what we can read by implication from the poem. Indeed the presence of a human being is not even mentioned in the poem, but we feel, nevertheless, that the poem is an expression of a human being; it involves an ordering and therefore an *interpretation.*

How is this true?

First, we know that the poet has assumed a particular view of the sea to the exclusion of other possible views. The sea here is, for example, not a stormy one. Second, the poet has been rigorously selective with the details which he actually puts into the poem.

This selection is not, it should be clear, performed at random. There must always be some principle of selection, some general feeling governing it, if the finished poem is not to appear incoherent. The sea in the poem has here been arranged by the poet so as to create a particular impression, and this impression implies the interpretation of life which is the theme of the poem.

Let us look at the poem to see how this interpretation is made available to us.

The poet has chosen, as it were, one billow on which the attention can be directed and which can give a kind of focus for the poem. The concentration on the single billow has another advantage, for while the sea as a whole, though agitated, does not progress, the single billow does seem to move forward. The eyes of the reader seem to be directed to a single billow advancing toward him as though he were standing on shore, or perhaps on a ship at sea. Only those qualities of the billow are singled out for comment that will not distract him from a concentrated gaze at the billow itself; the poet does not comment on the general scene. There is no direct reference, even, to the fact that the billow approaches the spectator but we gather this from the nature of the billow's movement. In the third stanza with the line

On—on—on—

we get an impression of increased speed, an impression not only from the words but from the additional accent in the line (no other line has more than two accents) that implies the hurry and piling up as the billow approaches. Further, this stanza gives a reference to the temperature of the billow, "cold-flushing," and "chill-rushing," as though on its nearer approach the spectator could almost tell the coldness of the water, something one could not think of in connection with a distant wave. Then with the last rush the billow spends itself on the beach and there is only the thin line of receding foam; or if we think of the observer on shipboard, the billow passes into the distance. This effect is supported by the repetition of the line

Hush—hushing . . .

We have here a process working itself out to a natural fulfillment. Out of the beautiful and splendid tumult of the billow comes the moment of poise when the process is completed. The idea is not stated—the poem seems quite objectively descriptive—but the poem has been so arranged that the effect is communicated to the reader. Even less does the poet present an application of his idea, as is the case in some poems; he does not moralize. He does not say, for instance, that the billow is like man's life, or that the billow shows us the process of struggle and fulfillment, or that nature always holds out a promise of peace, or anything of that sort. It might be possible to write a poem about the sea that would say these things and that would not necessarily be better or worse than "The Main-Deep," but it would be a different kind of poem. James Stephens leaves the reader, apparently, as close to the simple experience of looking at the sea as possible; but he has given an interpretation because, by his management of the materials, he has made the sea give the reader one feeling, the feeling of peace and fulfillment, and not any of the almost innumerable other feelings which the sea might be used by a poet to suggest. The reader may or may not take the step himself of attributing a specific application to the poem. The poem may be richer and more exciting if the reader does not fix on one specific application of the feeling and idea; for if he does leave it so, the poem has potential in it an attitude one might take toward many different experiences of life.

The following poems obviously bear a close resemblance to "The Main-Deep" in their method of objective presentation.

Pear Tree

H. D. [*1886–1961*]

Silver dust
lifted from the earth,
higher than my arms reach,
you have mounted.
O silver,
higher than my arms reach
you front us with great mass;
no flower ever opened
so staunch a white leaf,
no flower ever parted silver
from such rare silver;

O white pear,
your flower-tufts,
thick on the branch,
bring summer and ripe fruits
in their purple hearts.

Heat

H. D. [*1886–1961*]

O wind, rend open the heat,
cut apart the heat,
rend it to tatters.

Fruit cannot drop
through this thick air—

fruit cannot fall into heat
that presses up and blunts
the points of pears
and rounds the grapes.

Cut through the heat—
plow through it,
turning it on either side
of your path.

EXERCISE

1. "Pear Tree," like "The Main-Deep," may be taken as a poem about a natural process working itself out to fulfillment. Both Stephens and H. D. accept and celebrate the process; they do not bemoan the swift passage of time or the constant changes of life. But despite this similarity, we may detect some differences in attitude. To begin with, in H. D.'s poem we have not only the natural object—the tree—but also the poet confronting the tree, with lifted arms. Does not this give the impression of the reverential, the worshipful? If so, then the tree carries some hint of deity in itself, an active embodiment of the power of the life process. And this notion is supported by the fact that the poet does not regard the pear blossom as a thing brought forth by the season; instead, the pear blossoms "bring summer and ripe fruits." How far do you think we need to push this idea of a religious attitude in H. D.'s poem? What would we mean by the word *religious* in this connection? Try to state what difference you sense between H. D.'s attitude and that of Stephens.

2. Why does H. D. call the pear blossom "Silver dust / lifted from the earth"? Is there some relation between this phrase and what we have said above?

3. Read "Pear Tree" aloud several times and try to grasp its rhythm. Be sure that you give some value to line units. How would you describe the difference between the rhythm here and that of "The Main-Deep"? Does the difference seem to you in any way appropriate?

4. "Heat," like "Pear Tree," may be taken as a poem celebrating the natural process. But how does the attitude here differ from that of the previous poem? To be explicit, we know that fruit can fall through heat, and that heat ripens the

fruit. Why, if the poet celebrates fruitfulness and fulfillment, does she call for the wind?

A Brisk Wind

William Barnes [*1801–1886*]

The burdock leaves beside the hedge,
The leaves upon the poplar's height,
Were blown by windblasts up on edge,
And showed their undersides of white;
And willow trees beside the rocks,
All bent gray leaves, and swung gray boughs,
As there, on wagging heads, dark locks
Bespread red cheeks, behung white brows.

EXERCISE

1. Suppose the first four lines of "A Brisk Wind" were revised as follows:

> The burdock leaves beside the hedge
> All showed their undersides of white,
> And in the copse by the lane's edge
> Some leaves were snatched from the poplar's height.

What would be lost? What leap of perception?

2. Notice that the human figures in the scene are not specified. We have only the heads bowed into the wind. Is this more, or less, vivid than a fuller description would be?

3. The appearance of the wagging heads comes at the climax of the poem. Or is it a climax? What seems to be implied about man and nature here? How much identification do you feel with the scene? Why?

In a Station of the Metro

Ezra Pound [*1885–*]

The apparition of these faces in the crowd;
Petals on a wet, black bough.

Suppose Pound had written:

> The apparition of these faces in the crowd;
> Dead leaves caught in the gutter's stream.

Or:

> The apparition of these faces in the crowd;
> Dry leaves blown down the dry gutter.

What would be the difference?

We cannot say that there would be any loss in logic or common sense. The comparison—for the poem is based on a single metaphor, a comparison in the form of an identification—of the faces in the crowd to leaves caught in the water in a gutter or blown down a dry gutter by a gust of wind has just as much basis as does the comparison of the faces to white petals on a bough. The subway station does bear a certain resemblance to a gutter—more, in fact, than it bears to a bough. And the stream of people hurrying down bears likewise a resemblance to a stream of water, as the ordinary use of the word *stream* in this connection indicates. Or we might say that the roar of the subway train and the gust of its passing remind one of the wind; and the comparison of the faces to leaves is as "reasonable" as the comparison to petals. In a subway station, too, we expect the confusion of the crowd, people apparently being driven here and there by forces over which they have no control, perhaps a sense of unreality.

What, then, do the revisions lose?

They lose the shock of surprise, the suddenness of the perception. The comparisons in the revised versions are, we may say, too logical, too commonsensical, too reasonable, too literal. They are *merely* comparisons, with no inner significance, and when we encounter them we say, "Sure—and what of it?" There has been no leap of the poet's imagination, and therefore there is nothing to stir the reader's imagination.

In the original version of the poem, however, we observe that a new and surprising comparison is exactly what Pound gives us. The petals on a wet black bough, the white faces against the dimness—the comparison does embody a leap of the imagination, a shock of surprise. And yet, in the midst of the novelty, we sense that it, too, has a logical basis. The poet has simply focused upon the significant quality for the comparison, discarding other qualities, more obvious qualities. And the shock of surprise takes us to the poem's meaning.

A new and surprising interpretation is exactly what Pound's new and surprising comparison gives us. Even in this most unlikely place, we catch a glimpse of something beautiful, fresh, and pure, and in that momentary lift of the heart, sense an interpretation potentially applicable to a great deal of experience.

EXERCISE

1. We have said that the poem is based on a single metaphor. But the word *apparition* brings another metaphor, though a subordinate one, into the poem. What does this metaphor do for the poem?

2. Here is what Pound himself writes of the origin of his poem:

> Three years ago in Paris I got out of a "Metro" train at La Concorde, and saw suddenly a beautiful face, and then another and another, and then a beautiful child's face, and then another beautiful woman, and I tried all that day to find words for what this had meant to me, and I could not find any words that seemed to me worthy, or as lovely as that sudden emotion. . . .

He continues:

> I wrote a thirty-line poem, and destroyed it because it was what we call work "of second intensity." Six months later I made a poem half that length; a year later I made the following . . . sentence:
>
> "The apparition of these faces in the crowd:
> Petals on a wet, black bough."
>
> I daresay it is meaningless unless one has drifted into a certain vein of thought. In a poem of this sort one is trying to record the precise instant when a thing outward and objective transforms itself, or darts into a thing inward and subjective.*

We have not seen the early versions of this poem, but can you follow Pound's reasoning in rejecting them? How does the

* *Gaudier-Brzeska,* London, John Lane, 1916, pp. 100, 103.

last line of Pound's letter relate to the function of all description in poetry?

Dust of Snow

Robert Frost [*1874–1963*]

The way a crow
Shook down on me
The dust of snow
From a hemlock tree

Has given my heart
A change of mood
And saved some part
Of a day I had rued.

EXERCISE

1. This poem, like "In a Station of the Metro," is about a "change of mood." Develop the similarity (and dissimilarity) of theme.

2. Suppose "Dust of Snow" had been a poem in *free verse* (*Note on Versification*), as follows:

A crow, black on snow-whitened hemlock, shook snow-dust on me, passing:
My heart's mood is changed, and some part of the day saved.

What the poem presumably states is substantially the same as in the original version. Do you sense any difference in general feeling—and hence about what the poem means? If so, try to put it into words.

3. Is the method of Frost's poem more like that of "Pippa's Song" or "The Main-Deep"?

The Eagle

Alfred, Lord Tennyson [*1809–1892*]

He clasps the crag with crooked hands;
Close to the sun in lonely lands,
Ring'd with the azure world, he stands.

The wrinkled sea beneath him crawls;
He watches from his mountain walls,
And like a thunderbolt he falls.

EXERCISE

1. Taken at a perfectly literal level, what qualities of "eagleness" does the poem present? What qualities of the literal eagle are omitted? Why? What is the poet's attitude toward the qualities presented? How much identification do you feel with the eagle?

2. Suppose the first line read

He clasps the crag with crooked claws.

That would be more accurate as description, would it not? But, clearly, something would have been lost. The very fact of the *distortion*—the use of the word *hands* for claws—wakes up the imagination. We might go so far as to say that our human sense of gripping is in the hand, and the eagle in the poem really grips harder when we sense the claws as hands. And, at the same time, as the identification is set up between claws and hands, our own hands take on something of the hardness, scaliness, and sharpness of the claw; our own human sense of gripping is accentuated.

What we have here is a comparison (claws to hands), but the comparison is implied, is given in the form of an identification, an interpenetration of qualities; it is a metaphor. It is to be distinguished from a stated comparison, such as that to a thunderbolt in the last line, a simile.

The use of simile and metaphor may make description more vivid. A mere listing of qualities gives a rather flat description; it may be accurate but it does not stir the imagination. A new perception—a sharp detail shrewdly noticed—will catch the attention and make us create fully the image suggested. Likewise, a good metaphor or simile, by the fact that the points of similarity (the sense of gripping, the sense of thrust and fall) are drawn from the midst of differences, emphasizes what is essential, and embodies a new vision of reality.

3. What do you think is the most vivid line in the poem? Does it involve a metaphor?

4. Descriptive vividness, as we have said in the Foreword, is one of the most important qualities of all poetry. But a comparison may do more than wake up our imagination to the vividness of an image; it may make the imagination seize on certain ideas, and additional comparisons implied by the original comparison. Take the line:

He watches from his mountain walls.

Mountains are, literally, not walls. So we have a metaphor. The metaphor is, as a matter of fact, a rather worn-out one—a *cliché* (*Glossary*). Mountains are often compared to walls. But when the mountain walls become the watch tower or fortress, as it were, of the eagle, do we get something fresh and forceful about the eagle? If so, what?

5. Various critics have pointed out that the use of the word *hands* in the first line leads to the human identification with the eagle and makes the eagle an image for certain human qualities. But would the poem still work this way if *hands* (despite its force as a metaphor) were not used? Do we have elsewhere such a clue, such an invitation to project our human concerns into a poem?

6. Why are the lands of the eagle "lonely"?

7. Let us make a revision of the last line:

And he falls like a thunderbolt.

Ignoring the question of rhyme, what has been lost here?

Spring

William Shakespeare [1564–1616]

When daisies pied and violets blue
  And lady-smocks all silver-white
And cuckoo-buds of yellow hue
  Do paint the meadows with delight,
The cuckoo then, on every tree,
Mocks married men; for thus sings he,
                "Cuckoo;
Cuckoo, cuckoo": O, word of fear,
Unpleasing to a married ear!

When shepherds pipe on oaten straws,
  And merry larks are ploughmen's clocks,
When turtles tread, and rooks, and daws,
  And maidens bleach their summer smocks,
The cuckoo then, on every tree,
Mocks married men; for thus sings he,
                    "Cuckoo;
Cuckoo, cuckoo": O, word of fear,
Unpleasing to a married ear!

Winter

William Shakespeare [*1564–1616*]

When icicles hang by the wall,
  And Dick the shepherd blows his nail,
And Tom bears logs into the hall,
  And milk come frozen home in pail,
When blood is nipped and ways be foul,
Then nightly sings the staring owl,
                    "Tu-whit, tu-who!"
A merry note,
While greasy Joan doth keel[1] the pot.

When all aloud the wind doth blow,
  And coughing drowns the parson's saw,
And birds sit brooding in the snow,
  And Marian's nose looks red and raw,
When roasted crabs[2] hiss in the bowl,
Then nightly sings the staring owl,
                    "Tu whit, tu-who!"
A merry note,
While greasy Joan doth keel the pot.
                    (From *Love's Labour's Lost*)

EXERCISE

"Spring" presents a pleasant world of birds and flowers—a world in which the very meadows are painted "with delight."

1 skim
2 crab-apples

"Winter," on the contrary, gives us a world of ice and snow, of frost-bitten fingers and greasy kitchen-maids. We can see that the descriptive details have been selected in terms of this basic contrast. We can elaborate the contrast further: in addition to the general opposition of spring and winter, there are more particular contrasts. Outdoor scenes dominate one poem; indoor, the other. Youthful merry-making balances humdrum piety and domesticity; the beautiful and romantic are set over against the drab and comfortable.

1. In view of this general pattern, why has the poet introduced the cuckoo's song into the one poem; the owl's, into the other? (The cuckoo's song is "unpleasing to a married ear" because the Elizabethans associated its call with the taunting of cuckolds.)

2. Does the poet really think that the hooting of the owl is merry? (Compare "Proud Maisie," p. 51.)

3. Granting that the two little poems are quite "objective," and do not pretend to present any explicit interpretation of life, still do they not suggest an attitude toward the world of our experience? Could you suggest what this attitude is?

To Spring

William Blake [*1757–1827*]

O thou with dewy locks, who lookest down
Through the clear windows of the morning, turn
Thine angel eyes upon our western isle,
Which in full choir hails thy approach, O Spring!

The hills tell one another, and the listening
Valleys hear; all our longing eyes are turned
Up to thy bright pavilions: issue forth,
And let thy holy feet visit our clime.

Come o'er the eastern hills, and let our winds
Kiss thy perfumèd garments; let us taste
Thy morn and evening breath; scatter thy pearls
Upon our love-sick land that mourns for thee.

O deck her forth with thy fair fingers; pour
Thy soft kisses on her bosom; and put
Thy golden crown upon her languished head,
Whose modest tresses were bound up for thee.

EXERCISE

1. Spring is addressed as a godlike being—more specifically under the guise of an oriental prince coming in state to visit his betrothed. Is this *allegorical* (*Glossary*) figure adopted merely for prettification and decoration? Or does it have a more significant justification?

2. Compare the language of this poem with that of the Song of Solomon in the King James Version of the Bible. A poem, of course, inheres in its language, and the language implies the attitude and feeling in a poem. On the basis of a difference in the kind of language, how would you compare the attitude in this poem with that of Shakespeare's pair?

3. Compare the attitude of "To Spring," by Blake, with "Pear Tree," by H. D. (p. 86).

4. Read "To Spring" aloud several times. How would you compare the rhythms with those of Shakespeare's poems? Of "Written in March"? Of "Pear Tree"?

Summer and Winter

Percy Bysshe Shelley [*1792–1822*]

It was a bright and cheerful afternoon,
Towards the end of the sunny month of June,
When the north wind congregates in crowds
The floating mountains of the silver clouds
From the horizon—and the stainless sky
Opens beyond them like eternity.
All things rejoice beneath the sun; the weeds,
The river, and the corn-fields, and the reeds;
The willow leaves that glance in the light breeze,
And the firm foliage of the larger trees.

It was a winter such as when birds die
In the deep forests; and the fishes lie
Stiffened in the translucent ice, which makes
Even the mud and slime of the warm lakes
A wrinkled clod as hard as brick; and when,
Among their children, comfortable men
Gather about great fires, and yet feel cold:
Alas, then, for the homeless beggar old!

EXERCISE

1. Locate the instances of sharp observation. Would you say that this poem is realistic in temper? Compare the rhythm here with that of Shakespeare's two poems.

2. How do you take the word *comfortable* here? In the sense of "well-fleshed"? Of "well-off"? Of "well-housed"? Of "easy in their minds"? Of simply "out of the weather"? Or in all senses at once?

3. Does the word *cold* here carry any doubleness, or depth of meaning? If you feel that it does now, do you think it would have such a meaning if the last line were not in the poem?

4. What does this poem imply about man's relation to nature?

5. How would you compare the poet's attitude here with that in Shakespeare's two poems?

A Dirge

John Webster [*1580?–1625?*]

Call for the robin-redbreast and the wren,
Since o'er shady groves they hover,
And with leaves and flowers do cover
The friendless bodies of unburried men.
Call unto his funeral dole
The ant, the field-mouse, and the mole,
To rear him hillocks that shall keep him warm,
And, when gay tombs are robbed, sustain no harm;

But keep the wolf far thence, that's foe to men,
For with his nails he'll dig them up again.

EXERCISE

1. The robin was fabled to do this office for the dead—compare the old ballad of "The Children in the Wood." * But can you account for the wren? Is the wren an appropriate bird for this poem?

2. The poem seems to be saying that nature is kindly toward man, and buries the bodies of men who have been abandoned by humankind. But the wolf is a part of nature too. Why has the poet selected the birds and animals that he has? And why has he included in this poem the warning against the wolf?

3. Is "gay" a proper adjective to use with "tombs"? What is a *gay* tomb? Can you defend the use of the phrase here?

4. What is this poem "about"—if it is about anything?

Cavalry Crossing a Ford

Walt Whitman [*1819–1892*]

A line in long array where they wind betwixt green islands,
They take a serpentine course, their arms flash in the sun—
hark to the musical clank,
Behold the silvery river, in it the splashing horses loitering
stop to drink,
Behold the brown-faced men, each group, each person a picture, the negligent rest on the saddles,
Some emerge on the opposite bank, others are just entering
the ford—while,
Scarlet and blue and snowy white,
The guidon flags flutter gayly in the wind.

EXERCISE

Is this a mere assemblage of details or is there some principle of organization? That is our first question. For one thing, there is a hint of movement; there is the "serpentine course" be-

* *Oxford Book of Ballads*, p. 854.

tween the green islands, the command seen as a unit. But the unity quickly dissolves into the details. The poet, we become aware, is quite consciously insisting on this fact; he says that each group, even each person, is a picture that can be regarded individually. Having fractured his general impression into these individual "pictures," he then begins to reassemble the whole. Again we begin to get a sense of the column as a unit, the head emerging on the far bank, the rear entering the stream. But still the scene has not come into sharp focus. It is only when our eyes fix on the guidons fluttering "gayly" that everything is drawn together.

Not only the composition of the whole picture is drawn together, but we get a feeling of how the men who, for a moment, had become individual, just men watering their horses as casually and lazily as a farmer after a day in the field, are jerked back into their places in the unit, losing their identity in the whole. So the mere matter of mechanical focus becomes, as it were, a lead to the human feeling of the poem.

Let us glance at another mechanical detail. Line 5 ends with the word *while,* preceded by a dash, followed by a comma, left hanging at the end. So we have a sense of suspense here; it is as though we are asking, "While what?" But the poet holds off the answer, and in the next line enumerates the colors. This, too, gives suspense; for we do not know what the colors are to describe—they float vaguely, confusedly before us, qualities unattached to any object. Then, in the last line come the guidons, and after the two devices of suspense, our eye, and our curiosity, comes to a rest, fulfilled. We have been made to "want" the guidons.

1. What is gained by the direct address used by the speaker of the poem? To whom is he speaking?

2. What view does the poet take toward the fact that the individual men, after the moment of pause, are drawn into the unit of the column? Does he seem to resent this or applaud it? How would you relate your answer to the last paragraph of the comment given above?

3. What is the effect of the word *gayly?* Is it to be taken in reference to your answer to the question above? Or is it to be

taken as an ironical reference to the natural business of a military organization? Or to both? If to both, is there a necessary contradiction involved?

Nightingales

Robert Bridges [*1844–1930*]

Beautiful must be the mountains whence ye come,
And bright in the fruitful valleys the streams wherefrom
  Ye learn your song:
Where are those starry woods? O might I wander there,
  Among the flowers, which in that heavenly air
    Bloom the year long!

Nay, barren are those mountains and spent the streams:
Our song is the voice of desire, that haunts our dreams,
  A throe of the heart,
Whose pining visions dim, forbidden hopes profound,
  No dying cadence nor long sigh can sound,
    For all our art.

Alone, aloud in the raptured ear of men
We pour our dark nocturnal secret; and then,
  As night is withdrawn
From these sweet-springing meads and bursting boughs of May,
  Dream, while the innumerable choir of day
    Welcome the dawn.

The idea of this poem might be stated somewhat crudely as follows: the greatest beauty does not spring from pleasure but from pain, not from happiness but from sorrow, not from satisfaction, but from desire. It is, we might say, a kind of conquest of pain and sorrow and desire. But how does the idea become incorporated into a poem? The poet does not say in so many words that this is his idea or theme; instead, he has put it in a form that appeals to our imagination.

First, we observe that the poem is composed of two parts, an address to the nightingales by the poet (the first stanza) and the reply of the nightingales (the second and third stanzas). Given as a prose paraphrase the poem might be stated in this way: The poet says that, since the song of the nightingales is so beautiful, they must come from a place where the beauty of the mountains and the music of streams in the fruitful valleys instructs them; and that he, who lives in a far less beautiful place, longs to wander where the flowers in that heavenly air never wither and where there is no change from perfect beauty. But the birds reply to him that the land from which they come is a harsh place with spent streams, and that the beauty of their song comes, not from satisfaction, but from desire which is so great and so hopeless that it can never be fully expressed even in their song. At night, they add, they pour their song into the ears of men, and then with the coming of dawn on the spring landscape, dream while the birds of the day sing with pleasure.

Obviously, this paraphrase does not exhaust even the meaning of the poem that can be reduced to statement. (It is entirely lacking, of course, in the kind of meaning that comes to us from the nature of the poetic form. See "Afterword" to Section I.) One might even add to this paraphrase a statement of the theme of the poem, and the description would remain incomplete. What are some of the things that are absent from the condensed paraphrase and the general statement of the idea?

First, this poem, like many poems, carries with it an allusion to a special piece of information, the Greek myth concerning the woman who, after a tragic experience, was turned into the nightingale. Tereus raped Philomela and then cut out her tongue and cut off her hands lest she tell her sister Procne, Tereus's wife, what had happened to her. But Philomela managed to weave the story into a tapestry and showed it to Procne. The sisters revenged themselves upon Tereus by killing his son and serving his body to Tereus as food. Philomela was turned into a nightingale; Procne, into a swallow; and Tereus, into the hawk who pursues them.

The poem would still make sense to a person who was unacquainted with the suppressed reference to the myth, but a knowledge of the myth does support the meaning of the poem.

But dismissing the implied allusion, we can strike on other implications in the poem that are necessary to a full appreciation. In the first stanza an important instance is involved. Why does the poet in addressing the nightingales express a wish to wander in the beautiful land from which he assumes they have come? There is the answer that anyone likes agreeable surroundings. Then we realize that this land is a kind of mythical paradise where there is no decay or change, a static perfection, such a place as men in a world of change, struggle, and decay dream of. This land of the nightingales implies, then, all men's longing for a kind of other-worldly peace and happiness. But something more is implied here. The speaker evidently is a poet and in the present world is compelled to create his imperfect beauty by effort; he feels that if he inhabited that other land his poems might be as perfect and as spontaneous as the song of the nightingales.

The implications of the second stanza depend on these of the first, and merely involve a correction of the mistaken beliefs implied in the first stanza. But the third stanza raises some new issues, and becomes richer as we contemplate it. First, what is the "dark nocturnal secret"? It is of course the song of the nightingales. The bird sings at night and the use of "dark" seems merely to support and emphasize the use of "nocturnal." The bird also sings from some hidden or secret place, and not in the open. So far the phrase seems only a very good poetic statement about the song. But it carries further a truth about life, that beauty comes from desire, struggle, and pain and not from easy perfection. It is a dark truth, a truth usually hidden, and it may be a depressing truth. But—and this takes us back to the "raptured ear" of the previous line—it is a paradoxical fact that the statement of this dark secret does not depress but exalts the hearer more than the merely pleasant songs of the "innumerable choir of day" can do.

The poet makes the nightingales serve as a *symbol* (*Glossary*) to express his idea. He has developed the implications of the image so that it is unnecessary for him to argue his point; we seize on it in seizing on the image itself. The poet is not merely describing his own pleasure in the song of nightingales, or merely trying to make the reader who has no acquaintance with nightingales appreciate the poem fully; he is, instead, using the image of the nightingale to make us respond, emotionally and intellectually, to an interpretation of human experience.

EXERCISE

1. Compare the theme of this poem with those of "The Main-Deep," "Pear Tree," and "Hell Gate." Try to state differences as well as similarities.

2. What poems earlier in this section does "Nightingales" most resemble in diction and rhythm? (Such a poem need not have similar theme or subject matter.) What does the kind of diction indicate about the poet's attitude toward his subject? Notice how the poet threads his rather complicated sentences through the complicated stanza form, without doing violence to either. Can you make any comment on how this sense of formal control modifies the bare theme of the poem?

Rocky Acres

Robert Graves [*1895–*]

This is a wild land, country of my choice,
  With harsh craggy mountain, moor ample and bare.
Seldom in these acres is heard any voice
  But voice of cold water that runs here and there
  Through rocks and lank heather growing without care.
No mice in the heath run nor no birds cry
For fear of the dark speck that floats in the sky.

He soars and he hovers, rocking on his wings,
  He scans his wide parish with a sharp eye,
He catches the trembling of small hidden things,
  He tears them in pieces, dropping from the sky:
  Tenderness and pity the land will deny
Where life is but nourished from water and rock,
A hardy adventure, full of fear and shock.

Time has never journeyed to this lost land,
  Crakeberries and heather bloom out of date,
The rocks jut, the streams flow singing on either hand,
  Careless if the season be early or late.
  The skies wander overhead, now blue, now slate:
Winter would be known by his cold cutting snow
If June did not borrow his armor also.

Yet this is my country beloved by me best,
The first land that rose from Chaos and the Flood,
Nursing no fat valleys for comfort and rest,
Trampled by no hard hooves, stained with no blood.
Bold immortal country whose hill-tops have stood
Strongholds for the proud gods when on earth they go,
Terror for fat burghers in far plains below.

EXERCISE

1. There is clearly some similarity between this poem and "Nightingales." The land of the nightingales is, we are told, a barren, difficult place, but the place from which their perfection of song springs. The poet of "Rocky Acres" expresses a preference for harsh, craggy land, but he does not say why. Why?

2. What kind of man do you take the speaker to be?

3. In what sense is the country of his choice a "bold, immortal country"? Examine both adjectives in the light of the poem.

4. Compare the diction and rhythms of this poem with those of "Nightingales." Locate some words and phrases in "Rocky Acres" which could not be expected in "Nightingales." How do you relate any differences to differences between the speakers of the poems and between their attitudes toward their respective subjects?

Desert Places

Robert Frost [*1874–1963*]

Snow falling and night falling fast oh fast
In a field I looked into going past,
And the ground almost covered smooth in snow,
But a few weeds and stubble showing last.

The woods around it have it—it is theirs.
All animals are smothered in their lairs.
I am too absent-spirited to count;
The loneliness includes me unawares.

And lonely as it is that loneliness
Will be more lonely ere it will be less—

A blanker whiteness of benighted snow
With no expression, nothing to express.

They cannot scare me with their empty spaces
Between stars—on stars where no human race is.
I have it in me so much nearer home
To scare myself with my own desert places.

Let us assume that the poem had been written without the last stanza. It would still be a poem, and a good one, but a very different one from the poem we know. Such a poem would differ from "The Main-Deep," for instance, in several particulars. In the first place, the reader knows who the observer is. A man, at dusk, is passing an open field where snow is falling. The poem is quickly defined as *his* observation. In the second place, the man, in the second stanza, indicates a relation between himself and the empty field on which the snow falls, although he does not definitely state it. The snow-covered field, in its desolation, stands as a kind of symbol for the man's own loneliness. And since this relation is established for us in the second stanza, what follows in the third, though it is stated only in application to the field, comes to us as having application to the loneliness of the man who is observing. Then follow the lines:

A blanker whiteness of benighted snow
With no expression, nothing to express.

As implied here, it does not matter what happens to the man now or what he does, for nothing can have any further meaning.

If the poem be taken as ending there, the process used by the poet to give his effect is very easily defined: the observer describes a natural scene which becomes for the reader a symbol of the observer's own despairing state of mind. The scene in nature has been presented so that it serves to communicate a human meaning.

But the poem in reality does not end with the third stanza, and the last stanza introduces a new element into the poem—that is, the poet's own analysis and statement, an element that is almost wholly lacking from previous poems in this section.

The last stanza is not introduced with a transition from the earlier part; the observer does not say that after looking at the empty field he lifted his eyes to the sky and remembered what he had been told about the great emptiness of the stars and the interstellar spaces. But the reader understands that, and by the very abruptness of the shift gets a more dramatic effect, as though the man had jerked himself from his musing on the field to look at the sky and then make his comment. This comment, in summary, says this: a man who has known the desolation possible to human experience cannot be frightened or depressed by mere desolation in nature. And though this comment emphasizes the loneliness of the man, it gives us a different impression of him and gives a different total impression of the poem. It is not an impression of mere despair, for the man, we feel, has not been overcome by his own "desert places," but has mastered them.

He does not make this statement in so many words, but his attitude is implied. A reader analyzing the poem can almost base this implication of the man's attitude on the use of the single word *scare*. The man says,

> They cannot scare me with their empty spaces.

He does not use *terrify,* or *horrify,* or *astound*—any word that would indicate the full significance of human loneliness and despair. Instead, he uses the word *scare,* which is an understatement, a common, colloquial word. One "scares" children by telling them ghost stories, or by jumping at them from behind curtains. But by the use of the word in the poem the man is made to imply that he is not a child to be so easily affected. Knowledge of the infinite emptiness of space, which astronomers may give him, cannot affect him, for he knows, being a grown man, that the loneliness of spirit can be greater than the loneliness of external nature. But in the last line the word *scare* is repeated, and its *connotations* (*Glossary*) are brought into play in the new connection:

> To scare myself with my own desert places.

That is, the man has had so much experience of life, is so truly mature, that even that greater loneliness of the spirit cannot make him behave like a child who is afraid of the dark or of ghost stories. Even in his loneliness of spirit he can still find strength enough in himself.

EXERCISE

1. We have seen how the use of the colloquial word *scare* is put into meaningful contrast with other elements of the poem. Can you find other instances of such a contrast? What about some of the rhymes?

2. Can you locate more elevated phrases and rhetorical patternings set into contrast with the colloquial and realistic elements? In this connection, what about changes in rhythm?

Inversnaid

Gerard Manley Hopkins [*1844–1889*]

This darksome burn, horseback brown,
His rollrock highroad roaring down,
In coop and in comb the fleece of his foam
Flutes and low to the lake falls home.

A windpuff-bonnet of fáwn-fróth
Turns and twindles over the broth
Of a pool so pitchblack, féll-frowning,
It round and rounds Despair to drowning.

Degged with dew, dappled with dew
Are the groins of the braes that the brook treads through,
Wiry heathpacks, flitches of fern,
And the beadbonny ash that sits over the burn.

What would the world be, once bereft
Of wet and of wildness? Let them be left,
O let them be left, wildness and wet;
Long live the weeds and the wilderness yet.

EXERCISE

1. Do you think it appropriate that this poem should follow "Desert Places"?

2. Gerard Manley Hopkins was a Jesuit priest. Does this seem a strange poem for a priest to have written?

3. Examine the structure of the sentence which composes the first stanza. Why does the poet use this complicated and dif-

ficult structure to build up to the statement that the burn falls home to the lake? Would it have been better, as well as simpler, to start with the statement that the burn falls into the lake and then attach the descriptive elements?

4. Some of the images are, at first glance, difficult. Take, for instance, the "rollrock highroad"—what is it? And what is "fawn-froth"? An important consideration is involved in this question. We want poetry to seem immediate and vivid—we want the sense of meaning embodied in and shining, with exciting directness, from the events and images and language of a poem. But sometimes we have to make ourselves ready to receive that meaning. And sometimes looking up words in a dictionary or puzzling a little over images is the simplest thing we have to do. Sometimes, for instance, we can get ready only by living enough—or exercising our imaginations enough—to find certain kinds of experience significant.

5. There are a number of unusual words here. Look them all up in the Oxford English Dictionary. Are any of them old words—obsolete—or from dialects? Try replacing all the unusual words with ordinary ones which the dictionary gives by way of definition. What differences do you find in the effect?

6. The rhythms of Hopkins's poetry are often uncommon. (The accents here are provided by the poet to help the reader catch a movement which he might ordinarily miss.) How do Hopkins's unusual rhythms affect you? Do you detect any difference between the rhythm of the first three stanzas and that of the last? What is the effect of this? Does it make sense to you?

7. Compare the theme of this poem with that of "Rocky Acres," by Robert Graves, and that of "Nightingales," by Robert Bridges.

The Yew in the Graveyard *

Alfred, Lord Tennyson [*1809–1892*]

Old Yew, which graspest at the stones
  That name the under-lying dead,
  Thy fibers net the dreamless head,
Thy roots are wrapped about the bones.

* This poem is Number II of *In Memoriam*. The title is attached by the editors.

The seasons bring the flower again,
  And bring the firstling to the flock;
  And in the dusk of thee, the clock
Beats out the little lives of men.

O not for thee the glow, the bloom,
  Who changest not in any gale,
  Nor branding summer suns avail
To touch thy thousand years of gloom:

And gazing on thee, sullen tree,
  Sick for thy stubborn hardihood,
  I seem to fail from out my blood
And grow incorporate into thee.

EXERCISE

1. The basic situation of the poem is this: a man oppressed by grief stares at the old yew in the churchyard and envies its "stubborn hardihood." What is this "hardihood"? In other words, what human attitude does the yew embody and why should a man envy it? What does the last line mean? Compare the theme of this poem with those of "Desert Places" and "Rocky Acres."

2. Suppose line 3 were changed to

> Thy fibers clasp the dreamless head.

What would be gained or lost? What would be the effect on the line that follows it?

3. Suppose line 6 were changed to

> And bring the new lamb to the flock.

What differences do we have, not only in meaning and association, but in sound?

4. What does the word *branding* mean?

To Autumn

John Keats [*1795–1821*]

Season of mists and mellow fruitfulness,
  Close bosom-friend of the maturing sun:
Conspiring with him how to load and bless

With fruit the vines that round the thatch-eaves run;
To bend with apples the mossed cottage-trees,
And fill all fruit with ripeness to the core;
To swell the gourd, and plump the hazel shells
With a sweet kernel; to set budding more,
And still more, later flowers for the bees,
Until they think warm days will never cease,
For Summer has o'er-brimmed their clammy cells.

Who hath not seen thee oft amid thy store?
Sometimes whoever seeks abroad may find
Thee sitting careless on a granary floor,
Thy hair soft-lifted by the winnowing wind;
Or on a half-reaped furrow sound asleep,
Drowsed with the fume of poppies, while thy hook
Spares the next swath and all its twinèd flowers:
And sometimes like a gleaner thou dost keep,
Steady thy laden head across a brook;
Or by a cider-press, with patient look,
Thou watchest the last oozings hours by hours.

Where are the songs of Spring? Ay, where are they?
Think not of them, thou hast thy music too,—
While barrèd clouds bloom the soft-dying day,
And touch the stubble-plains with rosy hue;
Then in a wailful choir the small gnats mourn
Among the river sallows, borne aloft
Or sinking as the light wind lives or dies;
And full-grown lambs loud bleat from hilly bourn;
Hedge-crickets sing: and now with treble soft
The red-breast whistles from a garden-croft;
And gathering swallows twitter in the skies.

EXERCISE

1. Compare and contrast the mood of this poem with that of "Heat," by H. D., that of "Winter," by Shakespeare, and that of "The Yew in the Graveyard," by Tennyson. Why would we suggest the last poem for this purpose?

2. Note that after the predominantly visual imagery of the first two stanzas, the last stanza emphasizes auditory imagery. Why is the shift of imagery especially appropriate?

3. In this poem autumn is personified. What personality is indicated? What does descriptive detail in each of the three

stanzas contribute to the definition of that personality? How is this personality related to the mood of the poem—and the theme?

4. In connection with the theme of the poem, read the following comment:

> The whole stanza presents the paradoxical qualities of autumn, its aspects of both lingering and passing. This is especially true of the final image of the stanza. Autumn is the season of dying as well as of fulfilling. Hence it is with "*patient* look" that she (or he?) watches "the last oozings hours by hours." Oozing, or steady dripping, is, of course, not unfamiliar as a symbol of the passage of time.
>
> It is in the last stanza that the theme emerges most conspicuously. . . .*

What elements in the last stanza do continue the presentation of the paradoxical qualities of autumn? On what attitude may we say that the poem comes to rest?

5. Why, as a matter of fact, do swallows gather in the skies? What meaning does this have for the poem?

6. This poem has often been admired for its richness and appropriateness of rhythm. Get fully soaked in the poem and then discuss this topic.

7. The poem has also been admired for its precise and suggestive diction. Locate words and phrases which seem to justify this admiration. Or do you find any?

8. Compare the theme of this poem with those of "The Main-Deep" and "Pear Tree."

Composed upon Westminster Bridge, Sept. 3, 1802

William Wordsworth [1770–1850]

Earth has not anything to show more fair:
Dull would he be of soul who could pass by
A sight so touching in its majesty:
This city now doth like a garment wear
The beauty of the morning; silent, bare,

* Leonard Unger and William Van O'Connor: *Poems for Study*, New York, Rinehart and Company, 1953, p. 455.

Ships, towers, domes, theaters, and temples lie
Open unto the fields, and to the sky;
All bright and glittering in the smokeless air.
Never did sun more beautifully steep
In his first splendor valley, rock, or hill;
Ne'er saw I, never felt, a calm so deep!
The river glideth at his own sweet will:
Dear God! the very houses seem asleep;
And all that mighty heart is lying still!

EXERCISE

The description of the city given in this poem is general rather than particular—we are presented with a panorama rather than with a detailed scene. The description does not abound in bold comparisons or in striking realistic details. Yet many readers have testified to the power and excitement of the poem. Try to determine why the poem is successful. The following questions may be helpful in this enterprise.

1. Does the spectator seem to manifest surprise? Why?
2. What is the point in his saying that the city is "open" unto the fields and to the sky? Is it not always "open"?
3. Does the river not always glide "at his own sweet will"? Why is the spectator struck with this fact? What are the implications of the fact?
4. What is the point in comparing the city to scenes of natural beauty?
5. If the city were less quiet, would it seem to the spectator less "alive" or more "alive"?
6. In the light of your answer to Question 5, can you justify the last two lines? Ordinarily, the comparisons made in these lines ("houses . . . asleep" and the city as a "mighty heart") might seem trite.

Preludes

T. S. Eliot [*1888–*]

I

The winter evening settles down
With smell of steaks in passageways.
Six o'clock.

The burnt-out ends of smoky days.
And now a gusty shower wraps
The grimy scraps
Of withered leaves about your feet
And newspapers from vacant lots;
The showers beat
On broken blinds and chimney-pots,
And at the corner of the street
A lonely cab-horse steams and stamps.
And then the lighting of the lamps.

II

The morning comes to consciousness
Of faint stale smells of beer
From the sawdust-trampled street
With all its muddy feet that press
To early coffee-stands.
With the other masquerades
That time resumes,
One thinks of all the hands
That are raising dingy shades
In a thousand furnished rooms.

III

You tossed a blanket from the bed,
You lay upon your back, and waited;
You dozed, and watched the night revealing
The thousand sordid images
Of which your soul was constituted;
They flickered against the ceiling.
And when all the world came back
And the light crept up between the shutters
And you heard the sparrows in the gutters,
You had such a vision of the street
As the street hardly understands;
Sitting along the bed's edge, where
You curled the papers from your hair,
Or clasped the yellow soles of feet
In the palms of both soiled hands.

IV

His soul stretched tight across the skies
That fade behind a city block,
Or trampled by insistent feet

At four and five and six o'clock;
And short square fingers stuffing pipes,
And evening newspapers, and eyes
Assured of certain certainties,
The conscience of a blackened street
Impatient to assume the world.

I am moved by fancies that are curled
Around these images, and cling:
The notion of some infinitely gentle
Infinitely suffering thing.

Wipe your hand across your mouth, and laugh;
The worlds revolve like ancient women
Gathering fuel in vacant lots.

EXERCISE

1. The first two sections of this poem describe a winter evening and a winter morning in a city. The description in these sections is objective, but it establishes a mood and attitude. Discuss the mood and attitude. What effect do the last three lines of the second section give?

2. In the third section, one of the people whose hand will raise dingy shades is addressed. Out of her own misery she has "a vision of the street"—an awareness of the general loneliness and defeat. Why does the poet say that the street hardly understands this vision? What is the implication of *masquerades* here?

3. In the fourth section another character is referred to, a man who is sensitive enough to be constantly affected by the life he sees around him—a life which appears to be dominated by a meaningless routine of satisfying animal requirements, the "certain certainties." Ironically, the poet calls this assurance of these certainties the only "conscience" that the street has; and the street seems to impose its own standards on the entire world. Then (in line 48) the poet announces himself as a commentator on the scenes he has presented. What attitude does he take? Whom is he addressing in the last three lines? How do the last two lines serve as a symbolic summary of the poem? Is the poet ready to wipe his own hand across his mouth—the gross gesture of satisfied appetite—and laugh at human suffering?

4. Before attempting to answer the last question, it may be well to consider carefully the comparison that dominates the last three lines. Is there a realistic basis for the comparison? Does an old woman gathering chips—or anyone, for that matter, who keeps his eyes fixed on the ground—tend to move in circles? What are the "worlds" referred to? May they be the planets revolving in the solar system? If so, what is implied? Is the poet prepared to say that man is merely a trivial mechanism in a mechanistic universe?

5. This poem, like "Composed upon Westminster Bridge," gives a view of London, but there is more than a century between the two poems. What elements (language, rhythms, specific references, images, or whatever else seems relevant) seem to make each poem belong to its own age and not the age of the other? Do you think, in the light of the issues raised by Question 4, that it would be harder for Wordsworth to write his poem now? Why? But can we assume that in 1802 it was easy for him to take his particular view? Compare and contrast the view of human nature in the two poems.

6. Compare, on the basis of theme, both poems to "In the Station of the Metro," by Pound.

Ode to the West Wind

Percy Bysshe Shelley [*1792–1822*]

I

O, wild West Wind, thou breath of Autumn's being,
Thou, from whose unseen presence the leaves dead
Are driven, like ghosts from an enchanter fleeing,

Yellow, and black, and pale, and hectic red,
Pestilence-stricken multitudes: O, thou,
Who chariotest to their dark wintry bed

The wingèd seeds, where they lie cold and low,
Each like a corpse within its grave, until
Thine azure sister of the spring shall blow

Her clarion o'er the dreaming earth, and fill
(Driving sweet buds like flocks to feed in air)
With living hues and odors plain and hill:

Wild Spirit, which art moving everywhere;
Destroyer and preserver; hear, O, hear!

II

Thou on whose stream, 'mid the steep sky's commotion,
Loose clouds like earth's decaying leaves are shed,
Shook from the tangled boughs of Heaven and Ocean,

Angels of rain and lightning: there are spread
On the blue surface of thine airy surge,
Like the bright hair uplifted from the head

Of some fierce Mænad, even from the dim verge
Of the horizon to the zenith's height,
The locks of the approaching storm. Thou dirge

Of the dying year, to which this closing night
Will be the dome of a vast sepulcher,
Vaulted with all thy congregated might

Of vapors, from whose solid atmosphere
Black rain, and fire, and hail will burst: O hear!

III

Thou who didst waken from his summer dreams
The blue Mediterranean, where he lay,
Lulled by the coil of his crystalline streams,

Beside a pumice isle in Baiæ's bay,
And saw in sleep old palaces and towers
Quivering within the wave's intenser day,

All overgrown with azure moss, and flowers
So sweet, the sense faints picturing them! Thou
For whose path the Atlantic's level powers

Cleave themselves into chasms, while far below
The sea-blooms and the oozy woods which wear
The sapless foliage of the ocean, know

Thy voice, and suddenly grow gray with fear,
And tremble and despoil themselves: O hear!

IV

If I were a dead leaf thou mightest bear;
If I were a swift cloud to fly with thee;
A wave to pant beneath thy power, and share

The impulse of thy strength, only less free
Than thou, O, uncontrollable! If even
I were as in my boyhood, and could be

The comrade of thy wanderings over heaven,
As then, when to outstrip thy skiey speed
Scarce seemed a vision; I would ne'er have striven

As thus with thee in prayer in my sore need.
Oh! lift me as a wave, a leaf, a cloud!
I fall upon the thorns of life! I bleed!

A heavy weight of hours has chained and bowed
One too like thee: tameless, and swift, and proud.

V

Make me thy lyre, even as the forest is:
What if my leaves are falling like its own!
The tumult of thy mighty harmonies

Will take from both a deep, autumnal tone,
Sweet though in sadness. Be thou, spirit fierce,
My spirit! Be thou me, impetuous one!

Drive my dead thoughts over the universe
Like withered leaves, to quicken a new birth!
And, by the incantation of this verse,

Scatter, as from an unextinguished hearth
Ashes and sparks, my words among mankind!
Be through my lips to unawakened earth

The trumpet of a prophecy! O, wind,
If Winter comes, can Spring be far behind?

EXERCISE

Study the poem, and fix upon elements you find puzzling, interesting, pleasing, and significant. Frame a rather full set of exercises around those elements. Then compare your exercises with those prepared by other students. Do some of their questions deepen your sense of the poem? A good question is sometimes harder to make than a good answer.

The Woodspurge

Dante Gabriel Rossetti [*1828–1882*]

The wind flapped loose, the wind was still,
Shaken out dead from tree and hill:
I had walked on at the wind's will,—
I sat now, for the wind was still.

Between my knees my forehead was,—
My lips, drawn in, said not Alas!
My hair was over in the grass,
My naked ears heard the day pass.

My eyes, wide open, had the run
Of some ten weeds to fix upon;
Among those few, out of the sun,
The woodspurge flowered, three cups in one.

From perfect grief there need not be
Wisdom or even memory:
One thing then learnt remains to me,—
The woodspurge has a cup of three.

EXERCISE

Why is this poem especially appropriate to place here after we have studied descriptive poems? Or is it?

III

Metrics

FOREWORD

We have said ("Afterword," Section I, p. 75) that concentration and intensity are two of the qualities that tend to distinguish the poetic treatment of a subject from the prose treatment; and we related these qualities to the emphasis on form in poetry. The form of poetry, we said, is more closely organized than is the form of prose. As an example of this principle we indicated the greater selectivity in use of detail, the emphasis on suggestiveness, and the importance in the placing of details in relation to the central intention of a poem. For example, we indicated the importance of the line, "That kindles my mother's fire" in "The Wife of Usher's Well" (p. 40), and the implications of the phrase "our dark nocturnal secret" in "Nightingales" (p. 102). These things indicate the close-knit organization of various elements which one finds in poetry. Some of the same types of organization are to be found in prose as well as in poetry, but poetry *tends* toward a higher degree of formal organization than does prose. For example, the poor choice of words on the basis of connotation is much less damaging to a novel than to a poem. The damaged novel may still give some satisfaction, but the poem in which the writer has given little attention to connotation would certainly be a complete failure.

This tendency toward a high degree of organization in poetry is most obvious in the use of *rhythmical* language (*Glossary*). Some people, in fact, are accustomed to think that the use of rhythmical language is what chiefly distinguishes poetry from prose. But the distinction made on this basis can in the end be one only of degree and not of kind. This is obviously true when we reflect that by its very nature language, whether in prose or poetry, involves rhythm. In any prose whatsoever we feel a rise and fall of emphasis: we do not pronounce each syllable with precisely the same emphasis. We may say, however, that even if there is not an absolute difference between prose and poetry on the basis of rhythm, there is still a very important relative difference. A consideration of the following extracts from essays, stories, and poems may make clear what the relative difference is.

(1)

> As a sample of popular interest it may be noted that a single talk last spring by Professor MacMurry on psychology brought 17,000 requests for the supplementary aid-to-study pamphlet, and one by Professor Burt on the study of the mind brought 26,000.
> (From "The Level of Thirteen-Year-Olds," William Orton)

(2)

> But verse, you say, circumscribes a quick and luxuriant fancy, which would extend itself too far on every subject, did not the labor which is required to well-turned and polished rime, set bounds to it. Yet this argument, if granted, would only prove that we may write better in verse, but not more naturally.
> (From "An Essay of Dramatic Poesy," John Dryden)

(3)

> If there be any truth in astrology, I may outlive a jubilee; as yet I have not seen one revolution of Saturn, nor hath my pulse beat thirty years, and yet, excepting one, have seen the ashes of, and left underground, all the kings of Europe; have been contemporary to three emperors, four grand signiors, and as many popes: methinks I have out-

lived myself, and begin to be weary of the sun; I have shaken hands with delight in my warm blood and canicular days; I perceive I do anticipate the vices of age; the world to me is but a dream or mock-show, and we all therein but pantaloons and antics, to my severer contemplations.

(From *Religio Medici,* Sir Thomas Browne)

(4)

These and all else were to me the same as they are to you,
I loved well those cities, loved well the stately and rapid river,
The men and women I saw were all near to me,
Others the same—others who look back on me because I looked forward to them
(The time will come, though I stop here today and tonight).

(From "Crossing Brooklyn Ferry," Walt Whitman)

(5)

These our actors,
As I foretold you, were all spirits, and
Are melted into air, into thin air:
And, like the baseless fabric of this vision,
The cloud-capped towers, the gorgeous palaces,
The solemn temples, the great globe itself,
Yea, all which it inherit, shall dissolve,
And, like this insubstantial pageant faded,
Leave not a wrack behind.

(From *The Tempest,* William Shakespeare)

(6)

The gale, it plies the saplings double,
It blows so hard, 'twill soon be gone:
Today the Roman and his trouble
Are ashes under Uricon.

(From "On Wenlock Edge," A. E. Housman)

If one will read, preferably aloud, the specimens given above, it will be clear that all of them are, to some degree, rhythmical, even the first one with its dull, flat, matter-of-fact statement. Indeed, if we read carefully we can see that the specimens form, roughly speaking, a sort of ascending scale in regard to regularity and emphasis of the rhythm. If one hears specimens 1 and 6 read aloud, he can easily detect the difference; the rhythm of specimen 6 is much more systematized than that of specimen 1.

But if specimens 1 and 6 represent extremes of regularity and irregularity, what of a comparison between specimens 3 and 4 or between 4 and 5? Specimen 3 is taken from a work in *prose,* specimen 4 from a *poem;* yet a person hearing the two read aloud might not very easily distinguish them on this basis. Evidently there are degrees, as we have said, of regularization of rhythm, and the distinction between verse, with its regularized rhythm, and prose, with its freer rhythm, is not an absolute one.

In English verse this ordering is related to a pattern of accented and unaccented syllables.* By *meter* we mean the measure of the verse according to the line. The unit of measure is called the *foot,* a unit composed, in English verse, of one accented and one or more unaccented syllables. Names have been given to the various types of foot. (For full discussion of the general subject, see Note on Versification.) For instance, the most common foot in English poetry is called the *iambic foot;* it is composed of one unaccented and one accented syllable. The following line is composed of iambic feet:

Is this the face that launched a thousand ships

We can mark the divisions into feet and the accents as follows:

Ĭs thís | thĕ fáce | thăt láunched | ă thóu | sănd shíps

The line may be described as *iambic pentameter;* that is, it is composed of five iambic feet.

Because of the prominence of meter in poetry and perhaps because of the amount of attention which is usually given to

* Some attempts have been made to measure English verse in terms of time, even by a system of musical notation in which syllables have the duration of full notes, half notes, and so on. It is our considered opinion that such schemes provide neither theoretically nor practically an adequate description of *English* verse. Mention must be made here, however, of free verse (see pp. 172–80) and what is sometimes called "strong-stress verse," a descendant of the old native English meter. Its occurrence in modern English poetry tends to be sporadic and incidental. For discussion, see pages 568–70.

the technique of *versification* (*Note on Versification*), people sometimes tend to confuse verse with poetry, forgetting that *verse is only one of the instruments which the poet uses to gain his effect (Introduction,* pp. 16–20). This confusion is avoided if we realize that it is entirely possible to have verse without having a poetic effect. To illustrate the fact that verse, as such, does not give the poetic effect and is not to be confused with poetry, we can point to the following line, which provides an example of iambic pentameter:

A Mr. Wilkerson, a clergyman

We can scan it as follows:

Ă Mίst | ĕr Wίlk | ĕr són | ă clérg | y̆ mán

Or it would be possible to construct a pattern of pure nonsense that could be accurately scanned.

Investigation sad or verbally
Reveal unvision here this house no cat
Divest warm compromise imperially
What yes untold unwicked hiss nor that.

These lines are in regular iambic pentameter. They are arranged, furthermore, in the form of a simple stanza, the *quatrain* (*Note on Versification*). No one would maintain that the mere fact that these unrelated words are put into a metrical pattern creates poetry. To have poetry the words must be related in other ways as well. Verse is simply one of many instruments—narrative, dramatic incident, figurative language, logical sense of words, associations of words—at the poet's disposal. Our present interest is, then, to see some of the ways in which this element of verse works in making its contribution to the poetic effect, and to see some of its relations to the other elements used by the poet; for one must always remember that poetry is the result of a combination of relationships among the elements and does not inhere specially in any one of them (*Introduction,* pp. 16–20).

We have said that verse represents a specialization of rhythm in language. Rhythm is, of course, a basic function of all life. In our very bodies it is the most constant fact of which we are aware—the beat of the heart, the drawing of breath, the movement in walking.* Our awareness of the whole objective world is constantly referred to the rhythm of the seasons, of day and night, of the solar system. In addition to the connection of rhythm with all sorts of basic processes, the more intense states of emotion tend to seek a rhythmical expression. The life of primitive people or the habits of children or the nature of religious rituals all testify to this psychological fact. And we know how the moans of a person in great grief or pain tend to assume a rhythmical pattern. Considerations of this sort may help to indicate why verse has become traditionally associated with poetry. For poetry, though not *merely* emotional nor to be defined as the "expression of pure emotion" (*Introduction,* pp. 12–14), often treats experiences of great emotional intensity and does attempt to do justice to the emotional elements in experience.

Perhaps because of considerations of this sort, writers have stressed the hypnotic power exerted by verse upon the hearer. In stressing this hypnotic power, such writers are thinking, it should be pointed out, not of the apparent sluggishness and dullness of the hypnoidal state, but of the increased concentration of attention and suggestibility. It is, in fact, the *attention-catching* quality of rhythm that is sometimes prominent. It is this that makes Theodore Roethke, in beginning his discussion of verse technique, seize on the lines

> Hinx, minx, the old witch winks,
> The fat begins to fry.†

The person in the hypnoidal condition hangs upon every word of the hypnotist and attends to, and accepts, even the slightest

* By its organization of rhythm, so different from the verbal structure in a typically logical sentence—by its more or less strong accents—the word order in verse echoes the internal motions of the poet, and of the reader. "Indeed, it models itself on these internal motions; it is their external and communicative aspect. . . . The movements and attitudes of our muscles—those in our organs, those hidden in the body, as well as those of the face, and especially those mobile and sensitive muscles associated with the responses of sight and taste—translate our psychological impressions and ideas." (Telescoped translation by Stanley Burnshaw, from pp. 298, 299, 493, of André Spire's *Plaisir poétique et plaisir musculaire,* New York, Vanni, 1949.) See also "Introduction" to *The Poem Itself,* by Stanley Burnshaw, New York, Holt, Rinehart and Winston, 1960.

† Cleanth Brooks and Robert Penn Warren, eds.: *Conversations on the Craft of Verse,* pamphlet and tape recording, New York, Holt, Rinehart and Winston, 1960.

suggestion. One of the most interesting statements about this aspect of verse comes from Coleridge who says that meter tends "to increase the vivacity and susceptibility both of the general feelings and of the attention. . . . As a medicated atmosphere, or as a wine during animated conversation, they [the anticipations set up by the meter] act powerfully, though themselves unnoticed." *

Or, as William Butler Yeats has put it: "The purpose of rhythm, it has always seemed to me, is to prolong the moment of contemplation, the moment when we are both asleep and awake, which is the one moment of creation, by hushing us with an alluring monotony, while it holds us waking by variety, to keep us in that state of perhaps real trance, in which the mind liberated from the pressure of the will is unfolded in symbols." †

Whatever may be the merits of these speculations about the way in which rhythm is rooted in our biological heritage or about its general psychological effects, we are concerned here with a more limited and perhaps more important matter. What is the significance of verse in any given poem? Even if verse does exercise hypnotic effect, we still have to face the fact that of many poems using verse some are "good" and some are "bad." The fact that the hypnotic spell "works" in some instances and not in others leaves us with the necessity of studying the stipulated spell in relation to other elements in the poetry. If this were not so, every poem in regular and strongly marked meter would simply overcome us.

What does verse accomplish? It is one aspect of the greater formality, or closer organization, of poetry as contrasted with other literary modes. Verse is a means for controlling the use of language. The metrical pattern—that is, the pattern of accents—once we have grasped it as a pattern, sets up the unconscious expectation that the pattern will continue. This sense of pattern, though it may seem mechanical, and even trivial, has far-reaching consequences. For one thing, it is a powerful force in establishing a pervasive impression of unity. The same thing, we may add, applies to stanza pattern. The act of threading a meaningful statement through an intricate stanza pattern—for an example, look back at "Nightingales,"

* *Biographia Literaria,* Chapter XVIII.

† *Ideas of Good and Evil,* London, A. H. Bullen, 1903, pp. 247, 248.

p. 100—in itself imparts a certain formality to the utterance and focuses our attention on it in a special way.

Furthermore, since poetry, frequently in defiance of common sense, proceeds by its own imaginative logic, it is just as well that its unity be validated by the unwavering system of sounds. It is the authority of the meter, we might say, that promises us that the poem will ultimately make sense. It promises also that it will make sense in all of its parts; by insisting on this continuity and unity, it gives a perspective on each part.

Once a pattern of rhythm is established, variations from it register forcibly, and this fact leads us to the second important function of meter. The skillful poet finds in verse a most subtle instrument for regulating emphasis, for underlining the connections between ideas, for pointing up contrasts—in other words, for lifting utterance to a dramatic significance. Indeed, in great poetry the movement of the verse seems indivisible from the movement of the thought and feeling, and the verse seems to be an embodiment of the meaning.

In the first section of the book (pp. 38–41) we discussed the folk ballad "The Wife of Usher's Well." But in that discussion we did not concern ourselves at all with the metrical pattern of the poem, and indeed we passed over the whole matter of the sound of the poem and the management of sound effects. But these are important, and it is time to take into account the way in which they contribute to the total meaning of the poem and condition the effect that it makes upon the reader.

Here follows a partial scansion of the poem:

There lived | a wife | at Ush | er's Well,
  And a weal | thy wife | was she;
She had | three stout | and stal | wart sons,
  And sent | them oer | the sea.

They had | na been | a week | from her,
  A week | but bare | ly ane,
Whan word | came to | the carl | ine wife
  That her | three sons | were gane.

They hadna been a week from her,
  A week but barely three,
Whan word came to the carlin wife
  That her sons she'd never see.

"I wish the wind may never cease,
  Nor fashes in the flood,
Till my three sons come hame to me,
  In earthly flesh and blood."

It fell about the Martinmass,
  When nights are lang and mirk,
The carlin wife's three sons came hame,
  And their hats were o the birk.

It neither grew in syke nor ditch,
  Nor yet in ony sheugh;
But at the gates o Paradise,
  That birk grew fair eneugh.

^"Blow | ^up | the fire, | my maid | ens,
  Bring wat | er from | the well;
For a' | my house | shall feast | this night,
  Since my | three sons | are well."

And she | has made | to them | a bed,
  She's made | it large | and wide,
And she's taen | her man | tle her | about,
  Sat down | at the bed- | side.
^

^Up | then crew | the red, | red cock,
  And up | and crew | the gray;
The eld | est to | the young | est said,
  " 'T is time | we were | away."

The cock | he had | na crawd | but once,
  And clappd | his wings | at a',
When the young | est to | the eld | est said,
  "Brother, | we must | awa.

"The cock doth craw, the day doth daw,
  The channerin worm doth chide;
Gin we be mist out o our place,
  A sair pain we maun bide.

"Fare | ye weel, | my moth | er dear!
  Fareweel | to barn | and byre!
And fare | ye weel, | the bon | ny lass
  That kin | dles my moth | er's fire!"

Note that each stanza consists of four lines (that is, the stanza is a quatrain); that the first and third lines consist of four feet (each of which we have marked off with a vertical line); and that the second and fourth lines consist of three feet; and note further that the second and fourth lines are rhymed. We can describe the stanza thus: (4, 3, 4, 3) with a rhyme scheme (xaya). Note further that the typical foot is an *iamb*. Examples are *There lived* and *a wife*. Remember that in scansion we are making a count of *sounded* syllables. Thus, since the *-ed* of *lived* is silent, the foot is properly marked *There lived,* not *There lived;* and on the same principle, in line 31, *-tle her* is a foot, for the *-tle* in *mantle* is pronounced as a syllable.

How do we arrive at the normal foot and the number of feet that make up a normal line? By reading and listening to the beat of several lines—for any particular foot or line may be irregular. Line 2, for example, begins with an anapaest (two unaccented syllables followed by an accented syllable) instead of what we have determined is the normal foot, an iamb.

Indeed, few poems are completely regular, and the irregularities—the departures from the established and expected pattern—may be deeply expressive. In our discussion of poems in this book, we shall usually concern ourselves with the irregularities and variations: what is normal does not often call for special comment.

A poem that had no variation would seem mechanical and dull. But to say this is not at all to say that the more irregular the poem, the better it is. All variation would amount to no variation—or, to put it in a slightly different way, only in so far as we have the sense of a norm can there be any variation at all. A sensed pattern—a norm of expected recurrence—is the prerequisite for meaningful departure.

In this poem, as in most poems, the variations are of two kinds: there are substituted feet—in this poem usually an anapaest substituted for an iamb as in lines 2, 12, 20, 31, 32, 39, and 48; and there are varyingly heavy secondary accents instead of the normal unstressed syllable—*Bring wat-* in line 26 or *Fareweel* in line 46.* Some of these variations are of no special consequence. The substituted anapaests in lines 2 and 12, for instance, may seem to do little more than give us a

* A secondary accent (marked //) means a degree of accent heavier than that found in an unaccented syllable, but less heavy than a full or primary accent. How much less heavy? That, we shall not attempt to define. The degree of stress denoted by a secondary accent will, according to circumstances, vary from something almost as light as an unaccented syllable right on up to something practically as heavy as that of a primary accent. In the interests of simplicity, we shall limit ourselves to this one symbol for all degrees of intermediate stress. One symbol will suffice for our purposes, for the purpose of scansion is not to record all the nuances of a dramatic and expressive reading of the poem, but simply to indicate the basic pattern and the main deviations from it.

It is only proper, however, to indicate other ways in which the situation involving juxtaposed accents can be treated. Some authorities would call *Fareweel* a spondee, marking it *Fareweel* (or, to indicate *length* of syllables, *Fāreweēl*). In the classical languages, of course, the concept of the spondee makes sense, for the measure of verse in the classical languages is the length of time required to pronounce syllables, and two successive *long* syllables can certainly occur. But in English a spondee would be a foot consisting of two successive *accented* syllables, and there is some question as to whether the genius of the English language does not insure that one of the syllables always gets a little more stress than the other. But a foot like *Fareweel* does approximate an accented spondee and there is no harm done if the student wants to mark it *Fareweel,* though he may find it awkward sometimes to have to mark down *five* accents in a line whose meter calls for only four, or to mark six or more accents in a *pentameter* line.

There is still another way to deal with the situation to be found in a foot like *Fareweel.* The accent may be said to "hover" between the two syllables of the foot, and the student may prefer to mark the foot so as to signify a hovering accent, thus *Fareweel,* reserving the sign // for syllables in which the accent is not heavy enough to compete with the primary accent. But this is a refinement that he *need* not employ. The important thing is to recognize that some of the finest expressive effects in verse arise through juxtaposition of accents so nearly equal that it is difficult to resolve their claims to primacy.

vigorously stressed movement that accords with the "folk" quality of the ballad. (The student, however, should read these lines aloud, in context, and see what he thinks.)

Other variations are clearly expressive—though sometimes the effect is subtle and hard to state. Consider line 40:

/ ˘ // / ˘ /
Brother | we must | awa.

The trochee (a foot consisting of an accented followed by an unaccented syllable) and the relatively heavy accent on *we*—*we* is obviously an important word here and the sense demands some stress on it—give a heavy emphatic movement to this line, an effect entirely appropriate. (We can, if we prefer, state the situation in slightly different terms: the use of a trochee as the first foot of the line tends to throw more stress upon *we*, and an extra stress on this word is appropriate in the context.) In any case, the fact that *four* rather than three syllables in this line get a relatively heavy stress makes good dramatic and expressive sense.

Consider also the last stanza. As we indicated on page 40, this stanza marks the climax of the poem. Does the metrical situation here met with aid in the development of the dramatic effect? Is the system of stresses and pauses enforced by the metrical pattern and its variations meaningful?

Note that we have scanned line 45 as containing a *defective foot* (that is, a foot lacking an unaccented syllable—‸ *Fare*). But in whatever way we choose to scan the line—we might treat *Fare ye* as a trochee and regard *weel* as a defective foot—we are going to come out with a seven-syllable line. Accustomed to eight syllables, we are likely to slow our reading in order to make up for the missing syllable. But whether we do this or not, the line is so arranged that the important word *Fare* gets a strong stress. In the next line (line 46), though in normally unaccented position, it gets a heavy secondary accent—almost as heavy as *weel*, for such is its value in the combined word *farewell*, as it is ordinarily pronounced. In line 47, *fare* is again stressed heavily, for it is here the accented syllable of a normal iamb. This three-fold repetition of *fare* (though it is made with a slight shift each time in the value of its stress) does much to endow the youngest brother's speech with its special poignancy. We are here dealing with a fine point, granted; but the effect secured through the stress-pause relations is not fanciful. Note how much would be lost in a perfectly regular meter:

So fare ye well, my mother dear!
And fare ye well, the byre
And fare ye well, the bonny lass
That lights my mother's fire.

Perhaps we should say a word about line 25, the least regular line in the ballad. In whatever fashion we decide to scan the line, adopting the scansion given on page 127 or some other, we shall have to confront these basic facts. (1) There are only seven syllables though the normal count is eight. (2) *Blow* and *up,* even though there is no intervening unaccented syllable, both demand a heavy stress. (3) The basic pattern of the poem employs a rising accent (in this case, iambic), which means that it will be difficult not to treat the seventh syllable as a *feminine ending* (an extra unstressed syllable not connected with any particular foot; *Note on Versification*). This last item compels us to revise (1): there are actually available only six, not seven, syllables with which to fill out a line that normally is composed of four iambic feet.

It is a consideration of these facts that has caused us to adopt the scansion printed on page 127, that is, to scan the line so as to account for four heavy stresses such as all the other odd lines in the poem have. Dramatically the juxtaposed stresses (∧ *Blów* ∧ *úp*) make perfect sense. The excitement and authority of the mother's command to her maidens is well expressed in the stressing of three of the first four syllables in the line. In the next line, we get an echo of this effect when the opening word *Bring* demands a relatively heavy secondary stress—indeed, one nearly as strong as the stressed syllable *wat-* that follows it

EXERCISE

1. Scan stanzas 2, 3, 4, 5, and 10.

2. Note the word *three* as accented in this poem. Where would you mark it as unaccented (if anywhere)? Where would you mark it with a secondary accent (if anywhere)? How important is the word in this context? Does it vary in importance?

Absent Yet Present

Edward Bulwer-Lytton, Lord Lytton [1803–1873]

As the flight of a river
  That flows to the sea
My soul rushes ever
  In tumult to thee.

A twofold existence
  I am where thou art;
My heart in the distance
  Beats close to thy heart.

Look up, I am near thee,
  I gaze on thy face;
I see thee, I hear thee,
  I feel thine embrace.

As a magnet's control on
  The steel it draws to it,
Is the charm of thy soul on
  The thoughts that pursue it.

And absence but brightens
  The eyes that I miss,
And custom but heightens
  The spell of thy kiss.

It is not from duty,
  Though that may be owed,–
It is not from beauty,
  Though that be bestowed;

But all that I care for,
  And all that I know,
Is that, without wherefore,
  I worship thee so.

Through granite it breaketh
  A tree to the ray;
As a dreamer forsaketh
  The grief of the day,

My soul in its fever
  Escapes unto thee;
O dream to the griever!
  O light to the tree!

A twofold existence
  I am where thou art;
Hark, hear in the distance
  The beat of my heart!

EXERCISE

The first stanza of this poem may be scanned as follows:

As the flight | of a ri | ver
  That flows | to the sea
My soul | rushes e | ver
  In tu | mult to thee.

As with most anapaestic poems in English, there are many iambic substitutions. The first and third lines have feminine endings, which may be indicated as in the scansion above.

1. Scan the next three stanzas.

2. Is the verse happily chosen for this poem? Note that "I" in line 9, "thee" in line 11, and "thou" in line 38 are important rhetorically and deserve emphasis. Does the metrical pattern throw emphasis upon them? Do the metrical pattern and the rhetorical pattern in this poem pull against each other or in harmony with each other?

The Bells of Shandon

Francis Mahony [*1805–1866*]

With deep affection,
And recollection,
I often think of
      Those Shandon bells,
Whose sounds so wild would,
In the days of childhood,

Fling around my cradle
      Their magic spells:
On this I ponder
Where'er I wander,
And thus grow fonder,
      Sweet Cork, of thee;
With thy bells of Shandon,
That sound so grand on
The pleasant waters
      Of the River Lee.

I've heard bells chiming
Full many a clime in,
Tolling sublime in
      Cathedral shrine,
While at a glib rate
Brass tongues would vibrate—
But all their music
      Spoke naught like thine;
For memory, dwelling
On each proud swelling
Of the belfry knelling
      Its bold notes free,
Made the bells of Shandon
Sound far more grand on
The pleasant waters
      Of the River Lee.

I've heard bells tolling
Old Adrian's Mole in,
Their thunder rolling
      From the Vatican,
And cymbals glorious
Swinging uproarious
In the gorgeous turrets
      Of Notre Dame;
But thy sounds were sweeter
Than the dome of Peter
Flings o'er the Tiber,
      Pealing solemnly—
O, the bells of Shandon
Sound far more grand on
The pleasant waters
      Of the River Lee.

There's a bell in Moscow,
While on tower and kiosk O
In Saint Sophia
    The Turkman gets,
And loud in air
Calls men to prayer
From the tapering summits
    Of tall minarets.
Such empty phantom
I freely grant them;
But there's an anthem
    More dear to me,—
'Tis the bells of Shandon,
That sound so grand on
The pleasant waters
    Of the River Lee.

Perhaps the most obvious reason for the failure of this poem is the lack of any real dramatic quality (*Introduction,* p. 20). Notice how little development there is. The poem gives nothing more than the statement that the bells have such and such effect, and a statement of their superiority to other bells. The statement is mere repetition, the list of bells merely a catalogue which lengthens the poem without developing the experience. The whole experience is vague and undramatic, and the statement of it is rambling and monotonous. This deficiency in structure is matched by a comparable deficiency in the monotonous and inexpressive rhythm.

One notices that the handling of the meter is mechanical and inflexible. We continue at the same trot whether the subject is the bells of Shandon or those of Notre Dame or—not bells at all—the cry of the muezzin. In spite of some few variations, the tripping speed of the rhythm sweeps away any effect of contrast or development. Instead of being coordinated with the other elements in the poem, the rhythm has broken loose from the other elements and dominates the poem; the jog-trot metrical pattern is emphasized, apparently, as an end in itself.

But the domination by the meter goes to even greater extremes. Sentence structure is warped and twisted to conform to the demands of the meter. There is no real adaptation of the movement to fit expressive pause and emphasis. There are, for example, no pauses within the lines such as we should find in normal speech. Instead, there is a dead and monotonous beat. The metrical pattern in this poem, far from being one of the instruments used by the poet to get certain effects, actually distorts the sense.

All these distortions are, as a matter of fact, quite deliberate, for the poem is a parody, a high-spirited spoof on the work of the Irish poet Thomas Moore.* The comic point of the parody is made by the conscious violations of the principle of the relation to meaning.

EXERCISE

1. Scan "The Bells of Shandon." (Note that many of the lines have feminine endings.) Locate some instances where the meter seems especially to distort the sense.

2. Examine the rhyme scheme and the nature of some of the rhymes; for example, *Shandon* and *grand on, Mole in* and *tolling*. Locate rhymes that seem forced and strained. Do such rhymes accord with the burlesque spirit of the poem?

RHETORICAL VARIATION

It must have already occurred to the student that the rhythm of any individual line of poetry as actually experienced by the reader conforms only approximately to the metrical scheme as indicated by the scansion. (Indeed, as we have already said, all that the scansion can be expected to do is to mark out the pattern of accents and the accepted variations and substitutions.) No line of verse, however regular the pattern of accents may seem to be, reads with a purely mechanical regularity. Consider, for example, the following line:

Not marble, nor the gilded monuments
(Shakespeare, Sonnet 55)

This line of iambic pentameter scans with absolute regularity:

Nŏt már | blĕ nór | thĕ gíld | ĕd món | ŭ ménts

* See "The Rogueries of Tom Moore," in Mahony's *The Reliques of Father Prout.*

Metrical considerations call for an accent on every second syllable. Furthermore, the pressure of metrical regularity pushes in the direction of an *equal* accent on every second syllable. The situation might be graphed as follows:

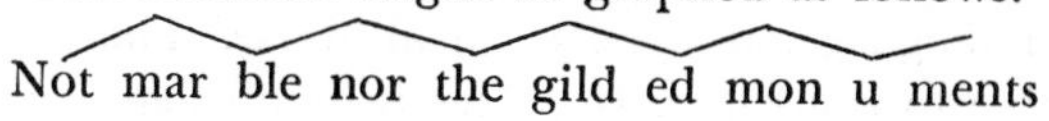

Not mar ble nor the gild ed mon u ments

But obviously some accented syllables are more important than others. Considerations of sense, of expressiveness, of rhetorical emphasis see to that. To read the line as graphed would be to read in a purely mechanical sing-song. In an expressive reading the conjunction *nor* could not receive so much emphasis as *mar-*, the stressed syllable of the noun *marble;* nor could *-ments* (in *monuments*) receive as much emphasis as that which falls on *mon-*. If we graph the line taking into account what may be called *rhetorical variation,* we get something like this:

Not mar ble nor the gild ed mon u ments *

In this line, as in all verse, two principles are at work: (1) a principle of metrical regularity which conditions our reading toward a fixed recurrence of stress and tends to level out divergencies from the norm; and (2) a principle of dramatic and rhetorical emphasis which demands stresses that sometimes coincide with those of the metrical pattern and sometimes diverge from them. The characteristic rhythm of a piece of verse comes from the interplay of these two principles. There is not only an interplay—there is a positive tension, which is necessary if verse is to have vitality and its unique expressiveness.

When the meter as such dominates meaning, we approach doggerel. As Robert Frost says, "You save it [a poem] from doggerel" by "having enough dramatic meaning in it for the other thing to break the doggerel. But it mustn't break *with* it. I said years ago that it [verse in which the meter and the

* If there is difference of level among the accented syllables, there is undoubtedly also difference of level among the unaccented syllables—just as there is great difference of level among the syllables marked with secondary accents (see p. 129*n*). *But we do not suggest that these nuances ought to, or can be, indicated in the scansion.* To do so would be to make that system of notation intolerably complicated and would defeat the real purpose of scansion which is to indicate succinctly what the *basic* pattern of regularity is. (See p. 129*n*.)

meaning have a proper relation] reminds me of a donkey and a donkey cart; for some of the time the cart is on the tugs and some of the time on the hold-back." *

As this factor of rhetorical variation exists by the very nature of language, it appears in all verse. The competent poet is able to control it. In "The Bells of Shandon," quite deliberately, for the sake of parody, it has been allowed to get out of control. The result is that parts of the poem have to be read as mechanical sing-song with a distortion of the sense or, if one reads them according to sense, the metrical pattern is distorted past recognition. For instance:

> There's a bell | in Mos | cow,
> While on tow | er and kiosk | O!
> In Saint | Sophi | a
>   The Turk | man gets,
> And loud | in air
> Calls men | to pray | er
> From tap | ering sum | mits
>   Of tall | minarets

Here we may see that the exclamation *O* in the second line, which by all sense requirements should be heavily accented, is treated according to the metrical pattern as a weak syllable.†

The student might look back over the discussion of "The Wife of Usher's Well" for examples of the proper relationship between metrical and rhetorical stress. In this poem, the metrical pattern does not override and distort the natural emphases. Instead, the system of stresses and pauses accords beautifully with the development of the drama. A general consideration of this poem in contrast with "The Bells of Shandon" will show that the meter, the rhetorical variations, and

* Brooks and Warren, eds.: *Conversations on the Craft of Verse,* pamphlet and tape recording.

† But a good poet can, on occasion, do even this successfully and meaningfully. Note that in the poem by Burns quoted on page 17, the exclamation *O* is successfully put in a metrically weak position. See Yeats's comment, pp. 17–18.

the other factors, such as imagery, supplement and corroborate each other. That is, we have a real coherence and unity.

In discussing some of the ways in which a good poet keeps his verse from becoming monotonous by endowing it with flexibility and proper expressiveness, we should say a further word about the use of pauses in verse. Good verse accommodates itself to a variety of pauses as does expressive language generally. (It is only mechanical, sing-song verse that tends to override and even to obliterate these pauses: see p. 135.) There is usually, however, one principal pause, the *caesura* (*Glossary*), within the verse line, especially if the verse has as many as four or five feet. This pause is to be distinguished from secondary pauses in the line. Variation of the placing of the caesura is one important means of avoiding monotony in verse. Notice how the caesura is varied in the following sonnet. (We have marked the caesuras in the first four lines.)

Like as the Waves

William Shakespeare [*1564–1616*]

Like as the waves || make towards the pebbled shore,
So do our minutes || hasten to their end;
Each changing place || with that which goes before,
In sequent toil || all forwards do contend.
Nativity, once in the main of light,
Crawls to maturity, wherewith being crown'd,
Crooked eclipses 'gainst his glory fight,
And Time, that gave, doth now his gift confound.
Time doth transfix the flourish set on youth,
And delves the parallels in beauty's brow;
Feeds on the rarities of nature's truth,
And nothing stands but for his scythe to mow:
  And yet, to times in hope my verse shall stand,
Praising thy worth, despite his cruel hand.

EXERCISE

1. Scan the poem.
2. Mark the caesuras in lines 5 through 14.
3. Are there any lines that seem to lack a caesura? Are

there any that seem to have more than one principal pause?

4. Can it be said that the relative monotony in the placement of the caesura in the first four lines (in contrast to its placement in the rest of the sonnet) is actually in this context expressive, and therefore justified?

5. Do the caesuras in lines 5 through 14 grow out of the "rhetorical situation" in the lines? Do they accord with the rhetorical emphasis?

To Heaven

Ben Jonson [*1573–1637*]

Good and great God! can I not think of thee,
But it must straight my melancholy be?
Is it interpreted in me disease,
That, laden with my sins, I seek for ease?
O be thou witness, that the reins [1] dost know
And hearts of all, if I be sad for show;
And judge me after, if I dare pretend
To aught but grace, or aim at other end.
As thou art all, so be thou all to me,
First, midst, and last, converted One and Three!
My faith, my hope, my love; and, in this state,
My judge, my witness, and my advocate!
Where have I been this while exiled from thee,
And whither rapt, now thou but stoop'st to me?
Dwell, dwell here still! O, being everywhere,
How can I doubt to find thee ever here?
I know my state, both full of shame and scorn,
Conceived in sin, and unto labor born,
Standing with fear, and must with horror fall,
And destined unto judgment, after all.
I feel my griefs too, and there scarce is ground
Upon my flesh t' inflict another wound;
Yet dare I not complain or wish for death
With holy Paul, lest it be thought the breath
Of discontent; or that these prayers be
For weariness of life, not love of thee.

[1] loins

EXERCISE

1. Scan this poem.
2. Can you justify the frequent trochaic substitutions and the frequent use of secondary accents on rhetorical grounds? Consider in particular the first ten lines.
3. Where do the caesuras fall in lines 1, 2, 10, 11, and 12?
4. Discuss the whole system of pauses in line 15? How are they forced by metrical and rhetorical considerations?

Rose Aylmer

Walter Savage Landor [1775–1864]

Ah, what | avails | the scep | tred race,
  Ah, what | the form | divine!
What ev | ery vir | tue, ev | ery grace!
  Rose Ayl | mer, all | were thine.

Rose Ayl | mer, whom | these wake | ful eyes
  May weep, | but nev | er see,
A night | of mem | ories and | of sighs
  I con | secrate | to thee.

This poem seems perfectly straightforward in its statement. But the statement alone does not give us the poem—that is, other factors are required to make the statement come alive for us. One thing that serves very obviously to convert the bare statement into poetry is the use made of the various elements which we have previously discussed in this general section.

In the first stanza, in the first foot of every line, we may note the heavy secondary accent,* and the length of the first syllable

* The secondary accent is so strong that if one makes use of the concept of the hovering accent at all, he will have to mark these accents as hovering—*Ah, what, What ev-*, and so on. For the question of length, see p. 148.

of the foot. These factors tend to give an unusual emphasis to those feet, especially since the remainder of each line is characterized by a very positive difference between accented and unaccented syllables; and those feet, by the repetitions, set the basic attitude of questioning. The marked regularity of the metrical pattern of each line, the definite stop at the end of each line, and the repetition involved in the first three lines—all of these factors contribute to a formal and elevated tone. (We can notice the formal tone supported, further, by the repetitive balance of the first and second lines, which is repeated by the balance within the third line. "What every virtue" is balanced against "[what] every grace." And we can notice how the distinction between the first and second parts of the line is marked by the pause, which tends to cause greater emphasis to fall on the first syllable of *every*.)

The first line of the second stanza, with the repetition of the name *Rose Aylmer,* picks up the metrical pattern characteristic of the first stanza, providing a kind of transition between the rhythm characteristic of the first stanza and that characteristic of the second. The difference in the rhythm of the second stanza is caused chiefly by the run-on lines, the absence of the secondary accents on the initial syllables of the last three lines, and the metrical accenting of syllables not usually accented. We may try to relate some of these special details to the meaning of the poem.

The first run-on line serves to emphasize the word *weep:* since the sense unit is so radically divided by the line end, when we do pick up the rest of the clause at the beginning of the second line, it comes with a feeling of emphatic fulfillment, which is further supported by the marked pause after the word *weep.* The emphasis on the word *weep* is, of course, rhetorically right because it is set over in contrast with the word *see* at the end of the second line. And we may also observe how the alliteration of the word *weep* with the word *wakeful* in the preceding line helps to mark the association of the two ideas: it is not merely weeping which is to be contrasted with seeing, but the lonely weeping at night when the sense of loss becomes most acute.

The third line is also a run-on line, giving a kind of balance to the structure of the stanza, which functions as do the various balances of structure in the first stanza. Although neither the first line nor the third line of the second stanza is punctuated at the end, we can see that the tendency to run on into the next line is not so strong in the third line as in the first; we can see that the phrase "whom these wakeful eyes" strikes us with a more marked sense of incompleteness than does the phrase "A night of memories and of sighs." This is especially true because the first of the two phrases, coming early in the stanza, is less supported by a context, by the sense of things preceding it. But, even though the tendency to run on is not so strong in the third line as in the first, the tendency is still marked; and such a tendency to *enjambment* (*Note on Versification*) fixes our attention on the clause, "I consecrate," which begins the last line, and forces a pause after that clause.

The word *consecrate,* which is thereby emphasized, is very important. We can see how important it is, and how effective it is in avoiding a sentimental or stereotyped effect, by substituting other words which convey approximately the same meaning. For instance, the lines might be rewritten

A night of memories and of sighs
  I now will give to thee.

We immediately see a great difference. The re-written passage tends toward sentimentality. The word *consecrate* means "to set apart perpetually for sacred uses"; it implies the formality and impersonality of a ceremony. This implication in conjunction with the formality of tone, which has already been discussed in connection with the technique of the first stanza, helps to prevent any suggestion of self-pity.

Another technical feature appears in the use of the word *consecrate,* which does not appear in the re-written line

I now will give to thee.

The word *consecrate* is accented in ordinary usage on the first syllable. But when the word is used in this poem, meter dictates an additional accent on the last syllable, for the line is to be scanned as follows:

Ĭ cón | sĕcráte | tŏ theé.

Thus the metrical situation tends to give the word an emphasis which it would not possess in ordinary prose usage; and this is appropriate because of the importance of the word in the poem.

EXERCISE

1. What would have been the difference in effect if the poet had written, in the next to the last line, "an age" instead of "a night"?
2. Discuss the effect of the accent on the ordinarily unimportant word *and* in the same line.

We began the discussion of the meter of this poem by asking why the poem is so much more rich and moving than any bare statement of its content, and we attempted to show in the course of our discussion that whereas in part this is due to the dramatization and the diction, the meter is largely responsible for the way in which the poem comes alive for us. More specifically, this sense of vitality and significance is gained in three ways: (1) The handling of the meter is flexible enough to give the dramatic impression of speech without violating the impression of a metrical pattern. (2) The metrical variations are never arbitrary but are used to secure the proper degree of emphasis on words where the meaning is focused. (3) The development of the idea of the poem is made alive and significant by being underscored by the metrical contrast between the first and second stanzas.

People sometimes make the mistake of supposing that very particular effects are attached to particular metrical situations. They will identify a special emotion or idea with a special movement of verse, and perhaps assume the movement of the verse to be *the* cause. That is, they assume that a particular metrical situation would convey the effect even to a person who did not understand the language in which the poem was written. In opposition to this view I. A. Richards writes as follows:

> . . . if the meaning of the words is irrelevant to the form of the verse, and if this independent form possesses aesthetic virtue [can transmit the effect without regard to

actual meaning of the words involved], as not a few have maintained . . . , it should be possible to take some recognised masterpiece of poetic rhythm and compose, with nonsense syllables, a double or dummy which at least comes recognisably near to possessing the same virtue.

> J. Drootan-Sussting Benn
> Mill-down Leduren N.
>   Telamba-taras oderwainto weiring
> Awersey zet bidreen
> Ownd istellester sween
>   Lithabian tweet ablissood owdswown stiering
> Apleven aswetsen sestinal
> Yintomen I adaits afurf I gallas Ball.

If the reader has any difficulty in scanning these verses, reference to Milton, *On the Morning of Christ's Nativity* [ll. 113–20] will prove of assistance, and the attempt to divine the movement of the original before looking it up will at least show how much the sense, syntax, and feeling of verse may serve as an introduction to its form. But the illustration will also support a subtler argument against anyone who affirms that the mere sound of verse has *independently* any considerable aesthetic virtue. For he will *either* have to say that this verse is valuable (when he may be implored to take up his pen at once and enrich the world with many more such verses, for nothing could be easier), *or* he will have to say that it is the differences *in sound* between this purified dummy and the original which deprive the dummy of poetic merit. In which case he will have to account for the curious fact that just those transformations which redeem it as sound, should also give it the sense and feeling we find in Milton. A staggering coincidence, unless the meaning were highly relevant to the effect of the form.

Such arguments (which might be elaborated) do not tend to diminish the power of the sound (the inherent rhythm) *when it works in conjunction with sense and feeling*. . . . In fact the close co-operation of the form with the meaning—modifying it and being modified by it in ways that though subtle are, in general, perfectly intelligible—is the chief secret of Style in poetry. But so much mystery and obscurity has been raised around this relation by talk about the *identity* of Form and Content, or about the extirpation of the Matter in the Form, that

> we are in danger of forgetting how natural and inevitable their co-operation must be.*

The real point is this: the meter, no more than any other single element in a poem, gives absolute effects; that is, the particular poetic effect in any case does not inhere in the meter alone. But the meter, as our analysis of "Rose Aylmer" indicates, can be used by the poet as a highly important element to combine with the other elements in order to give the total result which is the poem.

The great value of exercise in scansion and other technical analysis is that it makes us really attend to elements in poetry that are sometimes neglected. Ordinarily we are so conditioned to the use of language as a sign on a page that we forget sound is an essential part of it. Poetry (as well as good prose) uses language in its fullness. Even when we read poetry or prose silently, if we are trained and sensitive readers, we are aware sub-vocally of the rhythm and texture of the language and are affected by them. If we do not have this ability naturally, we can cultivate it by exercise and study that make us focus our attention upon that aspect of language.

This is not to say that any system of indicating scansion, certainly not the rather rudimentary system suggested in this book, will render the enormous subtlety, the complication and shading, of rhythm and texture in language when it is well used. We must depend upon the tact and discrimination of our ear to do that. But the use of a system will help us. It will give us a sort of standard, however crude, to which we can refer the actual language. And it is to the actual language that we always want to come back. That is where the poetry exists.

Furthermore, we must not assume that a poet begins by selecting a meter and then makes his poem conform to it. The more natural situation is one in which the urgency of feeling establishes the basic rhythm, and thus leads toward the particular metrical system. As the poet Marianne Moore has said, "Meter is a matter of conviction." † Or, as Theodore Roethke puts it, "Rhythm must move as a mind moves." ‡

* *Practical Criticism,* New York, Harcourt, Brace and Company, 1929, pp. 232–233.

† Letter to the editors.

‡ Brooks and Warren, eds.: *Conversations on the Craft of Verse,* pamphlet and tape recording.

Ah, Sunflower

William Blake [*1757–1827*]

Ah, Sunflower, weary of time,
  Who countest the steps of the sun;
Seeking after that sweet golden clime
  Where the traveller's journey is done;

Where the Youth pined away with desire,
  And the pale virgin shrouded in snow,
Arise from their graves, and aspire
  Where my Sunflower wishes to go!

EXERCISE

This poem is prevailingly anapaestic in meter. This meter often tends to give a mechanical effect. (See pp. 133, 135.) But this poem does not give such an effect, and, as a matter of fact, is characterized by its delicate and lingering rhythm. We can notice that the first foot in lines 1, 2, and 7 constitute iambic substitutions. Relate these substitutions to the context. But the most important item in securing the characteristic rhythm of this poem is the use of what might be called the secondary accent on the first syllable of the anapaest. For example, the following line might be scanned:

// ◡ / ◡ ◡ / // ◡ /
Seeking aft | er that sweet | golden clime

The first and the third feet are obviously different in effect from the second foot, which is a normal anapaest. The effect of this situation in the anapaest corresponds to that hovering effect given by the secondary accent in an iambic foot. This retardation of the anapaest is what one poet has said we can't "afford to miss" in this poem.

> For example, "Seeking after that sweet golden clime." You can't afford to hurry over "golden." It's just as important as "sweet.". . . Yes, and this one: "And the pale virgin shrouded in snow." There you can't possibly subordinate your "virgin" to "pale" and "shrouded." And so that's very bold. . . . I think it may be that "vir-

gin". . . . comes out stronger in its unaccented position than it would otherwise. . . . We have to overcome our initial impulse to subordinate it and drive on to "shroud—" then, don't we? So we set it up and it emerges more significant to us.*

Work out the scansion of the entire poem.

QUANTITATIVE VARIATION AND ONOMATOPOEIA

There is another factor that influences rhythm and yet finds no specific place in the scansion of English verse. Some syllables—those containing long vowels or clusters of consonants—take longer to pronounce than others. The meter of Greek and Latin poetry is indeed based upon the count (and the distribution) of "long" and "short" syllables. Though this is not true of English meter, and though in general the length of the syllable in English verse tends to ride along with the incidence of stress, still what may be called the *quantitative aspect* (*Glossary*) of language does exist and has its influence on the felt rhythm.

One iambic foot, for example, may be longer than another iambic foot, or one iambic pentameter line longer than another. Both of the following lines are iambic pentameter:

> 'Mid hushed, cool-rooted flowers fragrant-eyed
> (From "Ode to Psyche," John Keats)

> How soon they find fit instruments of ill
> (From *Rape of the Lock,* Alexander Pope)

But a normal reading of the Keats line will take longer than a normal reading of the Pope line. In the Keats line, the foot *cool-root-,* though it can be treated as an iamb, has two long syllables. This length, coupled with the fact that *cool* takes a rather heavy secondary accent—rhetorical considerations demand this—slows the reading of the foot and helps to give a grave and deliberate emphasis to the middle portion of the line. The quantitative aspect of verse is constantly interplaying with the strictly metrical aspect. The mere fact of this inter-

* John Crowe Ransom, in Brooks and Warren, eds.: *Conversations on the Craft of Verse,* pamphlet and tape recording.

play gives a certain vitality to verse. But the good poet is able to control the quantitative factor in language, as in the line quoted from Keats, in order to produce (or assist in producing) special effects.

At this point it may be proper to say a word about what is usually called *cacophonous effects* (*Glossary*). The difficulty in pronouncing certain consonants in succession may very measurably slow down the pronunciation of a line. Consider line 10 of "Sound and Sense" (below). In moving from *Ajax* to *strives,* the reader must negotiate the consonants *k-s-s-t-r;* from *strives* to *some, v-z-s;* and from *rock's* to *vast, k-s-v.* An aspect of the general difficulty is the pronunciation in succession of the same or related consonants; for example, *s* and *s* or *s* and *z.* The difficulty of such transitions makes the line too "labor," as Alexander Pope puts it. Sometimes, however, a transition may be retarded without being intrinsically unpleasant. For instance, such a combination may be one of the factors in lengthening the foot *cool-root-.* The consonants *l* and *r* are both liquids and it is impossible to move from one to the other without making a slight pause. In view of such instances as *cool-root-, cacophonous* is not always a satisfactory term for such forced pauses.

Sound and Sense

Alexander Pope [*1688–1744*]

True ease in writing comes from art, not chance,
As those move easiest who have learned to dance.
'T is not enough no harshness gives offense,
The sound must seem an echo to the sense:
Soft is the strain when Zephyr gently blows,
And the smooth stream in smoother numbers flows:
But when loud surges lash the sounding shore,
The hoarse, rough verse should like the torrent roar:
When Ajax strives some rock's vast weight to throw,
The line too labors, and the words move slow;
Not so, when swift Camilla scours the plain,
Flies o'er th' unbending corn, and skims along the main.
Hear how Timotheus' varied lays surprise,
And bid alternate passions fall and rise!

(From "An Essay on Criticism")

EXERCISE

Though this passage is written in iambic pentameter couplets, there is actually a great deal of variety in the verse. Moreover, Pope is practicing in this passage what he is preaching: he is making the sound "seem an echo to the sense."

1. Indicate the instances of secondary accents.
2. As we have noted, Pope sometimes uses cacophonous effects. Locate them. What use is the poet making of them?
3. Note that one line has twelve syllables rather than the normal ten. Is this an instance of clumsiness on the poet's part, or is it calculation?

In regard to the relation of verse effects to the meaning, it may be well to comment on the special relation which is called *onomatopoeia* (*Note on Versification*). The word means properly *name-making*. Words imitative of their own literal meanings are *onomatopoeic*—for example, *bang, fizz, hiss, crackle, murmur, moan, whisper, roar*. We may observe that all of the words listed here denote special sounds. *The sound of a word can be imitative only of a sound, and only to such words can the term* onomatopoeia *be strictly applied.* An example often given is found in the following lines from Tennyson's "Princess":

> The moan of doves in immemorial elms,
> And murmuring of innumerable bees.

We have here only two strictly onomatopoeic words, *moan* and *murmuring*. But the poet, in each line, supports and extends the particular onomatopoeic effect by repeating the sounds found in the onomatopoeic word. For instance, in the first line, the *m* and *o* are repeated in "i*mm*e*mo*rial el*m*s." Since the particular sound association has been already established by the denotation of *moan*, the repetitions of the sounds become part of the onomatopoeic effect. The same principle is at work in the next line.

It is important to insist upon at least a relatively strict interpretation of the term onomatopoeia and of onomatopoeic effects, for it is very easy for an unwary critic to attribute to onomatopoeia effects which arise from other causes. Such critics attribute a particular imitative meaning to the sound of a word, when at best only a general suitability can actually be observed. For example, here is what one critic has written of a certain line of Edna St. Vincent Millay's poetry:

> But she gets many different effects with clusters of unaccented syllables. With the many *f*'s and *r*'s and *th*'s a fine feeling of fluffiness is given to one line by the many unaccented syllables:
>
> / / / /
> Comfort, softer than the feathers of its breast,
>
> sounds as soft as the bird's downy breast feels.

But another critic challenges this interpretation, as follows:

> . . . The effect [is said to be] a fine feeling of fluffiness and a softness as of the bird's downy breast, while the cause is said to be the many unaccented syllables, assisted by the many *f*'s, *r*'s and *th*'s. But I will substitute a line which preserves all these factors and departs from the given line mainly by rearrangement:
>
> / / / /
> Crumpets for the foster-fathers of the brats.
>
> Here I miss the fluffiness and the downiness.*

In the same way, one might imagine a critic stating that the following line by Keats is onomatopoeic, and identifying the suggestion of coolness and repose with the presence of certain vowel and consonant sounds:

> 'Mid hushed, cool-rooted flowers fragrant-eyed.

The line gives a suggestion of coolness and repose, *but the effect is not to be identified with specific vowels or consonants, nor are specific vowels and consonants to be defined as the cause of the impression.* What one can say of the sound effect of the line is this. The scarcely resolved accentuation of the foot *cool-root-* and the length and sonority of the vowels repeated in the foot emphasizes these words, which with the accented word *hushed* just preceding, set the whole impression of coolness and repose; but the words set this impression

* John Crowe Ransom: *The World's Body,* New York, Charles Scribner's Sons, 1938, pp. 96–97.

primarily by their literal meanings. The function of the verse as such is highly important, but important in supporting and stressing the meaning.

To sum up, we may say that analysis of the elements of verse may be extremely valuable for any reader of poetry. But such analysis runs into absurdity when the reader begins to forget the cardinal principle which has already been stated several times: poetry is a result of a relationship among various elements and does not ever inhere specially in any single element. It is the fusion of all the elements that counts. As Robert Bridges has said, "The fusion of sound and sense is the magic of the greatest poetry." * And our study of the technical aspects of verse is simply a way of deepening our appreciation of the meaning of poetry.

The Blindness of Samson

John Milton [*1608–1674*]

O loss of sight, of thee I most complain!
Blind among enemies, O worse than chains,
Dungeon, or beggary, or decrepit age!
Light, the prime work of God, to me is extinct,
And all her various objects of delight
Annulled, which might in part my grief have eased,
Inferior to the vilest now become
Of man or worm; the vilest here excel me,
They creep, yet see, I dark in light exposed
To daily fraud, contempt, abuse and wrong,
Within doors, or without, still as a fool,
In power of others, never in my own;
Scarce half I seem to live, dead more than half.
O dark, dark, dark, amid the blaze of noon,
Irrecoverably dark, total eclipse
Without all hope of day!
O first created beam, and thou great Word,
Let there be light, and light was over all;
Why am I thus bereaved Thy prime decree?
The sun to me is dark
And silent as the moon.
When she deserts the night

* *Collected Essays,* London, Oxford University Press, 1936, Vol. X, p. 225.

Hid in her vacant interlunar cave.
Since light so necessary is to life,
And almost life itself, if it be true
That light is in the soul,
She all in every part; why was the sight
To such a tender ball as th' eye confined?
So obvious and so easy to be quenched,
And not as feeling through all parts diffused,
That she might look at will through every pore?
Then had I not been thus exiled from light;
As in the land of darkness yet in light.
To live a life half dead, a living death,
And buried; but O yet more miserable!
Myself, my sepulcher, a moving grave.

(From *Samson Agonistes*)

EXERCISE

In Milton's play, Samson speaks this passage under the following circumstances: he has been betrayed by his wife Delilah to his enemies the Philistines, who have blinded him and chained him to the mill as a slave. See *Judges:* Chapter 16.

1. Discuss metrical variation in the first five lines of this passage and in line 14. For *free verse* see the discussion on pp. 175–180.

2. What is the reason for the unusual grammatical construction in lines 17 and 18?

3. Why, in lines 20 and 21, does Samson say that the sun is silent as the moon? Since the sun is, of course, silent, what is served by this statement?

4. Comment on metrical variation in line 35.

FURTHER EXERCISES

1. Locate the onomatopoeic and quasi-onomatopoeic effects in the "Ode to the West Wind" (p. 115). How are these related to the development of the poem?

2. Scan lines 39–42 of "Preludes" (p. 112). How does the metrical effect support the meaning here? Does the meter of lines 53–55 seem to "go to pieces"? Is this the result of clumsiness on the part of the poet? What is the approximate effect? And how is it related to the theme of the poem?

3. Scan lines 25–34 of "Out, Out" (p. 24). What substitutions do you find? What instances of rhetorical variation? Can you justify them in terms of the meaning of the poem?

4. Note the heavy accents in the fourth stanza of "Proud Maisie" (p. 51). What effect do they give? Is the effect dramatically justified?

5. Study the "Ode to the West Wind" (p. 115) as an instance of the principle of rhetorical variation.

6. In many of the lines of "Composed upon Westminster Bridge" (p. 111), the first syllable of the line is heavily accented (the first foot being a trochee substituted for the expected iamb, or else having a heavily stressed secondary accent). Why has the poet handled his meter in this fashion? Can you justify him?

7. Scan "Proud Maisie" (p. 51). Is the metrical pattern used effectively to support the rhetorical pattern?

8. Are there any instances of onomatopoeia in the last stanza of "To Autumn" (p. 109)? Are the metrical variations in the last stanza mere metrical tricks or are they closely related to the meaning of the poem? How are they related?

9. Are there any instances of onomatopoeia in "Sound and Sense" (p. 149)? Where? How is the onomatopoeic effect supported by other elements in the line?

RHYME

All of our previous discussion in this section of the book has been concerned with aspects of rhythm. We have pointed out that rhythm is a constant factor in all use of language, and that its use in verse is a special adaptation. But there are other factors that tend to shape and bind poetry, factors that are not ever-present in the use of language. These are *alliteration, assonance, consonance,* and *rhyme* (*Note on Versification*). All of these involve the element of repetition of identical or of related sounds; and it is this repetition that gives the impression of a binding of the words together. Alliteration, for instance, is sometimes called "front rhyme."

In poetry written during the Old English period the device of alliteration was used regularly for the purpose of defining a verse scheme. The following lines illustrate, in modern

English, the way alliteration was used to give lines unity, just as meter tends to unify a line:

> Now *B*eowulf *b*ode in the *b*urg of the Scyldings,
> *l*eader be*l*ovèd, and *l*ong he ruled
> in *f*ame with all *f*olk, since his *f*ather had gone
> a*w*ay from the *w*orld, till a*w*oke an heir . . .*
> (From *Beowulf,* translated by Francis B. Gummere)

But now alliteration is not used in verse according to any regular scheme. Where it occurs frequently, as in the work of Swinburne, it often impresses the reader as a mechanical and monotonous mannerism or a too gaudy decoration. Most poets use it with discretion to give a line or a group of lines a greater unity or to emphasize the words alliterated. In the following lines we can see how alliteration is used to emphasize and support the contrast in the second line and to relate the contrast to the word, *forgot:*

> Hast thou *f*orgot me then, and do I seem
> Now in thine eye so *f*oul, once deemed so *f*air
> (From *Paradise Lost,* Book II)

Assonance may sometimes serve the same purposes of binding or emphasis. In the following line from Keats, one already given for other illustration, we can see a good example of assonance used for emphasis:

> 'Mid hushed, c*oo*l-r*oo*ted flowers fragrant-eyed

We have already pointed out the effect of the secondary accent in the foot c*oo*l-r*oo*t- and of the length and sonority of the vowel sound (p. 148). The repetition of this vowel sound, that is, the assonance, lends even greater emphasis. Let us examine another example:

> Or Alum styptics w*i*th contract*i*ng pow'r
> Shr*i*nk h*i*s th*i*n essence like a r*i*veled flow'r;
> Or, as *I*xion f*i*xed, the wretch shall feel
> The g*i*dd*y* motion of the whirl*i*ng M*i*ll . . .
> (From *The Rape of the Lock,* Canto II)

* For the survivals of this meter in modern English, see *old native meter* under Note on Versification. Robert Graves's "Rocky Acres" (p. 103) among the poems already studied is perhaps the one best scanned according to such a metrical scheme.

Here it is obvious that the sustained assonance, involving both accented and unaccented syllables, gives a high degree of unification. We can also see that emphasis is secured by the repetition in new combinations of the vowel sounds of the more important syllables. But the quality of the particular "run" here is of some significance, for the tight frontal sound is appropriate to, and supports, the general idea of the passage. (See also L. C. Knights on "No More Be Grieved," pp. 166–67; and the analysis of "Lucifer in Starlight," pp. 347–48.)

Consonance involves a similarity between patternings of consonants. In the following lines we see consonance serving to link lines in the same way as rhyme (see also *slant rhyme* in Note on Versification):

> You are the one whose part it is to *lean,*
> For whom it is not good to be *alone.*
> Laugh warmly turning shyly in the *hall*
> Or climb with bare knees the volcanic *hill.* . . .
>
> (From "III," *Poems,* by W. H. Auden)

Consonance does not serve merely as slant rhyme, but may occur internally in a single line or in several lines to serve the same general function as assonance. This use, however, is much rarer than the use of mere alliteration or assonance.

Rhyme is the most emphatic binder used in English verse. Alliteration, assonance, and consonance may be regarded as types of rhyme; that is, they are forms of resemblance in sound. But it is usual to confine the use of the term *rhyme* to instances of end-rhyme. There are several types of rhyme, *masculine, feminine, weak,* and so on (*Note on Versification*).

Rhyme serves usually, as we have already said, to bind lines together into larger units of composition. We have already seen that the metrical scheme of a single line does its work by setting up in the mind of the hearer or reader an anticipation of regular recurrence. In the same way a fixed pattern of rhyming, a *rhyme scheme,* will, in conjunction with a fixed pattern of line lengths, a stanza, define a group of lines as a unit. In stanzas where rhyme is employed, the rhyme emphasizes the stanza pattern by marking the end of each line unit. But rhyme, it should be said, is sometimes used irregularly; in such cases, it still exerts a binding and unifying effect, though much less forcefully. In addition, irregular rhyme may appear as a device of emphasis, in so far as it has not been used consistently in the poem or passage. The basic function of rhyme, however, has already been described: the unifying and "forming" function, which is most positively exhibited in the reinforcing of the line pattern of stanzas.*

FURTHER EXERCISES

1. Is the alliteration used in "Proud Maisie" (p. 51) merely decorative? Or is it functional?

2. What use of alliteration does Pope make in "Sound and Sense" (p. 149)? Note particularly the effect of the alliteration in lines 5–6.

3. In "Preludes" (p. 112), is the arrangement of the rhymes purely haphazard and capricious? Or can you find any sort of justification for it?

STANZA FORMS

There are many different stanza forms in use in English poetry. A student may consult the Note on Versification for definition of the more common of them. A knowledge of the stanza types is important, of course; but *any given type of stanza must be regarded as an instrument at the poet's disposal and not as a thing important in itself.* The same instrument may be used for widely different purposes. Any given type of stanza is used in conjunction with so many other poetic factors that a reader must be very wary of attributing special effects to special stanza forms. Only the most general principles may be arrived at concerning stanza forms considered in isolation from other poetic factors. For instance, it is fair to say that complicated stanza forms such as the *Spenserian stanza* (*Note on Versification*) offer disadvantages for use in long narrative poems because the involved form may become monotonous and may impede the movement of the action. But the folly of asserting,

* Although the function of rhyme as a structural factor is emphasized here, there is, of course, a pleasure intrinsic in rhyme itself. Children, for example, delight even in nonsense rhymes. But the functional use of rhyme is much more important than the "decorative" use (*Note on Versification*).

as many people have, that the *sonnet* (*Note on Versification*) is especially adapted for love poetry will be demonstrated by the following pair of sonnets:

How Do I Love Thee?

Elizabeth Barrett Browning [*1809–1861*]

How do I love thee? Let me count the ways.
I love thee to the depth and breadth and height
My soul can reach, when feeling out of sight
For the ends of Being and ideal Grace.
I love thee to the level of everyday's
Most quiet need, by sun and candle-light.
I love thee freely, as men strive for Right;
I love thee purely, as they turn from Praise.
I love thee with the passion put to use
In my old griefs, and with my childhood's faith.
I love thee with a love I seemed to lose
With my lost saints,–I love thee with the breath,
Smiles, tears, of all my life!–and, if God choose,
I shall but love thee better after death.

(From *Sonnets from the Portuguese*)

On the Late Massacre in Piedmont

John Milton [*1608–1674*]

Avenge, O Lord, thy slaughtered saints, whose bones
Lie scattered on the Alpine mountains cold;
Ev'n them who kept thy truth so pure of old,
When all our fathers worshipped stocks and stones,
Forget not: in thy book record their groans
Who were thy sheep, and in their ancient fold
Slain by the bloody Piedmontese, that rolled
Mother with infant down the rocks. Their moans
The vales redoubled to the hills, and they
To heav'n. Their martyred blood and ashes sow
O'er all th' Italian fields, where still doth sway
The triple Tyrant that from these may grow
A hundredfold, who, having learnt thy way,
Early may fly the Babylonian woe.

These sonnets have precisely the same rhyme scheme, both being examples of what is called the *Italian sonnet* (*Note on Versification*). But the difference in subject and treatment is obvious, and this simple example should indicate why one should be extremely cautious in assuming that any effect or subject matter is absolutely associated with a particular stanza form. The proper approach to the study of the significance of stanza form may be through this question: *How does the poet use his stanza form in any given poem to produce the special effect of that poem?*

In answering this question in any instance, one must bring into play all the principles which have been previously discussed in this section. But there are still other principles which must be taken into consideration in answering this question. In particular, there is the consideration of the relation of the rhetorical structure, not only to the metrical pattern within the line, which we have already discussed, but also to the stanza pattern itself. Obviously the distribution of pauses within the lines and of pauses at the ends of lines will have an important bearing on the general effect of any stanza form. Stanzas that have a large number of marked pauses at the ends of lines tend to be strongly defined; stanzas that have many run-over lines, or enjambments, tend to give an impression of fluidity and speed. But the effects of the distribution of pauses at the ends of lines are constantly conditioned by the rhythms used within the lines themselves and by the distribution and emphasis of pauses within the lines. To sum up, we may say that the relation of rhetorical pauses to the line pauses of a stanza provides a principle of vital vibration analogous to that provided by the relation of rhetorical accent to metrical accent.

The student has already encountered a number of rhyme schemes and stanza forms in the earlier pages of this book—blank verse, for example, in "Out, Out" (p. 24), and "Ulysses" (p. 59); octosyllabic couplets in "Hell Gate" (p. 52); pentameter (or heroic) couplets in "To Heaven" (p. 140) and "Sound and Sense" (p. 149); terza rima in "Ode to the West Wind" (p. 115); various kinds of quatrains in "Dust of Snow" (p. 91), "Ah, Sunflower" (p. 147), "Lord Randal" (p. 46), "Desert Places" (p. 104), "Proud Maisie" (p. 51); and such elaborate patterns as the sonnet, for example, "Like as the Waves"

(p. 139), or the eleven-line stanza of "To Autumn" (p. 109). But it cannot be too much emphasized that a mere knowledge of stanza forms as abstract and mechanical patterns has little to do with the reading of poetry. The student's aim should be to see what the poet has been able to do with the particular form that he has chosen.

A Deep-Sworn Vow

William Butler Yeats [*1865–1939*]

Others because you did not keep
That deep-sworn vow have been friends of mine;
Yet always when I look death in the face,
When I clamber to the heights of sleep,
Or when I grow excited with wine,
Suddenly I meet your face.

The theme of this poem is the lasting impression made by a love affair which has been broken off, apparently long ago, and which has been superseded by other relationships. On the conscious level of the mind, the loved one has been forgotten, but the image is still carried indelibly imprinted on the deeper, unconscious mind. When we come to consider how this theme is made concrete and forceful in its statement in the poem, we must consider, of course, matters like diction, imagery, structure of incidents, and so on. For example, there is the contrast of the informality of the opening lines of the poem and the note of excitement with which the poem ends. One notices also the arrangement of the three instances which the lover gives of the moments when the face suddenly appears to him: at moments of great danger, in sleep when the subconscious is released, and in moments of intoxication. The last item balances the first: the poet does not intend to falsify the experience by saying, "Only when I look death in the face, I remember you." The memory comes also when the occasion is one of no seriousness at all—merely one of conviviality. And yet the three classes of occasions, though they contrast with each other in their associations, all reinforce one particular idea: the face appears when concern for the immediate, self-conscious everyday existence has been let down—for whatever reason.

Yet important as are all the details of this sort, we shall have to examine the metrical arrangement and rhyme scheme of this poem before we can account for its effectiveness. The poem may be scanned as follows:

> Others | because | you did | not keep |
> That deep | sworn vow | have been friends | of mine; |
> Yet al | ways when | I look | death in | the face, |
> When I clam | ber to | the heights | of sleep, |
> Or when | I grow | exci | ted with wine, |
> Suddenly | I meet | your face. |

The poem is highly irregular. There is a considerable variation in the kinds of lines, trimeter, tetrameter, and pentameter; though the basic foot is of two syllables, some feet have three. Moreover, there are, one notices, many feet having secondary accents. But the irregularities in this poem are far from haphazard.

The tone of the first lines, we have already pointed out, is that of calm, unexcited statement. There is no anger or bitterness toward the woman who did not keep her vow. And this tone is supported by the rhythm of the line. One notices that the poet does not emphasize the word *you,* but the word *others.* The accent is thrown on the first syllable of *others,* and the word *you* does not receive a metrical accent at all, though, of course, rhetorical considerations throw some emphasis on it, and there is, because of the competition between metrical and rhetorical considerations, a weighting of the foot *you did* and of the foot *not keep.**

The second line is highly irregular. There is a heavy secondary accent in the foot *sworn vow,* and the accented syllables

* Some readers will prefer to mark these feet thus:

you did not keep,

feeling that *you* and *not* are quite as heavily accented as *did* and *keep.* See footnote page 129*n*. The important thing to remember is that the scansion is simply a pointer to variations of which we should be aware but cannot hope to define adequately short of a very elaborate system of notation.

here, plus the foregoing accented syllable, *deep,* urge the reader to give all three syllables decided emphasis, and force him to pause before going on with the rest of the line. One notices, also, that the sense unit does not terminate with the end of the first line but runs on rapidly to the second. The important phrase, "deep-sworn vow," is thus isolated, as it were, for emphasis.

The attempt to reassert the metrical pattern at the end of the second line forces rather heavy accent to be placed on the words, *friends* and *mine.* This is proper, for the word *friends* is important. The speaker has carefully chosen this word rather than some other word, such as, say, *lovers.* The quieter, more guarded word is important for the tone which the poet wishes to establish in the opening lines of the poem. The word *friends* stands as a correlative of the word *others.*

The next three lines of the poem are more regular, and in the three instances of memory which the poet gives, the basic pattern is more clearly affirmed and established in the reader's mind. One notices, however, that in the third line, the syllable *-ways* receives a rather definite secondary accent. The word *always* is, thus, emphasized and dwelt upon—quite properly, for it is the important word here. In this same line there is also a rather marked pause between the words *look* and *death,* because both words get a rather emphatic accent.*

The fourth line, with the exception of one detail, the substitution of an anapaest for an iamb in the first foot, is regular, and asserts the pattern which has been obscured to some extent by the variations of lines 2 and 3.

The fifth line has a rapid movement which accords with the sense of the line and with the effect of rapid, casual, even careless excitement. The movement may be accounted for in its metrical aspect as follows: The last foot of the line represents an anapaestic substitution for the expected iamb, and the extra syllable speeds up the end of the line. This added

* In connection with this pause, see also the Exercise on "In Tenebris, I" (p. 169). Some readers will prefer to scan line 3 as follows:

    //   /   //   /   ˘   /   /   ˘   ˘   /
    Yet al | ways when | I look | death | in the face
                              ^

making *death* a defective foot, the lost unaccented syllable being compensated for by the extra syllable in the last foot (anapaest substituted for iamb).

speed results from the following special situation. The fact that the first syllable of the last foot, *-ted,* is an integral part of the word *excited* demands that the anapaest be given unusual speed if the syllable *-ted,* is to be drawn into the last foot at all. (Contrast the situation in this anapaest with the situation in the anapaest at the beginning of the fourth line. See Exercise on "Ah, Sunflower," p. 147.)

Moreover, this last substitution helps to bring into sharper focus the substitution made in the last line of the poem, where a dactyl is substituted for the iamb in the first foot. The abrupt shock given by this substitution (the accent on the syllable *sud-* follows immediately after the heavy accent on the word *wine*) and the pause after *suddenly* prepare us for the climax of the poem, which appears in the phrase, "I meet your face." Other factors in the last line tend to underscore the climax. The line has only three accents, two less than line three, and one less than any other line. The reader, conditioned to the longer line, is prompted to take this line more slowly. The reader is further encouraged to do this by the fact that the word *your,* from rhetorical considerations, demands a decisive accent. The pause after *suddenly* and the strong successive accents on *meet, your,* and *face* give an effect of reserved and solemn statement.

One observes that the rhyme scheme is a, b, c, a, b, c. But *c* is a repetition, and not a rhyme. The repetition suggests that death's face, at moments of crisis when the speaker meets it, is somehow associated for him with the face of the lost love. The reader expects the rhyme, and the repetition, therefore, comes with an appropriate shock. The face is, as it were, echoed, and echoed at the climactic point of the poem, where the meter has helped to prepare us to receive the whole implication.

EXERCISE

1. Consider the image in line 4. We usually think of sleep as passive. What is gained, if anything, by using a figure here of strenuous activity as in mountain-climbing?

2. Can you suggest why the poet chose to make the last line a trimeter, one foot shorter than any other line in the poem?

3. Can you imagine why the poet used a heavy caesura in the last line after several lines containing rather light caesuras?

After Long Silence

William Butler Yeats [*1865–1939*]

Speech after long silence; it is right,
All other lovers being estranged or dead,
Unfriendly lamplight hid under its shade,
The curtains drawn upon unfriendly night,
That we descant and yet again descant
Upon the supreme theme of Art and Song:
Bodily decrepitude is wisdom; young
We loved each other and were ignorant.

The dramatic situation implied by the poem is easily defined. The two lovers are in a shadowed room alone, the lamplight being almost hidden by the shade. One of the lovers is speaking to the other, and before we comment on what he says, several points may be rehearsed. The lovers are evidently old. The relationship has not been a constant one, for we are told that all other lovers are "estranged or dead." The first line suggests that there has been a long silence after they have "descanted" upon the "supreme theme of Art and Song." (The nature of this theme will be discussed later.) This silence has been broken by more talk on the same subject, apparently now the only subject left to them, and one of the lovers makes the comment which constitutes the poem itself.

The speaker says, in effect, this: one lover can no longer take pleasure in the physical beauty of the other (for the lamplight, which would reveal the decay of age, is described as "unfriendly"). Furthermore, the outside world has no more use for them (for the world outside their drawn curtains is likewise "unfriendly"). It is right that, having passed through the other phases of their lives, they should now talk of the "theme of Art and Song," which is "supreme" because it involves the interpretation of their own previous experience. Wisdom, the power to reach an interpretation, comes only as the body decays. The poet sees the wisdom as a positive gain, but at the same time he can regret the time of beauty and youth when the lovers could dispense with wisdom. The basic point of the poem is the recognition, with its attendant pathos, of the fact that man cannot ever be complete—cannot, that is, possess beauty and wisdom together.

Why is the poem so much richer and more moving than the bare statement of our summary? In part, one would say, because the poet has dramatized the general statement—that is, he has made us feel that the idea as embodied in the poem has behind it the weight of experience involving real people. In part, one would say, because of the suggestiveness of the images used in the first four lines. And other reasons for the dramatic power of the poem will occur to the reader. But surely one of the most important reasons for the power of the poem is the beautiful adaptation of the verse to the rest of the poem so that we are made to read it with full expressiveness.

EXERCISE

This poem is written in iambic pentameter, but the first line is highly irregular, and there are several substitutions made in the course of the poem. There are also some very interesting and expressive secondary accents forced by rhetorical considerations.

1. Scan the poem. (If there seem to be alternative ways of handling certain lines, after consideration, choose the one that seems to be the simplest. What is important is that one should take into account—whatever the particular scansion adopted—the accents and secondary stresses that actually occur in the line.)

2. In line 3, how does the metrical situation throw emphasis upon the idea of light hidden?

3. Line 6 is metrically very interesting. Note the instance of internal rhyme. How does it work with the other factors—what are these other factors?—to throw emphasis upon the word *theme?* What is the rhetorical justification for special emphasis upon this word?

4. In line 7, the last word, *young,* is obviously an important word, a pivotal word in the poem. How does the metrical

situation in the line work to throw special stress upon this word? Where does the caesura fall in this line?

5. Notice the number of approximate rhymes in this poem: *dead-shade, descant-ignorant,* and *Song-young.* Are these defects in the poem? Are they signs that the poet was incompetent or careless? Or can you defend them as probably calculated and certainly justified?

No More Be Grieved

William Shakespeare [*1564–1616*]

No more be grieved at that which thou hast done,
Roses have thorns, and silver fountains mud,
Clouds and eclipses stain both Moon and Sun,
And loathsome canker lives in sweetest bud.
All men make faults, and even I in this,
Authorizing thy trespass with compare,
My self corrupting salving thy amiss,
Excusing thy sins more than thy sins are:
For to thy sensual fault I bring in sense,
Thy adverse party is thy Advocate,
And 'gainst myself a lawful plea commence,
Such civil war is in my love and hate,
That I an accessory needs must be,
To that sweet thief which sourly robs from me.

The following analysis of this poem has been made by a modern critic:

> The first four lines we may say, both in movement and imagery, are . . . straightforward. The fifth line begins by continuing the excuses, 'All men make faults,' but with an abrupt change of rhythm Shakespeare turns the generalization against himself: 'All men make faults, and even I in this,' *i.e.* in wasting my time finding romantic parallels for your sins, as though intellectual analogies ('sense') were relevant to your sensual fault. The painful complexity of feeling (Shakespeare is at the same time tender towards the sinner and infuriated by his own tenderness) is evident in the seventh line, which means both,

'I corrupt myself when I find excuses for you' (or 'when I comfort myself in this way') and 'I'm afraid I myself make you worse by excusing your faults'; and although there is a fresh change of tone towards the end (the twelfth line is virtually a sigh as he gives up hope of resolving the conflict), the equivocal 'needs must' and the sweet-sour opposition show the continued civil war of the emotions.

Some such comment as this was unavoidable, but it is upon the simplest and most obvious of technical devices that I wish to direct attention. In the first quatrain the play upon the letters *s* and *l* is mainly musical and decorative, but with the change of tone and direction the alliterative *s* becomes a hiss of half-impotent venom:

> All men make faults, and even I in thi*s*,
> Authorizing thy tre*s*pa*ss* with compare,
> My *s*elf corrupting *s*alving thy ami*ss*,
> Excu*s*ing thy *s*in*s* more than thy *s*ins are:
> For to thy *s*en*s*ual fault I bring in *s*en*s*e . . .

The scorn is moderated here, but it is still heard in the slightly rasping note of the last line,

> To that sweet thief which sourly robs from me.

From the fifth line, then, the alliteration is functional: by playing off against the comparative regularity of the rhythm it expresses an important part of the meaning, and helps to carry the experience alive into the mind of the reader.*

The Expense of Spirit in a Waste of Shame

William Shakespeare [*1564–1616*]

> The expense of spirit in a waste of shame
> Is lust in action; and till action, lust
> Is perjured, murderous, bloody, full of blame,
> Savage, extreme, rude, cruel, not to trust;
> Enjoyed no sooner but despisèd straight;

* L. C. Knights, "Shakespeare's Sonnets," from *Explorations*, New York, George W. Stewart, 1947, p. 65.

Past reason hunted; and no sooner had,
Past reason hated, as a swallowed bait,
On purpose laid to make the taker mad:
Mad in pursuit, and in possession so;
Had, having, and in quest to have, extreme;
A bliss in proof, and proved, a very woe;
Before, a joy proposed; behind, a dream.
All this the world well knows; yet none knows well
To shun the heaven that leads men to this hell.

EXERCISE

Taking suggestions from Knights's discussion of "No More Be Grieved," write an interpretation of this sonnet.

In Tenebris, I

Thomas Hardy [*1840–1928*]

Wintertime nighs;
But my bereavement pain
It cannot bring again:
Twice no one dies.

Flower-petals flee;
But since it once hath been,
No more that severing scene
Can harrow me.

Birds faint in dread:
I shall not lose old strength
In the lone frost's black length:
Strength long since fled!

Leaves freeze to dun;
But friends cannot turn cold
This season as of old
For him with none.

Tempests may scath;
But love cannot make smart

Again this year his heart
  Who no heart hath.

  Black is night's cope;
But death will not appall
One who, past doubtings all,
  Waits in unhope.

EXERCISE

This poem would not be regarded as euphonious. As a matter of fact, there are a number of pauses forced by cacophonous combinations. Are such pauses functional in this poem or are they an indication of inferior craftsmanship? Write a complete analysis of the poem which will deal with this problem.

Slow, Slow, Fresh Fount

Ben Jonson [*1573–1637*]

Slow, slow, fresh fount, keep time with my salt tears;
  Yet slower, yet, O faintly gentle springs:
List to the heavy part the music bears,
  Woe weeps out her division, when she sings.
    Droop herbs, and flowers;
    Fall grief in showers;
    Our beauties are not ours:
      O, I could still
(Like melting snow upon some craggy hill,)
      Drop, drop, drop, drop,
Since nature's pride is, now, a withered daffodil.

(From *Cynthia's Revels*)

EXERCISE

1. What is the meaning of *division* in line 4?
2. What is the meaning of the last line? How is your interpretation of the meaning supported by the preceding lines?
3. Write a metrical analysis of this poem.

The Poplar-Field

William Cowper [1731–1800]

The poplars are fell'd, farewell to the shade
And the whispering sound of the cool colonnade,
The winds play no longer, and sing in the leaves,
Nor Ouse on his bosom their image receives.

Twelve years have elaps'd since I first took a view
Of my favorite field and the bank where they grew,
And now in the grass behold they are laid,
And the tree is my seat that once lent me a shade.

The blackbird has fled to another retreat
Where the hazels afford him a screen from the heat,
And the scene where his melody charm'd me before,
Resounds with his sweet-flowing ditty no more.

My fugitive years are all hasting away,
And I must ere long lie as lowly as they,
With a turf on my breast, and a stone at my head,
Ere another such grove shall arise in its stead.

'Tis a sight to engage me, if any thing can,
To muse on the perishing pleasures of man;
Though his life be a dream, his enjoyments, I see,
Have a being less durable even than he.

Binsey Poplars felled 1879

Gerard Manley Hopkins [1844–1889]

My aspens dear, whose airy cages quelled,
Quelled or quenched in leaves the leaping sun,
Are felled, felled, are all felled;
  Of a fresh and following and folded rank
      Not spared, not one
      That dandled a sandalled
    Shadow that swam or sank
On meadow and river and wind-wandering weed-winding bank.

O if we but knew what we do
When we delve or hew—
Hack and rack the growing green!
Since country is so tender
To touch, her being só slender,
That, like this sleek and seeing ball
But a prick will make no eye at all,
Where we, even where we mean
To mend her we end her,
When we hew or delve:
After-comers cannot guess the beauty been.
Ten or twelve, only ten or twelve
Strokes of havoc únselve
The sweet especial scene,
Rural scene, a rural scene,
Sweet especial rural scene.

EXERCISE

Miss Elizabeth Drew discusses the difference in expression (including the metrical expression) between the Cowper and Hopkins poems on the felling of a favorite row of trees.

> The tripping rhythm [of the first two stanzas of "The Poplar-Field"] at once destroys any sense of grief in the situation, and except for the neat antithesis in the last line, the language is banal in the extreme. So is the final sentiment.
>
> 'Tis a sight to engage me, if anything can,
> To muse on the perishing pleasures of man;
> Though his life be a dream, his enjoyments, I see,
> Have a being less durable even than he.
>
> Hopkins also laments the loss of the shade, the shadow and the wind, but how differently!
>
> . . . Here [the first stanza of "Binsey Poplars"] the life and light and movement of the poplars before they were cut down, and the poet's delight in their ever-changing beauty is created in every word of the description. First not only the beauty, but the power of the trees that could quell and quench even the leaping sun, then the springing curving line of them, and their loosely shifting slipper-

like shadows on field and river and bank. And woven into the description, the poet's grief at man's outrage against this lovely scene. The heavy tolling doom of "all felled, felled, are all felled," and "not spared, not one" are the center of his emotion:

> Ten or twelve, only ten or twelve
> Strokes of havoc unselve
> The sweet especial scene.

That's the tragedy. This was something unique, with its own especial being. But Hopkins's "especial" voice remains; his extraordinary individual use of precise or invented words to create his unique vision and personal intensity of feeling.*

1. Does a scansion of the two passages of poetry enable you to corroborate Miss Drew's judgment?

2. Compare and contrast the use of rhetorical variation in the two poems. Notice also that both poems make a good deal of use of alliteration. Is it more than mere ornament?

Red Wheelbarrow

William Carlos Williams [*1883–1963*]

So much depends
upon
a red wheel
barrow
glazed with rain
water
beside the white
chickens.

This poem is in *free verse,* which, as the name implies, is verse that does not conform to a fixed pattern. But there is no knife-edge line between formal verse and free verse, just as there is no knife-edge line between verse and prose (see p. 120). Rather, there is a shading off from a scrupulous meter

* *Poetry: a Modern Guide to Its Understanding and Enjoyment,* New York, Dell Publishing Company, 1959, pp. 75–76.

toward greater and greater informality. Over the years there has been much debate about locating the precise point where informality in free verse becomes so marked that free verse should not be called verse at all.* There is certainly a point where the sense of form can be lost (except the form dictated by the principles of prose—syntax, grammar, and the like), but discussion that aims at fixing theoretically such a point is fruitless.

What most obviously distinguishes a piece of free verse from prose? It is the lining on the page. Even in the dreariest piece of writing that aspires to be free verse, the fact of its being set off in lines has some significance. It is significant, for one thing, because it pretends to be significant. That is, we have to dwell on the line as a unit, even if, by ordinary standards, we can find no unity.† The very arbitrariness of the slashing across the prose sentence may be important. The line set off by this slashing, whatever its content, is brought into special focus; it makes a special claim on our attention by the mere fact of being set off; the words demand to be looked at freshly. And the whole composition makes, we may say, an important negative claim—the claim of *not* being prose. The only line of "Red Wheelbarrow" that is not absolutely arbitrary is the first, which does have a certain intrinsic structure, the structure of a clause. The lining is so arbitrary that we have to see the poem in print before we have any notion that it is intended as a poem at all. But the very arbitrariness *is* the point. We are forced to focus our attention upon words, and details, in a very special way, a puzzling way. Now the poem itself is about that puzzling portentousness that an object, even the simplest, like a red wheelbarrow, assumes when we fix attention exclusively upon it. Reading the poem is like peering at some ordinary object through a pin prick

* We must keep firmly in mind that we are talking about *verse* and not poetry. Poetic effects—the exciting turn of phrase, the metaphor that opens up a dazzling perception, and so on—may appear in prose. Such effects must, of course, appear in any poem, in meter or free verse, if the poem is to be truly a poem.

† Associated with this is the fact that writers of free verse tend to emphasize typographical features—the visualized line is more significant in free verse than in formal verse, where the heard, or felt, meter defines the line. The most famous name in this connection is that of E. E. Cummings (pp. 185, 209, 446).

in a piece of cardboard. The fact that the pin prick frames it arbitrarily endows it with a puzzling, and exciting, freshness that seems to hover on the verge of revelation. And that is what the poem is actually about: "So much depends"—but what, we do not know.

Let us look at another poem by the same author:

Poem

By the road to the contagious hospital,
under the surge of the blue
mottled clouds driven from the
northeast—a cold wind. Beyond, the
waste of broad, muddy fields,
brown with dried weeds, standing and fallen,

patches of standing water,
the scattering of tall trees.

All along the road the reddish,
purplish, forked, upstanding, twiggy
stuff of bushes and small trees
with dead, brown leaves under them
leafless vines—

Lifeless in appearance, sluggish,
dazed spring approaches—

They enter the new world naked,
cold, uncertain of all
save that they enter. All about them
the cold, familiar wind—

Now the grass, tomorrow
the stiff curl of wild-carrot leaf.

One by one objects are defined—
It quickens: clarity, outline of leaf,

But now the stark dignity of
entrance—Still, the profound change
has come upon them; rooted, they
grip down and begin to awaken.

The most striking feature of this poem is the apparent arbitrariness of the lining. The first line has a phrasal unity, but each of the next three lines ends with a violent slashing across the sense structure—*blue* without its noun, and *the,* twice, without its noun. Such run-overs can, of course, occur in formal verse, but when there is a formal meter, the fact of the meter makes the effect less arbitrary: the metrical order at least substitutes for the order of grammar, syntax, and rhetoric. Here the apparent arbitrariness makes us take a special look. And in this instance, given the special look, the arbitrariness of the lining also fuses with the content to create the effect of openness, blankness, bareness, a sense of the late winter scene.

The arbitrariness of the lining implies, we have said, a claim of not being prose. But free verse cannot exist merely by this negative claim and by this arbitrariness. Consistent arbitrariness would cease to be significant. So we find the denial of the prose sentence being set off against recurrent acceptance of the logic of the sentence—an acceptance indicated by using phrasal, clausal, and other units of sentence logic as the basis of the line, as in lines 1 and 6 of the passage above.

Sometimes we find a poem in which the sentence logic provides the general basis for the lining. Take, for example, "Pear Tree," by H. D. (p. 86). Every line is, intrinsically, set in reference to the sentence logic; each is a unit. But we observe that the elements used for the line differ greatly from line to line in their range—from the vocative "O silver" to the independent clause "you front us with great mass." There is, on the whole, less variety in such a poem as Whitman's "Cavalry Crossing a Ford" (p. 98), where each line is one, or more, full and very strongly marked sentence element. The one line—line 5—which departs from this, departs very significantly, as we have said earlier (p. 99), with the dangling word *while* at the end of the line.

The shifting relation of the line to the sentence, which we have been discussing, occurs, of course, in formal verse, and is there of great importance. The difference with free verse is, however, that with the withdrawal of the obvious principle of meter, the relation of line to sentence takes on an added emphasis. With the withdrawal of meter, the shifting relations between the arbitrary verse lines to the lines based on sentence logic, and the relation among the units of varying weight based on sentence logic, provide a device capable of great subtlety of effect.

We have been speaking of the withdrawal of meter. But this withdrawal is rarely absolute—and some critics go so far as to say that when it is absolute, free verse becomes nothing more than lined prose. Yvor Winters, T. S. Eliot, and many others hold that behind every successful example of free verse is the shadow of formal verse, the background, we may say, against which we are aware of the free verse. As Eliot puts it: "The ghost of some simple meter should lurk behind the arras in even the 'freest' verse; to advance menacingly as we doze and withdraw as we rouse. Or, freedom is only true freedom when it appears against the background of an artificial limitation."

Let us take an example in which we can see very clearly the background of formal meter against which a piece of free verse is developed. In Milton's *Samson Agonistes* the prevailing measure is blank verse; at certain moments this is broken up, and both the length of line and the structure of the foot are changed, but we have in our ear the echo of the blank verse. Here is a passage from the Chorus as it discovers the prisoner Samson brooding alone:

> This, this is he; softly a while
> Let us not break in upon him;
> O change beyond report, thought, or belief!
> See how he lies at random, carelessly diffus'd,
> With languish'd head unpropt,
> As one past hope, abandon'd
> And by himself given over;
> In slavish habit, ill-fitted weeds
> O'er worn and soild;
> Or do my eyes misrepresent? Can this be he,
> That Heroic, that renown'd,
> Irresistible Samson? whom unarm'd
> No strength of man, or fiercest wild beast could withstand;
> Who tore the lion, as the lion tears the kid,
> Ran on embattld armies clad in iron,
> And weaponless himself,
> Made arms ridiculous, useless the forgery

Of brazen spear and shield, the hammer'd cuirass,
Chalybean temper'd steel, and frock of mail
Admantean proof . . .

Certain lines in this passage are readily perceived, with some reasonable variation, as iambic pentameter, the meter of blank verse—lines 1,* 3, 15, 17, 18, and 19. Others can, with wrenching, by absorbing a number of accents as merely secondary in a telescoped foot, be put into the pattern. Still others here, though not pentameter, can be treated as iambic. But other lines burst entirely out of the pattern, even if Milton's metrical practice in blank verse is in itself somewhat violent and idiosyncratic. In fact, we may say that here, when the standard of the blank verse line is withdrawn, certain feet that, in Milton's practice of blank verse, could be absorbed, tend to take on another shape. In any case, all the freedom of this passage is clearly set against the declared background of formal verse.

Usually, however, the formal background of a piece of free verse is not declared. We have to sense it. Let us try to scan the first section of "Pear Tree," by H. D. (p. 86):

Silver dust
lifted from the earth,
higher than my arms reach,
you have mounted.
O silver,
higher than my arms reach
you front us with great mass;
no flower ever opened
so staunch a white leaf,
no flower ever parted silver
from such rare silver. . . .

* In line 1, the first two feet are defective, a strongly marked pause compensating for the missing unaccented syllables: ∧ This, | ∧ this | is he | softly | a while.

There may well be some disagreement about the scansion as marked here.* For instance, in line 4, some readers might wish to give a primary accent to *you,* or a primary accent to *O* in line 5. Or, again, in line 10, the first syllable of *silver* might be given a secondary accent. Even with such debatable lines, however, most people would probably sense a dimeter line from which develop the variations.

With the same concerns in mind, we may turn to the section of a poem by Yvor Winters with the poet's own scansion indicated:

/ /
Earth darkens and is beaded
/ // / //
with a sweat of bushes and
/ //
the bear comes forth:
/ //
the mind stored with
/ // / //
magnificence proceeds into
/ // / //
the mystery of Time, now
/ // /
certain of its choice of
/ // / //
passion but uncertain of the
// /
passion's end.
/
When . . .†

Again, there may be some debate about the scansion, although the poet himself has marked it thus. But even if we depart substantially from the scansion as given, we shall still find that there is a prevailing pattern under the variations—again a dimeter.

Let us return to the poem by Williams and mark the accentuation of the first six lines:

/ / /
By the road to the contagious hospital,
/ / /
under the surge of the blue
// / / /
mottled clouds driven from the

* In formal poetry the presence of the metrical pattern tends to prevent disagreement. In free verse there is, inevitably, more uncertainty.

† Yvor Winters, *Primitivism and Decadence,* New York, Arrows Editions, 1937, p. 103.

> northeast—a cold wind. Beyond, the
> waste of broad, muddy fields,
> brown with dried weeds, standing and fallen. . . .

Again there is room for some debate about the scansion. Some readers might, for instance, want to give the first syllable of *fallen,* in line 6, a primary accent, and call the line a four-beat variation from the three-beat norm. But most readers, going through the entire poem, would probably accept the three-beat norm, despite such possible variations, and feel trimeter as the ghost meter of the whole poem.

From our examples, we can begin to see emerging some general notions about free verse.

(1) In free verse the syllable count is scarcely relevant to the line; a number of syllables may cluster around, and be carried by, the accent. The accents that are to be counted are, by and large, the main rhetorical ones (though sometimes juxtaposition may determine an accent, as in metrical verse).

(2) The count of the main accents may be variable, variation being determined by rhetorical and rhythmical considerations taken in conjunction.

(3) Around the accents, a number of secondary accents may appear—and usually do appear. These secondary accents are the great determinants of the weight, speed, and flexibility of the verse.

(4) The relation of the verse line to the sentence line—the degree of arbitrariness in relation to the rhetorical, syntactical, and grammatical order—is more important in free verse than in formal verse. In formal verse the most important interplay is between the meter and the rhetorical consideration *within the line;* in free verse the most important interplay—the basis of the vital tension—is primarily between the verse line and the sentence line. This, of course, is subject to modification and enrichment by the interplay between the accents of the line and the secondary accents, plus the time of the varying number of unaccented syllables.

This is not to be taken as a final account of free verse. It is intended merely to be suggestive, and to lead the student to make his own study, thereby sharpening his awareness of the factors that enter into free verse.

EXERCISE

1. Scan the remainder of Williams's *Poem.*
2. Comment on the lining.

FURTHER EXERCISES

1. Try to justify the poet's choice of a stanza form in "Nightingales" (p. 100), particularly the use of the short third and sixth lines of the stanza.

2. Write a metrical analysis of I, II, and IV (lines 39–47) of "Preludes" (p. 112). Are the rhymes disposed whimsically? Or can an argument be made for the arrangement?

3. Using Knights's discussion of "No More Be Grieved" (pp. 166–67) as a model, write an account of Milton's use of metrical factors in "On the Late Massacre in Piedmont" (p. 158) Take particular account of substituted feet, secondary accents, alliteration, consonance, and quantitative variation.

IV

Tone

FOREWORD

The *tone* of a poem indicates the speaker's attitude toward his subject and toward his audience, and sometimes toward himself. The word is, strictly speaking, a metaphor, a metaphor drawn from the tone of voice in speech or song. In conversation we may imply our attitude—and hence our true meaning—by the tone in which we say something. The simple phrase, "Yes, indeed," may mean, merely by shifts of tone, anything from enthusiastic, or respectful, agreement to insolent denial. In ordinary life, a great part of our meaning—our basic attitude toward the *what* and the *whom* of any transaction—is indicated by the tone. In a poem this is also true, but the poet must depend on the words on a page to take the place of his expressive human voice; he must choose and arrange his words so that the poem will dictate to the reader the desired tone, with all the subtle modifications of meaning. Our concern here will be to understand something of how this may be accomplished.

Tone, in a poem, expresses attitudes. And this leads us back to what we have said before, that every poem, is, in one sense, a little drama. A poem is an utterance. There is someone who utters. There is a provocation to utterance. There is an audience. This is clearly true of poems in which characters speak, but it is also true of the most lyrical piece. Even the song expresses a human response, and the response is provoked by something, and it implies a hearer—even if only the self.

This is true, even, of a poem like "The Main-Deep," which is about as objective and impersonal as a poem can be. But the poem inheres in words, and someone must have framed them. Further, they have been framed to express the reaction of the speaker—here presumably the poet himself—to an occasion. The occasion is simple: the speaker, staring at the movement of a wave, finds that the wave embodies his own feeling about the life process.

Where, however, is the audience? It is shadowy, not specified. The poet might, as it were, be talking to himself. As in a lyric, in a meditative poem—a poem in which the poet seems to be talking to himself, thinking out loud—what is of obvious importance is the attitude toward the subject, toward what has provoked to utterance. But even in this talking to one's self, there is a sense of audience, and a law imposed by this sense. One can express one's self to one's self, and thereby understand one's self, only by treating one's self as an audience—and that means by respecting the form of what is said so that anyone quite distinct from the self might be able to get the full force and implication of what is being expressed.

In some poems we are scarcely aware of the identity of the speaker—"The Main-Deep" (p. 82), "The Eagle" (p. 91), or "In a Station of the Metro" (p. 88). In other poems, in varying degrees, a personality enters the poem—an "I"—and the attitude of the speaker becomes a very marked feature of the poem. In "Rocky Acres," by Robert Graves (p. 103), for instance, the "I" of the poem calls the wilderness the "country of my choice," and the description of the wilderness becomes, in an indirect fashion, a way of stating the attitude toward the world and other men held by the "I." Or in "Desert Places," by Robert Frost (p. 104), the form is focused on the "I" in a very personal way—without the challenge which the "I" makes to the snowy vacancy to do its worst, there would be no poem. Again, in "Preludes" (p. 112), at the very end, we find the lines

I am moved by fancies that are curled
Around these images, and cling:
The notion of some infinitely gentle
Infinitely suffering thing.

The entrance of the "I" into the poem, here at the end, is a definite statement of the attitude which the poet takes toward the subject, and which, presumably, he expects us to take toward it.

How much are we to identify such an "I" with the personality of the poet? Is the poem to be taken as straight autobiography? In such a poem as "A Deep-Sworn Vow," by Yeats (p. 160), the poet is speaking in his own person, autobiographically, to the lady with whom he had been in love for many years. We even know who she was—Maud Gonne, the famous Irish beauty and patriot.

There are, however, many shadings off from this kind of literal identification to a merely fictitious "I," and for present purposes the degree of autobiographical identification is not *necessarily* important. We are concerned with the fact that the speaker of the poem, whether historical or fictional, is expressing an attitude through his particular use of language. This becomes clear as soon as we think of such poems as "Ulysses," by Tennyson (p. 59), or "Hell Gate," by Housman (p. 52), in which the "I" is obviously fictitious—in which there can only be an imaginative identification.

This is not to say that a poet may not speak his deepest convictions and reveal his deepest self through an imaginative identification. But if we are to say that Tennyson identified himself with Ulysses, we must also remember that, in some degree at least, he identified himself with the speaker of the poem "The Lotos-Eaters," in which a view exactly opposed to that in "Ulysses" is expressed, an attitude of self-indulgent and voluptuous world-weariness. Or we come to instances in which there is more than one speaker, where there is a dialogue as objective as that in a drama, poems like "Lord Randal" (p. 46) or "Danny Deever" (p. 49). And this situation, in which there is a total distinction between the poet and the speaker, or speakers, in the poem, emphasizes the fact that the question of tone is concerned with the speaker *in* the poem, in the situation *of* the poem, and not with degrees of identification of a speaker with any historical person, the poet or any other. The poem is, in this perspective, a drama.

Thus far we have been emphasizing the fact of the speaker. But there is always the audience, too, and the question of the attitude of the speaker to the audience. We began our discussion, in fact, by referring to the shadowy, unspecified audience in "The Main-Deep." Sometimes, however, a poem is addressed to a real person, as we have already pointed out in "A Deep-Sworn Vow," here the lady with whom Yeats had actually been in love. But there clearly does not have to be a particular person, historical or fictional, to whom a poem is directed. The reader himself may be the audience—not in the broad and inevitable sense in which the reader is always the eavesdropping audience, but in a specific sense with the poet addressing him, the "you" of the poem, and adopting a clearly marked attitude toward him.

We have already pointed out how the "I" comes in at the end of "Preludes," and now let us remark how, just after that statement of pity, we find the "you" to whom the poem is addressed:

> Wipe your hand across your mouth and laugh;
> The worlds revolve like ancient women
> Gathering fuel in vacant lots.

In other words, the poet assumes that his audience will not sympathize with the attitude of pity, that the "you" may make the gross gesture of satisfied appetite and laugh at suffering—and may logically do so if we take the view that man is nothing but a mechanical detail in the great mechanism of the universe. The poet assumes this possible attitude on the part of his audience as a way of indicating, by ironical contrast, the kind of response he does desire, and of indicating his own awareness of the difficulty of arriving substantially at that human sympathy. And the complication of this use of the "you" may indicate how important the role of the "you" as audience may be, and often is.

The audience, however, does not have to be a person at all. In "To Heaven" (p. 140), Ben Jonson is addressing God;

in "Ah, Sunflower" (p. 147), Blake is addressing the flower; and in "To Autumn" (p. 109), Keats is addressing the season. There are, too, many poems addressed to abstractions, like Fame or Fear. Sunflowers and seasons have no ears and, literally, cannot be audiences, but they serve in one way or another as a dramatic focus for the human attitude with which the poem is concerned. The tone which Shelley adopts in addressing the West Wind is very different from that which John Clare finds natural to use to the pert little bird in "Little Trotty Wagtail," which we shall soon read.

Portrait

E. E. Cummings [*1894–1962*]

Buffalo Bill's
defunct
          who used to
          ride a watersmooth-silver
                                                  stallion
and break onetwothreefourfive pigeonsjustlikethat
                                                                  Jesus
he was a handsome man
                                        and what i want to know is
how do you like your blueeyed boy
Mister Death

This poem deals with what is a rather common theme, and treats that theme simply. Death claims all men, even the strongest and most glamorous. How does the poet in treating such a common theme manage to give a fresh and strong impression of it? He might, of course, have achieved this effect in a number of different ways, and as a matter of fact, the general device which he employs is not simply one device: it is complex. In this case, however, the most prominent element is the unconventional attitude which he takes toward a conventional subject, and in this particular poem, the matter of tone is isolated sufficiently for us to examine it rather easily (though we must not forget either that there are other matters to be examined in this poem or that tone is a factor in every poem).

In the first place, what is the difference between writing

> Buffalo Bill's
> defunct

and

> Buffalo Bill's
> dead?

The first carries something of a tone of conscious irreverence. The poet here does not approach the idea of death with the usual and expected respect for the dead. He is matter-of-fact, unawed, and even somewhat flippant and joking. But the things which he picks out to comment on in Buffalo Bill make a strong contrast with the idea of death. The picture called up is one of tremendous vitality and speed: for example, the stallion is mentioned and is described as "watersmooth-silver." The adjective contains not only a visual description of the horse which Buffalo Bill rode but a kinetic description is implied too. How was the horse "watersmooth"? Smooth, graceful in action. (The poet by running the words together in the next line is perhaps telling us how to read the line, running the words together to give the effect of speed. The way the poem is printed on the page is designed probably to serve the same purpose, the line divisions being intended as a kind of arrangement for punctuation and emphasis. But the odd typography is not of fundamental importance.) The "portrait" of Buffalo Bill given here after the statement that he is "defunct" is a glimpse of him in action breaking five claypigeons in rapid succession as he flashes by on his stallion—the sort of glimpse which one might remember from the performance of the Wild West show in which Buffalo Bill used to star. The exclamation which follows is exactly the sort of burst of boyish approval which might be struck from a boy seeing him in action or remembering him as he saw him. And the quality of "handsome" applies, one feels, not merely to his face but to his whole figure in action.

The next lines carry on the tone of unabashed, unawed, slangy irreverence toward death. Death becomes "Mister Death." The implied figure of the spectator at a performance of the Wild West show helps justify the language and manner of expression used here, making us feel that it is in character.

But the question as asked here strikes us on another level. It is a question which no boy would ask; it is indeed one of the old unanswerable questions. But here it is transformed by the tone into something fresh and startling. Moreover, the dashing, glamorous character of the old Indian fighter gets a sharp emphasis. The question may be paraphrased like this: Death, you don't get lads like him every day, do you? The way the question is put implies several things. First, it implies the pathos at the fact that even a man who had such enormous vitality and unfailing youthfulness had to die. But this pathos is not insisted upon; rather, it is presented indirectly and ironically because of the bantering and flippant attitude given in the question, especially in the phrases "Mister Death" and "blueeyed boy." And in the question, which sums up the whole poem, we also are given the impression that death is not terrible for Buffalo Bill—it is "Mister Death" who stands in some sort of fatherly and prideful relation to the "blueeyed boy."

In attempting to state what the tone is in this poem, we have, no doubt, somewhat distorted it. Moreover, we have certainly not given an exhaustive account of the tone of this poem. But what has been said above may perhaps let us see how important an element the tone inevitably is. In this case—a case in which, as we have already noted, it is easy to deal with the tone in some isolation—it is the *tone* which transforms what might easily be a hackneyed and dead poem into something fresh and startling.

Little Trotty Wagtail

John Clare [1793–1864]

Little trotty wagtail, he went in the rain,
And tittering, tottering sideways he ne'er got straight again,
He stooped to get a worm, and looked up to get a fly,
And then he flew away ere his feathers they were dry.

Little trotty wagtail, he waddled in the mud,
And left his little footmarks, trample where he would.
He waddled in the water-pudge, and waggle went his tail,
And chirrupt up his wings to dry upon the garden rail.

Little trotty wagtail, you nimble all about,
And in the dimpling water-pudge you waddle in and out;
Your home is nigh at hand, and in the warm pigsty,
So, little Master Wagtail, I'll bid you a good-bye.

EXERCISE

1. Does the poet manage to give a vivid sense of the bird? What details seem particularly effective?

2. What is the poet's attitude toward the bird? Does he think it cute, charming, funny, foolish, or what? In defining this attitude, what part is played by the realistic details in the description? By the humorous details in the description?

3. What is the effect on tone of the use of words like *tittering, water-pudge,* to *nimble,* and so on?

4. Note that in the first two stanzas, the bird is "he," but in the last stanza it is addressed as "you." Does this shift have any effect on the tone?

5. Read the poem aloud a number of times and try to catch the rhythm. Is this in an irregular pentameter, or is it to be resolved in the old native meter (see *Note on Versification*)? Can you relate your answer to this question to the tone of the poem?

His Prayer to Ben Jonson

Robert Herrick [1591–1674]

When I a verse shall make,
Know I have prayed thee,
For old religion's sake,
Saint Ben, to aid me.

Make the way smooth for me,
When I, thy Herrick,
Honoring thee, on my knee
Offer my lyric.

Candles I'll give to thee,
And a new altar;
And thou, Saint Ben, shalt be
Writ in my psalter.

An Ode for Ben Jonson

Robert Herrick [1591–1674]

Ah, Ben!
Say how or when
Shall we, thy guests,
Meet at those lyric feasts,
Made at the Sun,
The Dog, the Triple Tun;
Where we such clusters had,
As made us nobly wild, not mad?
And yet each verse of thine
Out-did the meat, out-did the frolic wine.

My Ben!
Or come again,
Or send to us
Thy wit's great overplus;
But teach us yet
Wisely to husband it,
Lest we that talent spend;
And having once brought to an end
That precious stock, the store
Of such a wit the world should have no more.

EXERCISE

Both "His Prayer to Ben Jonson" and "An Ode for Ben Jonson" were written by Herrick to the poet whom he regarded as his friend and master. (Consult the library for information concerning the relationship between the two poets.) In one of these poems the poet adopts a half-playful attitude and in the other an attitude of serious tribute.

1. Attempt to define this difference more closely and more fully; and relate the difference to metrical and other technical factors.

2. Note that in "His Prayer," Ben Jonson is addressed as if he were a saint (in whose honor candles are to be burned, and so on). Is the poet making fun of Jonson? Teasing him? Is the effect to destroy any sense of reverence for Jonson?

3. Which of the two poems indicates the deeper homage to Ben Jonson? Which the warmer affection? On what grounds do you make your distinction—if you can make a distinction? If you have some acquaintance with the poems of Herrick and of Jonson, decide which of these two poems more resembles Jonson's own style and which more resembles one of the characteristic styles of Herrick. How would you relate your answer here to the first two questions in this group?

4. Can you relate the differences in rhythm between these two poems to the difference in tone?

Channel Firing

Thomas Hardy [*1840–1928*]

That night your great guns, unawares,
Shook all our coffins as we lay,
And broke the chancel window-squares,
We thought it was the Judgment-day

And sat upright. While drearisome
Arose the howl of wakened hounds:
The mouse let fall the altar-crumb,
The worms drew back into the mounds,

The glebe cow drooled. Till God called, "No;
It's gunnery practice out at sea
Just as before you went below;
The world is as it used to be:

"All nations striving strong to make
Red war yet redder. Mad as hatters
They do no more for Christés sake
Than you who are helpless in such matters.

"That this is not the judgment-hour
For some of them's a blessed thing,
For if it were they'd have to scour
Hell's floor for so much threatening . . .

"Ha, ha. It will be warmer when
I blow the trumpet (if indeed

I ever do; for you are men,
And rest eternal sorely need)."

So down we lay again. "I wonder,
Will the world ever saner be,"
Said one, "than when He sent us under
In our indifferent century!"

And many a skeleton shook his head.
"Instead of preaching forty year,"
My neighbor Parson Thirdly said,
"I wish I had stuck to pipes and beer."

Again the guns disturbed the hour,
Roaring their readiness to avenge,
As far inland as Stourton Tower,
And Camelot, and starlit Stonehenge.

The situation in this poem is a fantastic one. The practice firing of battleships at night in the English Channel (and ironically enough this poem is dated by Hardy in April, 1914) disturbs the sleep of the dead at a church near the coast, and even frightens the church mouse that has been stealing crumbs left from the altar bread, and the worms that have crept out of the mounds. Then God speaks to the dead, telling them that the noise isn't the clap of doom, as they had thought, that it's just the world going about the same old business, with the same old disregard for the teachings of Christ. Then a preacher buried there, thinking how little good his forty years of work had accomplished, says that he regrets not having spent his time in worldly pleasure. Meanwhile the guns continue the firing. To make the situation even more fantastic, the person who speaks the poem is one of the skeletons of the churchyard.

If the situation is fantastic, at what sort of reality is the poet aiming? He is aiming to dramatize a theme, a certain view of human life, a fatalistic and somewhat ironical view of the persistence of evil in human life. The situation, then, is a little fable, or parable.

But what attitude does the poet expect us to take to the unreality of the situation? And how does he define the attitude that he does desire? He approaches the whole matter very casually, playing down rather than up the weird and ghostly element of the situation. A poorer poet, or even a good poet with a very different intention from that of Hardy, might have emphasized the horror of the scene. But Hardy domesticates that horror, as it were, for he puts the poem in the mouth of one of the skeletons; to the skeleton there is naturally nothing unusual and shocking in the surroundings. A poor poet would have emphasized the conventional devices for giving a weird effect, for instance, the dolorous howling of the hounds and the crawling of the grave worms, things that are the stage-properties of horror. Hardy uses these things, but he mixes them with the hungry little church mouse and the cow that is drooling over its cud in the meadow. There is, then, a casual and perhaps slightly ironical approach to the horror.

This casual tone is emphasized by the conversational quality. For instance, observe the effect of the running over of the first stanza into the second, and of the second into the third. This spilling over of a stanza to a full pause in the middle of the first line of the next stanza, breaks up the regular and stately movement of the verse, with a kind of tag. The content of each of these tags that spills over supports the same impression. In the first instance, we would get a much more serious effect if the statement should end with the line

We thought it was the Judgment-day.

But, no. Hardy makes the spill-over tag a kind of anticlimax, almost comic in its effect. The dead do not rise to the sound of the Judgment, filled with hope and terror. They merely sit up in their coffins, a little irritated at being bothered, like people who have been disturbed in their beds at night. The same kind of effect is attained in the tag that spills over into the third stanza,

The glebe cow drooled.

The effect here again is that of a kind of anticlimax and ironical contrast, for the drooling cow follows the grave worms, conventional creatures of horror.

When God speaks, the effect is still conversational and simple. He says: "The world is as it used to be"—a line that might be spoken by any one in ordinary talk. And He uses such a phrase as "Mad as hatters." He even makes a kind of sardonic joke about scouring the floors of hell, and another one, at which He himself laughs, about the time when the trumpet will be blown. And the same tone is held in the following stanzas of dialogue among the skeletons. The whole effect, thus far, is a mixture of the grotesque and the horrible with the comic and of the serious with the ironical.

But the tone of the last stanza changes abruptly. The movement becomes emphatic and stately, and the imagination is presented with a sudden panoramic vision of the whole English countryside at night with the sound of the great guns dying inland. All of this elevated poetic effect is more emphatic because of the contrast in abrupt juxtaposition with the earlier section of the poem.

Perhaps further details are worthy of comment. In the first section of the poem there is no such use of conventional poetic suggestiveness as in the last stanza with "Camelot" and "Stonehenge." The effectiveness of this suggestion is increased by the contrast. But we may ask ourselves how the aura of poetic suggestion about these names really works in the poem. Is it merely decoration, as it were, or does it have a direct reference to the meaning of the poem? On the slightest reflection, we see that the use of these place names, with their poetic associations, is really necessary and functional. The meaning is this: Even though the sound of modern heavy guns is contrasted with the medieval associations of Arthurian chivalry, with Camelot and the prehistoric Stonehenge, man's nature does not change. The starlit scene with the guns roaring in the distance becomes a kind of symbolic conclusion for the poem.

EXERCISE

1. We have mentioned the conversational tone of the opening of the poem. But examine the first line. Would you call this "conversational in tone"? Examine alliteration, assonance, quantitative emphasis, and use of secondary accents in the line.

2. What has led us to say that the movement of the last stanza is emphatic and stately?

3. Look at the strange form of the word *Christés* in the fourth stanza. Find out what it is—ask your teacher or go to a reference book on the history of the language. Then try, with reference to the whole poem, to explain the use of this form.

The Fury of Aerial Bombardment

Richard Eberhart [1904–   ]

You would think the fury of aerial bombardment
Would rouse God to relent; the infinite spaces
Are still silent. He looks on shock-pried faces.
History, even, does not know what is meant.

You would feel that after so many centuries
God would give man to repent; yet he can kill
As Cain could, but with multitudinous will,
No farther advanced than in his ancient furies.

Was man made stupid to see his own stupidity?
Is God by definition indifferent, beyond us all?
Is the eternal truth man's fighting soul
Wherein the Beast ravens in its own avidity?

Of Van Wettering I speak, and Averill,
Names on a list, whose faces I do not recall
But they are gone to early death, who late in school
Distinguished the belt feed lever from the belt holding pawl.

EXERCISE

1. This poem invites comparison with Hardy's "Channel Firing." Compare and contrast the poems in their attitudes toward war, in their attitudes toward God, and in their attitudes toward ordinary men.

2. In the last stanza, the "belt feed lever" and the "belt holding pawl" evidently refer to parts of a machine gun. What effect does this technical precision give? What is the effect on the tone of the poet's calling two particular names? What is the speaker's relation to these men? Is this relationship significant for the theme of the poem?

3. Discuss the tone of the first line of the first stanza, and the first line of the second.

4. We have seen how Hardy shifts the tone in the last stanza of "Channel Firing." Discuss that question in regard to this poem.

5. What is the meter of this poem? Note the many extra syllables that have to be absorbed (for example, lines 7, 10 and 15) in the line by substituted trisyllabic feet. Are these variations acceptable?

A Refusal to Mourn the Death, by Fire, of a Child in London

Dylan Thomas [*1914–1953*]

Never until the mankind making
Bird beast and flower
Fathering and all humbling darkness
Tells with silence the last light breaking
And the still hour
Is come of the sea tumbling in harness

And I must enter again the round
Zion of the water bead
And the synagogue of the ear of corn
Shall I let pray the shadow of a sound
Or sow my salt seed
In the least valley of sackcloth to mourn

The majesty and burning of the child's death.
I shall not murder
The mankind of her going with a grave truth
Nor blaspheme down the stations of the breath
With any further
Elegy of innocence and youth.

Deep with the first dead lies London's daughter,
Robed in the long friends,
The grains beyond age, the dark veins of her mother
Secret by the unmourning water
Of the riding Thames.
After the first death, there is no other.

EXERCISE

1. Why does the speaker refuse to mourn the death of the child? How does the fact of refusal set the tone of this poem?

2. The first sentence might perhaps be paraphrased as follows: "Never until the darkness that begets and humbles all tells me that hour of my own death will I utter any prayer or weep any tear to mourn the majesty of this child's death." How accurate is the paraphrase? Indicate why the poet has chosen his much more involved and intricate sentence.

3. Of this poem, Edith Sitwell, the poet, writes:

> In that great poem, "A Refusal to Mourn the Death, by Fire, of a Child in London," with its dark magnificent, proud movement, we see Death in its reality—as a return to the beginning of things, as a robing, a sacred investiture in those who have been our friends since the beginning of Time:—
>
> The grains beyond age, the dark veins of her mother.
>
> (Earth, her mother.) Bird, beast, and flower have their part in the making of mankind.
>
> And I must enter again the round
> Zion of the water bead
> And the synagogue of the ear of corn.
>
> (The water drop is holy, the wheat ear a place of prayer.) The "fathering and all humbling darkness" itself is a begetting force. Even grief, even tears, are a begetting. "The stations of the breath" are the Stations of the Cross.*

If death is, here, as Miss Sitwell says, "a return to the beginning of things," what is its relation to life? Does this poem celebrate death or life or the eternal round of becoming, the unending life of nature? In what sense is the tone of this poem "religious"?

* "Dylan Thomas," Atlantic Monthly, Vol. 193 (Feb. 1954). p. 45.

Ten Days Leave

W. D. Snodgrass [*1926–*]

He steps down from the dark train, blinking; stares
At trees like miracles. He will play games
With boys or sit up all night touching chairs.
Talking with friends, he can recall their names.

Noon burns against his eyelids, but he lies
Hunched in his blankets; he is half awake
But still lacks nerve to open up his eyes;
Supposing it were just his old mistake?

But no; it seems just like it seemed. His folks
Pursue their lives like toy trains on a track.
He can foresee each of his father's jokes
Like words in some old movie that's come back.

He is like days when you've gone some place new
To deal with certain strangers, though you never
Escape the sense in everything you do,
"We've done this all once. Have I been here, ever?"

But no; he thinks it must recall some old film, lit
By lives you want to touch; as if he'd slept
And must have dreamed this setting, peopled it,
And wakened out of it. But someone's kept

His dream asleep here like a small homestead
Preserved long past its time in memory
Of some great man who lived here and is dead.
They have restored his landscape faithfully:

The hills, the little houses, the costumes:
How real it seems! But he comes, wide awake,
A tourist whispering through the priceless rooms
Who must not touch things or his hand might break

Their sleep and black them out. He wonders when
He'll grow into his sleep so sound again.

EXERCISE

1. We may have noticed that the several preceding poems deal with the violence and grimness of war—although in "Channel Firing" the grimness is relieved with comic and satiric touches. "Ten Days Leave" deals with war, too, and deals with a loss caused by war. What is that loss?

2. The young soldier coming home finds the world changed. What is the nature of this change? Look at the imagery used to present the world of home. What tone is characteristic of the imagery in the first five stanzas?

3. In the last two stanzas and the couplet, locate the words or phrases which introduce irony. What motivates this irony? At what is it directed? Is it savage? Tolerant? Tender? How would you describe it?

4. What difference in tone might one imagine if the poem were addressed directly to the young soldier as a "you"? At whom is it directed? At a person of what level of experience and perception? How does this affect the tone?

5. Scan the first stanza. Read it aloud and try to see the relation of your scansion to the rhythm you feel. How would you remark on the rhythm and the tone of the poem?

The Leg

Karl Shapiro [*1913–*]

Among the iodoform, in twilight-sleep,
What have I lost? he first inquires,
Peers in the middle distance where a pain,
Ghost of a nurse, hastily moves, and day,
Her blinding presence pressing in his eyes
And now his ears. They are handling him
With rubber hands. He wants to get up.

One day beside some flowers near his nose
He will be thinking, *When will I look at it?*
And pain, still in the middle distance, will reply,
At what? and he will know it's gone,
O where! and begin to tremble and cry.

He will begin to cry as a child cries
Whose puppy is mangled under a screaming wheel.

Later, as if deliberately, his fingers
Begin to explore the stump. He learns a shape
That is comfortable and tucked in like a sock.
This has a sense of humor, this can despise
The finest surgical limb, the dignity of limping,
The nonsense of wheel-chairs. Now he smiles to the wall:
The amputation becomes an acquisition.

For the leg is wondering where he is (all is not lost)
And surely he has a duty to the leg;
He is its injury, the leg is his orphan,
He must cultivate the mind of the leg,
Pray for the part that is missing, pray for peace
In the image of man, pray, pray for its safety,
And after a little it will die quietly.

The body, what is it, Father, but a sign
To love the force that grows us, to give back
What in Thy palm is senselessness and mud?
Knead, knead the substance of our understanding
Which must be beautiful in flesh to walk,
That if Thou take me angrily in hand
And hurl me to the shark, I shall not die!

EXERCISE

1. The first three stanzas describe the amputation and the convalescence with a studied restraint and understatement. What of the tone of the fourth stanza? Does the reasoning in the fourth stanza—"the leg is his orphan"—become fantastic? What is the point of the fourth stanza?

2. What do you take to be the meaning of the last stanza? Does the speaker believe in personal immortality? Are the last lines akin to the Biblical "Yea, though He slay me, yet will I trust him"? Or is there another meaning?

3. What is the tone of the fifth stanza? Does it have the tone of a prayer? How is it prepared for by the preceding stanzas? How does it complete the poem?

The Death of the Ball Turret Gunner

Randall Jarrell [1914–   ]

From my mother's sleep I fell into the State
And I hunched in its belly till my wet fur froze.
Six miles from earth, loosed from its dream of life,
I woke to black flak and the nightmare fighters.
When I died they washed me out of the turret with a hose.

EXERCISE

1. How does the imagery emphasize the brevity of the gunner's life? Is the imagery consistent? What is his "wet fur"? Does the imagery hint that he remains an embryo—is never really "born"?

2. Try to characterize the tone of the poem. Does it seem ragingly bitter? Or coldly bitter? Or what?

3. Why does the poet say that the gunner had fallen into "the State"? Why not into "the world"? What is the grammatical antecedent of "its" in line 2? But to what does the "its" refer in the action of the poem? Do we find here a blur, a confusion—or a meaningful doubleness?

4. Can it be said that this poem is about "identity of the individual in the modern world"? Explain your view.

A City Shower

In Imitation of Virgil's Georgics

Jonathan Swift [1667–1745]

Careful observers may foretell the hour
(By sure prognostics) when to dread a shower.
While rain depends, the pensive cat gives o'er
Her frolics, and pursues her tail no more;
Returning home at night, you'll find the sink
Strike your offended sense with double stink.
If you be wise, then, go not far to dine:
You'll spend in coach-hire more than save in wine.

A coming shower your shooting corns presage,
Old aches will throb, your hollow tooth will rage.
Sauntering in coffee-house is Dulman seen;
He damns the climate, and complains of spleen.
  Meanwhile, the south, rising with dabbled wings,
A sable cloud athwart the welkin flings,
That swilled more liquor than it could contain,
And, like a drunkard, gives it up again.
Brisk Susan whips her linen from the rope,
While the first drizzling shower is borne aslope:
Such is that sprinkling which some careless quean
Flirts on you from her mop, but not so clean:
You fly, invoke the gods; then, turning, stop
To rail; she, singing, still whirls on her mop.
Not yet the dust had shunned th' unequal strife,
But aided by the wind, fought still for life;
And, wafted with its foe by violent gust,
'Twas doubtful which was rain and which was dust.
Ah! where must needy poet seek for aid,
When dust and rain at once his coat invade?
Sole coat! where dust cemented by the rain
Erects the nap, and leaves a cloudy stain!
  Now in contiguous drops the rain comes down,
Threatening with deluge this devoted town.
To shops in crowds the daggled females fly,
Pretend to cheapen goods but nothing buy.
The templar spruce, while every spout's abroach,
Stays till 'tis fair, yet seems to call a coach.
The tucked up seamstress walks with hasty strides,
While streams run down her oiled umbrella's sides.
Here various kinds, by various fortunes led,
Commence acquaintance underneath a shed.
Triumphant Tories and desponding Whigs
Forget their feuds, and join to save their wigs.
Boxed in a chair, the beau impatient sits,
While spouts run clattering o'er the roof by fits,
And ever and anon with frightful din
The leather sounds; he trembles from within.
So when Troy chairmen bore the wooden steed,
Pregnant with Greeks impatient to be freed
(Those bully Greeks, who, as the moderns do,
Instead of paying chairmen, ran them through),
Laocoön struck the outside with his spear,

And each imprisoned hero quaked for fear.
  Now from all parts the swelling kennels flow,
And bear their trophies with them as they go:
Filths of all hues and odor seem to tell
What street they sailed from by their sight and smell.
They, as each torrent drives with rapid force,
From Smithfield or St. 'Pulchre's shape their course,
And in huge confluence joined at Snowhill ridge,
Fall from the conduit prone to Holborn bridge.
Sweepings from butchers' stalls, dung, guts, and blood,
Drowned puppies, stinking sprats, all drenched in mud,
Dead cats, and turnip tops, come tumbling down the flood.

EXERCISE

At first glance this poem is merely a description of a street of eighteenth-century London in a shower, introduced by a few remarks on how to predict a change of weather. The first of the signs is casual and innocent enough: the cat stops chasing her tail and goes "pensive." The second, too, may be taken merely at face value—a fact, though a peculiarly unpleasant one, which indicates rain. Let us for the moment take it at its face value, but even so the image is there of sewage accumulating, filth backed up waiting for the flushing the rain may give.

Next we have the advice to the "you" of the poem—a citizen of London. It is, on the surface, friendly advice, but it really says: You don't go to dine because you like your host; you go, hypocritically, to save money. So here we move to a comment on a fault in human nature. In other words, the satiric intention of the poem is unmasked, and now we vaguely sense that the accumulated filth that gives the stench in the sink is not merely the literal sewage; it takes on a metaphorical weight, an image for the accumulation of human defect and error that must be purged. So with the old aches that, literally, presage the shower. They come, we now feel, not merely from corns and cavities; they are related, somehow, to moral failings, the dull ache of conscience in a person not willing to face honestly the fact of his character and situation.

The poem now moves into the overt description of the street in the rain. Let us examine the details in the light of the now apparent satirical attitude of the poem.

1. Such a poem as this will not succeed unless the literal descriptive material is striking—physical facts and social types and attitudes. Indicate some of the details which you feel are shrewdly observed. (Here, no doubt, you will find a good many unfamiliar words, such as *spleen, welkin, quean, daggled, templar, cheapen.* Look them up in the Oxford English Dictionary.)

2. Many of the details of the poem involve the dirty, the ugly, the unsavory—the stench of a sink, a drunkard vomiting, the waste from butcher stalls, and so on. What is the relation of this fact to the attitude of the poet toward his subject? How is it used to establish the tone of the poem?

3. In contrast to the realistic details mentioned above, we find such language as

> A sable cloud athwart the welkin flings,

or

> You fly, invoke the gods.

And we find the beau trapped in his sedan chair by the rain compared to the Greeks in the wooden horse craftily introduced into Troy, and the poet using the elevated language and the long simile modeled on the use of the simile by Homer. This is, we quickly understand, *mock-heroic* (*Glossary*). But why is the mock-heroic tone used here? To deflate what pretensions? Why does the poet call the Greeks "bully"? Locate words or phrases of this sort besides those we have mentioned.

4. What does Swift think of the poet, the templar, the "daggled females," the seamstress, the beau in his sedan chair? In relation to the beau, inspect the basis of comparison in the couplet:

> Those bully Greeks, who, as the moderns do,
> Instead of paying chairmen, ran them through.

How does the comparison fit the Greeks? How does it fit the beau?

5. Examine the couplet:

> Triumphant Tories and desponding Whigs
> Forget their feuds, and join to save their wigs.

What is the satiric point here? What, in other words, is the value of a wig set against? (If necessary, find in some reference book, or history of England in the eighteenth century, the meaning of Whig and Tory.)

6. What is the significance of naming the districts of London?

7. All the filth of the city, we are told, is being flushed out by the rain to "come tumbling down the flood"? Suppose the poet had (with an appropriate rhyme, of course) used the word *gutter* or *sewer* or *torrent* instead of *flood?* What would be the difference? How significant for the satiric point of the poem is the reminder of the Biblical deluge?

8. If there is a reminder of the Biblical deluge, why doesn't Swift dwell more on the vice and depravity of the city?

9. Who is the "you" of the poem? What is Swift's attitude toward him?

10. Try to describe the tone of the poem.

To a Young Heir

Samuel Johnson [*1709–1784*]

Long-expected one-and-twenty,
  Ling'ring year, at length is flown:
Pride and pleasure, pomp and plenty,
  Great * * * * * * *, are now your own.

Loosened from the minor's tether,
  Free to mortgage or to sell,
Wild as wind, and light as feather,
  Bid the sons of thrift farewell.

Call the Betsies, Kates, and Jennies,
  All the names that banish care;
Lavish of your grandsire's guineas,
  Show the spirit of an heir.

All that prey on vice and folly
  Joy to see their quarry fly:
There the gamester, light and jolly,
  There the lender, grave and sly.

Wealth, my lad, was made to wander,
  Let it wander as it will;

Call the jockey, call the pander,
  Bid them come and take their fill.

When the bonny blade carouses,
  Pockets full, and spirits high—
What are acres? What are houses?
  Only dirt, or wet or dry.

Should the guardian friend or mother
  Tell the woes of willful waste,
Scorn their counsel, scorn their pother;—
  You can hang or drown at last!

EXERCISE

1. In "A City Shower," Swift, under the guise of a casual description, made a serious comment on the life of London. Here, under the guise of sympathetic advice, Johnson says what to the "Young Heir"?

2. How much does Johnson identify himself with the attitude of the heir? The heir is a "bonny blade"—a gay dashing young fellow, above such vulgar considerations as property—and generous, even generous to a fault. Take the phrase "Wild as wind." Isn't there some hint of approbation in this—applause at the sense of freedom and strength? Even if it is made ambiguous by the phrase "light as feather"? Ambiguity of attitude—an irony that pretends to give approbation, praise, and sympathy even while it condemns—is at the very center of the poem. It sets the tone of the poem. What other examples of this ironical tone can you isolate in the poem?

3. How would you characterize the rhythm of the poem? How would you describe the relation of this rhythm to the tone of the poem?

The Maimed Debauchee

John Wilmot, Earl of Rochester [*1647–1680*]

As some brave Admiral, in former war
  Deprived of force, but pressed with courage still,
Two rival fleets appearing from afar,
  Crawls to the top of an adjacent hill;

From whence (with thoughts full of concern) he views
  The wise and daring conduct of the fight:
And each bold action to his mind renews
  His present glory, and his past delight.

From his fierce eyes flashes of rage he throws,
  As from black clouds when lightning breaks away,
Transported thinks himself amidst his foes,
  And absent, yet enjoys the bloody day.

So when my days of impotence approach,
  And I'm by love and wine's unlucky chance
Driven from the pleasing billows of debauch,
  On the dull shore of lazy temperance;

My pains at last some respite shall afford,
  While I behold the battles you maintain:
When fleets of glasses sail around the board,
  From whose broadsides volleys of wit shall rain.

Nor shall the sight of honorable scars,
  Which my too forward valor did procure,
Frighten new-listed soldiers from the wars;
  Past joys have more than paid what I endure.

Should some brave youth (worth being drunk) prove nice
  And from his fair inviter meanly shrink,
'Twould please the ghost of my departed vice,
  If, at my counsel, he repent and drink.

Or should some cold-complexioned sot forbid,
  With his dull morals, our night's brisk alarms,
I'll fire his blood, by telling what I did
  When I was strong, and able to bear arms.

I'll tell of whores attacked, their lords at home,
  Bawd's quarters beaten up, and fortress won,
Windows demolished, watches overcome,
  And handsome ills by my contrivance done.

With tales like these I will such heat inspire
  As to important mischief shall incline;
I'll make him long some ancient church to fire,
  And fear no lewdness they're called to by wine.

Thus statesmanlike I'll saucily impose,
   And safe from danger, valiantly advise,
Sheltered in impotence, urge you to blows,
   And being good for nothing else, be wise.

EXERCISE

1. How apt is the comparison with which the poem opens? And how inapt? Consider the contrast between the aptness and the inaptness. Could this be the reason for its use here? Of what in "A City Shower" does this remind you?

2. The speaker does not only compare himself to the old admiral; he compares the life of debauchery to war. How apt is this? What is the point here?

3. In the last stanza, is the life of debauchery the only thing satirized?

4. What is the attitude of the speaker to the life of debauchery? To himself? How much ironical ambiguity do you detect here? How could you compare the poem on this point with "To a Young Heir"?

5. Comment on the following items: "dull shore of lazy temperance," "honorable scars," "fire his blood," "handsome ills," "important mischief." Why are these grouped together? Do you see any other words or phrases which might have been added to this list?

6. In the Foreword to this section we have said that knowledge of biographical identification is not *necessarily* important in determining the tone of a poem, that the poem is, in this perspective, a drama and establishes its own tone. This is not to say that such biographical information about the poet, a person he addresses, or a person he writes about, may not be interesting and important. It will not make a poem better or worse; it will not change, that is, what the poet has made of his materials. But it may make us understand better how poems come to be written, it may help us to grasp more fully the implications of a poem, or since poems are about human concerns, it may enrich our responses. With these considerations in mind, look up the biography of John Wilmot, Earl of Rochester. How much identification of Rochester and the speaker in the poem do you think exists? How do you think this may modify the question of the speaker's attitude toward

himself? Do you find that you have had to modify your view of the speaker's attitude toward himself, or do you merely feel it more sharply?

Kind of an Ode to Duty

Ogden Nash [*1903–*]

O Duty,
Why hast thou not the visage of a sweetie or a cutie?
Why glitter thy spectacles so ominously?
Why art thou clad so abominously?
Why art thou so different from Venus
And why do thou and I have so few interests mutually in common between us?
Why art thou fifty per cent martyr
And fifty-one per cent Tartar?

Why is it thy unfortunate wont
To try to attract people by calling on them either to leave undone the deeds they like, or to do the deeds they don't?
Why art thou so like an April post-mortem
On something that died in the ortumn?
Above all, why dost thou continue to hound me?
Why art thou always albatrossly hanging around me?

Thou so ubiquitous,
And I so iniquitous.
I seem to be the one person in the world thou art perpetually preaching at who or to who;
Whatever looks like fun, there art thou standing between me and it, calling yoo-hoo.
O Duty, Duty!
How noble a man should I be hadst thou the visage of a sweetie or a cutie!
But as it is thou art so much forbiddinger than a Wodehouse hero's forbiddingest aunt
That in the words of the poet, When Duty whispers low, Thou must, this erstwhile youth replies, I just can't.

EXERCISE

1. Do you get some idea of the person who speaks the poem? He presents himself, in a sense, as a rather undependable sort, inclined to dodge obligations and evade duties. Do you get the impression that this is a complete picture?

2. If you do not feel that the speaker of the poem is undependable, why do you think he is repudiating "Duty"? Is there a distinction between "Duty" with the capital *D* and the ordinary duties of life? Is there any relation between this distinction (if you think it exists) and the fact that "Duty" hangs "albatrossly" around, and has a face like the "forbiddingest aunt"?

3. The title of "Kind of an Ode to Duty" reminds us of a very different "Ode to Duty," the one by Wordsworth. Look that up and read it. The last line of "Kind of an Ode" echoes another poem:

> When Duty whispers low, *Thou must,*
> The youth replies, *I can.*
> (From "Voluntaries," Ralph Waldo Emerson)

How do these facts connect with the meaning of the "Kind of an Ode"? What is the satire directed at? Duty in general, or certain attitudes toward Duty?

4. Study the meter, rhyme scheme, and rhythm of "Voluntaries" and of Wordsworth's "Ode," and compare and contrast them with the corresponding aspects of "Kind of an Ode," with its irregular lengths of line, slapdash rhymes, and sprawling stanzas. What do you make of this? How are these facts related to tone?

The Season 'Tis, My Lovely Lambs

E. E. Cummings [*1894–1962*]

the season 'tis, my lovely lambs,

of Sumner Volstead Christ and Co.
the epoch of Mann's righteousness

the age of dollars and no sense.
Which being quite beyond dispute

as prove from Troy (N. Y.) to Cairo
(Egypt) the luminous dithyrambs
of large immaculate unmute
antibolshevistic gents
(each manufacturing word by word
his own unrivalled brand of pyro
-technic blurb anent the (hic)
hero dead that gladly (sic)
in far lands perished of unheard
of maladies including flu)

my little darlings, let us now
passionately remember how—
braving the worst, of peril heedless,
each braver than the other, each
(a typewriter within his reach)
upon his fearless derrière
sturdily seated—Colonel Needless
To Name and General You know who
a string of pretty medals drew
(while messrs jack james john and jim
in token of their country's love
received my dears theorder of
The Artificial Arm and Limb)

—or, since bloodshed and kindred questions
inhibit unprepared digestions,
come: let us mildly contemplate
beginning with his wellfilled pants
earth's biggest grafter, nothing less;
the Honorable Mr. (guess)
who, breathing on the ear of fate,
landed a seat in the legislat-
ure whereas tommy so and so
(an erring child of circumstance
whom the bulls nabbed at 33rd)

pulled six months for selling snow

EXERCISE

1. What is the tone of this poem? Relate to the tone the poet's puns, forced rhymes, slang expressions, and irreverently used clichés.

2. Does the poet merely delight in disfiguring whatever stuffed shirts conveniently present themselves? Is his satire briskly irresponsible? Or does it stem from a positive set of values? How would you justify the satiric method used here?

As a Plane Tree by the Water

Robert Lowell [*1917–*]

Darkness has called to darkness, and disgrace
Elbows about our windows in this planned
Babel of Boston where our money talks
And multiplies the darkness of a land
Of preparation where the Virgin walks
And roses spiral her enameled face
Or fall to splinters on unwatered streets.
Our Lady of Babylon, go by, go by,
I was once the apple of your eye;
Flies, flies are on the plane tree, on the streets.

The flies, the flies, the flies of Babylon
Buzz in my ear-drums while the devil's long
Dirge of the people detonates the hour
For floating cities where his golden tongue
Enchants the masons of the Babel Tower
To raise tomorrow's city to the sun
That never sets upon these hell-fire streets
Of Boston, where the sunlight is a sword
Striking at the withholder of the Lord:
Flies, flies are on the plane tree, on the streets.

Flies strike the miraculous waters of the iced
Atlantic and the eyes of Bernadette
Who saw Our Lady standing in the cave
At Massabielle, saw her so squarely that

Her vision put out reason's eyes. The grave
Is open-mouthed and swallowed up in Christ.
O walls of Jericho! And all the streets
To our Atlantic wall are singing: "Sing,
Sing for the resurrection of the King."
Flies, flies are on the plane tree, on the streets.

EXERCISE

1. This poem teems with religious references and allusions—Babel, Babylon, the Virgin, Saint Bernadette, the tree by the water (Psalm 1), Jericho, and, possibly, the flies of the Egyptian plague. Yet the poem associates them with a modern American city, Boston. What is the point of this association?

2. On what ground would you compare this poem with Jonathan Swift's poem about London, "A City Shower" (p. 200)?

3. We have implied by the previous question that this poem has an important satirical element. But with what tone does the poem end?

Horace Paraphrased

Isaac Watts [*1674–1748*]

There are a number of us creep
Into this world to eat and sleep,
And know no reason why they're born
But merely to consume the corn,
Devour the cattle, fowl and fish,
And leave behind an empty dish.
The crows and ravens do the same,
Unlucky birds of hateful name;
Ravens or crows might fill their places,
And swallow corn and carcases.
Then if their tombstone when they die
Ben't taught to flatter and to lie,
There's nothing better will be said
Than that "They've eat up all their bread,
Drank up their drink and gone to bed."

EXERCISE

With the foregoing satirical poems in mind, prepare a set of questions on "Horace Paraphrased." Be sure that you do not ask questions to which you yourself cannot give a reasonable answer.

Mr. Flood's Party

Edwin Arlington Robinson [*1869–1935*]

Old Eben Flood, climbing alone one night
Over the hill between the town below
And the forsaken upland hermitage
That held as much as he should ever know
On earth again of home, paused warily.
The road was his with not a native near;
And Eben, having leisure, said aloud,
For no man else in Tilbury Town to hear:

"Well, Mr. Flood, we have the harvest moon
Again, and we may not have many more;
The bird is on the wing, the poet says,
And you and I have said it here before.
Drink to the bird." He raised up to the light
The jug that he had gone so far to fill,
And answered huskily: "Well, Mr. Flood,
Since you propose it, I believe I will."

Alone, as if enduring to the end
A valiant armor of scarred hopes outworn,
He stood there in the middle of the road
Like Roland's ghost winding a silent horn.
Below him, in the town among the trees,
Where friends of other days had honored him,
A phantom salutation of the dead
Rang thinly till old Eben's eyes were dim.

Then, as a mother lays her sleeping child
Down tenderly, fearing it may awake,
He set the jug down slowly at his feet
With trembling care, knowing that most things break;

And only when assured that on firm earth
It stood, as the uncertain lives of men
Assuredly did not, he paced away,
And with his hand extended paused again:

"Well, Mr. Flood, we have not met like this
In a long time; and many a change has come
To both of us, I fear, since last it was
We had a drop together. Welcome home!"
Convivially returning with himself,
Again he raised the jug up to the light;
And with an acquiescent quaver said:
"Well, Mr. Flood, if you insist, I might.

"Only a very little, Mr. Flood—
For auld lang syne. No more, sir; that will do."
So, for the time, apparently it did,
And Eben evidently thought so too;
For soon amid the silver loneliness
Of night he lifted up his voice and sang,
Secure, with only two moons listening,
Until the whole harmonious landscape rang—

"For auld lang syne." The weary throat gave out,
The last word wavered; and the song being done,
He raised again the jug regretfully
And shook his head, and was again alone.
There was not much that was ahead of him,
And there was nothing in the town below—
Where strangers would have shut the many doors
That many friends had opened long ago.

Mr. Flood is a drunken derelict, an outcast, a disgrace to the community, a friendless and poverty-bit old nuisance. But once he had been young and full of hope, with a comfortable home and, presumably, wife and children, and in those happy days all the doors of the town would have been hospitably open to him. The main fact of the poem is the falling away of Mr. Flood, and the main emotion of the poem is pity at his ruin. Poetry, in general, deals with emotion, and one of the dangers all poems run, especially those involving strong emotions, is that the reader will feel tricked, or bullied, into his response—that he will feel that the poet is insisting on an emotion which is not justified.

Our first question is: Do we feel that the desired response is justified by this poem? Nobody can tell you the answer to this question. You simply have to submit yourself to the poem as fully as possible, and then, in candor, see how you feel. But assuming that you feel the poem to be at least moderately successful—as many readers have felt—then we have another question: How has the poet presented the poem so that the intended emotion is actually available?

In general we may say that the poet has not insisted upon his own response (or ours) to Mr. Flood's ruin. He has, rather, presented Mr. Flood's own response to the situation; that is the central event of the poem. Mr. Flood, coming home alone by moonlight, with his jug, stops and has a party by himself, Mr. Flood and "Mr. Flood" meeting after a long separation, drinking decorously like two gentlemen sitting at their snug leisure, toasting each other. There is no swinish self-indulgence here. Everything is correct and mannerly:

> "Only a very little, Mr. Flood—
> For auld lang syne. No more, sir; that will do."

Then the two Mr. Floods sing in moonlight, two old friends celebrating their long association.

Taken in itself this is a comic scene—the standard comedy of the drunk trying to be sober. Robinson is not afraid to make his drunkard funny, and because he is not afraid to make him genuinely funny, he can elicit a pathos which is far this side of mawkish and generalized pity. The humor gets its point and edge from the pathos, but it also undergirds and guarantees the pathos.

We can appreciate the straight comedy, but even as we appreciate it we are aware that it is modified by three facts.

First, the scene which Mr. Flood, in his alcoholic dignity, enacts on the lonely road is a scene which, under happier circumstances, might very well have been taking place, this very moment, with a real friend, behind one of the severely closed doors down in the town, Mr. Flood talking over old times with a respectable citizen and a good bottle. This contrast, implied but never stated, is always at the back of our consciousness.

We are amused by the comedy, but pity is mixed with the amusement.

As the second fact to modify the comedy, something else enters our reaction too: a sneaking admiration for Mr. Flood's gallantry in not giving way to self-pity and sodden drunkenness—not yet, anyway—and in maintaining, even in his ruin, some fiction of dignity and social decorum. The point is that Mr. Flood, by not making a direct bid for sympathy, succeeds in attracting it.

The third fact that modifies the comic effect is the running commentary by the poet himself, as he presents Mr. Flood in action. In the commentary we shall find the same sort of complication which we have noticed in our own reaction.

Let us look at the commentary in the first stanza. The poet says that Mr. Flood is "alone," that his remote house is "forsaken" but is as much as he will ever know "On earth again of home." So far, we find the poet insisting on our sympathy for his character. But two things come in to modify this direct bid for sympathy.

Take the word *warily*. The word does carry some sense of the hunted animal, and in that sense continues the direct bid for our sympathy. As soon as we know the poem, however, the word gives us, also, the beginning of the comedy: Old Eben peering this way and that to be sure that he is alone before his little charade. More important, to modify the direct bid is the phrase "having leisure." This is another comic touch, a joke: There's no reason why Eben shouldn't stop if he wants to, leisure is all he does have. But the phrase slips incidentally into the structure of the sentence, as we would use it about a man of business who ordinarily did not have leisure, and this casualness makes the humor wry and controlled. So in the first stanza, in a minor way, the complication of the poem has been initiated.

With the third stanza the commentary seems, at first glance anyway, to make only the direct bid. We find the phrases "valiant armor" and "scarred hopes outworn." They are direct, yes. But they are too direct; that is, the phrases remind us of all the clichés of chivalric poetry about knights and derring-do, and when applied to the likker-soaked old derelict they are mock-heroic, too grand, merely funny.

Then we find Mr. Flood, holding up his jug, literally compared to Roland, the hero of the Old French epic *The Song of Roland,* the nephew of Charlemagne, who, as commander of the rear guard of the Emperor's army in the mountains of Spain, held off an overwhelming force of the Moors and refused, until the very end, to blow his famous horn for help. Some readers have felt that the association of the village drunk with Roland is too romantic, too obviously and arrantly a bid for our sympathy: as Roland called for help to his far-off friends, so Mr. Flood summons up the old days of friendship and dignity. The association is, in fact, extreme, but it is perfectly consonant with the realism of the preceding part of the poem. The gesture of lifting the jug, and the shape of the jug, evoke with literal accuracy the gesture Roland made. Mr. Flood is a ghostly Roland and his horn is a silent one, unless we hear the gurgle of the whiskey. The episode is, again, a piece of mock-heroic banter, but something of the grandeur of Roland rubs off on Mr. Flood.

As we have the mock-heroic in the third stanza, so in the fourth, we have what we may call the mock-sentimental modifying the direct bid for sympathy. We may even take the image of the mother and child to be a smuggled-in reminder of the time of Mr. Flood's happier fortune. But when the child suddenly becomes jug, the effect goes comic. But look at the phrase "knowing that most things break." Again as with the phrase in the first stanza, "having leisure," this phrase is slipped casually into the sentence, in an unemphatic participial construction. Yet this phrase, in its incidental construction, is the thing the poem is about—the instability of human happiness.

Mr. Flood finished his party "with only two moons listening" to the song celebrating his happier days. So the scene ends with a last joke at the old drunk's expense. Are we prepared now to accept the direct statement of Mr. Flood's sad situation? Has the poet, in other words, done enough justice to the various aspects of the situation to allow us to accept the pathos as real and not as sentimental self-indulgence? To do justice to the situation—that is what a poet is obligated to try to do.

EXERCISE

1. What is the tone of the last four lines of the poem? How do you feel about them?

2. In the fourth stanza, look at the clause "as the uncertain lives of men / Assuredly did not." How is it related to the main idea of the poem? What is its syntactical relation to the sentence in which it appears? What observation might your answers to these two questions lead you to make?

3. Explore the implications for the poem of the word *secure* in line 47.

4. How do we take the word *harmonious* in line 48?

5. State the theme of the poem. Is it merely "the instability of human happiness"? Or does it involve some attitude toward that fact?

Stopping by Woods on a Snowy Evening

Robert Frost [*1874–1963*]

Whose woods these are I think I know.
His house is in the village though;
He will not see me stopping here
To watch his woods fill up with snow.

My little horse must think it queer
To stop without a farmhouse near
Between the woods and frozen lake
The darkest evening of the year.

He gives his harness bells a shake
To ask if there is some mistake.
The only other sound's the sweep
Of easy wind and downy flake.

The woods are lovely, dark and deep.
But I have promises to keep,
And miles to go before I sleep,
And miles to go before I sleep.

EXERCISE

1. Why does the speaker stop by the woods? (The horse thinks it queer that he stops; the owner of the woods, it is implied, would also think it queer if he could see him.)

2. Does the speaker drive on with reluctance? What does this implied reluctance tell us about the motive for stopping?

3. What attitude toward nature is implied in this little poem? The woods are "lovely, dark, and deep" and make some deep appeal to the speaker. Note that it is not an appeal that is felt by the sub-human (the horse) or the practical man (the owner of the woods) and that it is an appeal that is finally resisted by even the speaker himself: "But I have promises," and so on.

Wessex Heights

Thomas Hardy [*1840–1928*]

There are some heights in Wessex, shaped as if by a kindly hand
For thinking, dreaming, dying on, and at crises when I stand,
Say, on Ingpen Beacon eastward, or on Wylls-Neck westwardly,
I seem where I was before my birth, and after death may be.

In the lowlands I have no comrade, not even the lone man's friend—
Her who suffereth long and is kind; accepts what he is too weak to mend:
Down there they are dubious and askance; there nobody thinks as I,
But mind-chains do not clank where one's next neighbor is the sky.

In the towns I am tracked by phantoms having weird detective ways—
Shadows of beings who fellowed with myself of earlier days:
They hang about at places, and they say harsh heavy things—
Men with a frigid sneer, and women with tart disparagings.

Down there I seem to be false to myself, my simple self that was,
And is not now, and I see him watching, wondering what crass cause

Can have merged him into such a strange continuator as this,
Who yet has something in common with myself, my chrysalis.

I cannot go to the great gray Plain; there's a figure against the moon,
Nobody sees it but I, and it makes my breast beat out of tune;
I cannot go to the tall-spired town, being barred by the forms now passed
For everybody but me, in whose long vision they stand there fast.

There's a ghost at Yell'ham Bottom chiding loud at the fall of the night,
There's a ghost in Froom-side Vale, thin lipped and vague, in a shroud of white,
There is one in the railway-train whenever I do not want it near,
I see its profile against the pane, saying what I would not hear.

As for one rare fair woman, I am now but a thought of hers,
I enter her mind and another thought succeeds me that she prefers;
Yet my love for her in its fulness she herself even did not know;
Well, time cures hearts of tenderness, and now I can let her go.

So I am found on Ingpen Beacon, or on Wylls-Neck to the west,
Or else on homely Bulbarrow, or little Pilsdon Crest,
Where men have never cared to haunt, nor women have walked with me,
And ghosts then keep their distance; and I know some liberty.

EXERCISE

1. The speaker of the poem is obviously a man haunted by the past, but he can escape from the oppressive memories by going to certain heights in his native county where he feels outside his experience, as before birth or after death. He is a man who has not come to terms with the pains, frustrations, and losses of life. Are we to take it that when he goes to the hills of Wessex he simply forgets those aspects of his experience, or that he has a different attitude toward them, sees them in a different perspective? Perhaps we can arrive at no

certain answer to this question, but the last line of the first stanza and the last line of the poem may give some evidence. Too, we may ask if our impression of the speaker, after we have thought over the poem, is of a man who seeks nothing more than flight.

2. This is a poem in which the speaker inspects his fundamental view of experience, and his relation to the world. Inevitably this involves an attitude toward himself. He knows himself a "lone man." We should like to know what makes him "lone." Perhaps the poem is confused and does not give any indication, but let us assume that it is not and pursue the question.

a. What view does he have about his own weaknesses or failings of character?

b. Does he accept the standard, conventional opinions of his society?

c. Why do the ghosts of friends of early days sneer at and disparage him? Had the old companions always done so? Or are we to take it there has been some self-betrayal—a betrayal of the older "simple self" which has become the "strange continuator"? Are we to take it that the present man is no longer "simple"? By the way, how much is this man like an ordinary man?

d. There is the hint of a love story that has come to a bad end. Does the man feel himself the victim? What is his view of the woman? Does he blame her? Or does he seem to take the blame? Or is he now prepared to think of the ruin of his love without blaming anyone?

e. In connection with the last question, we may return to the word *chrysalis* in line 16. The old self, we are told, was the chrysalis of the present "strange continuator." A chrysalis is a stage in a natural development, an inevitable development. Are we forcing things too much to relate this image to the question of blame, and the attitude in line 28?

3. Some important imagery of the poem uses the ghosts. If you did not know the author of this poem, would you, on the basis of your acquaintance with "Channel Firing," be likely to assign it to Hardy? Why? For instance, look at the phrase "phantoms having weird detective ways." Phantoms are ordinarily thought of as "weird"; it is a word in keeping with the

expected spooky atmosphere. The word *detective,* however, comes with a shock. It belongs to the world of hard fact, ratiocination, and deduction. But we quickly become aware of a peculiar rightness in the word. The ghosts pursue the speaker of the poem with some kind of relentless, secret logic. There is even the sense that they may pursue in punishment for some crime, or at least shortcoming. We can see, furthermore, that the detective in himself has some qualities in common with the ghost—stealth, shadowlike ease, and so on. When other ghosts appear in the poem, do you find something of the same doubleness in the presentation—the conventionally spooky and the realistic? What is at stake here?

4. How can you relate line 26 to the ghosts of the poem?

5. Read the poem aloud until you feel that you have a firm sense of its rhythms. Is there much variety in the rhythm? Can you relate the shifts in rhythm in the poem to the general idea of Exercise 3?

6. Scan line 20. What is the effect, in contrast with the movement of the preceding line and in relation to the content, of the massing of heavy accents at the end of the line?

7. The reader is likely to feel (a) that this is a clumsy poem, marred by a number of lapses of tone (lines 8, 9, 20, 23, 32, for example) or (b) that it is a remarkably fine poem, with brilliantly dramatic and expressive shifts of tone. How do you feel about it? Try to justify your answer.

The Pilgrims

Adelaide Anne Procter [*1825–1864*]

The way is long and dreary,
The path is bleak and bare;
Our feet are worn and weary,
But we will not despair;
More heavy was Thy burden,
More desolate Thy way;—
O Lamb of God who takest
The sin of the world away,
  Have mercy on us.

The snows lie thick around us
In the dark and gloomy night;
And the tempest wails above us,
And the stars have hid their light;
But blacker was the darkness
Round Calvary's Cross that day:—
O Lamb of God who takest
The sin of the world away,
  Have mercy on us.

Our hearts are faint with sorrow,
Heavy and hard to bear;
For we dread the bitter morrow,
But we will not despair:
Thou knowest all our anguish,
And Thou wilt bid it cease,—
O Lamb of God who takest
The sin of the world away,
  Give us Thy peace!

Even though the work of Adelaide Procter, who is known now only as the author of "The Lost Chord," was once greatly admired by Charles Dickens, most modern readers of poetry would find this poem bad. Most readers who admire it probably do so because they approve of the pious sentiment expressed in it. Such readers go to poetry merely to have their own beliefs and feelings flattered or to find what they would call "great truths" or "worth-while ideas" expressed in an agreeable form. Such readers do not go to poetry for anything that poetry, as poetry, can give them, but for something that they might get, though in not so compact and pleasant a form, in a sermon or a collection of adages.

"The Pilgrims" can be appreciated only because of something the reader may bring to it (an uncritical and sentimental piety) and not because of anything it brings to the reader. A truly pious person who was also an experienced reader of poetry might, as a matter of fact, have his piety offended rather than sustained by this poem. He might feel it as stupid, trivial, and not worthy of the subject.

He might feel this because the business of a poem is to sharpen and renew the experience of the subject. But the present poem does nothing to accomplish that purpose. It is composed of worn-out materials, stereotyped images and phrases. The trouble is not that the basic idea of salvation through the Christ has been used in poetry before. Basic ideas, or themes, of poetry are relatively limited in number and occur again and again. Numerous fine poems (several in this book) have been written on this theme, and others in all probability will be written. But if a poem is successful, the reader feels it as a new experience; it is again proved, as it were, by the fact that the poem provokes a new response to it, by new devices of dramatization, new images and combinations of images, new shades of feeling in expression, new phrasing, new combinations of rhythm.

"The Pilgrims" has a serious theme and one about which a body of emotional response might easily gather. But if that response is stereotyped, if the theme merely appeals to what is called the *stock response* (*Glossary*), the seriousness or interest of the theme loses all value. Now Adelaide Procter, apparently, responded to her theme in a perfectly stereotyped way. The attitude developed in the poem is *conventional* (*Glossary*) in a bad sense.

This failure to bring any freshness to the theme, to make it into something the reader could experience as new, is indicated by the numerous clichés in the poem. The poem is built up of such phrases: the way is *long and dreary;* the path *bleak and bare;* the snows *lie thick;* the tempest *wails;* the stars *hide* their *light;* hearts are *faint with sorrow,* and so on. In every instance the poet has used a phrase that dulls the reader's perception of the scene rather than stimulates it. In other words, the poet has made no real attempt to visualize, or make the reader visualize, the objects. Nothing strikes the reader with the force of a new perception, and the total effect is vague. (By the very nature of language every poem must employ certain stereotyped expressions; the poet may even deliberately use clichés to set a certain tone [see "A Litany," p. 250].)

This defect in the use of detail is paralleled by a similar defect in the general dramatic framework of the poem. Life is presented as a journey over difficult country in bad weather. This basic comparison has been used innumerable times, and does not in itself bring any poetic or dramatic freshness to the theme. It could be effective only if the detail work were adequate. But that is not the case. The clichés, the poorly visualized imagery, and the mechanical rhythms all help to dull the reader's response.

Lead, Kindly Light

John Henry Newman [*1801–1890*]

Lead, kindly Light, amid the encircling gloom,
  Lead thou me on;
The night is dark, and I am far from home;
  Lead thou me on:
Keep thou my feet; I do not ask to see
The distant scene; one step enough for me.

I was not ever thus, nor prayed that thou
  Shouldst lead me on;
I loved to choose and see my path; but now
  Lead thou me on.
I loved the garish day, and, spite of fears,
Pride ruled my will: remember not past years.

So long thy power hath blest me, sure it still
  Will lead me on
O'er moor and fen, o'er crag and torrent, till
  The night is gone;
And with the morn those angel faces smile
Which I have loved long since, and lost awhile.

EXERCISE

1. In this hymn, as in "The Pilgrims," there is the basic image of a journey through the darkness, a journey that will end in morning light. Is this (and the subsidiary imagery) used more responsibly in this hymn?

2. Is the basic image used more interestingly—less monotonously—here than in "The Pilgrims"? If your answer is yes, give your reasons.

3. Scan this hymn. Are the substitutions and the use of secondary accents expressive? What is the effect of the short second and fourth lines in each stanza?

Ulalume–A Ballad

Edgar Allan Poe [*1809–1849*]

The skies they were ashen and sober;
  The leaves they were crispéd and sere—
  The leaves they were withering and sere.
It was night, in the lonesome October
  Of my most immemorial year:
It was hard by the dim lake of Auber,
  In the misty mid region of Weir:
It was down by the dank tarn of Auber,
  In the ghoul-haunted woodland of Weir.

Here once, through an alley Titanic,
  Of cypress, I roamed with my Soul—
  Of cypress, with Psyche, my Soul.
These were days when my heart was volcanic
  As the scoriac rivers that roll—
  As the lavas that restlessly roll
Their sulphurous currents down Yaanek
  In the realms of the Boreal Pole.

Our talk had been serious and sober,
  But our thoughts they were palsied and sere—
  Our memories were treacherous and sere;
For we knew not the month was October,
  And we marked not the night of the year
  (Ah, night of all nights in the year!)
We noted not the dim lake of Auber
  (Though once we had journeyed down here)—
We remembered not the dank tarn of Auber,
  Nor the ghoul-haunted woodland of Weir.

And now, as the night was senescent
  And star-dials pointed to morn —
  As the star-dials hinted of morn—
At the end of our path a liquescent

And nebulous luster was born,
Out of which a miraculous crescent
Arose with a duplicate horn—
Astarte's bediamonded crescent
Distinct with its duplicate horn.

And I said—"She is warmer than Dian;
She rolls through an ether of sighs—
She revels in a region of sighs.
She has seen that the tears are not dry on
These cheeks, where the worm never dies,
And has come past the stars of the Lion,
To point us the path to the skies—
To the Lethean peace of the skies—
Come up, in despite of the Lion,
To shine on us with her bright eyes—
Come up through the lair of the Lion,
With love in her luminous eyes."

But Psyche, uplifting her finger,
Said—"Sadly this star I mistrust—
Her pallor I strangely mistrust:
Ah, hasten!—ah, let us not linger!
Ah, fly!—let us fly!—for we must."
In terror she spoke, letting sink her
Wings till they trailed in the dust—
In agony sobbed, letting sink her
Plumes till they trailed in the dust—
Till they sorrowfully trailed in the dust.

I replied—"This is nothing but dreaming:
Let us on by this tremulous light!
Let us bathe in this crystalline light!
Its Sibyllic splendor is beaming
With Hope and in Beauty to-night:—
See!—it flickers up the sky through the night!
Ah, we safely may trust to its gleaming,
And be sure it will lead us aright—
We surely may trust to a gleaming,
That cannot but guide us aright,
Since it flickers up to Heaven through the night."

Thus I pacified Psyche and kissed her,
And tempted her out of her gloom—

And conquered her scruples and gloom;
And we passed to the end of the vista,
But were stopped by the door of a tomb—
By the door of a legended tomb:
And I said—"What is written, sweet sister,
On the door of this legended tomb?"
She replied—"Ulalume—Ulalume!—
'Tis the vault of thy lost Ulalume!"

Then my heart it grew ashen and sober
As the leaves that were crispéd and sere—
As the leaves that were withering and sere;
And I cried—"It was surely October
On *this* very night of last year
That I journeyed—I journeyed down here!—
That I brought a dread burden down here—
On this night of all nights in the year,
Ah, what demon hath tempted me here?
Well I know, now, this dim lake of Auber—
This misty mid region of Weir—
Well I know, now, this dank tarn of Auber,
This ghoul-haunted woodland of Weir."

Said *we,* then—the two, then—"Ah, can it
Have been that the woodlandish ghouls—
The pitiful, the merciful ghouls—
To bar up our way and to ban it
From the secret that lies in these wolds
From the thing that lies hidden in the wolds
Have drawn up the specter of a planet
From the limbo of lunary souls—
This sinfully scintillant planet
From the Hell of the planetary souls?"

"Ulalume" raises some questions about suggestiveness and atmosphere in poetry. Poe is sometimes praised because of an ability to create a mood. All poetry, indeed, has this quality. But why do admirers of Edgar Allan Poe usually connect these things especially with him? Perhaps the best way to approach this particular matter will be to try to analyze the poem as a whole.

What is it about? The element of incident may be summarized as follows: A man, engaged in conversation with

Psyche, his soul, walks through a mysterious landscape. He and his soul are so preoccupied that they do not notice the setting nor do they even know what month of the year it is, even though, as it is pointed out, they have been here before and this night marks a mysterious and important anniversary. Then a light appears, which the man takes to be Astarte, and not Diana, that is, love and not chastity. Psyche is terrified by this and wishes to flee, but the man overcomes her scruples and persuades her to follow the light. They stumble upon a tomb, which, Psyche tells the man, is the tomb of his lost love, Ulalume. Then the man remembers that, precisely a year before, he had brought the body to the tomb. This discovery being made, both the man and Psyche simultaneously say that the sight of Astarte's crescent has been conjured up, perhaps, by the merciful ghouls to prevent them from stumbling on the tomb. But they had failed to heed the warning.

This is, apparently, an allegorical way of saying that love (or the semblance of love, for the crescent is defined as "the specter of a planet") only leads him to the door of the tomb where Ulalume is buried.

But all of this leaves a great many questions, even questions that should have factual answers, without answer. For instance, what significance, if any, is possessed by the following lines:

> It was hard by the dim lake of Auber,
> In the misty mid region of Weir:
> It was down by the dank tarn of Auber,
> In the ghoul-haunted woodland of Weir.

The poet returns to similar descriptions during the course of the poem and evidently attaches considerable importance to them. He is trying to give an unreal, mysterious atmosphere to the poem. These places have no historical or geographical existence; the reference to them is supposed to tease the reader with mysterious implications in the same way as do the later references to Mount Yaanek and "the stars of the Lion." The details of the first description are directed to the same end: "the ghoul-haunted woodland." It is the kind of suggestiveness used in romantic ghost stories, a kind of atmosphere that we can accept only if we do not inspect its occasion too closely—

for dank tarns and ghoul-haunted woodlands are stage-sets, we might say, that are merely good for frightening children. We accept them only if we happen to be willing to forego our maturity and make a temporary concession. The process whereby the poet has created his atmosphere is too transparent, too obvious; we feel that we humor him by accepting it.

One might justify the general atmosphere of the poem, perhaps, by saying that the whole poem is unrealistic, is a kind of fable (though this justification would not necessarily excuse the poet for the particular manner by which the atmosphere is given, the stale devices of mystification). But even in such a poem as this the reader can expect that the parts all contribute something directly to the poem, that they be consistent among themselves, and that the devices of mystification bear some relation to the business of the poem and do more than indicate a love of mystification merely for its own sake (see "Channel Firing," p. 190). What, then, about the ghouls that haunt the woodland of Weir? A ghoul, according to the dictionary, is a "demon who robs graves and feeds on corpses." But these are pitiful ghouls that summon up ghosts of planets from "the Hell of the planetary souls," in order to save the man from finding the tomb. The situation might be something like this: The poet could not let the planet of Astarte appear as a fact in itself; it was a ghost of a planet. He felt that he had to account for its presence. Arbitrarily he chose ghouls to serve this purpose. He had used the word *ghoul-haunted* earlier in the poem and so had some preparation for the reference; ghouls may provoke in the reader a kind of shudder of supernatural mystery and horror. But the reader feels that this has little or no real reference to the meaning of the poem. It may be said to contribute to the atmosphere of the poem, but otherwise it does not connect with the meaning of the poem; it simply does not pull its weight in the boat.

One might compare this rather disorderly use of suggestion in "Ulalume," the use of the place names, the ghouls, and so on, with the use made in other poems in this collection. For instance, one can see how the suggestions of the names Camelot, Stourton Tower, and Stonehenge in "Channel Firing," by Hardy, directly contribute to the meaning of the poem itself. (See p. 193.) Or one can see how, in a similar fashion, suggestion is employed in poems like "Ode on a Grecian Urn" (p. 431) and "Ode to a Nightingale" (p. 424), by Keats, to develop and present the actual theme of a poem as well as to create an atmosphere. We feel that in the poems by Hardy and Keats, who are poets with great differences between them, the atmosphere is not only appropriate to the poem in question, but that the suggestion actually helps us to the meaning of the experience in the poem; the devices used by the poet will stand a logical definition and inspection. It is no surprise, after studying "Ulalume" in this respect, to discover that Poe could make the following remark about poetry in general: "Poetry, above all things, is a beautiful painting whose tints, to minute inspection, are confusion worse confounded, but start boldly out to the cursory glance of the connoisseur." * That is, Poe expected poetry to stand little analysis, and to affect only the person who gave it a "cursory glance," a superficial reading. It is no wonder, then, that much of Poe's work is very vague and confused, for he said that poetry has for its "object an *indefinite* instead of a *definite* pleasure." But really good poetry will stand a great deal of close inspection, even poetry that is simple and unambitious. We feel that the parts all contribute definitely to the total meaning of the poem.

We may apply the same line of reasoning to another feature of "Ulalume," the rhythm. In this connection we may quote again from Poe: ". . . presenting perceptible images with definite, poetry with *indefinite* sensations, to which music is an *essential,* since the comprehension of sweet sound is our most indefinite conception." Poe, then, holds that the function of the rhythms of poetry is to lull the reader; to increase the indefiniteness of the impression; to prevent him, in fact, from having the impulse to analyze the poem closely; to contribute to the general atmosphere; to have a hypnotic effect on the reader. One may notice that in "Ulalume," by consequence, there is an emphatic beat of rhythm that becomes monotonous, that there is a lack of variation in the rhythmic effects of the poem.

* Letter to Elam Bliss, Preface to *Poems,* 1831.

Aldous Huxley has this to say about Poe's handling of his meter in this poem:

> These lines protest too much (and with what a variety of voices!) that they are poetical, and, protesting, are therefore vulgar. To start with, the walloping dactylic meter is all too musical. Poetry ought to be musical, but musical with tact, subtly and variously. Meters whose rhythms, as in this case, are strong, insistent and practically invariable offer the poet a kind of short cut to musicality. They provide him (my subject calls for a mixture of metaphors) with a ready-made, reach-me-down music. He does not have to create a music appropriately modulated to his meaning; all he has to do is to shovel the meaning into the moving stream of the meter and allow the current to carry it along on waves that, like those of the best hairdressers, are guaranteed permanent. . . . A quotation and a parody will illustrate the difference between ready-made music and music made to measure. I remember (I trust correctly) a simile of Milton's:—
>
> Like that fair field
> Of Enna, where Proserpine gathering flowers,
> Herself a fairer flower, by gloomy Dis
> Was gathered, which cost Ceres all that pain
> To seek her through the world.
>
> Rearranged according to their musical phrasing, these lines would have to be written thus:—
>
> Like that fair field of Enna,
> where Proserpine gathering flowers,
> Herself a fairer flower,
> by gloomy Dis was gathered,
> Which cost Ceres all that pain
> To seek her through the world.
>
> The contrast between the lyrical swiftness of the first four phrases, with that row of limping spondees which tells of Ceres' pain, is thrillingly appropriate. Bespoke, the music fits the sense like a glove.
>
> How would Poe have written on the same theme? I have ventured to invent his opening stanza.
>
> It was noon in the fair field of Enna,
> When Proserpina gathering flowers—
> Herself the most fragrant of flowers,

Was gathered away to Gehenna
  By the Prince of Plutonian powers;
Was borne down the windings of Brenner
  To the gloom of his amorous bowers—
Down the tortuous highway of Brenner
  To the god's agapemonous bowers.

The parody is not too outrageous to be critically beside the point; and anyhow the music is genuine Poe. That permanent wave is unquestionably an *ondulation de chez Edgar.* The much too musical meter is (to change the metaphor once more) like a rich chasuble, so stiff with gold and gems that it stands unsupported, a carapace of jewelled sound, into which the sense, like some snotty little seminarist, irrelevantly creeps and is lost. This music of Poe's—how much less really musical it is than that which, out of his nearly neutral decasyllables, Milton fashioned on purpose to fit the slender beauty of Proserpine, the strength and swiftness of the ravisher and her mother's heavy, despairing sorrow! *

Luke Havergal

Edwin Arlington Robinson [*1869–1935*]

Go to the western gate, Luke Havergal,
There where the vines cling crimson on the wall,
And in the twilight wait for what will come.
The leaves will whisper there of her, and some,
Like flying words, will strike you as they fall;
But go, and if you listen, she will call.
Go to the western gate, Luke Havergal—
Luke Havergal.

No, there is not a dawn in eastern skies
To rift the fiery night that's in your eyes;
But there, where western glooms are gathering,
The dark will end the dark, if anything:
God slays Himself with every leaf that flies,
And hell is more than half of paradise.
No, there is not a dawn in eastern skies—
In eastern skies.

* *Vulgarity in Literature,* London. Chatto and Windus, 1930, pp. 28, 30–31.

Out of a grave I come to tell you this,
Out of a grave I come to quench the kiss
That flames upon your forehead with a glow
That blinds you to the way that you must go.
Yes, there is yet one way to where she is,
Bitter, but one that faith may never miss.
Out of a grave I come to tell you this—
To tell you this.

There is the western gate, Luke Havergal,
There are the crimson leaves upon the wall.
Go, for the winds are tearing them away,—
Nor think to riddle the dead words they say,
Nor any more to feel them as they fall;
But go, and if you trust her she will call.
There is the western gate, Luke Havergal—
Luke Havergal.

EXERCISE

1. Compare and contrast this poem with "Ulalume."

2. What paradoxes does the poet use? What is their effect upon the tone of the poem?

3. Discuss the rhythm of the poem. Does it suggest an incantation? Is the rhythm used to conceal weaknesses in the poem? Or does it strengthen the poem by emphasizing and enforcing the meaning of the poem?

4. The "she" of lines 6, 21, and 30 is evidently the dead woman to whom Luke wishes to be reunited. Who then is the "I" who speaks the poem? What is meant by the fact that the "I" has come "Out of a grave" to tell this to Luke?

Voices

Walter de la Mare [*1873–1956*]

Who is it calling by the darkened river
  Where the moss lies smooth and deep,
And the dark trees lean unmoving arms,
  Silent and vague in sleep,

And the bright-heeled constellations pass
  In splendor through the gloom;
Who is it calling o'er the darkened river
      In music, "Come!"?

Who is it wandering in the summer meadows
  Where the children stoop and play
In the green faint-scented flowers, spinning
  The guileless hours away?
Who touches their bright hair? who puts
  A wind-shell to each cheek,
Whispering betwixt its breathing silences,
      "Seek! seek!"?

Who is it watching in the gathering twilight
  When the curfew bird hath flown
On eager wings, from song to silence,
  To its darkened nest alone?
Who takes for brightening eyes the stars,
  For locks the still moonbeam,
Sighs through the dews of evening peacefully
      Falling, "Dream!"?

EXERCISE

1. This poem, like "Ulalume" and like "Luke Havergal," attempts to build up the effect of an incantation. In this regard, is it more or less successful than "Ulalume" or "Luke Havergal"?

2. Like most poems that attempt to build up incantatory effects, "Voices" relies heavily upon elaborate rhythms and upon sound effects generally. Consider carefully the handling of metrical factors in this poem and especially the use of run-on lines. (Note, for example, lines 5–6, 7–8, 10–11, 11–12, 13–14, 18–19, 23–24.) What effect is gained by concluding each stanza with a very short line?

3. Does this poem attempt to work up an indefinite and vague "poetic" mood? Or does the poem have a definite and meaningful structure?

4. Can you answer the questions put by the poem? Who *is* calling? Who is watching?

Bells for John Whiteside's Daughter

John Crowe Ransom [1888–   ]

There was such speed in her little body,
And such lightness in her footfall,
It is no wonder her brown study
Astonishes us all.

Her wars were bruited in our high window.
We looked among orchard trees and beyond,
Where she took arms against her shadow,
Or harried unto the pond

The lazy geese, like a snow cloud
Dripping their snow on the green grass,
Tricking and stopping, sleepy and proud,
Who cried in goose, Alas,

For the tireless heart within the little
Lady with rod that made them rise
From their noon apple-dreams, and scuttle
Goose-fashion under the skies!

But now go the bells, and we are ready;
In one house we are sternly stopped
To say we are vexed at her brown study,
Lying so primly propped.

The first stanza is based on two clichés: first, "Heavens, won't that child ever be still, she is driving me distracted"; and second, "She was such an active child, who would have thought she would just up and die?" In fact, the whole poem develops these clichés, and depends on the irony created by putting them side by side: the child you wished would just be still a minute is now very still, and for good.

Such a savage irony is not the business of the poem; it is merely the basis of the poem. The poem is concerned to move toward an attitude that may responsibly be taken in the face of this savage irony. The irony itself is masked, not dwelt on and exploited. To begin, we find *brown study* and not some phrase which would insist on a full response of pity or grief at the child's death. *Brown study*—the understated description of the child in the stillness of death—reminds us of those moments of pensiveness which come so surprisingly in the child's activity, those moments into which a grown-up cannot enter. This brown study does more than merely surprise. It astonishes those accustomed to the child's constant movement. But the word *astonishes,* too, for all its force is an understatement—a masking of the savage irony.

In the second, third, and fourth stanzas, we find an account of the ordinary activities of the child—her little naughtinesses that disturbed a grown-up at work inside the "high window." We notice, however, that the activities are not realistically described. They are given with the flavor of the fanciful story book, a world in which geese are whiter than nature, and grass greener, and geese speak and say, "Alas," and have apple-dreams. Notice how the phrase "little lady with rod" works: the detached primness of "little lady"; the formal, stiff effect gained by the omission of the article before *rod;* the slightly unnatural use of the word *rod* itself, which sets some distance between us and the scene (perhaps with the hint of the fairy story, the magic wand, the magic rod—not, anyway, a common everyday stick).

But how does this fairy-tale atmosphere relate to the poem? It is, again, a way of masking the savage irony. But it is also a way of going beyond it, of moving toward the responsible attitude that may be taken to the occasion of grief. It is as though, already, even while the child is lying in her coffin, the facts of her life and death have begun to take on the beauty of the tale—a hint of the time to come when the rawness of bereavement will be healed over and the bereaved family can take comfort in the charm of a child now beyond the accidents of time.

These stanzas, however, have another tie into the main business of the poem. The little girl, in her excess of energy, had warred against her shadow. Is it crowding matters too hard to surmise that the shadow here achieves a sort of covert symbolic significance? The little girl lost her war against her "shadow," which was always with her. Certainly, the phrase "tireless heart" has a rich ironic suggestion—for the heart had tired all too soon. And the geese which say "Alas!" at the bothersome activity of the child are uttering, unwittingly, the proper word for a deeper sadness and regret. The stanzas have masked the savage irony, they have understated it, but at the same time they have done two other things. Even in the masking they have made reference to the brute fact that needs the masking; and in the hints of the fairy tale they are indicating a hope of resolving, and escaping from, the savage underlying irony.

The last stanza states that now "we are ready." We, the bereaved, have summoned up enough of fortitude, self-control—something—to deal with the "stern" fact.

EXERCISE

1. What is the attitude brought to this occasion? The key is in the word *vexed*. Look back at our comment on the word *scared* in "Desert Places," by Frost (p. 104). Do you find a similar effect here? Do you find, too, in the associations of the word anything that would carry us back again to the underlying clichés? What about the repetition of "brown study"? What do you make of the phrase "primly propped"? Does it, too, tie back into the poem? If so, how?

2. As a kind of footnote on our discussion, what significance, if any, do you find in the fact that the author of this poem, though a father, had never lost a child?

After the Burial

James Russell Lowell [*1819–1891*]

Yes, faith is a goodly anchor;
  When skies are sweet as a psalm,
At the bows it lolls so stalwart,
  In its bluff, broad-shouldered calm.

And when over breakers to leeward
  The tattered surges are hurled,
It may keep our head to the tempest,
  With its grip on the base of the world.

But, after the shipwreck, tell me
  What help in its iron thews,
Still true to the broken hawser,
  Deep down among sea-weed and ooze?

In the breaking gulfs of sorrow,
  When the helpless feet stretch out
And find in the deeps of darkness
  No footing so solid as doubt,

Then better one spar of Memory,
  One broken plank of the Past,
That our human heart may cling to,
  Though hopeless of shore at last!

To the spirit its splendid conjectures,
  To the flesh its sweet despair,
Its tears o'er the thin-worn locket
  With its anguish of deathless hair!

Immortal? I feel it and know it,
  Who doubts it of such as she?
But that is the pang's very secret—
  Immortal away from me.

There's a narrow ridge in the graveyard
  Would scarce stay a child in his race,
But to me and my thought it is wider
  Than the star-sown vague of Space.

Your logic, my friend, is perfect,
  Your moral most drearily true;
But, since the earth clashed on *her* coffin,
  I keep hearing that, and not you.

Console if you will, I can bear it;
  'T is a well-meant alms of breath;
But not all the preaching since Adam
  Has made Death other than Death.

It is pagan; but wait till you feel it,—
  That jar of our earth, that dull shock
When the plowshare of deeper passion
  Tears down to our primitive rock.

Communion in spirit! Forgive me,
  But I, who am earthly and weak,
Would give all my incomes from dreamland
  For a touch of her hand on my cheek.

That little shoe in the corner,
  So worn and wrinkled and brown,
With its emptiness confutes you,
  And argues your wisdom down.

Many readers have found this poem disturbing. They find it disturbing because, on one hand, they know that it was written as the expression of a deep personal grief, and on the other hand, they think that it is a bad poem. We tend to feel that as an expression of deep personal emotion this poem should be respected, and yet our own critical sense finds the poem a cruel parody of the emotion. We are, in other words, up against a very complicated problem—that of distinguishing between the sincerity of the writer *as a man* and the integrity of the poem *as a work of art.* We do assume that a man's personality and character bear some relation to the work he performs. We instinctively feel that a bad job of grass-cutting or a good job of bookkeeping, everything else being equal, indicates something about the character of the workman. But we also know that there is no easy point-to-point equation, that the relationship is a very deep and complex one. There is no easy solution to this problem, but at least we can keep the two ideas quite distinct and try to deal with them without confusion.

To begin, we may inquire about the reasoning of those readers who have found this poem unsatisfactory. Even such readers would have to grant, we feel sure, that the poem proposes a real subject: the difficulty of making the brute pain of bereavement accept an ideal consolation, here the consolation of the Christian promise of immortality. But such readers might answer that the poem insists too much. It repeats, over and over, the difficulty of accepting consolation. Friends have offered, presumably, various comforting arguments—the idea of immortality, the hope of communion in spirit, and so on; and the poem is a series of refutations, each coming back to what the poem calls the "sweet despair" of the flesh. The sweet despair is, naturally, offered to us in a series of images; or rather the images are offered to us as a validation of the sweet despair. We find "the thin-worn locket," the "anguish of deathless hair," the "incomes from dreamland," the little shoe "worn and wrinkled and brown." And suddenly we are aware that this is the lingo of the popular song and the advertising agency. Nothing is freshly perceived or freshly put and thus able to give us a sense of reality; and yet everything is directed to a crude assault on our emotions. We are, as it were, being bullied into sympathy, and being human, we resent being bullied. This kind of emotional bullying is ordinarily called sentimentality.

The poem insists, over and over again, on the difficulty of accepting consolation. In other words, the poem does not go anywhere. The subject is not developed; it ends where it began. We do not have the sense of a human being really grappling with his situation, really trying to make sense of it. And therefore we have the monotony, the lack of a sense of drama. The poet has not even tried to hint at the depth and fullness of the subject. The poem, for all its insistence on the absoluteness of feeling, is thin and mechanical. It resembles a childish tantrum more than a mature effort to make sense of an emotional shock. Some sense of depth and control, even in the most modest poem, is what we want. We here have sentimentality instead of depth, repetition instead of control.

It may be said that we are implying that there is no place for a poem that is a pure and instinctive expression of emotion. In one sense that accusation is justified. The purest and most instinctive expression of emotion is a scream, and a scream is not poetry. The emotion, to enter poetry, requires at least the shaping into words, and that shaping process means control. The emotion has, in moving over into the world of words, been drained of its animal urgency, has been held out, as the philosopher George Santayana says, "at arm's length." We can recapture, and then only by imagination, the old urgency only if the verbal relations (and their implications) are properly controlled and if the human drama is adequately hinted at. And all this means that the emotion has moved into interpretation. An attitude has been implied toward it.

There are many ways in which this can be done, as many ways as there are good poets, and many good poets, in fact some of the very best, have given us a pure lyric cry, a pure utterance of feeling. No—they have given us what, because of the subtlety of the handling, *seems* like the pure cry of feeling. The control is always there, and in the simplest poem, when it is good, and even when it is gay, the hint of depth.

EXERCISE

1. Study the rhythm of "After the Burial," and then go back to Aldous Huxley's remarks on the rhythm of "Ulalume" (pp. 232–33). In "After the Burial" do you find the rhythm "walloping," too? If so, how would you relate that to what has been said above about the poem? This implies what attitude toward the reader? And hence about the tone of the poem?

2. Scan the poem. Then turn to "Ah, Sunflower," by Blake (p. 147), which is, generally speaking, in the same meter. What makes the difference in the over-all effect?

On My First Son

Ben Jonson [*1573–1637*]

Farewell, thou child of my right hand, and joy;
My sin was too much hope of thee, loved boy.
Seven years thou wert lent to me, and I thee pay,
Exacted by thy fate, on the just day.
O, I could lose all father now. For why
Will man lament the state he should envy?
To have so soon 'scaped world's, and flesh's, rage,
And if no other misery, yet age?
Rest in soft peace, and, asked, say here doth lie
Ben Jonson, his best piece of poetry.
For whose sake, henceforth, all his vows be such,
As what he loves may never like too much.

EXERCISE

1. One critic remarks of this poem:

> This pointed epigrammatic series of couplets is very skillful and concentrated, and we do feel emotion behind it.

> Yet somehow the emotion is weakened by the obvious artfulness of it. The poet can think too cleverly about the situation to carry conviction. We stay too much on the surface of the words, and are too much occupied with the intellectual intricacy of verbal meaning.*

But the poem, like the preceding one, is written by a father who has actually lost a child. How do you feel about what the critic has said?

2. With reference to the points discussed in connection with "After the Burial," write a comment on the tone of this poem.

On His Blindness

John Milton [*1608–1674*]

When I consider how my light is spent
Ere half my days in this dark world and wide,
And that one talent which is death to hide
Lodged with me useless, though my soul more bent
To serve therewith my Maker, and present
My true account, lest he returning chide,
"Doth God exact day-labor, light denied?"
I fondly ask. But Patience, to prevent
That murmur, soon replies, "God doth not need
Either man's work or his own gifts. Who best
Bear his mild yoke, they serve him best. His state
Is kingly: thousands at his bidding speed,
And post o'er land and ocean without rest;
They also serve who only stand and wait."

EXERCISE

1. The sonnet obviously alludes to the Parable of the Talents (see Matthew 25:14–30). What is meant by the one talent that is death to hide? Is the poem a development of, or a reversal of, the meaning of the parable? Or, perhaps, both?

2. Does Patience answer the question, or does Patience show that the question is badly framed?

* Elizabeth Drew: *Poetry: a Modern Guide to Its Understanding and Enjoyment,* New York, Dell Publishing Company, 1959, p. 123.

3. This poem, like the two preceding ones, is autobiographical. Milton's blindness, as we know, was real. Yet we find here, as we do not find in "After the Burial," a high degree of control and dramatic depth. Try to indicate, by close reference to the poem, how this is true. Do not forget the question of meter and rhythm. Is this poem sentimental? Is it personally sincere? How important to you is the question of the personal sincerity? Does the poem make sense to you in its own terms?

Piano

D. H. Lawrence [*1885–1930*]

Softly, in the dusk, a woman is singing to me;
Taking me back down the vista of years, till I see
A child sitting under the piano, in the boom of the tingling strings
And pressing the small, poised feet of a mother who smiles as she sings.

In spite of myself, the insidious mastery of song
Betrays me back, till the heart of me weeps to belong
To the old Sunday evenings at home, with winter outside
And hymns in the cozy parlor, the tinkling piano our guide.

So now it is vain for the singer to burst into clamor
With the great black piano appassionato. The glamor
Of childish days is upon me, my manhood is cast
Down in the flood of remembrance, I weep like a child for the past.

EXERCISE

Suppose the poem ran as follows:

Softly, in dusk a woman is singing to me;
Taking me back down the vista of years, till I see
Myself as a happy child in the old Sunday evenings at home,
Singing hymns in the pleasant parlor inside
With the tinkling piano our guide,
While outside the wind raised its clamor—

Outside in the wintry gloom.
I am taken back down the years. The glamor
Of childish days is upon me, my manhood is cast
Down in the flood of remembrance, I weep like a child for the
past.

What would be lost? What difference in tone can you see?

Western Wind

Anonymous

Western wind, when will thou blow,
The small rain down can rain?
Christ, if my love were in my arms
And I in my bed again!

We have said that in those poems which give, or rather *seem* to give, the pure lyric cry, the pure utterance of feeling, there is always, when the poem is good, a hint of the depth and complexity of experience. The poem before us is celebrated as a poem which does give, in about as pure a form as possible, the simple cry of the heart—the cry of loneliness for the absent beloved. But under the apparent simplicity and power of the effect, it may not be so simple after all; and the hint of complexity may be what substantiates the effect of power and simplicity, working on us unconsciously to give us a sense of freedom, not in having denied certain aspects of experience, but in having absorbed them.

Let us notice a contrast in tone between the first two lines and the fourth line, with the third line as a kind of transition between them. The first two lines give the pure romantic cry, the cry that the wind and the rain come to relieve the aridity and deadness of the lover's loneliness. This is expansive; it would involve all nature in a response to the lover's plight. Even the third line continues something of this expansive treatment; that is, the exclamation "Christ" continues the excitement of the earlier part, and too the phrase "in my arms" has a romantic implication. But with the last line a change occurs. The generalized romantic excitement, with its expansiveness and vagueness, is all at once brought down to the realistic and literal, with all the realistic and literal implications:

And I in my bed again!

The tone of the last line works to make the whole poem more credible and acceptable. It gives a context—a hint of the full human context—for the romantic cry. Therefore we "believe" the cry. Awareness of context: can we say that that is another way of saying what we sometimes mean when we use the phrase "poetic sincerity," as contrasted with personal sincerity?

EXERCISE

1. Do you find any other realistic detail that we have not mentioned?
2. Suppose the last line read:

Then my soul might bloom again.

What difference would this make to you?

When Love Meets Love

Thomas Edward Brown [1830–1897]

When love meets love, breast urged to breast,
God interposes,
An unacknowledged guest,
And leaves a little child among our roses.

We love, God makes: in our sweet mirth
God spies occasion for a birth.
Then is it His, or is it ours?
I know not—He is fond of flowers.

O, gentle hap!
O, sacred lap!
O, brooding dove!
But when he grows
Himself to be a rose,
God takes him—where is then our love?
O, where is all our love?

EXERCISE

1. In this little poem does God become a "guest," though entertained unawares, or does the poet seem to make of God a Peeping Tom?

2. What is the effect of "spies" (line 6)? What is the effect of line 8?

3. Is it reasonable to suppose that the author was here trying to give some complexity of tone, but simply was not aware of some of the absurd or comic implications? (This is not to say, of course, that comic implications may not be used for serious effects, as in "Mr. Flood's Party.")

4. Conceding that the idea behind this poem is a serious and profound one (the idea of love as a sacramental act), does the poem render the idea worthily, or does it debase the idea? In other words, is the poem incoherent and sentimental?

O, Wert Thou in the Cauld Blast

Robert Burns [*1759–1796*]

O, wert thou in the cauld blast
  On yonder lea, on yonder lea,
My plaidie to the angry airt,
  I'd shelter thee, I'd shelter thee.
Or did misfortune's bitter storms
  Around thee blaw, around thee blaw,
Thy bield should be my bosom,
  To share it a', to share it a'.

Or were I in the wildest waste,
  Sae black and bare, sae black and bare,
The desert were a paradise,
  If thou wert there, if thou wert there.
Or were I monarch of the globe,
  Wi' thee to reign, wi' thee to reign,
The brightest jewel in my crown
  Wad be my queen, wad be my queen.

EXERCISE

1. In the first stanza the speaker does not claim that he can take the loved one out of the storm, or fully protect her. Actually what he can promise is a very small and inadequate thing, to wrap her in his plaid against the angry quarter from which the wind comes. As for misfortune, he can do even less. His bosom will be the beloved's "bield," her comfort, but only because of his willingness to share all misfortune with her. What is the effect of this realism and understatement?

2. Many readers have felt that the second stanza is much inferior to the first. For one thing, we may feel that "wildest waste," "paradise," "monarch of the globe," and "jewel" are very conventional and abstract. They give our imagination nothing specific to fix on like the simple gesture of a lover spreading his ineffectual plaid against the weather. We may also feel that the overstatement and extravagance of the last stanza (wilderness becoming paradise, the fantasy of a world reign) get too far away from experience; or rather, that the stanza does not have the half-playful, or humorous, or ironic tone which might make such extravagance acceptable, and significant. But granting all this, what was Burns trying to do here? For instance, would the last stanza be more acceptable, or less, if it stood alone?

Song

Edmund Waller [*1606–1687*]

Go, lovely Rose,
Tell her that wastes her time and me,
That now she knows,
When I resemble her to thee,
How sweet and fair she seems to be.

Tell her that's young,
And shuns to have her graces spied,
That hadst thou sprung
In deserts where no men abide,
Thou must have uncommended died.

Small is the worth
Of beauty from the light retir'd:
Bid her come forth,
Suffer herself to be desir'd,
And not blush so to be admir'd.

Then die, that she
The common fate of all things rare
May read in thee,
How small a part of time they share,
That are so wondrous sweet and fair.

EXERCISE

1. In line 2, why does the poet write "wastes her time and me"? How does this differ from "wastes her time and mine"?

2. Consider the word *suffer* in line 14. Look the word up in the Oxford English Dictionary. Among the meanings listed you will find that of "permitting" or "tolerating," which is clearly the main, or threshold, meaning here. But in the context does the word also seem to hint at two other ideas which are central to the poem—the ideas of love and death, of sensuality and decay? What effect does this have on a poem which, taken superficially, is a piece of deft and charming *vers de société?*

Envoi (1919)

Ezra Pound [1885–   ]

Go, dumb-born book,
Tell her that sang me once that song of Lawes:
Hadst thou but song
As thou hast subjects known,
Then were there cause in thee that should condone
Even my faults that heavy upon me lie,
And build her glories their longevity.

Tell her that sheds
Such treasure in the air,
Recking naught else but that her graces give
Life to the moment,
I would bid them live

As roses might, in magic amber laid,
Red overwrought with orange and all made
One substance and one color
Braving time.

Tell her that goes
With song upon her lips
But sings not out the song, nor knows
The maker of it, some other mouth,
May be as fair as hers,
Might, in new ages, gain her worshippers,
When our two dusts with Waller's shall be laid,
Siftings on siftings in oblivion,
Till change hath broken down
All things save Beauty alone.

EXERCISE

Waller's "Song" (see above) was set to music by Henry Lawes, seventeenth-century musician and friend of Milton.

1. Compare the theme of this poem with that of Waller's "Song."
2. What is the speaker's attitude toward the girl "that sang me once that song of Lawes"?
3. Does Pound's poem gain from a knowledge of Waller's poem? How does it differ from it in tone?

A Litany

Sir Philip Sidney [1554–1586]

Ring out your bells, let mourning shows be spread;
For Love is dead.
  All Love is dead, infected
With plague of deep disdain;
  Worth, as nought worth, rejected,
And Faith fair scorn doth gain.
  From so ungrateful fancy,
  From such a female franzy,
    From them that use men thus,
    Good Lord, deliver us!

Weep, neighbors, weep! do you not hear it said
That Love is dead?
  His death-bed, peacock's folly;
His winding-sheet is shame;
  His will, false-seeming holy;
His sole executor, blame.
  From so ungrateful fancy,
  From such a female franzy,
    From them that use men thus,
    Good Lord, deliver us!

Let dirge be sung and trentals rightly read,
For Love is dead.
  Sir Wrong his tomb ordaineth
My mistress Marble-heart,
  Which epitaph containeth,
"Her eyes were once his dart."
  From so ungrateful fancy,
  From such a female franzy,
    From them that use men thus,
    Good Lord, deliver us!

Alas! I lie, rage hath this error bred;
Love is not dead.
  Love is not dead, but sleepeth
In her unmatchèd mind,
  Where she his counsel keepeth,
Till due desert she find.
  Therefore from so vile fancy,
  To call such wit a franzy,
    Who Love can temper thus,
    Good Lord, deliver us!

A litany is a form of liturgical prayer, with invocations, supplications, and responses. "Good Lord, deliver us" is one of the reiterated responses in the Litany that is printed in the Book of Common Prayer, with which, of course, Sir Philip Sidney was familiar. And so Sidney's references to it here help to define the special tone of the poem. The death of Love is being treated as if it were a kind of public calamity, one such as the outbreak of the dreaded plague, that might properly call for a recital of the Litany. Indeed, there is more than a hint of this in the first stanza with its call for ringing the church bells, its reference to mourning shows, and its remark that Love is dead, having been "infected / With plague." A very private matter, the ill fortune of the speaker's love affair, is being treated as if it were a matter of public concern. The apparently solemn pronouncement of the first lines is thus seen to be undercut with mocking irony by the end of the stanza.

It is true that the speaker has gone on to say not merely that "Love is dead" but to add that "All Love is dead," as if the failure of his own love affair proved that there was no such thing as love in the world. But that tends to be a natural human reaction. His loved one is disdainful; she rejects true worth, scorns fair faith, and is indeed acting with characteristic female madness (*franzy,* or as we should spell it, *frenzy*). How seriously does the speaker take his plight? He is not owlishly solemn about it. There is some spirited exaggeration, there is a definite ingredient of self-mockery, and something that might be called simply high spirits.

These shadings of the general tone of mockery come out more clearly in the second stanza. The speaker begins this stanza by demanding that the neighbors weep. It is as if the poet should querulously nudge the people next to him and say, "Why don't you make an appropriate response?" The movement of the first two lines helps to convey this sense of mocking impatience. In the first stanza there is a heavy pause after the long first line, so that the short line

For Love is dead

comes as a solemn—we later realize that it is a mock-solemn—announcement. In the second stanza, in the first line, a heavy pause occurs after the second *weep* so that we hurry on rapidly through the sense-unit: "Do you not hear it said / That Love is dead?"

But in his self-mockery the poet does not abandon his original figure. He retains it, for ironical effect, exaggerating it somewhat, for the purpose of making it a vehicle for his bitter scorn. The little allegory of the death of love is thus made a piece of conscious frippery for the poet to exhibit ironically for laughter. He pictures love on a death bed made of peacock feathers and the gorgeousness of the bed itself increases the irony. The peacock, incidentally, is a stock figure of overweening pride. It is appropriate therefore that its feathers should furnish forth love's death bed. The poet goes on to elaborate for the purposes of mockery all the other appurtenances of a human death—the winding-sheet, the will, the executor.

The third stanza, which carries on this elaboration, contains several elliptical constructions which the reader must be aware of if he is to understand the grammar: "Sir Wrong ordaineth (that is, solemnly proclaims) my mistress's Marbleheart as his (love's) tomb which containeth (the) epitaph 'Her (the mistress's) eyes were once his (love's) dart.' " The irony of this last clause would be more apparent to a reader of Sidney's own time than perhaps to a modern reader, for in Elizabethan time certain mannerisms of love poetry were flourishing. These mannerisms grew from the tradition of Petrarch, the Italian poet of the fourteenth century who first popularized the love sonnet. In what came to be known as the Petrarchan tradition, the lover's mistress was often ridiculously idolized; her beauty was superlative; her eyes gave death-dealing glances; the devotion of the lover could only be described in extravagant terms. The imagery used here in the description of Love's tomb is Petrarchan; princely tombs were made of marble, and the hardness of the lady's heart, its marblelike quality, makes it appropriate that it should be Love's tomb. She once furnished Love with his darts, supplying him with the bright beams of her eyes (with an allusion to the belief that love flashed from a beautiful woman's eyes). But the imagery here is plainly mock-heroic. Sidney has used these clichés ironically, expecting the reader to recognize their stereotyped quality. They help define the appropriate tone. (See "The Pilgrims," p. 222.)

But with the fourth stanza the tone is abruptly changed again. The poet suddenly tells us in the first line that he has been lying. The meter of the first four lines of this stanza reflects the change in tone. Consider the system of pauses. There is a definite pause after *lie.* The sense demands it, but in addition the meter supports it. Sidney has substituted a trochee for the expected iamb in the third foot. Compare, for example,

Alas! | I lie, | rage hath | this er | ror bred

with

Alas! | I lie, | for rage | this er | ror bred.

The first demands more than usual stress on *rage* and it demands a heavy pause after *I lie.* (See analysis of "After Long Silence," pp. 164–65.)

There is, of course, a heavy pause after *bred,* but the poet has done something else to throw emphasis on the statement that "Love is not dead." In the three earlier stanzas the second line reads, "For Love is dead," "That Love is dead," and "For Love is dead." All of these are regular iambic lines, and we have become accustomed to expect that pattern at this point in each stanza. But in this stanza the poet makes a trochaic substitution in the first foot and writes:

Love is not dead.

The result is a slight shock—the other pattern having been established in our minds—and a slowing down of the line: this is appropriate because this is the turning point of the poem. The poet has used still another device, repetition, and the statement is emphasized as it is swept along into the full line: "Love is not dead, but sleepeth."

The flow of the verse through this part of the stanza with the run-on line and the volume given to *unmatchèd* by pronouncing it as a trisyllable, gives a sense of triumphant assurance after the halting pauses of the first part of the stanza.

The tone is that which a man might use who has come to himself and finds that the precious thing which he has believed lost is not lost at all. This tone is supported not only by the movement of the verse but also by the contrast of the imagery of the last stanza with the Petrarchan frippery of the two preceding stanzas.

Moreover, the refrain which has been used to castigate his mistress is now turned on himself and the belief to which he has been previously giving expression. It should be pointed out that *fancy* in Elizabethan times could mean "love" and that this is the common meaning of the word as used by Shakespeare. Line 7 could mean therefore that the speaker asks to be delivered "From so ungrateful a love." But in line 37, *fancy* clearly means supposition: To call such discernment as his mistress has displayed a "franzy" is a "vile fancy"—a base imagination.

This poem reveals a basic shift in tone, and the changes in tone correspond to a very definite psychological structure. It is as if a lover stated to himself the fact that his love was dead; then went on to parade his grief in scorn and revulsion; and finally, having vented his irony—his anger now having spent itself and cleared the air—turned suddenly to see that love was not dead at all, and that his mistress, far from being whimsical and cruel, was justified, his temporary revulsion having the effect of letting him see her real nature better. We do not of course have to read this dramatic interpretation into the poem. But the development of tone in a poem always conforms, in so far as the work is successful, to a psychological structure; for, as we have said, every poem is a little drama (*Introduction,* p. 20).

Cynara

Ernest Dowson [*1867–1900*]

Last night, ah, yesternight, betwixt her lips and mine
There fell thy shadow, Cynara! thy breath was shed
Upon my soul between the kisses and the wine;
And I was desolate and sick of an old passion,
  Yea, I was desolate and bowed my head:
I have been faithful to thee, Cynara! in my fashion.

All night upon mine heart I felt her warm heart beat,
Night-long within mine arms in love and sleep she lay;
Surely the kisses of her bought red mouth were sweet;
But I was desolate and sick of an old passion,
  When I awoke and found the dawn was gray:
I have been faithful to thee, Cynara! in my fashion.

I have forgot much, Cynara! gone with the wind,
Flung roses, roses, riotously with the throng,

Dancing, to put thy pale, lost lilies out of mind;
But I was desolate and sick of an old passion,
  Yea, all the time, because the dance was long:
I have been faithful to thee, Cynara! in my fashion.

I cried for madder music and for stronger wine,
But when the feast is finished and the lamps expire,
Then falls thy shadow, Cynara! the night is thine;
And I am desolate and sick of an old passion,
  Yea, hungry for the lips of my desire:
I have been faithful to thee, Cynara! in my fashion.

EXERCISE

This poem, like "A Litany," by Sidney, deals with the subject of lost love. Dowson centers his poem on a paradox: "I have been faithful to thee, Cynara! in my fashion." Presumably, he felt that the use of this paradox would lend a sharpness, a sense of precise statement, and a toughness that would help him to avoid the sentimental and trite in treating his subject.

1. Assuming that there is an element of truth in the paradox, and that a successful poem might be based upon it, the question remains: Is this a successful poem?

2. Does the speaker seem to enjoy feeling sorry for himself? Does he enjoy recalling what a sad dog he has been? In this connection, consider how much of the poem is taken up with recounting his past exploits.

3. How well (or ill) do the "pale, lost lilies" (in contrast with the riotous roses) suggest the personality of Cynara?

4. Does the paradox develop as the poem proceeds? Does repetition enrich its meaning or weaken it? Suppose that we reversed the order of the last three stanzas. Would transposing them make any difference?

Blame Not My Cheeks

Thomas Campion [1567–1620]

Blame not my cheeks, though pale with love they be;
The kindly heat unto my heart is flown,
To cherish it that is dismaid by thee,

Who art so cruel and unsteadfast grown:
For nature, called for by distressèd hearts,
Neglects and quite forsakes the outward parts.

But they whose cheeks with careless blood are stained,
Nurse not one spark of love within their hearts,
And, when they woo, they speak with passion feignèd,
For their fat love lies in their outward parts:
But in their breasts, where love his court should hold,
Poor Cupid sits and blows his nails for cold.

EXERCISE

1. A poem exists in itself, it is a self-fulfilling structure. But it exists in the special world in which it was written, and we must understand something of that world in order to understand the poem. For example, this poem, like "A Litany," can be most fully understood against the background of the Petrarchan tradition. In "A Litany," as we have seen, Sidney uses the Petrarchan imagery and attitudes with a mock-heroic intention, knowing that they are clichés and using them ironically as clichés, and in the end sets the clichés in contrast to a sudden, direct statement. In "Blame Not My Cheeks," the speaker takes the attitude of the abject, pale, pining lover of the Petrarchan tradition, and contrasts himself with full-blooded, robust men who pretend to sincere love but really seek only to gratify appetite. But the speaker of the poem does this with a kind of flickering irony that both denies and accepts the contrast. Let us look at the details of the poem. Let us begin by the simple task of looking up the word *kindly* in the Oxford English Dictionary. Do you now feel that the poem is enriched? Explain.

2. Lines 3 and 4 with the "dismayed" lover and the "cruel and unsteadfast" mistress state the Petrarchan cliché. Scan these lines. How many secondary accents are there? What is the effect of this weighty rhythm in conjunction with the staleness—the ironic staleness, we might say—of the content of the lines? Is there a hint of reality introduced into the clichés?

3. Contrast the rhythm of lines 3 and 4 with that of lines 5 and 6. The content of lines 5 and 6 is, too, Petrarchan, but with the tripping movement do we sense that here the Pe-

trarchan "explanation" of the lover's paleness is offered with a touch of ironic glibness?

4. Let us take a series of words, and examine as fully as we may their range of possible meanings in the poem: *parts, careless, stained, fat love.* Notice how if the first impression of meaning is literal (as with *stained*—the flush of health), the meaning moves over into a metaphoric (morally stained), or how, if the first impression is metaphoric (as with *fat love*), we move over to various possible literal applications. Do not these words, the more we dwell on their meanings and references in the poem, fortify the impression of grossness, fleshiness, sensuality? If this is true, does this work toward an acceptance, because of a sudden burst of realism, of the Petrarchan distinction between the true and the false lover?

5. Look at the word *lies.* What do you make of it?

6. How is the speaker's attitude toward himself, the subject, and the audience addressed, reflected in the closing image of the poor, naked little Cupid shivering beside a fireless hearth? Is this supposed to be pathetic, ridiculous, or what?

7. Can we say that the theme of the poem involves a distinction between true love and false love, unselfish love and selfish love, soul and body? What does the speaker make of the distinction? In other words, what is the poem about?

Delight in Disorder

Robert Herrick [*1591–1674*]

A sweet disorder in the dress
Kindles in clothes a wantonness:
A lawn about the shoulders thrown
Into a fine distraction:
An erring lace, which here and there
Enthralls the crimson stomacher:
A cuff neglectful, and thereby
Ribbands to flow confusedly:
A winning wave (deserving note)
In the tempestuous petticoat:
A careless shoe-string, in whose tie
I see a wild civility:
Do more bewitch me, than when art
Is too precise in every part.

EXERCISE

F. W. Bateson has analyzed as follows the attitudes implicit in this poem:

> The impression of a surprising richness, and almost grandeur (as of a painting by Titian), with a certain tantalizing quality, that Herrick's poem leaves, is primarily due to the skill with which he has exploited the ambiguous associations of the epithets. On the surface his subject is the 'Delight in the Disorder' of the title—a disorder, that is, of costume. But a second subject is hinted at, though not protruded: a delight in disorder, not of costume but of manners and morals. It is not only the clothes but their wearers too whom he would have *sweet, wanton, distracted, erring, neglectful, winning, tempestuous, wild,* and *bewitching* rather than *precise.** The poem, in fact, instead of being the mere *jeu d'esprit* that it would seem to be, is essentially a plea for paganism. There are three themes: (1) untidiness is becoming; (2) the clothes are the woman; (3) anti-Puritanism. But the success of the poem depends upon the fact that the themes are not isolated

* These adjectives, as we have seen, have at least two levels of application. But in poetry a word may have even more multiform associations and applications, giving a sense of mass and depth of meaning. In a good poem the words are continually interacting with each other to qualify and specialize meanings. Consider, for example, the word *intrinsicate* in the following passage from Shakespeare's *Antony and Cleopatra* (V, 2) where Cleopatra, taking up the asp, says to it:

> Come, thou mortal wretch,
> With thy sharp teeth this knot intrinsicate
> Of life at once untie; poor venomous fool,
> Be angry and dispatch.

Professor I. A. Richards (*The Philosophy of Rhetoric,* New York, Oxford University Press, 1936, pp. 64–65) comments as follows:

"Edward Dowden, following the fashion of his time in making Shakespeare as simple as possible, gives 'intricate' as the meaning here of *intrinsicate.* And the Oxford Dictionary, sad to say, does likewise. But Shakespeare is bringing together half a dozen meanings from *intrinsic* and *intrinse:* 'Familiar,' 'intimate,' 'secret,' 'private,' 'innermost,' 'essential,' 'that which constitutes the very nature and being of a thing,'—all the medical and philosophic meanings of his time as well as 'intricate' and 'involved.' What the word does is exhausted by no one of these meanings and its force comes from all of them and more. As the movement of my hand uses nearly the whole skeletal system of the muscles and is supported by them, so a phrase may take its powers from an immense system of supporting uses of other words in other contexts."

See also pages 249 and 257–58.

> and contrasted but grow out of and into each other. The suspension between the various meanings produces a range of reference that none of them would have alone.*

Indicate other words and phrases in the poem which would support Bateson's view.

Winter Remembered

John Crowe Ransom [*1888–*]

Two evils, monstrous either one apart,
Possessed me, and were long and loath at going:
A cry of Absence, Absence, in the heart,
And in the wood the furious winter blowing.

Think not, when fire was bright upon my bricks,
And past the tight boards hardly a wind could enter,
I glowed like them, the simple burning sticks,
Far from my cause, my proper heat and center.

Better to walk forth in the murderous air
And wash my wound in the snows; that would be healing;
Because my heart would throb less painful there,
Being caked with cold, and past the smart of feeling.

And where I went, the hugest winter blast
Would have this body bowed, these eyeballs streaming,
And though I think this heart's blood froze not fast
It ran too small to spare one drop for dreaming.

Dear love, these fingers that had known your touch,
And tied our separate forces first together,
Were ten poor idiot fingers not worth much,
Ten frozen parsnips hanging in the weather.

EXERCISE

1. What is the dramatic situation implied in this poem? Who is speaking to whom, and under what circumstances?

2. Literally, the speaker is saying that he did *not* spend the

* *English Poetry and the English Language,* Oxford, Oxford University Press, 1950, pp. 42–43.

winter of his absence in thinking of his loved one. How can this fact become a proof of the intensity of his love?

3. What justification is there for comparing the fingers to frozen parsnips? What is the effect of the comparison? Do you see any relation in method between the end of this poem and the end of "Blame Not My Cheeks"?

4. How would you define the tone of this poem?

5. The theme of this poem, like that of "Blame Not My Cheeks," involves the question of body and soul. What does this poet make of it?

They Flee from Me

Sir Thomas Wyatt [*1503?–1542*]

They flee from me, that sometime did me seek
With naked foot, stalking in my chamber.
I have seen them gentle, tame, and meek,
That now are wild, and do not remember
That sometime they put themself in danger
To take bread at my hand; and now they range
Busily seeking with a continual change.

Thanked be fortune it hath been otherwise
Twenty times better; but once, in special,
In thin array, after a pleasant guise,
When her loose gown from her shoulders did fall,
And she me caught in her arms long and small,
Therewith all sweetly did me kiss,
And softly said: "Dear heart, how like you this?"

It was no dream: I lay broad waking
But all is turned, thorough my gentleness,
Into a strange fashion of forsaking;
And I have leave to go of her goodness:
And she also to use newfangleness.
But since that I so kindly am served,
I would fain know what she hath deserved.

EXERCISE

1. Who, or what, is the "they" of the first stanza? What is the meaning of the word *stalk* here? Look up its meanings in

the sixteenth century, in the Oxford English Dictionary. Do you think it an error in judgment that the poet did not identify the "they" more clearly? If not, why not? Is the word *naked* a surprising one to use in this connection? What are its meanings at the time of the poem? What is its primary meaning in the poem—its meaning as applied to the foot of the "they"? But does it have a secondary meaning—one which, by a kind of metaphorical force, gives a preparation for the second stanza? Explain your view.

2. What is the speaker's attitude toward himself in the first stanza? Does he think it somehow logical and natural that the "they" have deserted him?

3. If the lady referred to in the love scene in the second stanza has, like the "they" of the first stanza, deserted him, why does he thank fortune?

4. In the third stanza, the speaker says that the love scene was no dream. Why might it have been thought one? Because of time and place of the episode? Or because now, after desertion, it seems impossible to believe it to have been a fact? Or both? What do you make of the word *strange?* What is the attitude, the tone, when the speaker says that he has leave to go by the lady's goodness? Is the conclusion of the poem one that we might expect to find in a poem in the Petrarchan tradition?

5. In a very early printing of the poem in an anthology called *Tottel's Miscellany* (1557), the editor has printed line 20 as follows:

> But since that I unkindly so am served.

Had the editor improved Wyatt's poem, or did he misunderstand the tone of it? To answer this, look up the word *kind* in the Oxford English Dictionary, and see what meanings would have been available to Wyatt. Would any of those meanings return us to the first stanza, in which it is implied that "they" naturally range? Or is there, in line 20, a doubleness of meaning which allows for the above idea, with its acceptance of desertion, but which also embodies an ironical attack on the beloved?

6. In Tottel's version we find the first line of the third stanza given as follows:

> It was no dream: for I lay broad awaking.

Study the scansion of the two versions. Presumably Tottel was trying to regularize the meter. What did he gain, or lose? Consider the following remark by E. M. W. Tillyard, a modern critic: "The strong stresses on *lay broad waking* create a profound feeling of wonder." * Would you agree with this?

Lay Your Sleeping Head, My Love

W. H. Auden [*1907–*]

Lay your sleeping head, my love,
Human on my faithless arm;
Time and fevers burn away
Individual beauty from
Thoughtful children, and the grave
Proves the child ephemeral:
But in my arms till break of day
Let the living creature lie,
Mortal, guilty, but to me
The entirely beautiful.

Soul and body have no bounds:
To lovers as they lie upon
Her tolerant enchanted slope
In their ordinary swoon,
Grave the vision Venus sends
Of supernatural sympathy,
Universal love and hope;
While an abstract insight wakes
Among the glaciers and the rocks
The hermit's sensual ecstasy.

Certainty, fidelity
On the stroke of midnight pass
Like vibrations of a bell,
And fashionable madmen raise
Their pedantic boring cry:
Every farthing of the cost,
All the dreaded cards foretell,

* *The Poetry of Sir Thomas Wyatt,* London, Chatto and Windus, 1949, p. 21.

Shall be paid, but from this night
Not a whisper, not a thought,
Not a kiss nor look be lost.

Beauty, midnight, vision dies:
Let the winds of dawn that blow
Softly round your dreaming head
Such a day of sweetness show
Eye and knocking heart may bless,
Find the mortal world enough;
Noons of dryness see you fed
By the involuntary powers,
Nights of insult let you pass
Watched by every human love.

EXERCISE

1. In this poem the speaker attempts to account for the facts which the illusion of love does not alter, and yet attempts to do justice to the intensity of the illusion itself. Is he successful or not? If successful, what sort of tone does he gain by his manner of procedure?

2. Why does he call his arm (line 2) "faithless"? Does this acknowledgment deny seriousness to his protestation of love, or does it intensify the seriousness?

3. What is the meaning of "Find the mortal world enough" (line 36)? May this line be said to summarize the theme of the poem?

The Going

Thomas Hardy [*1840–1928*]

Why did you give no hint that night
That quickly after the morrow's dawn,
And calmly, as if indifferent quite,
You would close your term here, up and be gone
Where I could not follow
With wing of swallow
To gain one glimpse of you ever anon!

Never to bid good-bye,
Or lip me the softest call,

Or utter a wish for a word, while I
Saw morning harden upon the wall,
    Unmoved, unknowing
    That your great going
Had place that moment, and altered all.

Why do you make me leave the house
And think for a breath it is you I see
At the end of the alley of bending boughs
Where so often at dusk you used to be;
    Till in darkening dankness
    The yawning blankness
Of the perspective sickens me!

    You were she who abode
    By those red-veined rocks far West,
You were the swan-necked one who rode
Along the beetling Beeny Crest,
    And, reining nigh me,
    Would muse and eye me,
While Life unrolled us its very best.

Why, then, latterly did we not speak,
Did we not think of those days long dead,
And ere your vanishing strive to seek
That time's renewal? We might have said,
    "In this bright spring weather
    We'll visit together
Those places that once we visited."

    Well, well! All's past amend,
    Unchangeable. It must go.
I seem but a dead man held on end
To sink down soon. . . . O you could not know
    That such swift fleeing
    No soul foreseeing—
Not even I—would undo me so!

EXERCISE

Hardy wrote this poem to his wife, who had died at night from a heart attack. One other piece of information may be useful: there had been some estrangement between the poet and his wife and for some years she had been accustomed to take trips away from home without previously telling her husband of her intention. So her dying without warning becomes a kind of extension of the ordinary habit of leaving unexpectedly.

1. Discuss contrast and shifts of tone in the poem. In doing so, the following considerations may be useful. The word *term,* as it appears in line 3, has some sense of the term of a lease or some other formal or legal arrangement. The phrase "great going" in the next to the last line of the second stanza has a Shakespearean or Elizabethan flavor—the sort of phrase that might have been used, say, of a royal progress. In the last line of the third stanza, the word *perspective* is precise and semitechnical.

2. The phrase "Not even I" in the last line of the poem comes in parenthetically, almost casually. How important, however, is this for the poem? What does it imply about the poet's attitude in the past toward his wife?

3. *Undo* (line 42) might seem too flat and tame a word to describe the change in him. Can you justify the choice of this word here?

4. How is the poem kept restrained and yet powerful in its effect? Consider in this connection, among other things, line 36 and the meter of line 42. How would you describe the tone of this poem?

5. Compare this poem with "Rose Aylmer" (p. 141) and with "Luke Havergal" (p. 233).

I Knew a Woman

Theodore Roethke [*1908–1963*]

I knew a woman, lovely in her bones,
When small birds sighed, she would sigh back at them;
Ah, when she moved, she moved more ways than one:
The shapes a bright container can contain!
Of her choice virtues only gods should speak,
Or English poets who grew up on Greek
(I'd have them sing in chorus, cheek to cheek).

How well her wishes went! She stroked my chin,
She taught me Turn, and Counter-turn, and Stand;
She taught me Touch, that undulant white skin;
I nibbled meekly from her proffered hand;
She was the sickle; I, poor I, the rake,
Coming behind her for her pretty sake
(But what prodigious mowing we did make).

Love likes a gander, and adores a goose:
Her full lips pursed, the errant note to seize;
She played it quick, she played it light and loose;
My eyes, they dazzled at her flowing knees;
Her several parts could keep a pure repose,
Or one hip quiver with a mobile nose
(She moved in circles, and those circles moved).

Let seed be grass, and grass turn into hay:
I'm martyr to a motion not my own;
What's freedom for? To know eternity.
I swear she cast a shadow white as stone.
But who would count eternity in days?
These old bones live to learn her wanton ways:
(I measure time by how a body sways).

EXERCISE

Develop a set of exercises based on the striking and significant features of this poem, and directed toward a description of the tone of the poem and a statement of its theme.

V

Imagery

FOREWORD

In reading the poems printed thus far in this book, we have had abundant opportunity to notice the importance of what might be called the sensuous envelope of the poem. Poems, it is true, are not merely pleasant nonsense. They "mean" something—often intensely, and that meaning may on occasion be elaborate and complicated. But poems characteristically express their meanings not through abstractions but through concrete particulars.

There is the pattern of sound: the poem invites us to read it aloud. And there is the reliance on imagery, visual imagery and every other kind.

In "The Wife of Usher's Well," for example, the concrete particulars are of immense importance: the specific command to the serving maids to blow up the fire, the bed "made . . . large and wide," the detail of the mother's throwing a "mantle" about her as she sits by her sons' bed, the crowing, not of vague, anonymous barnyard fowl, but of two specific birds, "the red, red cock" and the "gray" of this special farmyard. These details give life to the scenes described and enlist our sympathies. In poems like "The Eagle" and "The Main-

Deep" we may even have a momentary feeling that the concrete detail *is* the poem—that there is nothing to be found except the images.

The functions of imagery are various. As we have already pointed out, the images do much more than merely provide a setting or stimulate the imagination or furnish pictures pleasing in themselves (see pp. 83–86). Images, particularly as they function in comparisons of various sorts, are important devices for interpretation. On page 89, for example, we saw how Pound's choice of a particular comparison (the faces in the crowd are like petals on a wet, black bough) makes all the difference in the meaning of the poem. Some of the most important interpretative effects, however, are even less directly stated than is any comparison. Recall, for example, the use of the images at the end of Hardy's "Channel Firing" (p. 193). We are ostensibly given simply a panoramic vision of the part of the English countryside across which vibrates the thunder of the naval guns. But the place names as presented in this context are meaningful and provide a climactic "statement" for the poem.

Because imagery affects meaning in so many different and so many indirect ways, it is not easy to give a neat definition of what it does. It is not even easy to state what the function of a comparison is. One of the accounts of metaphor or simile that was popular a century or more ago (though it continues to be heard from time to time) holds that their function is twofold: to illustrate and to decorate. Or as Dr. Samuel Johnson put it in the eighteenth century: a good metaphor must "both illustrate and ennoble the subject."

In a rough and ready way, this formula does seem to deal with the intellectual and the emotional aspects of a comparison: the comparison renders the matter in question simpler and clearer and it brings to it some kind of emotional heightening. But this formula oversimplifies in two very serious ways. First, to say that a comparison *illustrates* suggests that it provides an *alternate* description, one that is simpler, more familiar, easier to grasp than the ordinary description. Often a comparison does this. For example, we may tell a child that the human heart is a *pump*. But in poetry, comparisons often offer the only means by which the author can describe for us the object or the situation he wishes to describe. Good comparisons may on occasion have to be intricate and difficult. One function of metaphor is to discover truth—not merely illustrate truth in the sense of simplifying it.

In like manner, to say that the function of a comparison is to *decorate* involves a partial falsification. To decorate implies adding some special coloring or ornamentation. But, if as we have just said in the last paragraph, a comparison may often offer the only means by which the poet can "say" what he wishes to say, then the comparison is structural, part of the primary statement and no ornamental accessory. In any case, "ennoble" is too restrictive a term. Effective metaphors need not refer to beautiful objects: as we shall see, much imagery is "neutral" and much (in satire, to take an obvious example) is positively ugly. (Look back at "A City Shower," p. 200.) Indeed, decorating and illustrating miss, as descriptions, the essential function of metaphor. Metaphor is a means to insight. The Spanish philosopher Ortega y Gasset goes so far as to say: "Its efficacy verges on magic, and it seems a tool for creation which God forgot inside one of His creatures when He made him." *

What has been said may well be illustrated from the discussion of Tennyson's poem, "The Eagle" (p. 91). In even so simple a poem as this the imagery is far more than mere setting: it has everything to do with what the poem "says"—with what it means. And the comparisons in this poem, both implied and declared, do more than illustrate and decorate. At all events, the "illustration" and "decoration" that they provide is no alternate statement or outward decoration of the sort that could be peeled off the poem, leaving the intrinsic poem there to make its primary statement. The imagery is an integral part of the poem: what Tennyson had wanted to say about the eagle, he could apparently say in no other fashion.

The same general points can, of course, be illustrated from a more subtle and complex piece of poetry. Here, for example, are two lines from Shakespeare's *Venus and Adonis* with the comment made upon them by Samuel Taylor Coleridge:

* *The Dehumanization of Art,* New York, Doubleday and Company, 1956, p. 30.

Look! how a bright star shooteth from the sky
So glides he in the night from Venus' eye.

How many images and feelings are here brought together without effort and without discord—the beauty of Adonis—the rapidity of his flight—the yearning yet helplessness of the enamoured gazer—and a shadowy ideal character thrown over the whole.*

A modern critic, I. A. Richards, has explored the Shakespeare passage further still. He comments:

Here . . . the more the image is followed up, the more links of relevance between the units are discovered. As Adonis to Venus, so these lines to the reader seem to linger in the eye like the after-images that make the trail of the meteor. Here Shakespeare is realizing, and making the reader realize—not by any intensity of effort, but by the fulness and self-completing growth of the response—Adonis' flight as it was to Venus, and the sense of loss, of increased darkness, that invades her. The separable meanings of each word, *Look!* (our surprise at the meteor, hers at his flight) *star* (a light-giver, an influence, a remote and uncontrollable thing) *shooteth* (the sudden, irremediable, portentous fall or death of what had been a guide, a destiny) *the sky* (the source of light and now of ruin), *glides* (not rapidity only, but fatal ease too), *in the night* (the darkness of the scene and of Venus' world now)—all these separable meanings are here brought into one. And as they come together, as the reader's mind finds cross-connexion after cross-connexion between them, he seems, in becoming more aware of them, to be discovering not only Shakespeare's meaning, but something which he, the reader, is himself making. His understanding of Shakespeare is sanctioned by his own activity in it. As Coleridge says: "You feel him to be a poet, inasmuch as for a time he has made you one—an active creative being." †

The student in reading any poem should be on the alert for the implications of the imagery and for the relation of the imagery to the full meaning of the poem. The imagery may

* Thomas Middleton Raysor, ed.: *Coleridge's Shakespearean Criticism*, Cambridge, Mass., Harvard University Press, 1930, Vol. I, p. 213.

† *Coleridge on Imagination,* New York, W. W. Norton and Company, 1950, pp. 83–84.

work in a fashion very different from that in the passage from Shakespeare just described by Richards. (And, of course, for that matter, the student may want to interpret Shakespeare's imagery in terms very different from those used by Richards.) What is to be stressed is the flexibility of imagery and the almost infinite variety of its uses. The degree of explicitness, the amount of ingenuity, in the comparison, the unpoetic and even shocking nature of the terms compared, the subtlety (or lack of it) in the metaphor, the elaboration of the figure or its swift telescoping—all of these will vary from poem to poem and from "good" poem to "good" poem. Perhaps all that we can fairly ask of any poem is that its imagery shall not be idle and meaningless, dead or inert, or distracting and self-serving, like some foolish ornament that merely calls attention to itself. Every bit of image ought to "make sense" and to aid the poem in *its* making sense—but, one must concede, there are many ways in which imagery may make its sense and we can only judge its efficacy in terms of the unique context of which it is a part.

Yet though our emphasis ought to rest upon the variety of functions that are legitimate and on a proper catholicity in the response of the reader, there may be some value as we begin this section of this book, in pointing out two divergent tendencies. At one extreme is the imagery characteristic of "metaphysical poetry." Here the comparisons tend to be quite explicit; the things compared may be shockingly different; they may be "unpoetic"—neutral or even ugly and unpleasant in their associations. There may be a display of ingenuity in the comparisons; there is frequently a show of logic or pseudologic; the comparisons may seem far-fetched. In general the principle of analogy is openly used and boldly used. Marvell's "Definition of Love" (p. 295) or Donne's "A Valediction: Forbidding Mourning" (p. 305) are good instances of this kind of poetry and display characteristic imagery. But the student has already encountered imagery of at least the general sort in such poems as "Blame Not My Cheeks" and "A Litany." (He will also find it in a good deal of twentieth-century poetry.)

At the other extreme, represented characteristically by some romantic poetry, the principle of analogy is more covertly used. Instead of metaphors that boldly declare that A is B, this poetry tends to make use of symbols—that is, images so used in a carefully arranged context that A comes to stand for and to suggest B—but the connection is left for the reader to infer. "Symbolist poetry" (as practiced by the French poets of the late nineteenth century) represents a very subtle and intricate poetry of this general kind. Somebody has described symbolist poetry as a poetry in which the metaphors have been reduced to one term—that is, made implicit rather than explicit. The first poem that we are to consider in this section, Wordsworth's "Yew-Trees," is poetry of this general kind, and discussion of it will provide an illustration of this imagery that looks on the surface like simple description (compare the poems in Section II) but which may come to carry a rather indefinite but quite powerful symbolism. The point to be made here is that in most poetry the imagery lies somewhere between the two extremes we have described. Both kinds of imagery are valid. Both can, on occasion, yield great poetry.*

Yew-Trees

William Wordsworth [1770–1850]

There is a Yew-tree, pride of Lorton Vale,
Which to this day stands single, in the midst
Of its own darkness, as it stood of yore:
Not loth to furnish weapons for the bands
Of Umfraville or Percy ere they marched
To Scotland's heaths; or those that crossed the sea
And drew their sounding bows at Azincour,
Perhaps at earlier Crecy, or Poictiers.
Of vast circumference and gloom profound
This solitary Tree! a living thing
Produced too slowly ever to decay;
Of form and aspect too magnificent
To be destroyed. But worthier still of note
Are those fraternal Four of Borrowdale,
Joined in one solemn and capacious grove;

* For a discussion of these two kinds of imagery, the student might profitably consult W. K. Wimsatt's "The Structure of Romantic Nature Imagery," *The Verbal Icon,* Lexington, Ky., University of Kentucky Press, 1954.

Huge trunks! and each particular trunk a growth
Of intertwisted fibers serpentine
Up-coiling, and inveterately convolved;
Nor uninformed with Phantasy, and looks
That threaten the profane;—a pillared shade,
Upon whose grassless floor of red-brown hue,
By sheddings from the pining umbrage tinged
Perennially—beneath whose sable roof
Of boughs, as if for festal purpose decked
With unrejoicing berries—ghostly Shapes
May meet at noontide; Fear and trembling Hope,
Silence and Foresight; Death the Skeleton
And Time the Shadow;—there to celebrate,
As in a natural temple scattered o'er
With altars undisturbed of mossy stone,
United worship; or in mute repose
To lie, and listen to the mountain flood
Murmuring from Glaramara's inmost caves.

This poem may appear to content itself with description for its own sake. Though even the casual reader is likely to be impressed with the magnificence of some of the phrasing—"in the midst / Of its own darkness," "Of intertwisted fibers serpentine / Upcoiling, and inveterately convolved," "as if for festal purpose decked / With unrejoicing berries"—he may wonder what the description leads to, if anything. The explicit statements made in the poem will be of scant assistance in this regard. For they amount to something like this: "There is in Lorton Vale a single yew tree of enormous age and size. But even more remarkable is the grove of four yew trees at Borrowdale." Indeed, the only main verbs in the poem are "is" (line 2) and "are" (line 14). Though the passage beginning "This solitary" (line 10) and ending "be destroyed" (line 14) is punctuated as if it were a sentence, it lacks a main verb. What this poem "says" is, structurally considered, said through its subordinate clauses, its appositives, its participles, and its adjectives. As a matter of fact, the poem says a great deal, but it says it indirectly. In great part, it says it through its imagery.

The size of the first yew tree, the aspect that makes it remarkable (the "pride of Lorton Vale") is not measured for us in terms of feet and inches. The dimension of space is converted into that of time: it is the mighty age of the tree on which the speaker dilates. In the Middle Ages the favorite wood for bows came from the yew tree, and the speaker imagines boughs from this venerable tree having furnished bows for soldiers of Earl Percy of Northumberland engaged on some raid across the Scottish border. Umfraville was at the battle of Bannockburn. The English under Henry V in 1415 won a decisive battle against the French at Agincourt. Crecy (1346) and Poitiers (1356) are the names of other famous English victories over the French. As the speaker imagines it, the substance of the great tree has intermingled with and become a part of history, but its vital principle continues. Centuries after the bows which it contributed to Percy's soldiers and centuries after the soldiers themselves have become dust, the tree is still alive, its continuity with the past unbroken.

One cannot claim originality for this association of a great tree with the passage of time and with history. It is an obvious one, and one that has occurred at one time or another to most of us. But the poet has invoked this connection quietly and unobtrusively, and the historical associations he has called up are rich, and the phrasing is powerfully suggestive. Thus it is said that the tree was "Not loth to furnish weapons" as if it took an interest in human affairs and out of its magnificence could yield, with a kind of princely largesse, its boughs to men. But at the same time the tree lives a mysterious life of its own beyond that of ephemeral men: it has long stood "in the midst / Of its own darkness" and again in "gloom profound." This sense of a life deeper and more mysterious than that of the passing generations of men is admirably summarized in lines 11–13. This "living thing" has been produced "too slowly ever to decay"—as if its fashioning had been so patient and careful as to preclude any internal weakness. Moreover, it is so "magnificent" "Of form and aspect" that it may be thought to overawe any man who might be tempted to bring it down.

The single yew ("This solitary tree") has been associated with history: it touches upon human affairs but transcends them with a deeper life of its own. The "fraternal Four of Borrowdale," on the other hand, rather suggest the mysterious forces and powers that play through or underlie the life of every successive generation. The accent in this instance is religious. The grove of yew trees provides an access to powers that are to be contemplated, propitiated, or worshiped. Indeed, the grove is a "natural temple" with pillars (line 20), floor (line 21), roof (line 23), and altars (line 30).

Here again, it ought to be observed, that the comparison of a grove of trees to a temple is not very original. It is old and obvious. But as with the tree-history comparison mentioned above, the stress here is not upon originality. The value resides in what is done with the otherwise trite comparison—in the richness of the associations evoked, the aptness of the phrasing, and the power of significance developed. (Compare the use of "mountain walls" in "The Eagle," p. 91.)

For one thing, the grove is rendered to the pictorial imagination with a brilliantly sharp but suggestive detail. Consider, for instance, the "grassless floor of red-brown hue." The earth is carpeted with needles, shed from the roof annually through the centuries. "Pining umbrage" would mean literally "wilting foliage." But a common meaning of *pine* applies to a human being's failing in vitality from longing or regret, and *umbrage* is powerfully associated with shade and shadow. (The word actually derives from the Latin word for *shadow*.) So the suggestions build up the sense of melancholy gloom, yet at no expense to the pictorial detail, for "pining" in its echo of "pine tree" accords with the pinelike foliage of needles that is "tinged / Perennially" from darkest green to reddish-brown.

Or consider lines 23–25. The red berries of the yew remind the speaker of the way in which a room might be decorated with boughs "for festal purpose" as, say, an English hall at Christmastime was decked with boughs bearing the red berries of the holly. But the fruit of the yew tree, the characteristic tree of the English graveyard, consists of "unrejoicing" berries.

The grove that makes this "natural temple," is, as we have been told in line 19, "Not uninformed with Phantasy, and looks / That threaten the profane." This rather involved statement may require pondering. The double negative states cautiously that the grove may be *informed* by (given form and character by? pervaded by? animated by?) "Phantasy" (imagination? fancy? hallucination? the visionary power?). The words that follow—"and looks / That threaten the profane"—do not clearly point to any one of these suggested possibilities. They too are vague in their general reference: the grove is "informed" by "looks" that are solemn and awesome.

These statements do not receive any concrete illustration until—after the rather detailed description of the grove—we come to line 25: here "ghostly Shapes / May meet at noontide." And the speaker, doubtless drawing upon his own imagination, and awed and inspired by the grove, describes some of these ghostly shapes: "Fear and trembling Hope," and so on. The strategy is a sound one: the vaguely portentous statement of line 19 only gradually is given specific and concrete development *after* we who read the poem are made to visualize the scene and begin to participate in it.

People do not see (or think they see) ghosts in broad daylight. Ghostly shapes may be met with in the grove at noontide because of its umbrageous gloom. Yet the situation is not really so simple as this. Much more is involved than the mere absence of light. It is a special kind of gloom and one that is rich in special associations. One might expect a Gothic church to be shadowy—with the "dim, religious light" of which Milton wrote—and among natural objects, one would expect to find this half-light in a cave. But trees ordinarily thrive on sunlight—grow upwards to the light—and so the darkness to be met with in this grove is extraordinary. It is as if a living organism were so venerable as to hold within itself some of the primeval darkness.

The force of this association will become plainer if we consider the character of some of the ghostly shapes that the speaker says haunt this place. At first glance they may seem a rather oddly assorted group: what has Silence to do with Foresight, or Hope with Death the Skeleton? Yet these figures have more in common than merely a general connection with solemn thought. All have to do with the contemplation of time and mortality. Indeed Time the Shadow and Death the Skeleton excite in man alternately Fear and trembling Hope, demand his Foresight and often awe him into silent contemplation. These ghostly shapes indeed find the appropriate place in the gloom cast by trees so old that they have outlived generations of men, themselves living chronicles.

The speaker imagines the ghostly shapes at some ceremony of united worship, but we are not told what they are worshiping. The emphasis is evidently on "united"—the shapes are imagined as joined in some solemn ritual. And this particular emphasis is heightened by the speaker's alternative interpretation of their action—an interpretation which sees them merely as listening, in "mute repose," to the same sound. The sound is, significantly, that of a stream ("the mountain flood"), and a stream running through caverns. Time is frequently likened to a stream, and a stream that runs murmuring through "inmost caves" is a sufficiently apt symbol of the flowing of time, especially conceived of as issuing from a dim and inaccessible past. The poem, thus, for all its quietness, rises to a kind of climactic effect in this last figure.

How might we summarize this poem? Perhaps by saying that certain awesome and venerable aspects of nature, like the ancient yew trees described in the poem, have a peculiar power to stir the imagination. They offer us an example of a kind of permanence in the midst of the ephemeral, a permanence that throws into sharp perspective the little lives of men. Man, himself a part of nature, is reminded of the awesome and mysterious depths of nature, and is at once heartened and sobered by the spectacle.

But the student may feel that this summary is erroneous or wrong in emphasis or that it is simply too specific. For the genius of the imagery of this poem is its massive character, its rich potentiality.

EXERCISE

1. A manuscript of "Yew-Trees" preserves the following additional lines which the poet decided to cancel before publication:

> Pass not the [? Place] unvisited—Ye will say
> That Mona's Druid Oaks composed a Fane
> Less awful than this grove: as Earth so long
> On its unwearied bosom has sustained
> The undecaying Pile: as Frost and Drought,

The Fires of heaven have spared it, and the Storms,
So for its hallowed uses may it stand
For ever spared by Man!

Do these lines suggest that the poet himself at first thought his poem needed a more definite "conclusion" than lines 1–33 afford? Is there any contradiction between what is said in this passage and in lines 10–13? Would you seek here Wordsworth's motive for lopping off this passage? Or do you find other reasons for the cancellation? Are the canceled lines necessary? Do lines 1–33 say all that Wordsworth wanted to say?

2. Wordsworth dictated the following note on this poem:

> [Grasmere, 1803.] These yew-trees are still standing, but the spread of that at Lorton is much diminished by mutilation. I will here mention that a little way up the hill, on the road leading from Rosthwaite to Stonethwaite, lay the trunk of a yew-tree, which appeared as you approached, so vast was its diameter, like the entrance of a cave, and not a small one. Calculating upon what I observed of the slow growth of this tree in rocky situations, and of its durability, I have often thought that the one I am describing must have been as old as the Christian era. The tree lay in the line of a fence. Great masses of its ruins were strewn about, and some had been rolled down the hillside and lay near the road at the bottom. As you approached the tree, you were struck with the number of shrubs and young plants, ashes, etc., which had found a bed upon the decayed trunk and grew to no inconsiderable height, forming, as it were, a part of the hedgerow. In no part of England, or of Europe, have I ever seen a yew-tree at all approaching this magnitude, as it must have stood. By the bye, Hutton, the old Guide, of Keswick, had been so impressed with the remains of this tree that he used gravely to tell strangers that there could be no doubt of its having been in existence before the flood.

Compare what is said in this note and what is said in lines 10–13. Is the contradiction important? In the light of it, can you justify lines 1–13? In what spirit are they to be read? Could the speaker of this poem state them with full dramatic propriety even though Wordsworth the man knew them to be false?

The Solitary Reaper

William Wordsworth [1770–1850]

Behold her, single in the field,
Yon solitary Highland Lass!
Reaping and singing by herself;
Stop here, or gently pass!
Alone she cuts and binds the grain,
And sings a melancholy strain;
O listen! for the Vale profound
Is overflowing with the sound.

No Nightingale did ever chaunt
More welcome notes to weary bands
Of travelers in some shady haunt,
Among Arabian sands:
A voice so thrilling ne'er was heard
In spring-time from the Cuckoo-bird,
Breaking the silence of the seas
Among the farthest Hebrides.

Will no one tell me what she sings?—
Perhaps the plaintive numbers flow
For old, unhappy, far-off things,
And battles long ago:
Or is it some more humble lay,
Familiar matter of today?
Some natural sorrow, loss, or pain,
That has been, and may be again?

Whate'er the theme, the Maiden sang
As if her song could have no ending;
I saw her singing at her work,
And o'er the sickle bending;—
I listened, motionless and still;
And, as I mounted up the hill,
The music in my heart I bore,
Long after it was heard no more.

EXERCISE

1. If we omit the second stanza, we are given an account of the situation and of the effect of the girl's song upon the trav-

eler. What, then, would be lost—if anything—had the poet decided to cancel the second stanza?

2. Consider as carefully as you can the meaning of the girl-bird comparison. In what specific ways does the song of the girl resemble the song of the birds? Is the poet simply suggesting that the girl's song is beautiful? Or is he defining its special quality and significance for the traveler who overhears it?

3. Go back to Wordsworth's sonnet "Composed upon Westminster Bridge" (p. 111). In that poem, as in "The Solitary Reaper," the poet comes upon a scene which gives him a sudden and, he feels, permanent expansion of spirit—a new vision. How would you describe this new vision?

The Goat Paths

James Stephens [*1882–1950*]

The crooked paths go every way
Upon the hill—they wind about
Through the heather in and out
Of the quiet sunniness.
And there the goats, day after day,

Stray in sunny quietness,
Cropping here and cropping there,
As they pause and turn and pass,
Now a bit of heather spray,
Now a mouthful of the grass.

In the deeper sunniness,
In the place where nothing stirs,
Quietly in quietness,
In the quiet of the furze,
For a time they come and lie
Staring on the roving sky.

If you approach they run away,
They leap and stare, away they bound,
With a sudden angry sound,
To the sunny quietude;
Crouching down where nothing stirs
In the silence of the furze,
Crouching down again to brood
In the sunny solitude.

If I were as wise as they,
I would stray apart and brood,
I would beat a hidden way
Through the quiet heather spray
To a sunny solitude;

And should you come I'd run away,
I would make an angry sound,
I would stare and turn and bound
To the deeper quietude,
To the place where nothing stirs
In the silence of the furze.

In that airy quietness
I would think as long as they;
Through the quiet sunniness
I would stray away to brood
By a hidden, beaten way
In the sunny solitude,

I would think until I found
Something I can never find,
Something lying on the ground,
In the bottom of my mind.

The general method of this poem is the simple one we became familiar with in the section of descriptive poems. A natural scene is presented to us and then is translated into an image for a human meaning. We see a hillside—not lush, rich, and green, but covered with heather and furze, the dry, prickly vegetation of an arid spot. The scene, however, has its own kind of beauty; the remote, sunlit hill is a place of peace. Height and sunlight give a sense of openness, an "airy quietness," but we must observe that there are "crooked paths," the hidden beaten ways, the "deeper quietude," where the goat may flee from human intrusion and crouch down to brood. The hillside combines, paradoxically enough, airy, sunlit openness and withdrawn secrecies, a solitude that permits identification with both earth and sky.

This solitude is inhabited by goats—creatures that, appropriately enough as we shall find, thrive on land that is spare and dry. How, additionally, are they characterized? They "stray"—absorbed into the peace of the "sunny quietness" in which urgent purposiveness would be out of keeping. But in their straying they exhibit a delicacy, an elegance, a fastidiousness—

> Cropping here and cropping there,
> As they pause and turn and pass,
> Now a bit of heather spray,
> Now a mouthful of the grass.

And they are moving toward some spot of deeper quietness where, after their fastidious grazing, they may lie

> Staring on the roving sky,

in their own present stillness absorbed into the unhurried, majestic motion of the sky. If they are disturbed, they will angrily bound away to resume their secret life. They are, we are told, "wise" goats. The poet wishes he were as wise as they.

What, however, is the wisdom for which he envies them—and for which presumably, we should envy them? It is the thing which the poet has never found, and will never, we assume, be able to find in the ordinary human striving and hurlyburly of life. If it is to be found at all, it will be found, we know, not in a lush green spot, but on the arid hill, among heather and prickly furze. It will be found in a secret spot of deeper quietude, but one open to the sun and roving sky. To change the image, it will not be found by an act of ordinary calculation and clear reasoning, but, as the poet says,

> In the bottom of my mind.

It will be found when the deepest impulses and needs are brought into harmony with all of one's being, a harmony, as it were, between the earthy secretness of the hidden ways and the openness of the roving sky, a harmony within the self and with the natural process of life and the world.

EXERCISE

1. Compare this poem with "The Main-Deep," by the same author (p. 82). How much similarity of idea do you find? Com-

pare it, on the same basis, with "Rocky Acres," by Robert Graves (p. 103), with "Expostulation and Reply" and "Composed upon Westminster Bridge," by William Wordsworth (pp. 10, 111), with "The Scoffers," by William Blake (p. 380), and with "Nightingales," by Robert Bridges (p. 100). What differences in tone do you find?

2. Why is it appropriate that the goats thrive in an arid, waste place?

3. Note the various repetitions of words and phrases in the poem, especially rhyme words, and the hypnotic effect this gives. How do you relate this to the tone of the poem? The poem has, too, a generally falling rhythm. How do you relate this to the tone of the poem?

4. Below we shall indicate some possible revisions. What differences would such changes make?

Line 6: Stray in sunny quietness
to: Walk in sunny quietness

Line 9: Now a bit of heather spray
to: Now a bit of heather leaf

Line 16: Staring on the roving sky
to: Staring on the sunny sky

Line 30: And should you come I'd run away
to: And should you come I'd rise and flee

When First I Came Here

Edward Thomas [*1878–1917*]

When first I came here I had hope,
Hope for I knew not what. Fast beat
My heart at sight of the tall slope
Or grass and yews, as if my feet

Only by scaling its steps of chalk
Would see something no other hill
Ever disclosed. And now I walk
Down it the last time. Never will

My heart beat so again at sight
Of any hill although as fair
And loftier. For infinite
The change, late unperceived, this year,

The twelfth, suddenly, shows me plain.
Hope now,—not health, nor cheerfulness,
Since they can come and go again,
As often one brief hour witnesses,—

Just hope has gone for ever. Perhaps
I may love other hills yet more
Than this: the future and the maps
Hide something I was waiting for.

One thing I know, that love with chance
And use and time and necessity
Will grow, and louder the heart's dance
At parting than at meeting be.

EXERCISE

Holding in mind the commentaries and questions concerning the previous poems in this section, frame a set of questions looking toward an interpretation of this poem.

Follow Thy Fair Sun, Unhappy Shadow

Thomas Campion [*1567–1620*]

Follow thy fair sun, unhappy shadow,
Though thou be black as night,
And she made all of light,
Yet follow thy fair sun, unhappy shadow.

Follow her whose light thy light depriveth,
Though here thou liv'st disgraced,
And she in heaven is placed,
Yet follow her whose light the world reviveth.

Follow those pure beams whose beauty burneth,
That so have scorchèd thee,
As thou still black must be,
Till her kind beams thy black to brightness turneth.

Follow her while yet her glory shineth:
There comes a luckless night,
That will dim all her light;
And this the black unhappy shade divineth.

Follow still since so thy fates ordainèd;
The sun must have his shade,
Till both at once do fade,
The sun still proud, the shadow still disdainèd.

In the previous poems in this section, the poet has taken a single item—the yew tree, the goats, and so on—and developed it with a weight of meaning. The method has been one of suggestion, so that the image becomes more and more massive with meaning, but with a meaning never quite analyzed. These poems give the sense of a slow growth of a never quite specified significance around the object, or event, contemplated.

With "Follow Thy Fair Sun," we find another method. Here, as before, we have one basic image—now the sun and a shadow—but the process is, we may say, analytical. That is, the poet does not work primarily by suggestion, but by listing and explicating quite systematically the ways in which the image becomes a metaphor; that is, the ways in which the image can be made to apply to the subject of the poem, here the relation of a lover and his beloved. So we have, very tidily, a series of statements, one to a stanza:

1. Though you are "black" (unhappy, unbeautiful), follow (as a shadow must follow the sun) your mistress (who is beautiful, powerful, free).
2. Though the light (beauty) of your mistress puts out your own (by contrast with her brilliance, by the fact that you are subordinate to her power), you must follow her whose power revives the world around her (at your cost, as it were).
3. Though her force has "scorched" you to blackness (as in stanza 2), she may yet turn your darkness to light (as she "revives" the world in stanza 2).
4. Follow her now for even her beauty and power is not eternal, as you (being a "shadow") might, from your own unhappiness, guess.

5. It is natural and inevitable (ordained by fate) that you should follow your mistress (as the shadow follows the sun) until death ends the story, with, very probably, your mistress still disdaining you.

In such a method the poet commits himself to precision in the working out of the metaphorical implications of his basic image. He may work with a far-fetched comparison—much more far-fetched than the present one—but he must, point by point, prove its final aptness. The poet must be consistent in developing his image, *if he has once committed himself to this method.* The commitment a poet makes is the important thing here, and there are various kinds of commitments. This is not to say that one method is better or worse than another, for great triumphs have been scored in all kinds of poetic styles. It is only to say that each method implies its own logic, and we should try to understand that logic.

EXERCISE

1. Let us not forget that the handling of the imagery is only one factor in a poem. What other factors here, do you think, contribute to the success of this poem?
2. Is this poem thoroughly consistent? Do you find any inconsistency, any lag in logic, between what is offered in stanza 3 and the conclusion of the poem?
3. Compare the tone of this poem with that of Wyatt's "They Flee from Me" (p. 261) and with that of Roethke's "I Knew a Woman" (p. 266).

Trees

Joyce Kilmer [*1886–1918*]

I think that I shall never see
A poem lovely as a tree.

A tree whose hungry mouth is pressed
Against the earth's sweet flowing breast;

A tree that looks to God all day,
And lifts her leafy arms to pray;

A tree that may in summer wear
A nest of robins in her hair;

Upon whose bosom snow has lain;
Who intimately lives with rain.

Poems are made by fools like me,
But only God can make a tree.

This poem has been very greatly admired by a large number of people. But it is a bad poem.

First, let us look at it merely on the technical side, especially in regard to the use Kilmer makes of his imagery. Now the poet, in a poem of twelve lines, makes only one fundamental comparison on which the other comparisons are based; this is the same method used by Housman in "To an Athlete Dying Young." In "Trees" this fundamental comparison is not definitely stated but is constantly implied. The comparison is that of the tree to a human being. If the tree is compared to a human being, the reader has a right to expect a consistent use to be made of the aspects of the human being which appear in the poem. But look at stanza two:

A tree whose hungry mouth is pressed
Against the earth's sweet flowing breast.

Here the tree is metaphorically treated as a sucking babe and the earth, therefore, as the mother—a perfectly good comparison that has been made for centuries—the earth as the "great mother," the "giver of life," and so on.

But the third stanza introduces a confusion:

A tree that looks to God all day,
And lifts her leafy arms to pray.

Here the tree is no longer a sucking babe, but, without warning, is old enough to indulge in religious devotions. But that is not the worst part of the confusion. Remember that the tree is a human being and that in the first stanza the *mouth* of that human being was the *root* of the tree. But now, if the branches are "leafy arms," the tree is a strangely deformed human being.

The fourth and fifth stanzas maintain the same anatomical

arrangement for the tree as does the third, but they make other unexpected changes: the tree that wears a "nest of robins in her hair" must be a grown-up person, a girl with jewels in her hair; the tree with snow on its bosom is a chaste and pure girl, for so the *associations* of snow with purity and chastity tell the reader; and the tree that "lives with rain" is a chaste and pure young woman who, although vain enough to wear jewels, is yet withdrawn from the complications of human relationships and lives alone with "nature," that is, rain, or might be said to be nunlike, an implication consonant with the religious tone of the poem.

Now it would be quite legitimate for the poet to use any one of the thoughts he wishes to convey about the tree (1. the tree as a babe nursed by mother earth, 2. the tree as a devout person praying all day, 3. the tree as a girl with jewels in her hair, or 4. the tree as a chaste woman alone with nature and God) and to create a metaphor for it, but the trouble is that he tries to convey all of these features by a single basic comparison to a person, and therefore presents a picture thoroughly confused.

For a moment it may seem possible to defend the poem by appealing to the title, "Trees," pointing out that no over-all consistency is called for: one tree is like the babe nursing at its mother's breast; another tree is a girl lifting her arms to pray, and so on. But this defense is probably more damaging than the charge it seeks to meet; for the poem provides no real basis for seeing one tree as babe and another as a devout young woman.

EXERCISE

1. Can you find any principle of progression in the poem? Some good poems do work, in part at least, by accumulation, but the accumulation should lead to a significant impression. Do you find such an impression? In other words, what leads us to the last couplet?

2. On what ground may one compare a tree and a poem? On any ground indicated in the poem? Or are they completely incommensurate? If they are, isn't the word *lovely* a nonsense word in the context of the first stanza?

3. Is there any basis for saying that God makes trees and fools make poems?

4. This has been a popular poem. To what does it appeal?

Cleopatra's Lament

William Shakespeare [*1564–1616*]

Cleopatra. I dreamed there was an Emperor Antony:
O! such another sleep, that I might see
But such another man.
Dolabella. If it might please ye,—
Cleopatra. His face was as the heavens, and therein stuck
A sun and moon, which kept their course, and lighted
The little O, the earth.
Dolabella. Most sovereign creature,—
Cleopatra. His legs bestrid the ocean; his reared arm
Crested the world; his voice was propertied
As all the tunèd spheres, and that to friends;
But when he meant to quail and shake the orb,
He was as rattling thunder. For his bounty,
There was no winter in 't, an autumn 'twas
That grew the more by reaping; his delights
Were dolphin-like, they showed his back above
The element they lived in; in his livery
Walked crowns and crownets, realms and islands were
As plates dropped from his pocket.
Dolabella. Cleopatra,—
Cleopatra. Think you there was, or might be, such a man
As this I dreamed of?
Dolabella. Gentle madam, no.

(From *Antony and Cleopatra,* Act V, Scene 2)

We have said that in "Follow Thy Fair Sun" and "Trees" the poet makes a commitment to develop consistently one basic image, and that this image is, to repeat a phrase we used in the Foreword, the sensuous envelope of the poem. But this is not the only kind of commitment a poet may make for the handling of his imagery. In the passage above we have a very different method.

We may begin our consideration of Cleopatra's speech by

reminding ourselves that it is from a play and by reconstructing the circumstances of its utterance. Antony is recently dead, and nothing now stands between the Egyptian queen and the vengeance of the conquering Octavius. Dolabella, the emissary of Octavius, has appeared before Cleopatra to arrange what amounts to the terms of surrender. As he tries to introduce himself, her mind leaps back to the days of her happiness. It is a "dream"—in shocking contrast to the present reality; and the image of Antony, now godlike in her recollection, is in shocking contrast to what any human being might be.

To picture the godlike quality of her lover is the intent, the drift of the passage, and Cleopatra starts with a comparison so extreme as to break any ordinary logic—Antony's face as the very heavens, with eyes like sun and moon lighting the little earth. But the violation of logic is an index to the force of feeling that now breaks out. We feel a dramatic grounding for the violence and elevation of the utterance—with its sense of dreamlike release and apocalyptic grandeur—which is not unlike the language of, say, the Book of Revelations, another attempt to utter the unutterable. Then we find the attempt of Dolabella to break in—the voice of realism demanding to be heard in the midst of the rapture of the vision.

With the next section Cleopatra begins with what seems to be a systematic description of the creature whose improbable face she has just sketched—how "his legs bestrid the ocean," how his arm was lifted, how his voice affected others. But this systematic description breaks into a series of images which have no consistent relation to the main image with which the passage begins, or with each other. Here again we feel that the breaking away from the systematic description is, like the violation of ordinary logic in the first big image, an index to the dramatic urgency, the power of the queen's feeling. Then, with the last image, we return to the first, the image of the godlike creature bestriding the world, with realms and islands like gold or silver "plates" dropped from his pockets in careless generosity. So the main image serves as a kind of envelope to hold the other inconsistent and unrelated images. Then, as further rounding out and tightening of the passage, the whole speech is again defined as a dream; the voice of everyday realism speaks.

In the central part of the passage we have what the textbooks call mixed metaphor: the bounty like an autumn, delights with dolphin backs, and so on. But here we not only find the images acceptable, we find them grandly expressive. We accept them because, on one level, we sense the dramatic urgency from which they spring and because, on another, we recognize the kind of commitment the poet is making. He does not pretend to give a system, as does the poet of "Trees"; the very violence of his general style and the exaggerated differences between one image and another indicate this. We refer each image back to the central intent, the central drift of the passage, the controlling idea of the passage, and accept or reject it by this reference. The images may, as is the case here with the return to the godlike figure in the end, be enclosed in some general image, but that is not our point. Our point is the very *discontinuity* of the individual images.

We have, then, two basic kinds of commitment in the use of images. In the first, as in "Follow Thy Fair Sun" and "Trees," the poet undertakes to give a series of images related to each other to form a consistent series—the image of the shadow following the sun, the image of the tree as a human being. This development of an image in a series of consistent manifestations carries the idea, the "argument," of the poem, which may or may not be actually stated. Let us make a little chart of this:

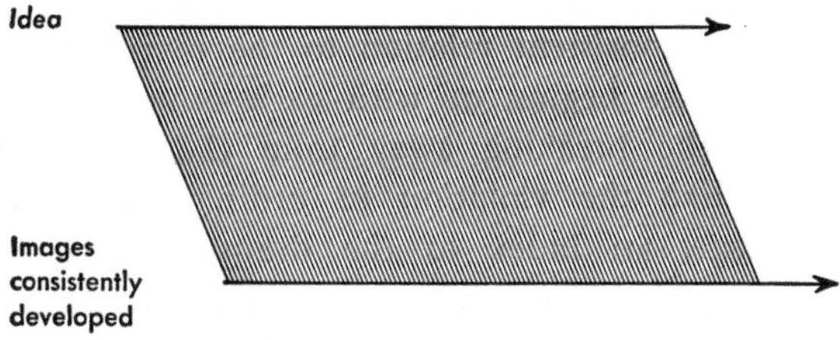

The progression of the idea, we may say, is totally projected into the imagery, and the imagery is as consistent as the argument it embodies. Continuity is the earmark of this method, and self-consistency in the use of imagery.

For the kind of commitment we find in "Cleopatra's Lament," we may make another chart:

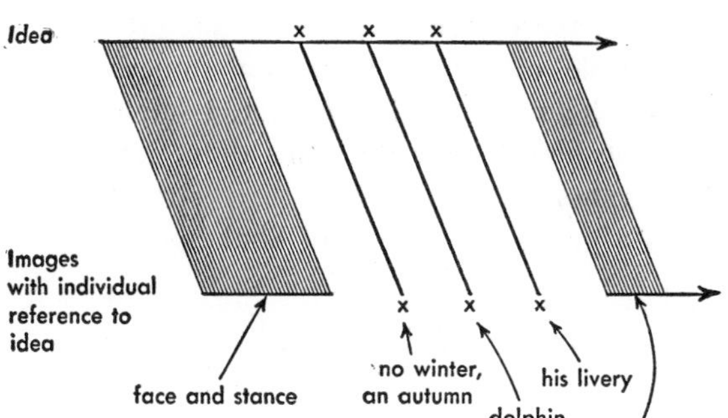

As we have said, the very point of this style is the discontinuity of the images. Each image must be guaranteed by its individual reference to the line of idea, of argument.

We might add that each image must be validated by its reference to the line of feeling, too—to the tone of the poem. We have indicated how the passion of Cleopatra breaks out in the intrinsic violence of her imagery as well as in the discontinuity. This kind of commitment in the use of imagery, however, is useful not only with poetry of high dramatic tension; it has other uses, as we shall see when we come to "The Definition of Love," by Andrew Marvell, where the leap from one image to the next is not an indication of a driving, overwhelming feeling, but of an alert, probing intellectuality trying to understand a feeling.

EXERCISE

1. Look at the word *crested* in line 10. The word itself is, clearly, a metaphor, condensed or submerged. But what is the image in the metaphor? The arm crests the world—an orb with a bent shape above. By reason of the word *crested,* and the warlike and chivalric temper of the passage, we are led to some sense of helmet with plume, perhaps mailed arm bent

above the plume, or some other heraldic device. In any case, the word carries a weight of possibility which affects the hearer *as possibility,* the speed and depth of mental association being what it is, even when we do not rationalize the metaphor. What do you make of the dolphinlike delights?

2. An example of mixed metaphor sometimes given in handbooks of rhetoric is: "Mr. Speaker, I smell a rat. Shall I nip him in the bud?" How does this differ from Cleopatra's "mixed" metaphors?

3. Here is a passage from one of Shakespeare's sonnets:

> O how shall summer's honey breath hold out
> Against the wreckful siege of battering days.
>
> (From Sonnet LXV)

If we are literal-minded and mistake the kind of commitment the poet is here making for his images, we get a mere hash. "Days" stands for Time, which, as the two critics René Wellek and Austin Warren have pointed out, "is then metaphorized as besieging a city and attempting, by battering-rams, to take it. What is attempting–city-like, or ruler of the city-like–to 'hold out' against these assaults? It is youth, metaphorized as summer, or more exactly, as the sweet fragrance of summer: the fragrance of summer flowers is to the earth as sweet breath is to the human body, a part of or adjunct of the whole. If one tries to fit together neatly in one image the battering siege and the breath, he gets jammed up. The figurative movement is rapid and hence elliptical." * The point these critics are making is that the reader should not try to fit the separate items neatly into one image. He should accept the rapid and elliptical reference to the line of idea.

Tomorrow and Tomorrow

I.

William Shakespeare [1564–1616]

> Tomorrow, and tomorrow, and tomorrow,
> Creeps in this petty pace from day to day,
> To the last syllable of recorded time;

* René Wellek and Austin Warren: *Theory of Literature,* New York, Harcourt, Brace and Company, 1949, p. 208.

And all our yesterdays have lighted fools
The way to dusty death. Out, out, brief candle;
Life's but a walking shadow; a poor player,
That struts and frets his hour upon the stage,
And then is heard no more: it is a tale
Told by an idiot, full of sound and fury,
Signifying nothing.

(From *Macbeth,* Act V, Scene 5)

II.

Sir William Davenant [*1606–1668*]

Tomorrow and tomorrow and tomorrow
Creeps in a stealing pace from day to day,
To the last minute of recorded time,
And all our yesterdays have lighted fools
To their eternal homes; out, out, that candle!
Life's but a walking shadow, a poor player
That struts and frets his hour upon the stage,
And then is heard no more. It is a tale
Told by an idiot, full of sound and fury,
Signifying nothing.

EXERCISE

The second version of this passage is a rewriting of the first. The intention of Sir William Davenant (a poet of a generation after Shakespeare) was to remove what he considered offenses against "correctness" and "reasonableness."

1. Analyze the passage from Shakespeare. Can you justify the transition from image to image? (Is an actor in any sense "a walking shadow"?)
2. Write a detailed comparison of the two passages.

The Definition of Love

Andrew Marvell [*1621–1678*]

My love is of a birth as rare
As 'tis for object strange and high:
It was begotten by Despair
Upon Impossibility.

Magnanimous Despair alone
Could show me so divine a thing,
Where feeble Hope could ne'er have flown
But vainly flapped its tinsel wing.

And yet I quickly might arrive
Where my extended soul is fixed,
But Fate does iron wedges drive,
And always crowds itself betwixt.

For Fate with jealous eye does see
Two perfect loves, nor lets them close:
Their union would her ruin be,
And her tyrannic power depose.

And therefore her decrees of steel
Us as the distant poles have placed,
(Though love's whole world on us doth wheel)
Not by themselves to be embraced,

Unless the giddy heaven fall,
And earth some new convulsion tear,
And, us to join, the world should all
Be cramped into a planisphere.

As lines, so loves oblique may well
Themselves in every angle greet;
But ours, so truly parallel,
Though infinite, can never meet.

Therefore the love which us doth bind,
But fate so enviously debars,
Is the conjunction of the mind,
And opposition of the stars.

This poem deals with a subject which may seem at first glance too narrow to afford very much scope, and which would seem to afford little opportunity to say anything very fresh and new. The intensity of one's love is surely a conventional enough theme. The poet might easily, in handling such a subject, fail to convey the sense of the intensity, or, in attempting to convey it, might easily overwrite his poem and find himself betrayed into hollow sounding exaggeration or embarrassing sentimentality. This is the problem which the poet faces here. The solution which he makes is not the only solution, of course. It is only one of the many possible solutions, as the great number of fine poems on the same theme will indicate, but a close examination of it may tell us a great deal about the use of imagery. For it is largely in terms of his imagery that this poet presents the complex and rich experience which the poem embodies.

The poet begins by stating the matter in terms of a paradox, and the shock of this paradox—the sharp break which it makes with the stale and conventional in general—allows him to state with no sense of overfacile, glib exaggeration that

My love is of a birth as rare
As 'tis for object strange and high.

The first word of the second stanza enforces the paradox. It lets us know that the poet is going to stand by his paradox. Despair is not *grim* or *harsh* or *cruel,* as one would anticipate, but *magnanimous.* His love is too divine to have been hoped for—it could only have been shown to him by Despair itself. Already the paradox has done something more than startle us out of an accustomed attitude; but the startling paradox is only a device to lead us to grasp the poet's attitude which is an attitude complex enough to perceive a magnanimity in the very hopelessness of attaining his love since only that hopelessness allows him to see the true and ideal character of his love.

The poet now proceeds to develop this paradox in terms of images. It is nothing less than fate that separates him from his love. Fate drives iron wedges between them. And the poet, having personified fate—having turned it into a person—provides the person with a motive. Fate itself would cease to exist if any complete perfection might be attained. Their love is so perfect that its consummation would be incompatible with a world ruled over by fate. That this should be prevented from happening is therefore not the result of one of fate's malicious caprices—the character of the love itself determines the "fate."

Notice at this point that the poet's attitude toward fate is not that of hysterical outrage. There is a calm reasoned tone here such as we have already found in the ability to see despair as "magnanimous." And yet this sense of reasonableness has been achieved *in the process* of making statements which ordinarily would seem the most outrageous exaggerations! His love is the highest possible; his love is too divine to be even hoped for. The result is that the statements are felt, not as outrageous statements to be immediately discounted, but as having the weight of reasoned truth.

In the fifth stanza the major paradox is given a decisive statement through an unusually fine figure. Fate has placed the two lovers as "far apart as the poles." This seems at first merely the conventional expression which we use to indicate great distance apart. But the poet immediately seizes on the implied figure and develops it for us. The two lovers are, like the poles of the earth, unable to touch each other; but though they are separated by the distance of the entire globe, they are the focal points in determining the rotation of the earth. Thus, the lovers, though separated, define the ideal nature of love. The world of love, like a globe, turns on the axis of their relationship. The exactness of the comparison gives force to his statement, and Marvell further stresses the exactness of the relationship between his own situation and the figure which he uses to illustrate it, by going on to state the only condition on which the poles might be united. The poles might be united only if the earth were suddenly compressed into a two-dimensional disc which would have no thickness at all—that is, into a *planisphere.* The associations of a technical word again support the sense of exact, calculated statement in the poem. The poet continues to expound the incredible nature of his love with the poise of a mathematician. Therefore we are more readily inclined to accept the statement.

The technical word also prepares somewhat perhaps for the figure which the poet uses in the seventh stanza. Loves "oblique," the loves of those who are not in perfect accord, are like lines which cross each other at an angle. Their very lack of parallelism forms the possibility of their meeting. His own love and that of his mistress accord with each other so perfectly that, though stretched to infinity, they could draw no nearer together. In this image, then, the poet finds exactly the illustration of the paradoxical relationship of which he is writing. The application of this image is made easier by the ordinary association of the idea of infinity with the idea of love; it is a conventional association in love poetry. But Marvell has taken the conventional association and, by developing it, has derived a renewed life and freshness.

The poem closes with another paradox, this time drawn from astrology. We say that stars are in *conjunction* when they are seen in the sky very close together; that they are in *opposition* when they are situated in opposite parts of the sky. According to astrology, moreover, planets in conjunction unite their influences. In opposition they fight against each other. Here the lovers' minds are in conjunction. They are united, but their stars (fate) are against them. This concluding comparison, then, combines the idea of the third and fourth stanzas with that of the fifth and sixth. In a way, it epitomizes the whole poem.

Is the poem merely an ingenious bundle of paradoxes? Some readers may dislike the very active play of the mind here, and will dislike also the exactness of the diction, and the imagery drawn from mathematics and kindred subjects. But does this ingenuity and exactness make the poem insincere? Does it not have indeed the opposite effect? The lover protesting his love is too often vague and rhetorical. He gives a sense of glibness and effusiveness. The effect of Marvell's imagery is not only one of freshness as opposed to stale conventionality—it is also one of calculation as opposed to one of unthinking excitement.

My Springs

Sidney Lanier [1842–1881]

In the heart of the Hills of Life, I know
Two springs that with unbroken flow
Forever pour their lucent streams
Into my soul's far Lake of Dreams.

Not larger than two eyes, they lie
Beneath the many-changing sky
And mirror all of life and time,
—Serene and dainty pantomime.

Shot through with lights of stars and dawns,
And shadowed sweet by ferns and fawns,
—Thus heaven and earth together vie
Their shining depths to sanctify.

Always when the large Form of Love
Is hid by storms that rage above,
I gaze in my two springs and see
Love in his very verity.

Always when Faith with stifling stress
Of grief hath died in bitterness,
I gaze in my two springs and see
A faith that smiles immortally.

Always when Charity and Hope,
In darkness bounden, feebly grope,
I gaze in my two springs and see
A Light that sets my captives free.

Always when Art on perverse wing
Flies where I cannot hear him sing,
I gaze in my two springs and see
A charm that brings him back to me.

When Labor faints, and Glory fails,
And coy Reward in sighs exhales,
I gaze in my two springs and see
Attainment full and heavenly.

O Love, O Wife, thine eyes are they,
—My springs from out whose shining gray
Issue the sweet celestial streams
That feed my life's bright Lake of Dreams.

Oval and large and passion-pure
And gray and wise and honor-sure;
Soft as a dying violet-breath
Yet calmly unafraid of death;

Thronged, like two dove-cotes of gray doves,
With wife's and mother's and poor-folk's loves,
And home-loves and high glory-loves
And science-loves and story-loves,

And loves for all that God and man
In art and nature make or plan,
And lady-loves for spidery lace
And broideries and supple grace

And diamonds and the whole sweet round
Of littles that large life compound,
And loves for God and God's bare truth,
And loves for Magdalen and Ruth,

Dear eyes, dear eyes and rare complete—
Being heavenly-sweet and earthly-sweet,
—I marvel that God made you mine,
For when He frowns, 'tis then ye shine!

This poem is sentimental.

Sentimentality often makes itself felt as a kind of strain, a strain on the part of the writer to convince the reader that he should respond in such and such a way. In this poem the strain most clearly manifests itself in the use the poet makes of imagery. In the discussion of "The Pilgrims" (pp. 223–25), it was said that the clichés of phrase and idea indicate a sentimental approach, the lack of any attempt on the part of the poet to investigate the real possibilities of the subject, and the poet's unconscious dependence on some sort of stock response in the reader. Both of these defects may indicate sentimentality, for both imply an attempt to get a response not justified in the poem itself. But let us try to study the imagery in Lanier's poem.

The first nine stanzas are constructed about one basic image, that of the springs, and the next four about another, that of the doves in a dove-cote. Now the image of the eyes as springs is given a kind of geographical location in an imaginary landscape. The springs (the eyes) are located, says the poet, in the midst of the Hills of Life, and by their overflow keep full the Lake of Dreams of the poet's soul. Is there any basis for what we might call the construction of this little piece of poetic landscape? Does anything really bind its parts together? The poet apparently means by the Hills of Life the difficulties that beset him. He has taken an abstraction, the general idea of difficulties, and has in his poem made it equivalent to the concrete objects, hills. This is really a cliché, but the poet has tried to save the comparison by giving it a relationship to the Springs. The comparison of eyes to pools or springs, however, is another cliché, equally dull. These two worn-out images could be given new strength only if the relationship established between them were really expressive and imaginatively justifiable.

But first we may observe that the two images are not arrived at by the same process. That of the hills is an identification of an abstraction (difficulties) with a concrete object (hills); that of the springs is an identification of one concrete object (eyes) with another concrete object (springs). The image of the Lake of Dreams is arrived at by the former process. Yet all of these three images are parts of the same landscape: the springs in the hills overflow into the lake. The reader feels that the poet has arbitrarily put these things together and that they do not really represent an imaginative insight.

There is no particular reason why, for instance, the Dreams should be represented by a lake rather than by any of a dozen other objects except that a lake fits the landscape better. As a matter of fact, as the poem goes on, we discover that the Lake of Dreams is not at all what we presume the poet to mean. In plain prose, the eyes of his wife encourage him in Love, Faith, Charity, Hope, Art, and Ambition. Yet we know that the poet does not mean to say that the things by which he lives, for instance, love, faith, and art, are illusions; he would maintain that they are realities. Or perhaps the poet does not mean the image in this sense; he may mean that the eyes of his wife encourage him to dream of worth-while things. This is more consistent with the general temper of the poem, but it bears no specific connection with the image itself.

Further, the poet was not really willing to stand by his identification of the eyes with springs, and he proceeds without dealing at all with one important inconsistency implied in the image. The springs, we remember, overflow. The springs are eyes. The most emphatic implication here is that of weeping, which is inconsistent with the meaning the poet has in mind. The poet should have solved this difficulty of implication for the reader or should have abandoned the image. Instead, he ignored the matter, which seems to argue that he himself really was not paying much attention to the full implication of what he was doing. In other words, there is a kind of vagueness here, and a kind of strain.

The personifications, the "Form of Love," "Faith," "Charity," and "Hope," bear no real relation to the scene in which they are put. For instance, how much close investigation can the relation between Charity and the basic scene of the springs, etc., be made to bear? In what darkness are Charity and Hope, personified as real persons, bound? Is there a dungeon or a cave near by? No provision has been made for this in the scene. And how can the Light that the poet sees in the spring set the "captives free"? It would have been perfectly possible for the poet to leap from one image to another in pursuit of his idea, *if he had not insisted on the formal connection between the two images* (see pp. 285–94).

The basic image of the eleventh, twelfth, and thirteenth stanzas, the image of the dove-cote and doves, shares the same quality of strain and artificiality. On what basis can we conceive of the love of science ("science-loves") or the love of fine lace ("lady-loves for spidery lace") or the love of fiction and poetry ("story-loves") as gray doves? It is a purely arbitrary equating of the two things. And the image becomes even more arbitrary and more complicated when we conceive, or try to conceive, of those doves in two dove-cotes which are a lady's eyes. The poet, by this use of imagery, is trying to force a reaction on the reader that is not justified by the material.

The Tear

Richard Crashaw [*1613?–1649*]

What bright soft thing is this,
  Sweet Mary, thy fair eyes' expense?
A moist spark it is,
  A wat'ry diamond; from whence
The very term, I think, was found,
The water of a diamond.

Oh! 'tis not a tear,
'Tis a star about to drop
From thine eye, its sphere;
The Sun will stoop and take it up.
Proud will his sister be to wear
This thine eye's jewel in her ear.

Oh! 'tis a tear,
Too true a tear; for no sad eyne,[1]
How sad soe'er,
Rain so true a tear as thine;
Each drop, leaving a place so dear,
Weeps for itself, is its own tear.

Such a pearl as this is,
(Slipped from Aurora's dewy breast)
The rose-bud's sweet lip kisses;
And such the rose itself, when vexed
With ungentle flames, does shed,
Sweating in too warm a bed.

Such the maiden gem
By the wanton Spring put on,
Peeps from her parent stem,
And blushes on the manly Sun:
This wat'ry blossom of thy eyne,
Ripe, will make the richer wine.

Fair drop, why quak'st thou so?
'Cause thou straight must lay thy head
In the dust? Oh no;
The dust shall never be thy bed:
A pillow for thee will I bring,
Stuffed with down of angel's wing.

Thus carried up on high,
(For to heaven thou must go)
Sweetly shalt thou lie,
And in soft slumbers bathe thy woe;
Till the singing orbs awake thee,
And one of their bright chorus make thee.

[1] eyes

There thyself shalt be
  An eye, but not a weeping one;
Yet I doubt of thee,
  Whether th'hadst rather there have shone
An eye of Heaven; or still shine here
In th' Heaven of Mary's eye, a tear.

EXERCISE

1. The images of this poem are usually condemned because they are too "far-fetched." But is this the point? Are the images any "farther fetched" than those in many poems that we have judged to be good? See "Cleopatra's Lament" (pp. 290–94).

2. Can it be argued that these comparisons are essentially "decorative"—that they do not develop the poem but merely say over and over that Mary Magdalene's tears are very precious?

3. Does the poem have any development in theme or attitude? Could the order of the stanzas be rearranged without affecting the poem? If so, what, if anything, does this tell us about the poem?

A Valediction: Forbidding Mourning

John Donne [*1573–1631*]

As virtuous men pass mildly away,
  And whisper to their souls, to go,
Whilst some of their sad friends do say,
  The breath goes now, and some say, no:

So let us melt, and make no noise,
  No tear-floods, nor sigh-tempests move,
'Twere profanation of our joys
  To tell the laity our love.

Moving of th' earth brings harms and fears,
  Men reckon what it did and meant,
But trepidation of the spheres,
  Though greater far, is innocent.

Dull sublunary lovers' love
  (Whose soul is sense) cannot admit
Absence, because it doth remove
  Those things which elemented it.

But we by a love, so much refined,
  That our selves know not what it is,
Inter-assurèd of the mind,
  Care less, eyes, lips, and hands to miss.

Our two souls therefore, which are one,
  Though I must go, endure not yet
A breach, but an expansion,
  Like gold to airy thinness beat.

If they be two, they are two so
  As stiff twin compasses are two,
Thy soul the fixed foot, makes no show
  To move, but doth, if th' other do.

And though it in the center sit,
  Yet when the other far doth roam,
It leans, and hearkens after it,
  And grows erect, as that comes home.

Such wilt thou be to me, who must
  Like th' other foot, obliquely run;
Thy firmness makes my circle just,
  And makes me end, where I begun.

EXERCISE

Write an analysis of this poem, taking into account the following topics:

1. The tone of the first two stanzas.

2. The implications of the imagery in the last four stanzas. (For instance, how do the associations one ordinarily has with compasses tend to give an impression of accuracy and conviction to the conclusion of the poem?)

3. The use of enjambment.

4. The use of alliteration and repetition.

5. The metrical situation in line 25.

6. The relationship of the various images to each other.

The Last Days of Alice

Allen Tate [*1899–*]

Alice grown lazy, mammoth but not fat,
Declines upon her lost and twilight age,
Above in the dozing leaves the grinning cat
Quivers forever with his abstract rage;

Whatever light swayed on the perilous gate
Forever sways, nor will the arching grass
Caught when the world clattered undulate
In the deep suspension of the looking-glass.

Bright Alice! always pondering to gloze
The spoiled cruelty she had meant to say
Gazes learnedly down her airy nose
At nothing, nothing thinking all the day:

Turned absent-minded by infinity
She cannot move unless her double move,
The All-Alice of the world's entity
Smashed in the anger of her hopeless love,

Love for herself who as an earthly twain
Pouted to join her two in a sweet one:
No more the second lips to kiss in vain
The first she broke, plunged through the glass alone—

Alone to the weight of impassivity
Incest of spirit, theorem of desire
Without will as chalky cliffs by the sea
Empty as the bodiless flesh of fire;

All space that heaven is a dayless night
A nightless day driven by perfect lust
For vacancy, in which her bored eyesight
Stares at the drowsy cubes of human dust.

We, too, back to the world shall never pass
Through the shattered door, a dumb shade-harried crowd,
Being all infinite, function, depth and mass
Without figure; a mathematical shroud

Hurled at the air—blessèd without sin!
O God of our flesh, return us to Your wrath
Let us be evil could we enter in
Your grace, and falter on the stony path!

EXERCISE

1. The "Alice" referred to in this poem is the heroine of *Alice in Wonderland* and *Alice Through the Looking-Glass.* How much of the imagery of the first five stanzas is derived from these two books?

2. What does Alice stand for in this poem? What does the absurdly but inhumanly logical world of the Looking-Glass (or of her Wonderland) stand for? Why is *our* plight (see line 29) like that of Alice? (Note how many figures suggest that the Alice of this poem has hypnotized herself—has locked herself into the world spun out of her own head.)

3. Comment on the meaning of such phrases as "Incest of spirit," "mathematical shroud," and "blessèd without sin." What is this poem about? The poem may be said to end with a prayer. How is the prayer related to the rest of the poem?

4. What kind of "commitment" does the poet make here for consistency in his use of imagery?

5. Can you relate the theme of this poem to that of Eliot's "Preludes" (p. 112)?

To His Coy Mistress

Andrew Marvell [*1621–1678*]

Had we but world enough, and time,
This coyness, Lady, were no crime.
We would sit down and think which way
To walk and pass our long love's day.
Thou by the Indian Ganges' side
Shouldst rubies find; I by the tide
Of Humber would complain. I would
Love you ten years before the Flood,
And you should, if you please, refuse
Till the conversion of the Jews.

My vegetable love should grow
Vaster than empires, and more slow;
An hundred years should go to praise
Thine eyes and on thy forehead gaze;
Two hundred to adore each breast,
But thirty thousand to the rest;
An age at least to every part,
And the last age should show your heart.
For, Lady, you deserve this state,
Nor would I love at lower rate.
 But at my back I always hear
Time's wingèd chariot hurrying near;
And yonder all before us lie
Deserts of vast eternity.
Thy beauty shall no more be found,
Nor, in thy marble vault, shall sound
My echoing song; then worms shall try
That long preserved virginity,
And your quaint honor turn to dust,
And into ashes all my lust:
The grave's a fine and private place,
But none, I think, do there embrace.
 Now therefore, while the youthful hue
Sits on thy skin like morning lew [1]
And while thy willing soul transpires
At every pore with instant fires,
Now let us sport us while we may,
And now, like amorous birds of prey,
Rather at once our time devour
Than languish in his slow-chapt power.
Let us roll all our strength and all
Our sweetness up into one ball,
And tear our pleasures with rough strife
Thorough the iron gates of life:
Thus, though we cannot make our sun
Stand still, yet we will make him run.

EXERCISE

1. Distinguish the three divisions of the logical structure of the poem. Comment upon the tone of each division.

[1] Warmth. Conjectured by H. M. Margoliouth. The 1681 text reads *glew*. Other conjectured readings are "dew" and "glow."

2. Someone has said that the imagery in the first part of the poem is playful, conversational, and absurd; that of the second section, grand; and that of the third section, exciting. Can you justify this characterization? Or is there too much interpenetration among the parts to justify the remark?

3. What does the poet mean by "amorous birds of prey"? Does this figure carry over into "tear our pleasures" (line 43)?

4. Define the attitude presented in the passage comprising lines 25 to 32.

5. What range of imagery do you find here—little or considerable variety?

Mariana

Alfred, Lord Tennyson [*1809–1892*]

"Mariana in the moated grange." *Measure for Measure*

With blackest moss the flower-plots
  Were thickly crusted, one and all;
The rusted nails fell from the knots
  That held the pear to the gable-wall.
The broken sheds looked sad and strange:
  Unlifted was the clinking latch;
  Weeded and worn the ancient thatch
Upon the lonely moated grange.
    She only said, "My life is dreary,
      He cometh not," she said;
    She said, "I am aweary, aweary,
      I would that I were dead!"

Her tears fell with the dews at even;
  Her tears fell ere the dews were dried;
She could not look on the sweet heaven,
  Either at morn or eventide.
After the flitting of the bats,
  When thickest dark did trance the sky,
  She drew her casement-curtain by,
And glanced athwart the glooming flats.
    She only said, "The night is dreary,
      He cometh not," she said;
    She said, "I am aweary, aweary,
      I would that I were dead!"

Upon the middle of the night,
  Waking she heard the night-fowl crow;
The cock sung out an hour ere light;
  From the dark fen the oxen's low
Came to her; without hope of change,
  In sleep she seemed to walk forlorn,
  Till cold winds woke the gray-eyed morn
About the lonely moated grange.
    She only said, "The day is dreary,
      He cometh not," she said;
    She said, "I am aweary, aweary,
      I would that I were dead!"

About a stone-cast from the wall
  A sluice with blackened waters slept,
And o'er it many, round and small,
  The clustered marish-mosses crept.
Hard by a poplar shook alway,
  All silver-green with gnarlèd bark:
  For leagues no other tree did mark
The level waste, the rounding gray.
    She only said, "My life is dreary,
      He cometh not," she said;
    She said, "I am aweary, aweary,
      I would that I were dead!"

And ever when the moon was low,
  And the shrill winds were up and away,
In the white curtain, to and fro,
  She saw the gusty shadow sway.
But when the moon was very low,
  And wild winds bound within their cell,
  The shadow of the poplar fell
Upon her bed, across her brow.
    She only said, "The night is dreary,
      He cometh not," she said;
    She said, "I am aweary, aweary,
      I would that I were dead!"

All day within the dreamy house,
  The doors upon their hinges creaked;
The blue fly sung in the pane; the mouse
  Behind the moldering wainscot shrieked,

Or from the crevice peered about.
  Old faces glimmered thro' the doors,
  Old footsteps trod the upper floors,
Old voices called her from without.
    She only said, "My life is dreary,
      He cometh not," she said;
    She said, "I am aweary, aweary,
      I would that I were dead!"

The sparrow's chirrup on the roof,
  The slow clock ticking, and the sound
Which to the wooing wind aloof
  The poplar made, did all confound
Her sense; but most she loathed the hour
  When the thick-moted sunbeam lay
  Athwart the chambers, and the day
Was sloping toward his western bower.
    Then said she, "I am very dreary,
      He will not come," she said;
    She wept, "I am aweary, aweary,
      O God, that I were dead!"

In Shakespeare's play *Measure for Measure,* Mariana is the young woman betrothed to Angelo. But Angelo has refused to marry her and she lives far away from the gay life of the capital, in the country at a "moated grange." In this poem Tennyson has tried to imagine her situation of lonely desperation. In describing the physical background of her *isolation,* he has enlarged on the hint afforded by the phrase "moated grange." A moated grange would be a large farmhouse fortified against attack by being enclosed within a moat. Many castles in the Middle Ages had moats, but few granges were moated unless they were in hard-to-defend flat country. The moated grange of the poem is surrounded by such a "level waste" marked by only a single tree, with dark fens all about it and with marsh vegetation filling up the disused moat.

But Tennyson's larger purpose in choosing this particular landscape to describe was to find a physical counterpart to the jilted woman's state of mind. For this poem has to do finally with the depiction of an interior, not an exterior, state of affairs. The refrain with its repetitions and its rhymed insistence upon the girl's weariness and her wish for death tell us that. Doubtless Mariana's state of frustration and depression could occur to a person living upon a mountain top, but the gray, monotonous countryside does accord well with Mariana's listless and despairing inactivity.

What, in fact, gives richness to the poem and delicate authenticity to the psychological representation is Tennyson's handling of detail in his description of landscape and house—both its exterior and its interior, both the sights and the sounds associated with it. Readers who find the poem obvious and superficial might profitably examine some of the descriptive detail before accepting such an estimate as final. And readers who find a special magic in the poem may find some of the sources of its power just here.

The poet's basis for selection of most of the detail is obvious: there are images of age and decay ("rusted nails," "ancient thatch," "moldering wainscot"), somber hues ("blackest moss," "dark fen," "blackened waters," "glooming flats"), and details that suggest the monotonous round of existence ("the slow clock ticking," the movement of the shadow in lines 51–56, the constant rustle of the poplar leaves in line 41). But there is a great deal of subtle particularity as well and there is variety of effect. Variety of a sort is highly necessary, for though Mariana's existence, as the poem depicts it, is monotonous, the poem itself must not be monotonous. If the poem has to become dull and listless in order to convey an experience of dull listlessness, then the poem has failed.

The following topics may suggest both the subtlety and variety of the descriptive detail:

(1) Images that have to do with the round of the day. The grange is seen throughout the round of the day: evening, morning, the "middle of the night," the gray of first light (line 31), the night toward moonset, the last glimmering just after the "flitting of the bats," and late afternoon ("the day / Was sloping toward his western bower"). The ostensible purpose is to describe the various aspects of Mariana's day, but the effect is to remind us of time—its slow passage and the loneliness which the woman feels in its every aspect.

(2) References to sleep and dreaming. Mariana wakes at midnight (lines 25–26) but the "gray-eyed morn" does not wake (line 31) until later. And the blackened waters of the moat,

whose "sleep" is mentioned at line 38, presumably do not wake at all: they are stagnant waters that sleep perpetually. It is suggested that the house and its setting are somehow asleep, even during the day, whereas the human occupant cannot sleep: she wakes at midnight, and while the moon is low in the sky, she watches in her casement-curtain "the gusty shadow sway." Closely related to these references to sleep are the several references to dreaming. Even when Mariana does sleep, her dreams are troubled: she seems "to walk forlorn." A little later in the poem the house itself is called "dreamy." Perhaps the adjective has some sense of "dreaming," but more probably—in terms of what follows—it means "dreamlike." The house seems filled with ghostly sights and sounds—unopened doors that creak upon their hinges, footsteps that seem to tread the upper floors, "Old faces" that glimmer through the doors, and "Old voices" that seem to call from outside. The adjective *old* suggests that the faces and footsteps are familiar, remembered from the past. In this lonely house, past and present, dream and reality, the imagined and the actual become confused.

(3) The distortion of the senses. As has just been suggested, it is hard to distinguish dream from fact in this "dreamy" house. Indeed, in the last stanza the poet tells us that the sparrow's chirrup, the clock's ticking, and the wind in the poplar "did all confound" Mariana's sense. But the sense of strangeness—amounting even to a distortion of the senses—is to be found in the very first stanza. The broken sheds "looked sad and strange." The world colored by her despair—even the ordinary and familiar world—seems unfamiliar, indeed, strange. There are also hints in the poem that Mariana's world is topsy-turvy in other ways. The cry of the night-fowl is described as a "crow," yet the crowing of the cock is called a song ("sung out"), just reversing our normal expectation. (How seriously should one take this reversal? Perhaps not very seriously, but the shift of terms is suggestive.)

It is, of course, in the last two stanzas that we are given the most emphatic instance of senses tightened to a preternatural intensity when the woman can believe for a moment that she sees the hidden mouse that seems to "shriek," when faces out of the past come "glimmering" through doorways, and when even a sparrow's chirrup on the roof "confounds" her sense. This is the climactic point toward which the poem has been moving. But for his culminating image, the poet, after the mention of the three sounds, shifts back once more to a visual image:

> but most she loathed the hour
> When the thick-moted sunbeam lay
> Athwart the chambers. . . .

Grammatically, the shift is abrupt, and one may wonder about the exact force of the word "but." Presumably the passage might be expanded in something like this fashion: All this heightening of innocent sounds to a mad intensity was loathsome to her, but most loathsome of all was "the hour / When" the image of the shaft of level light, swimming with flecks of dust, cut across the half-darkened room. This was the culminating horror of the day.

EXERCISE

1. "Mariana" is a poem which obviously might have been studied in Section II under the rubric Description. But from the foregoing paragraphs, it is plain that it might also have been reasonably placed among the poems of Section IV, those that offer special problems in tone. What is the tone of this poem? What attitude are we to take toward Mariana? The situation invites pity and, on the part of the lonely woman, might even seem to justify self-pity. But in spite of her repeated outcry, "I am aweary, aweary / I would that I were dead," the emotion of the poem is not excessive and the tone impresses us as one of restraint.

2. We have just been commenting on the general restraint of this poem: in this connection, what is the force of *only* in "She only said. . . ."

3. Note the change in the refrain in the last stanza. What is its significance? Does it help to provide a proper climax to the poem?

4. List the sounds mentioned in the poem. Have they been selected at random or is there a principle of selection?

5. Why does Mariana loathe most the hour of the "moted sunbeam"?

6. Why could Mariana not look "on the sweet heaven"?

7. Compare the use of imagery in this poem with that in Rossetti's "Woodspurge" (p. 118).

Doom Is Dark

W. H. Auden [*1907–*]

Doom is dark and deeper than any sea-dingle.
Upon what man it fall
In spring, day-wishing flowers appearing,
Avalanche sliding, white snow from rock-face,
That he should leave his house,
No cloud-soft hand can hold him, restraint by women;
But ever that man goes
Through place-keepers, through forest trees,
A stranger to strangers over undried sea,
Houses for fishes, suffocating water,
Or lonely on fell as chat,
By pot-holed becks
A bird stone-haunting, an unquiet bird.

There head falls forward, fatigued at evening,
And dreams of home,
Waving from window, spread of welcome,
Kissing of wife under single sheet;
But waking sees
Bird-flocks nameless to him, through doorway voices
Of new men making another love.

Save him from hostile capture,
From sudden tiger's spring at corner;
Protect his house,
His anxious house where days are counted
From thunderbolt protect,
From gradual ruin spreading like a stain;
Converting number from vague to certain,
Bring joy, bring day of his returning,
Lucky with day approaching, with leaning dawn.

EXERCISE

This poem gets much of its effect through its imagery which, though carefully general in its reference to the fate of all men, is at the same time very concrete and even shockingly particular. For example, "day-wishing flowers," "place-keepers" (things which are immobile), "houses for fishes," and so on.

1. The imagery of the first section suggests a primitive life in an upland glacial country—"pot-holed becks," for instance. On the other hand, at line 22 there is the image of the tiger, and the phrase "tiger's spring at corner" suggests the tropical animal encountered at the end of a city block. Is the imagery a meaningless jumble, or can you justify it?

2. What is the tone of the poem? (The last section sounds like a prayer.) What effect does the imagery have upon the tone? What effect does the rhythm have upon the tone?

Tears, Idle Tears

Alfred, Lord Tennyson [*1809–1892*]

Tears, idle tears, I know not what they mean,
Tears from the depth of some divine despair
Rise in the heart, and gather to the eyes,
In looking on the happy Autumn-fields,
And thinking of the days that are no more.

Fresh as the first beam glittering on a sail,
That brings our friends up from the underworld,
Sad as the last which reddens over one
That sinks with all we love below the verge;
So sad, so fresh, the days that are no more.

Ah, sad and strange as in dark summer dawns
The earliest pipe of half-awakened birds
To dying ears, when unto dying eyes
The casement slowly grows a glimmering square;
So sad, so strange, the days that are no more.

Dear as remembered kisses after death,
And sweet as those by hopeless fancy feigned

On lips that are for others; deep as love,
Deep as first love, and wild with all regret;
O Death in Life, the days that are no more!

(From *The Princess*)

EXERCISE

1. The subject of this poem, like that of "Ulalume" (p. 226), is vague. Why is it more "successful" than "Ulalume"?

2. Are the tears idle (that is, meaningless) or are they the most meaningful of tears? What occasion prompts them? Does the speaker himself know?

3. The days that are no more are called "sad" and "fresh" in stanza two; and in stanza three, "sad" and "strange." Why are they *fresh* and *strange?* Compare "sad and strange" in line 5 of "Mariana." Does the imagery of stanzas two and three throw any light on their freshness and strangeness? On their "wildness" (see line 19)?

4. What do the tears mean? Is this a weepy, sentimental poem or is it something quite different?

5. How can the poet say that the days that are no more are "deep as love, / Deep as first love, and wild with all regret" (lines 18–19)? How can days be *deep* and *wild?* What do these words come to mean in the context of the poem? Has their application to "days" been prepared for? How?

Mystery

Elizabeth Barrett Browning [*1806–1861*]

We sow the glebe, we reap the corn,
  We build the house where we may rest,
And then, at moments, suddenly,
We look up to the great wide sky,
Inquiring wherefore we were born . . .
  For earnest, or for jest?

The senses folding thick and dark
  About the stifled soul within,
We guess diviner things beyond,

And yearn to them with yearning fond;
We strike out blindly to a mark
  Believed in, but not seen.

We vibrate to the pant and thrill
  Wherewith Eternity has curled
In serpent-twine about God's seat;
While, freshening upward to his feet,
In gradual growth his full-leaved will
  Expands from world to world.

And, in the tumult and excess
  Of act and passion under sun,
We sometimes hear—oh, soft and far,
As silver star did touch with star,
The kiss of Peace and Righteousness
  Through all things that are done.

God keeps His holy mysteries
  Just on the outside of man's dream.
In diapason slow, we think
To hear their pinions rise and sink,
While they float pure beneath His eyes,
  Like swans adown a stream.

And, sometimes, horror chills our blood
  To be so near such mystic Things,
And we wrap round us, for defense,
Our purple manners, moods of sense—
As angels, from the face of God,
  Stand hidden in their wings.

And, sometimes, through life's heavy swound
  We grope for them!—with strangled breath
We stretch out hands abroad and try
To reach them in our agony,—
And widen, so, the broad life-wound
  Which soon is large enough for death.

EXERCISE

With close attention to the comments on "The Definition of Love" (pp. 295–99) and "My Springs" (pp. 299–303), write a comment on this poem. Consider especially the following topics:

1. The inferiority of the imagery in the first part of the third stanza to that in the second part.

2. The confusion of imagery in the fifth stanza.

3. The credibility of the statement that "horror chills our blood. . . ." (Does the word *horror* have any accurate application here? Or does it merely represent an attempt to gain dramatic force?)

4. The relation of the rhythm to the other elements in the poem.

5. The indefiniteness of the subject as compared to that of "Tears, Idle Tears."

At Melville's Tomb

Hart Crane [*1899–1932*]

Often beneath the wave, wide from this ledge
The dice of drowned men's bones he saw bequeath
An embassy. Their numbers as he watched,
Beat on the dusty shore and were obscured.

And wrecks passed without sound of bells,
The calyx of death's bounty giving back
A scattered chapter, livid hieroglyph,
The portent wound in corridors of shells.

Then in the circuit calm of one vast coil,
Its lashings charmed and malice reconciled,
Frosted eyes there were that lifted altars;
And silent answers crept across the stars.

Compass, quadrant and sextant contrive
No farther tides . . . High in the azure steeps
Monody shall not wake the mariner.
This fabulous shadow only the sea keeps.

This poem is a little elegy upon Herman Melville, the author of *Moby Dick,* the great American novel of the sea and whaling. The general meaning of the poem is easy enough. The poet says that the spirit of the writer whose imagination was so vividly engaged by the sea, and who saw such grandeur in man's struggle with it, though his body might be buried on land, would find its real abiding place in the sea:

> This fabulous shadow only the sea keeps.

The imagery of the poem, however, provoked the editor who first published the poem to write the poet to ask several questions concerning the detailed meanings:

> Take me for a hard-boiled unimaginative unpoetic reader, and tell me how *dice* can *bequeath an embassy* (or anything else); and how a calyx (*of death's bounty* or anything else) can give back a *scattered chapter, livid hieroglyph;* and how, if it does, such a *portent* can be *wound in corridors* (of shells or anything else).
>
> And so on. I find your image of *frosted eyes lifting altars* difficult to visualize. Nor do compass, quadrant and sextant *contrive* tides, they merely record them, I believe.
>
> All this may seem impertinent, but is not so intended. Your ideas and rhythms interest me, and I am wondering by what process of reasoning you would justify this poem's succession of champion mixed metaphors, of which you must be conscious. The packed line should pack its phrases in orderly relation, it seems to me, in a manner tending to clear confusion instead of making it worse confounded.*

The first part of the poet's reply to the editor's letter containing these questions was concerned with the general justification of comparisons which are not scientifically and logically exact. (This general consideration has already been raised in some degree in dealing with various poems discussed in this section.) The poet then undertook to analyze the implied points of reference behind his own use of imagery:

> . . . I'll . . . come at once to the explanations you requested on the Melville poem:
>
> > "The dice of drowned men's bones he saw bequeath
> > An embassy."
>
> Dice bequeath an embassy, in the first place, by being ground (in this connection only, of course) in little cubes

* This correspondence between Harriet Monroe and Hart Crane appeared in *Poetry: A Magazine of Verse.*

from the bones of drowned men by the action of the sea, and are finally thrown up on the sand, having "numbers" but no identification. These being the bones of dead men who never completed their voyage, it seems legitimate to refer to them as the only surviving evidence of certain messages undelivered, mute evidence of certain things, experiences that the dead mariners might have had to deliver. Dice as a symbol of chance and circumstance is also implied.

"The calyx of death's bounty giving back," etc.

This calyx refers in a double ironic sense both to a cornucopia and the vortex made by a sinking vessel. As soon as the water has closed over a ship this whirlpool sends up broken spars, wreckage, etc., which can be alluded to as *livid hieroglyphs,* making a *scattered chapter* so far as any complete record of the recent ship and her crew is concerned. In fact, about as much definite knowledge might come from all this as anyone might gain from the roar of his own veins, which is easily heard (haven't you ever done it?) by holding a shell close to one's ear.

"Frosted eyes lift altars"

refers simply to a conviction that a man, not knowing perhaps a definite god yet being endowed with a reverence for deity—such a man naturally postulates a deity somehow, and the altar of that deity by the very *action* of the eyes *lifted* in searching.

"Compass, quadrant and sextant contrive no farther tides."

Hasn't it often occurred that instruments originally invented for record and computation have inadvertently so extended the concepts of the entity they were invented to measure (concepts of space, etc.) in the mind and imagination that employed them, that they may metaphorically be said to have extended the original boundaries of the entity measured? This little bit of "relativity" ought not to be discredited in poetry now that scientists are proceeding to measure the universe on principles of pure *ratio,* quite as metaphorical, so far as previous standards of scientific methods extended. . . .

This correspondence raises some very interesting questions that frequently appear in connection not only with poems like this one by Hart Crane, but also with all poetry. People sometimes say: "But the poet couldn't have been thinking of all this when he wrote the poem." And in the sense in which they are using the term "thinking" they are right. The poet certainly did not draw up an analysis of his intention, a kind of blueprint, and then write the poem to specification. But it is only a very superficial view of the way the mind works that would cast the question into those terms. Does a finely trained pole-vaulter in the act of making his leap think specifically of each of the different muscles he is employing; or does a boxer in the middle of a round think of the details of his boxing form? Probably not, even though the vaulter or boxer may have acquired his form by conscious practice which involved detail after detail. Furthermore, at the moment of action, a competent coach would be able to analyze and criticize the performance in detail. In the same way, one might say that a poet, in his role as craftsman in the process of making a poem, does not work by blueprint specifications, but toward a sort of general objective which is conditioned by his "training"—by his previous study of his own responses, by his study of the detailed methods and effects in the work of other poets, and by his thinking about experience. The process of composing the poem is a process of exploring the full implications of the intended meaning and of finding a suitable structure. The process is probably one of movement by trial and error, governed by self-criticism.*

But to return to the matter of Crane's analysis of his own poem: in attempting to answer questions about his poem, Crane is obviously acting in the role of observer or critic, and one is not to confuse this process of analysis with the process that probably occurred in the actual composition. Moreover, one is not to suppose that the reader necessarily must duplicate the process of analysis in experiencing the force of the poem. But as the preliminary discipline of the poet extends and enriches his capacity for creation, so the process of study extends the reader's capacity for appreciation.

* See *How Poems Come About* (pp. 520–31).

Voyages

Hart Crane [*1899–1932*]

II

And yet this great wink of eternity,
Of rimless floods, unfettered leewardings,
Samite sheeted and processioned where
Her undinal vast belly moonward bends,
Laughing the wrapt inflections of our love;

Take this Sea, whose diapason knells
On scrolls of silver snowy sentences,
The sceptered terror of whose sessions rends
As her demeanors motion well or ill,
All but the pieties of lovers' hands.

And onward, as bells off San Salvador
Salute the crocus lusters of the stars,
In these poinsettia meadows of her tides,—
Adagios of islands, O my Prodigal,
Complete the dark confessions her veins spell.

Mark how her turning shoulders wind the hours,
And hasten while her penniless rich palms
Pass superscription of bent foam and wave,—
Hasten, while they are true,—sleep, death, desire,
Close round one instant in one floating flower.

Bind us in time, O seasons clear, and awe.
O minstrel galleons of Carib fire,
Bequeath us to no earthly shore until
Is answered in the vortex of our grave
The seal's wide spindrift gaze toward paradise.

VI

Where icy and bright dungeons lift
Of swimmers their lost morning eyes,
And ocean rivers, churning, shift
Green borders under stranger skies,

Steadily as a shell secretes
Its beating leagues of monotone,

Or as many waters trough the sun's
Red kelson past the cape's wet stone;

O rivers mingling toward the sky
And harbor of the phoenix' breast—
My eyes pressed black against the prow,
—Thy derelict and blinded guest

Waiting, afire, what name, unspoke,
I cannot claim: let thy waves rear
More savage than the death of kings,
Some splintered garland for the seer.

Beyond siroccos harvesting
The solstice thunders, crept away,
Like a cliff swinging or a sail
Flung into April's inmost day—

Creation's blithe and petaled word
To the lounged goddess when she rose
Conceding dialogue with eyes
That smile unsearchable repose—

Still fervid covenant, Belle Isle,
—Unfolded floating dais before
Which rainbows twine continual hair—
Belle Isle, white echo of the oar!

The imaged word, it is, that holds
Hushed willows anchored in its glow.
It is the unbetrayable reply
Whose accent no farewell can know.

EXERCISE

These two poems make use of a very rich and perhaps tangled imagery. The student ought to try to determine whether the imagery is confused, or whether it hangs together; and if so, on what principle the images are interrelated. Before beginning this examination, he might well reread what Crane has to say about the imagery used in "At Melville's Tomb."

1. What aspects of the sea are pictured by the imagery? Suggested by the imagery?

2. In the first poem the sea is referred to as if it were a goddess; in the second, the goddess Aphrodite (who was born of the seafoam), is referred to. What does the sea come to symbolize in these poems?

Because I Could Not Stop for Death

Emily Dickinson [*1830–1886*]

Because I could not stop for Death,
He kindly stopped for me;
The carriage held but just ourselves
And Immortality.

We slowly drove, he knew no haste,
And I had put away
My labor, and my leisure too,
For his civility.

We passed the school where children played,
Their lessons scarcely done;
We passed the fields of gazing grain,
We passed the setting sun.

We paused before a house that seemed
A swelling on the ground;
The roof was scarcely visible,
The cornice but a mound.

Since then 'tis centuries; but each
Feels shorter than the day
I first surmised the horses' heads
Were toward eternity.

EXERCISE

1. Look at the word *stop* in line 1. Does it mean the same thing here as in line 2? How does the word in line 1 relate to the meaning of line 7?

2. Are we to take it that the lady has died? Or is the poem about an awareness?

3. Here are comments on this poem by two well-known

critics. Read them carefully. Do you find any statements that you feel are wrong, or at least not supported by evidence in the poem? Do you find any that shed new light?

> If the word great means anything in poetry, this poem is one of the greatest in the English language. The rhythm charges with movement the pattern of suspended action back of the poem. Every image is precise and, moreover, not merely beautiful, but fused with the central idea. Every image extends and intensifies every other. The third stanza especially shows Miss Dickinson's power to fuse, into a single order of perception, a heterogeneous series: the children, the grain, and the setting sun (time) have the same degree of credibility; the first subtly preparing for the last. The sharp *gazing* before *grain* instills into nature a cold vitality of which the qualitative richness has infinite depth. The content of death in the poem eludes explicit definition. He is a gentleman taking a lady out for a drive. But note the restraint that keeps the poet from carrying this so far that it becomes ludicrous and incredible; and note the subtly interfused erotic motive, which the idea of death has presented to most romantic poets, love being a symbol interchangeable with death. The terror of death is objectified through this figure of the genteel driver, who is made ironically to serve the end of Immortality. This is the heart of the poem: she has presented a typical Christian theme in its final irresolution, without making any final statements about it. There is no solution to the problem; there can be only a presentation of it in the full context of intellect and feeling. . . . the idea of immortality is confronted with the fact of physical disintegration. We are not told what to think; we are told to look at the situation.*

> The only pressing technical objection to this poem is the remark that "Immortality" in the first stanza is a meretricious and unnecessary personification and that the common sense of the situation demands that Immortality ought to be the destination of the coach and not one of the passengers. The personification of death, however, is unassailable. In the literal meaning of the poem, he is apparently a successful citizen who has amorous but genteel intentions. He is also God. . . .

* Allen Tate: *On the Limits of Poetry,* New York, Swallow Press and William Morrow and Company, 1948, pp. 206–207.

. . . The third stanza is a symbolic recapitulation of life: the children playing, wrestling (more "labor") through the cycle of their existence, "in a ring"; the gazing grain signifies ripeness and the entranced and visionary gaze that first beholds the approach of death of which the setting sun is the felicitous symbol.

The last two stanzas are hardly surpassed in the whole range of lyric poetry. The visual images here are handled with perfect economy. All the poem needs is one or two concrete images—roof, cornice—to awake in our minds the appalling identification of house with grave. Even more compelling is the sense of pausing, and the sense of overpowering action and weight in "swelling" and "mound." This kinaesthetic imagery prepares us for the feeling of suddenly discerned motion in the last stanza, which with final dramatic tact presents us with but one visual image, the horses' heads. There are progressively fewer visible objects in the last three stanzas, since the seen world must be made gradually to sink into the nervously sensed world. . . .*

After Great Pain a Formal Feeling Comes

Emily Dickinson [*1830–1886*]

After great pain a formal feeling comes—
The nerves sit ceremonious like tombs;
The stiff Heart questions—was it He that bore?
And yesterday—or centuries before?

The feet mechanical go round
A wooden way
Of ground or air or Ought,
Regardless grown,
A quartz contentment like a stone.

This is the hour of lead
Remembered if outlived
As freezing persons recollect
The snow—
First chill, then stupor, then
The letting go.

* Richard Chase: *Emily Dickinson*, New York, William Sloane Associates, 1951, pp. 249–251.

EXERCISE

1. Some of the imagery used in this little poem is very bold. What, for example, do you make of line 2? How can nerves be said to *sit?* What is meant by sitting *ceremonious?* Why like *tombs?* What is the total image? Comment upon it.

2. What is meant by a "quartz contentment"? Why "quartz" and not some other stone? Can this figure be related to "wooden way" and "hour of lead"?

3. The experience of deep grief in stanza 3 is compared to death by freezing. What are the steps of this process? How carefully is the analogy worked out? What is the force of "Remembered if outlived"?

The Soul Selects

Emily Dickinson [*1830–1886*]

The soul selects her own society,
Then shuts the door;
On her divine majority
Obtrude no more.

Unmoved, she notes the chariot's pausing
At her low gate;
Unmoved, an emperor is kneeling
Upon her mat.

I've known her from an ample nation
Choose one;
Then close the valves of her attention
Like stone.

EXERCISE

1. What images are suggested in stanza 2 by "chariot's," by "emperor," and by "mat"? Is the collocation of the emperor and the door-mat absurd, or is it justified?

2. What images are suggested by the last two lines of the poem? What does *valves* mean here? Can the term be justified? Does it clash too much with the rest of the imagery?

3. Attempt to define the tone of this poem. In answering this question take into account, not only the imagery, but the stanza form that has been chosen.

Let Me Not to the Marriage of True Minds

William Shakespeare [1564–1616]

Let me not to the marriage of true minds
Admit impediments. Love is not love
Which alters when it alteration finds,
Or bends with the remover to remove:
O, no! it is an ever-fixèd mark
That looks on tempests and is never shaken;
It is the star to every wandering bark,
Whose worth's unknown, although his height be taken.
Love's not Time's fool, though rosy lips and cheeks
Within his bending sickle's compass come;
Love alters not with his brief hours and weeks,
But bears it out even to the edge of doom.
If this be error and upon me proved,
I never writ, nor no man ever loved.

EXERCISE

1. Work out in detail the implied as well as the developed images. What is the relation among the various images? Is the imagery inconsistent or confused?

2. What is the meaning of "Love's not Time's fool"? And of "bending sickle's compass"?

3. What is the tone of the poem? How does the poet avoid a tone of extravagant protestation?

As I Walked Out One Evening

W. H. Auden [1907–   ]

As I walked out one evening,
  Walking down Bristol Street,
The crowds upon the pavement
  Were fields of harvest wheat.

And down by the brimming river
  I heard a lover sing
Under an arch of the railway:
  "Love has no ending.

I'll love you, dear, I'll love you
  Till China and Africa meet,
And the river jumps over the mountain
  And the salmon sing in the street.

I'll love you till the ocean
  Is folded and hung up to dry,
And the seven stars go squawking
  Like geese about the sky.

The years shall run like rabbits,
  For in my arms I hold
The Flower of the Ages,
  And the first love of the world."

But all the clocks in the city
  Began to whirr and chime:
"O let not Time deceive you,
  You cannot conquer Time.

In the burrows of the Nightmare
  Where Justice naked is,
Time watches from the shadow
  And coughs when you would kiss.

In headaches and in worry
  Vaguely life leaks away,
And Time will have his fancy
  Tomorrow or today.

Into many a green valley
  Drifts the appalling snow;
Time breaks the threaded dances
  And the diver's brilliant bow.

O plunge your hands in water,
  Plunge them in up to the wrist;
Stare, stare in the basin
  And wonder what you've missed.

The glacier knocks in the cupboard,
  The desert sighs in the bed,
And the crack in the tea-cup opens
  A lane to the land of the dead.

Where the beggars raffle the banknotes
  And the Giant is enchanting to Jack,
And the Lily-white Boy is a Roarer,
  And Jill goes down on her back.

O look, look in the mirror,
  O look in your distress;
Life remains a blessing
  Although you cannot bless.

O stand, stand at the window
  As the tears scald and start;
You shall love your crooked neighbor
  With your crooked heart."

It was late, late in the evening,
  The lovers they were gone;
The clocks had ceased their chiming,
  And the deep river ran on.

This poem makes use of some of the ballad conventions. It is written in quatrains (though not in strict ballad measure); it makes use of the lover's promise (stanzas 2–5); it affects a kind of naïveté, and so on. Indeed, the opening line specifically echoes "The Sailor's Return," a ballad that Auden as editor included in the *Oxford Book of Light Verse*.*

Yet reminiscences of the ballad account for only some of the echoes to be heard in this poem. Others are from the lyrics of Tin Pan Alley. The promises made in love poems are often extravagant, but the extravagances met with in this poem obviously recall contemporary popular songs. There is the straining for effect in

* See Edward C. McAleer, *College English*, Vol. 18 (February, 1957), pp. 27–72. The first stanza reads:

As I walked out one night, it being dark all over,
The moon did show no light I could discover,
Down by a river side where ships were sailing,
A lonely maid I spied, weeping and bewailing.

> . . . the river jumps over the mountain
> And the salmon sing in the street.

There is the slangy hyperbole of

> I'll love you till the ocean
> Is folded and hung up to dry,
> And the seven stars go squawking
> Like geese about the sky.

There is the sentimental hyperbole of

> For in my arms I hold
> The Flower of the Ages,
> And the first love of the world.

The imagery here it at once tired and excessively violent, strident and awkwardly muffled. If the poem ended here we should have to regard it as a kind of disaster. Its badness could be justified only as deliberate—as a kind of conscious parody of a particular kind of bad poetry. But the poem does not end here and the value of the imagery of these stanzas can be fairly determined only by seeing their functions in the total context.

To sum up for the moment, the lover by the traditional "brimming river" but now in a modern urban environment ("Under an arch of the railway") voices the lover's universal claim to an eternal love, but voices it in a tired and sleazy idiom.

The lover, however, is at once answered by the clocks of the city which warn him not to be deceived by time into any notion that he can conquer time. But their warning is stated in imagery which is, on one level, as bold and extravagant as that in the stanzas spoken by the lover. Consider lines 25–28. Is Justice indeed naked in the burrows of the nightmare? Or consider lines 41–44. "The glacier knocks in the cupboard / The desert sighs in the bed" are statements which match the extravagance of "I'll love you, dear, I'll love you / Till China and Africa meet."

Yet the latter images make a kind of sense which those in the lover's vaunt do not. For example, the nightmare, the oppressive dream, may be said to be labyrinthine like a cave or like the winding burrow of an animal. And in such dreams justice—proper retribution—is to be found. One does not have to be much of a Freudian to see that in the elaborate and often curious symbolism of dreams our true plight is expressed and our evasions and self-deceptions reveal themselves. Or consider lines 41–42. In our more somber moods—or it may be in our more realistic insights into our true situations—the glacier, type of frozen sterility, declares itself in the most cozy corner of the household scene, the place where our food is kept; and the desert, type of infertility, is discovered in the bed of love itself.

The world of reality, the clocks are saying, is a baffling and topsy-turvy as the factitious world of the lover's song. It is a world that defeats normal expectations and whose true character can only be expressed in imagery which on at least one level matches the images used by the lover.

The imagery of the first part of the poem has thus been carefully selected to prepare for and indeed "set up" the later imagery. We can express this double function in terms of tone. Without this preparation, the tone of the speech of the clocks might have seemed simply heavy-handed with a kind of lugubrious moralism. If it does not seem so, it is because we are willing to modulate from one kind of extravagance into another. In short, we can believe that "the crack in the tea-cup opens / A lane to the land of the dead" because we have recognized and rejected the fatuity of "I'll love you till the ocean / Is folded and hung up to dry. . . ."

The next-to-last stanza which concludes the speech of the clocks matches the lover's song not only with another piece of extravagance but with another conception of love. Love as *agape* (translated as "charity" in the King James version of the Bible) is that which is enjoined in line 55. It is not merely the sweetheart but the neighbor who, it must be admitted, is a "crooked" neighbor, that "you shall love." More extravagantly difficult still, you must love him "With your crooked heart," an instrument apparently hopelessly inadequate for the task.

The last stanza is interesting and important for its effect on the rest of the poem. No miraculous change in the lover occurs. He presumably does not heed what the clocks say. Indeed there is no sign that the lover even hears what they have said. We are merely told that "The lovers they were gone." The clocks are again silent. The scene is what it was in the beginning: "The deep river ran on" as it had been when the lovers first approached it and as it will continue to do long after these lovers have gone.

EXERCISE

1. Lines 45–48 probably require a note. Line 46 is a reference to the story of Jack the Giant Killer. The Lily-white Boy, line 47, is a reference to the song "Green Grow the Rushes O" (the Dorsetshire version of which is also included by Auden in his *Oxford Book of Light Verse*): "Two, two for the lily-white boys." (Compare also line 15, "And the seven stars go squawking," to line 9 of "Green Grow the Rushes O"—"Seven for the seven stars in the sky.") Jill in line 48 is the companion of Jack in the nursery rhyme which tells how they went to fetch a pail of water. What use is made of these allusions?
2. In line 36, what is meant by "the diver's brilliant bow"?
3. What is the tone of this poem? Is it one of quiet moralizing, or of heavy-handed sermonizing, of bitter mockery, or of cynical disillusion, or what?
4. Relate as specifically as you can the poet's use of his imagery to his development of the tone.
5. Why are the clocks, the means by which time is measured, chosen by the poet to voice the warning against time? Time is often treated as a flowing stream. Is the brimming river in this poem related to the problem of time? If so, how? What is its relation to the clocks?
6. Compare the extravagance of the lover's promises in this poem with that of the promises made in "O, Wert Thou in the Cauld Blast," p. 247.

Among School Children

William Butler Yeats [1865–1939]

I

I walk through the long schoolroom questioning;
A kind old nun in a white hood replies;
The children learn to cipher and to sing,

To study reading-books and history,
To cut and sew, be neat in everything
In the best modern way—the children's eyes
In momentary wonder stare upon
A sixty-year-old smiling public man.

II

I dream of a Ledaean body, bent
Above a sinking fire, a tale that she
Told of a harsh reproof, or trivial event
That changed some childish day to tragedy—
Told, and it seemed that our two natures blent
Into a sphere from youthful sympathy,
Or else, to alter Plato's parable,
Into the yolk and white of the one shell.

III

And thinking of that fit of grief or rage
I look upon one child or t'other there
And wonder if she stood so at that age—
For even daughters of the swan can share
Something of every paddler's heritage—
And had that color upon cheek or hair,
And thereupon my heart is driven wild:
She stands before me as a living child.

IV

Her present image floats into the mind—
Did Quattrocento finger fashion it
Hollow of cheek as though it drank the wind
And took a mess of shadows for its meat?
And I though never of Ledaean kind
Had pretty plumage once—enough of that,
Better to smile on all that smile, and show
There is a comfortable kind of old scarecrow.

V

What youthful mother, a shape upon her lap
Honey of generation had betrayed,
And that must sleep, shriek, struggle to escape
As recollection or the drug decide,
Would think her son, did she but see the shape

With sixty or more winters on its head,
A compensation for the pang of his birth,
Or the uncertainty of his setting forth?

VI

Plato thought nature but a spume that plays
Upon a ghostly paradigm of things;
Solider Aristotle played the taws
Upon the bottom of a king of kings;
World-famous golden-thighed Pythagoras
Fingered upon a fiddle-stick or strings
What a star sang and careless Muses heard:
Old clothes upon old sticks to scare a bird.

VII

Both nuns and mothers worship images,
But those the candles light are not as those
That animate a mother's reveries,
But keep a marble or a bronze repose.
And yet they too break hearts—O Presences
That passion, piety or affection knows,
And that all heavenly glory symbolize—
O self-born mockers of man's enterprise;

VIII

Labor is blossoming or dancing where
The body is not bruised to pleasure soul,
Nor beauty born out of its own despair,
Nor blear-eyed wisdom out of midnight oil.
O chestnut tree, great rooted blossomer,
Are you the leaf, the blossom or the bole?
O body swayed to music, O brightening glance,
How can we know the dancer from the dance?

EXERCISE

1. The structure of the poem may be sketched briefly as follows: Stanza I gives the situation which stimulates the speaker to his reverie. Stanzas II, III, and IV present the relation of childhood to maturity and of maturity to age with reference to the speaker himself and to the woman he loves. Stanzas V and

VI extend the personal comment to a general one: would any mother, if she could see the old age of her child, feel that her own love and sacrifice had been justified? For even the greatest men, Plato, Aristotle, and Pythagoras, were, in old age, little better than scarecrows. Stanza VII goes on to comment that the images which people hold in affection and reverence always mock man's inability to realize them. Stanza VIII presents the idea that when the mind and body are in harmony, there is no distinction between the real and the ideal; the image and the actuality are one. Investigate the ways by which the imagery serves to present these ideas. (Consult the library for information concerning Leda, Quattrocento, Plato, Aristotle, Alexander the Great, who is referred to here as "king of kings," the meaning of the word *taws,* and Pythagoras.)

2. What are the interrelations among the images? Observe, for instance, that the story of Leda and the swan is alluded to in line 20.

3. Is it suggested that man should do away with all ideals, since none can be fully attained and all bruise man in his struggle to attain them? What does the speaker say on this point? In attempting an answer here, consider the evidence of imagery.

4. Why does the speaker refer to both nuns and mothers? How do the nuns and mothers complement each other in this poem?

5. What does the speaker mean by his last two questions (lines 61–64)? Is there a sense in which we literally cannot know the dancer apart from the dance?

The Fair Singer

Andrew Marvell [*1621–1678*]

To make a final conquest of all me,
Love did compose so sweet an enemy,
In whom both beauties to my death agree,
Joining themselves in fatal harmony;
That while she with her eyes my heart doth bind,
She with her voice might captivate my mind.

I could have fled from one but singly fair;
My disentangled soul itself might save,
Breaking the curlèd trammels of her hair;
But how could I avoid to be her slave,
Whose subtile art invisibly can wreathe
My fetters of the very air I breathe?

It had been easy fighting in some plain
Where victory might hang in equal choice;
But all resistance against her is vain
Who has th' advantage both of eyes and voice;
And all my forces needs must be undone,
She having gainèd both the wind and sun.

EXERCISE

Write an interpretation of the poem with special reference to the implications of the imagery and its relation to the tone.

VI

Theme: Statement and Idea

FOREWORD

In treating the poems in earlier sections of this book we have continually referred to the idea, the meaning, the theme. It could not be otherwise, for we cannot long consider rhythm, imagery, or tone in isolation. For one thing, poetry exists in the medium of words, and as the philosopher George Santayana * says, words inevitably carry with them some weight of idea; "the detail of things and the detail of ideas pass equally into his [the poet's] verse," and "it is only by the net of new connections which words throw over things, in recalling them, that poetry arises at all." A poem, then, even when presumably it is aiming at a direct expression of feeling or the direct presentation of an object, can only give what Santayana calls "an echo of crude experience," and "a theoretic vision of things at arm's length." The theme is as inevitable to poetry as are words.

Or to look at the matter another way, we can remember

* *Three Philosophical Poets,* New York, Doubleday and Company, 1953, p. 114.

that a mood implies an idea, as an idea implies a mood. The human being is a unity, and the slightest shift in feeling implies some new interpretation of things—which is susceptible of being stated as an idea. Or conversely, the slightest shift in our ideas implies some new stance of feeling, however minimal. To take this in relation to poetry, we may recall Keats's "Ode to Autumn" (p. 109), in which there is no statement of an idea, but in which the general mood built up by the rhythm and imagery leads us inevitably to a certain attitude toward life—that is, to an idea, a theme. And such a relation between mood and idea is at the root of all poetry.

All of this is a way of saying again what was said at the beginning of this book, that a poem, in so far as it is a good poem, is an organic unity in which all the elements are vitally interfused. We may abstract rhythm, or imagery, for discussion, but we know that we are making an abstraction, and that the thing we abstract is really an aspect of a whole. We make the abstraction, we study the aspect, merely in order to understand better the whole in its complex interrelations.

In this connection we may warn ourselves that what we want from poetry is not the idea as such—the theme as a slogan, a poster, or a piece of sampler work to hang on the wall. As far as poetry is concerned, an idea is worthless unless it is dramatized in the poem, unless it seems to grow out of the poem. Early in this book we said that every poem is a little drama, and we may now say that the theme of a poem is what the little drama amounts to. The theme embodies the attitude toward life that grows out of the little drama—the evaluation of human experience.

This kind of talk may sound very heavy and sober-sided when we put it over against the lightness, brightness, deftness, or even comedy of such poems as "Delight in Disorder," by Robert Herrick (p. 257), "Blame Not My Cheeks," by Thomas Campion (p. 256), "The Season 'Tis, My Lovely Lambs," by E. E. Cummings (p. 209), or "Kind of an Ode to Duty," by Ogden Nash (p. 208). But not all themes are somber—"Life is a jest," one poet wrote. Besides, even the lighthearted poem may have grown out of the confrontation of the deeper realities. It is even possible to argue that comedy, however lighthearted, is possible only because there is some urgency in the world which it treats lightheartedly; and humor and poetry have much in common, the warmth of feeling and the leap of imagination.

The theme of a poem, as we have said, amounts to a comment on human values, an interpretation of life. But what are we to make of poems in which the theme does not accord with our own feelings about life? This is a constant question, and one which can hardly be settled once and for all, but it may help us to think of our estimates of poems (or poets) as we think of our estimates of other people. We associate, more or less happily, with a great number of people, and with most of them we have, on some point or other, serious differences of opinion, taste, and values. But we manage to be friendly with most of them. We manage to recognize in many of them certain qualities which, despite our disagreements, can be valued and enjoyed. In people whom we respect we recognize some underlying good will, some attempt to make sense of things and deal honestly with them. In recognizing this fact about others, we discover in ourselves some tolerance and some power of sympathetic imagination that enables us to feel ourselves into another person's skin and to understand how the world looks to him. In this process of imaginative sympathy we realize that the world is complicated and the richer for its complications. We realize, too, that opinions, tastes, and values which are in some sense opposed to each other may each have a place, that to many questions there may be more than one answer, and that our own private convictions and dogmatic beliefs may have to be modified. In other words, imagination may teach us a little humility.

Indeed, no attitude or interpretation will invalidate a poem, if it is an attitude or interpretation that can conceivably be held by a serious and intelligent person in the dramatic situation stated or implied in the poem. Obviously, words like *serious* and *intelligent* do not mean the same thing to all people, and consequently there is a margin for disagreement in estimating poetry. But such disagreements, taken by and large over a long sweep of time, after contemporary prejudices have died, are relatively infrequent where first-rate work—or really poor work—is concerned.

The fact that no serious and intelligent attitude will in itself invalidate a poem is not to be taken as saying that one thing is as good as another. We each have to work out our own scale of values and try to justify it and live by it. But it does mean that when we encounter differences, we must try to understand their nature and try to find the underlying common ground that makes respect and appreciation possible.

What, then, is this common ground in poetry? The common ground is the understanding of the fact that, in so far as a theme is coherently developed through a poem, in so far as it actually flowers from the whole process of the poem, we are witnessing and taking part in the great human effort to achieve meaning through experience. It is only when the attitude involved in the poem comes as an over-simplified, and unvalidated, generalization, when the response which the poem demands is not warranted by the dramatic situation, when, to sum up, the poem is incoherent—it is only in these cases that we ordinarily reject a poem.

If we find the poem coherent, dramatically significant, we tend to take the leap of sympathetic imagination. We can appreciate it for the sense of the conquest over disorder and meaninglessness which it gives us. Perhaps this sense may be the very basis of the exhilaration we find in poetry—just as it may be the basis for the pleasure we take in watching the clean drive of an expert golfer or the swoop of a hawk, as contrasted with the accidental tumbling of a stone downhill. The sense of order and control in the vital act—that is what in a successful poem confirms us in the faith that experience itself may be made meaningful. And a poem is, in this sense, an image of our life process—and in being that, an enlightening image of ourselves.

In the poems which follow in this section we shall not be indulging ourselves in message-hunting. We do want to be able to state to ourselves as clearly as possible the theme of a poem, but we must be aware of the fact that our statement will always be little more than a brutal paraphrase. We must make our statement, but we make it in order to appreciate more keenly the modifications and extensions of meaning that the texture—the rhythm, the tone, the imagery—of the poem imposes.

Lucifer in Starlight

George Meredith [*1828–1909*]

On a starred night Prince Lucifer uprose.
Tired of his dark dominion swung the fiend
Above the rolling ball in cloud part screened,
Where sinners hugged their specter of repose.
Poor prey to his hot fit of pride were those.
And now upon his western wing he leaned,
Now his huge bulk o'er Afric's sands careened,
Now the black planet shadowed Arctic snows.
Soaring through wider zones that pricked his scars
With memory of the old revolt from Awe,
He reached a middle height, and at the stars,
Which are the brain of heaven, he looked, and sank.
Around the ancient track marched, rank on rank,
The army of unalterable law.

Some of the ways in which an idea finds expression in poetry have been treated more or less fully in many of the earlier discussions, especially in the section dealing with imagery. But the ways in which this process occurs are innumerable and, in fact, vary from poem to poem. In the present instance, "Lucifer in Starlight," the process is a fairly simple one.

An understanding of the poem depends on reference to some specific information that is not given in the poem itself. It presupposes a knowledge and interpretation of the Lucifer myth. Lucifer, the Archangel, rebelled against God, and as a result of his pride, which would not endure the divine dominion over him, was hurled out of heaven. But the subject not only carries with it the bare facts of the myth, but also associations derived from a treatment such as that in Milton's epic, *Paradise Lost,* which involves the rebellion of the angels, and his temptation of Man as a revenge against God. From the myth and its different treatments the reader knows that Lucifer may be taken as the incarnation of pride, and therefore as the principle of anarchy and disorder, in conflict with the principle of order in the universe.

Essentially, Meredith presents this same theme in his poem, but he has put his theme into a new set of terms, and though depending on the body of information and associations which the reader brings to the poem, has succeeded in creating a new poem. Meredith has made, as it were, a new myth, a kind of sequel to the more traditional treatments of the idea. Lucifer, who, as in Milton's *Paradise Lost,* maintains his pride even in the depth of Hell, is shown rising through the starry universe, above the sphere of the earth which is partially concealed from him by clouds. He is not now interested in the sinners on earth through whom, since the Fall of Man, he has been striking at God in revenge; apparently, in his "hot fit of pride" he is aiming at nothing less than a return to his old estate.

Meredith attempts to give as vivid a picture as possible of the enormous bulk of the Fiend, like a planet, flying so near the "rolling ball" of the earth that he shadows it, presumably, from the moon. One may notice that in giving this picture Meredith casts the mythical figure of the Fiend into the universe as we now conceive it, describing the earth revolving in its orbit, and does not use the fixed, central earth of the Ptolemaic conception, which Milton, for instance, used. This detail, though small in itself, gives a certain novelty to Meredith's treatment. It seems to imply, perhaps as a kind of undertone to the poem, that the old force of anarchy is still operating, despite changes in human conceptions, and trying to reach out, even beyond human affairs, to the very center of the universe.

But the real novelty in the new "myth" lies in the reason given by Meredith for Lucifer's failure to proceed with his present rebellion. He does not sink again because he encounters the divine force that once hurled him down. It is definitely stated in the poem that he passes through.

wider zones that pricked his scars
With memory of the old revolt from Awe.

But this does not deter him, for the reader will observe that he goes on, fearless, to another height, where, simply, he regards the stars, and then quietly sinks to his proper place. The stars, the poet says, are "the brain of heaven." Apparently, the recognition of this fact is what conquers the impulse of the Fiend. The order of the stars demonstrates the reasonable nature of the universe, against which it is useless to rebel. One need not call on an exhibition of the divine powers, the poet is saying, to conquer the impulse of anarchy and rebellion; the slightest understanding of the construction of the universe is enough. The perception of the stars, or of any other item of the ordered universe, not only may comfort man by assuring him that the universe in which he lives is a reasonable one, but may at the same time rebuke his pride, as it rebukes Lucifer, and may teach man humility.

We must remember that the meaning of a poem is not communicated by any single element of a poem—by the statements, symbols, or rhythms. We may say that the meaning of a poem is the result of all of these. We have seen earlier that a poet, for instance, does not merely put an idea into a verse form; he expects the verse to serve as part of the expression of the poem, for, otherwise, there would be no purpose in using verse at all. In this particular poem one can indicate some of the features of the verse that contribute to the total expression of the theme. The poem may be scanned as follows:

1. On a | starred night | Prince Lu | cifer | uprose.
2. Tired of | his dark | domin | ion swung | the fiend
3. Above | the rol | ling ball | in cloud | part screened,
4. Where sin | ners hug | their spec | ter of | repose.
5. Poor prey | to his | hot fit | of pride | were those.
6. And now | upon | his wes | tern wing | he leaned,
7. Now his | huge bulk | o'er Af | ric's sands | careened,
8. Now the | black plan | et shad | owed Arc | tic snows.
9. Soaring | through wi | der zones | that pricked | his scars
10. With mem | ories of | the old | revolt | from Awe,
11. He reached | a mid | dle height, | and at | the stars,
12. Which are | the brain | of heav | en, he looked, | and sank.
13. Around | the an | cient track | marched, rank | on rank,
14. The ar | my of | unal | tera | ble law.

One can observe that the relatively regular and heavy beat of the verse, the preponderance of monosyllables and secondary accents making for a retarded movement, and the many end-stop lines with light caesura support the impression of ponderous, sullen majesty which the image of Lucifer inspires.* But there are some more special details that are worthy of notice. The relative absence of heavy internal pauses in the lines makes such pauses come, by contrast, with a special emphasis. The first one appears in line 11 to give an emphatic preparation for the "stars," the word that raises the fundamental idea of the poem. In line 12 the pauses set off "he looked," and "and sank" so that the pauses contribute to the impression of Lucifer's taking a long and thoughtful inspection of the firmament and then slowly descending. In line 13 the fourth foot of the line is composed of the words *marched, rank,* but the foot gives a spondaic effect, because of the secondary accent, which occurs elsewhere as in the second foot, *black plan-* of line 8. This fact and the preparatory pause before *rank* give a powerful emphasis. In line 14 the most important idea, in fact, the most important idea of the poem, is contained in the word *unalterable.* This word is composed of five syllables. It is two syllables longer than any other in the poem, standing in contrast to the prevailing use of monosyllables. It is divided *un-al-ter-a-ble.* The accent falls on the second syllable, *al,* and the last three syllables tend to be slurred together. But in the iambic pentameter line in which the word appears in the poem, two of the regular metrical beats fall on syllables of the word:

un-ál-ter-á-ble.

This means that the entire word is given more force than is usual; and this is effective, because of the importance of the word in relation to the subject of the poem.

Concerning another technical factor Chard Powers Smith writes:

> Spoken sounds fall naturally into certain groups, the members of each group arising from approximately the same location in the vocal apparatus. In utterance, even in the silent utterance of reading to one's self, the sounds

* Of the 111 words in the poem 86 are monosyllables, 3 are trisyllables, and the rest, with the exception of *unalterable,* are disyllables. There are only two run-on lines, and only four cases of internal punctuation.

within any one group *feel* alike because the same vocal muscles come into play. It is upon this kinetic basis that assonance rests, quite as much as upon the actual auditory quality of words; it is upon this basis that the sensed similarity of sounds may be most easily explained. Intuitively we feel, for instance, that such a line as this is musically all of a piece:

The army of unalterable law.

The reason is that the principal vowel sounds—the *a* in "army," the first *a* in "unalterable" and the *a* in "law," along with the unimportant vowel sound in "of," all arise in the same region of the throat, while the *u*, second *a* and terminal *e* of "unalterable" arise from an adjoining region; and the dominant consonants—*r*, *m*, *n*, and *l*—are likewise all members of a single assonance group.

It will be observed in the line quoted, as in all cases, that it is the stressed syllables that dominate phonetically in any passage, those syllables that receive emphasis in normal prose utterance—quite independent of prosodic scansion. . . . In the line just quoted we may capitalize these stressed syllables, as follows:

the ARMy of UNALterable LAW.

These are the sounds which, made emphatic by the sense, are most intrusive and which, consequently, give the line its phonetic flavor. According as they do or do not fall into the same assonance group, according, that is, as they are or are not repetitions and variations in the same rhythms of sound, the passage is or is not musical in the present sense. Compared to these syllables, all the rest are of secondary importance.*

EXERCISE

1. What is the effect of metrical accent on the preposition *at* in line 11?

2. Compare Meredith's use of the stars as a symbol of order here with Eliot's use of them as a symbol of wearisome routine in "Preludes" (p. 112).

* *Pattern and Variation in Poetry*, New York, Charles Scribner's Sons, 1932, pp. 57–58.

1887

A. E. Housman [*1859–1936*]

From Clee to heaven the beacon burns,
  The shires have seen it plain,
From north and south the sign returns
  And beacons burn again.

Look left, look right, the hills are bright,
  The dales are light between,
Because 'tis fifty years tonight
  That God has saved the Queen.

Now, when the flame they watch not towers
  About the soil they trod,
Lads, we'll remember friends of ours
  Who shared the work with God.

To skies that knit their heartstrings right,
  To fields that bred them brave,
The saviors come not home tonight:
  Themselves they could not save.

It dawns in Asia, tombstones show
  And Shropshire names are read;
And the Nile spills his overflow
  Beside the Severn's dead.

We pledge in peace by farm and town
  The Queen they served in war,
And fire the beacons up and down
  The land they perished for.

"God save the Queen" we living sing,
  From height to height 'tis heard;
And with the rest your voices ring,
  Lads of the Fifty-third.

Oh, God will save her, fear you not:
  Be you the men you've been,
Get you the sons your fathers got,
  And God will save the Queen.

EXERCISE

This poem has to do with the celebration of the fiftieth year of Queen Victoria's reign. The second stanza provides a kind of key to the speaker's attitude. The beacons are lighted up and down the land and the people are singing

> Because 'tis fifty years tonight
>   That God has saved the Queen.

The last line comes with some shock: "God save the Queen (or King)" is a ritualistic phrase, a phrase grammatically petrified, as it were; and we are momentarily disconcerted at its being fitted into a matter-of-fact statement, with the change of tense and the other normal syntactical adjustments. The poet wants the shock; but the effect of the shock here is not playful but sobering. The rest of the poem is devoted to working out the implications of this wrenching of the phrase from its conventional context. Indeed, the poem may be described as a realistic and ironic examination of the real meanings of a phrase, usually so glibly and unthinkingly uttered.

Try to work out in detail some of the implications of this view of the poem.

Elegy

Written in a Country Churchyard

Thomas Gray [*1716–1771*]

The Curfew tolls the knell of parting day,
  The lowing herd wind slowly o'er the lea,
The plowman homeward plods his weary way,
  And leaves the world to darkness and to me.

Now fades the glimmering landscape on the sight,
  And all the air a solemn stillness holds,
Save where the beetle wheels his droning flight,
  And drowsy tinklings lull the distant folds;

Save that from yonder ivy-mantled tower
  The moping owl does to the moon complain
Of such, as wandering near her secret bower,
  Molest her ancient solitary reign.

Beneath those rugged elms, that yew-trees's shade,
  Where heaves the turf in many a mould'ring heap,
Each in his narrow cell for ever laid,
  The rude Forefathers of the hamlet sleep.

The breezy call of incense-breathing Morn,
  The swallow twitt'ring from the straw-built shed,
The cock's shrill clarion, or the echoing horn,
  No more shall rouse them from their lowly bed.

For them no more the blazing hearth shall burn,
  Or busy housewife ply her evening care:
No children run to lisp their sire's return,
  Or climb his knees the envied kiss to share.

Oft did the harvest to their sickle yield,
  Their furrow oft the stubborn glebe has broke;
How jocund did they drive their team afield!
  How bowed the woods beneath their sturdy stroke!

Let not Ambition mock their useful toil,
  Their homely joys, and destiny obscure;
Nor Grandeur hear with a disdainful smile
  The short and simple annals of the poor.

The boast of heraldry, the pomp of power,
  And all that beauty, all that wealth e'er gave,
Awaits alike th' inevitable hour.
  The paths of glory lead but to the grave.

Nor you, ye Proud, impute to These the fault,
  If Memory o'er their Tomb no Trophies raise,
Where through the long-drawn aisle and fretted vault
  The pealing anthem swells the note of praise.

Can storied urn or animated bust
  Back to its mansion call the fleeting breath?
Can Honor's voice provoke the silent dust,
  Or Flattery sooth the dull cold ear of Death?

Perhaps in this neglected spot is laid
  Some heart once pregnant with celestial fire;
Hands, that the rod of empire might have swayed,
  Or waked to ecstasy the living lyre.

But Knowledge to their eyes her ample page
  Rich with the spoils of time did ne'er unroll;
Chill Penury repressed their noble rage,
  And froze the genial current of the soul.

Full many a gem of purest ray serene,
  The dark unfathomed caves of ocean bear:
Full many a flower is born to blush unseen,
  And waste its sweetness on the desert air.

Some village-Hampden, that with dauntless breast
  The little Tyrant of his fields withstood;
Some mute inglorious Milton here may rest,
  Some Cromwell guiltless of his country's blood.

Th' applause of list'ning senates to command
  The threats of pain and ruin to despise,
To scatter plenty o'er a smiling land,
  And read their history in a nation's eyes,

Their lot forbade: nor circumscribed alone
  Their growing virtues, but their crimes confined;
Forbade to wade through slaughter to a throne,
  And shut the gates of mercy on mankind,

The struggling pangs of conscious truth to hide,
  To quench the blushes of ingenuous shame,
Or heap the shrine of Luxury and Pride
  With incense kindled at the Muse's flame.

Far from the madding crowd's ignoble strife,
  Their sober wishes never learned to stray;
Along the cool sequestered vale of life
  They kept the noiseless tenor of their way.

Yet ev'n these bones from insult to protect,
  Some frail memorial still erected nigh,
With uncouth rhymes and shapeless sculpture decked,
  Implores the passing tribute of a sigh.

Their name, their years, spelt by th' unlettered muse,
  The place of fame and elegy supply:
And many a holy text around she strews,
  That teach the rustic moralist to die.

For who to dumb Forgetfulness a prey,
  This pleasing anxious being e'er resigned,
Left the warm precincts of the cheerful day,
  Nor cast one longing ling'ring look behind?

On some fond breast the parting soul relies,
  Some pious drops the closing eye requires;
Ev'n from the tomb the voice of Nature cries,
  Ev'n in our Ashes live their wonted Fires.

For thee, who mindful of th' unhonored Dead
  Dost in these lines their artless tale relate,
If chance, by lonely contemplation led,
  Some kindred Spirit shall inquire thy fate,

Haply some hoary-headed Swain may say,
  "Oft have we seen him at the peep of dawn
Brushing with hasty steps the dews away
  To meet the sun upon the upland lawn.

"There at the foot of yonder nodding beech
  That wreathes its old fantastic roots so high,
His listless length at noontide would he stretch,
  And pore upon the brook that babbles by.

"Hard by yon wood, now smiling as in scorn,
  Mutt'ring his wayward fancies he would rove,
Now drooping, woeful wan, like one forlorn,
  Or crazed with care, or crossed in hopeless love.

"One morn I missed him on the customed hill,
  Along the heath and near his favorite tree;
Another came; nor yet beside the rill,
  Nor up the lawn, nor at the wood was he;

"The next with dirges due in sad array
  Slow through the church-way path we saw him borne.
Approach and read (for thou can'st read) the lay,
  Graved on the stone beneath yon agèd thorn."

THE EPITAPH

Here rests his head upon the lap of earth
  A youth to fortune and to fame unknown.
Fair Science frowned not on his humble birth,
  And Melancholy marked him for her own.

Large was his bounty, and his soul sincere,
Heaven did a recompense as largely send:
He gave to Misery all he had, a tear,
He gained from Heaven ('twas all he wished) a friend.

No farther seek his merits to disclose,
Or draw his frailties from their dread abode,
(There they alike in trembling hope repose)
The bosom of his Father and his God.

EXERCISE

This poem may be said to be, among other things, a speculation upon the proper place to be buried. The speaker contemplates the country churchyard where those are buried whose fortune entitled them to no more glorious grave. He compares with these humble graves the tombs of the rich and the famous as he imagines them standing in some great abbey church. As for himself, though "Fair Science frowned not on his humble birth," and he might have aspired to the rich abbey tomb, he chooses to be buried among "th' unhonored Dead."

1. Is the speaker saying that the villagers lack all vanity? Does he sentimentalize their innocence? Is he patronizing in his attitude toward them? If you are inclined to answer no, indicate your reasons with specific reference to the text of the poem.

2. Personification is frequently regarded as a weak and frigid device. Are the personifications effective in this poem? Or are they, as Coleridge complained of some personifications, simply abstract qualities spelled with a capital letter? What about Ambition, Grandeur, and Memory?

3. What is the nature of irony in lines 41–44? What is the special force of *animated?* Of *provoke?* Of *south?*

4. In line 4 the speaker refers to himself in the first person (*me*). In line 93 he seems to refer to himself in the second person (*thee*). Can you account for the shift, or if not, determine the person referred to as "thee"?

5. This poem makes a number of general statements about life. Are these statements insisted upon in isolation? Or do they grow out of the dramatic context of the poem?

6. Investigate the meanings of "homely joys" (line 30), "am-

mated bust" (line 41), "pleasing anxious being" (line 86), and "artless tale" (line 94). How are the meanings and submeanings related in the context?

If Poisonous Minerals

John Donne [*1573–1631*]

If poisonous minerals, and if that tree
Whose fruit threw death on else immortal us,
If lecherous goats, if serpents envious
Cannot be damned, Alas! why should I be?
Why should intent or reason, born in me,
Make sins, else equal, in me more heinous?
And mercy being easy, and glorious
To God, in his stern wrath why threatens he?
But who am I, that dare dispute with thee,
O God? O! of thine only worthy blood,
And my tears, make a heavenly Lethean flood,
And drown in it my sin's black memory;
That thou remember them, some claim as debt,
I think it mercy, if thou wilt forget.

The theme of this poem may be put as a question: What should be the attitude of sinful man toward God's justice? The theme is presented by a method quite different from that employed in "Lucifer in Starlight," in which the idea appears in terms of an obvious dramatic incident. Here no incident, no narrative element, appears directly. But this poem is, in one sense, dramatic in that, being a prayer, it is addressed by a sin-convicted man to God, and has therefore a special speaker and a special listener and is not merely a general thought or speculation. Being dramatic, it involves a special instance. But the handling of the idea is direct, in the form of argument. The question, then, is: How does the poet invest this argument with the emotional force necessary to poetic effect?

The argument may be briefly summarized as follows: Although it appears unjust that man, merely because he possesses the faculty of reason, should be damned for actions common to lower Nature and unpunished there, man should realize that God's treatment is not to be understood by human reason, and should therefore seek the remission of his sins through the double force of Christ's blood and his own repentance. This is a flat prose statement using none of the imaginative resources that can vivify language with poetic force. This statement, as prose, has an interest, not because of the form in which it is put, but because the idea it involves is a serious one in human experience. But as it stands, the reader must supply, by such application as his own imagination affords, the emotional force. One cannot say, however, that the seriousness of the theme of this poem permits the poet to employ successfully a more direct presentation through argument than is characteristic of most poems; for the theme of all effective poetry has, in some degree, a serious reference to human experience. Even such a poem as Herrick's "Delight in Disorder" (p. 258) which shows a playful or fanciful surface effect, has a concealed bearing on important elements of human life. In Donne's poem, then, the success of the more direct presentation of the idea is still dependent upon the way in which it is handled, on the total organization and structure of the poem, and not on the mere seriousness or importance of the idea as such.

We should study, then, the way in which the idea is handled and try to define some of the devices.

In the first paragraph, in comparing the poem with "Lucifer in Starlight," we said that it does, as a prayer, an address from a man to God, have a certain dramatic context. This dramatic effect is heightened in various incidental ways. First, the *octave* (*Note on Versification*) is composed of three questions, in an ascending order. A question is more provocative than a statement. This is especially true when the linking, as in this case, creates a kind of suspense, rising to a climax with

> . . . in his stern wrath why threatens he?

Then this is answered in the beginning of the sestet, not by a statement, but by another question:

> But who am I, that dare dispute with thee?

Second, the exclamatory effects, which occur twice in the poem, serve to heighten the dramatic quality. A poet must be very careful in using exclamation, for it frequently strikes the reader as an arbitrary attempt to force him to respond; the poet must, that is, be careful of the context and of preparation for his use of exclamation. But observe in this poem how the preparation has been made. The first case occurs in the fourth line with the word "Alas!" Let us shift the use to see what change would follow:

> Alas! if poisonous minerals and that tree.

Or, perhaps a better version:

> Alas! if poisonous minerals, if that tree.

In such cases the exclamation merely serves as a signal to the reader that the poet intends something important, and unless what follows does fulfill that promise, the reader feels cheated. Even if the reader feels that the exclamation is justified by what follows, such a use is essentially undramatic because unprepared for. By contrast observe how Donne introduces the exclamatory word just after the idea of damnation has been given, and just before that idea receives a personal application:

> . . . if serpents envious
> Cannot be damned, Alas! why should I be?

It is as though the cry were wrung from some one by the sudden full awareness of the meaning of damnation. The same principle is applied in the second instance. The cry "O God? O!" occurs at the point where the thought of the sonnet turns. The first line of the sestet has just stated that human reason cannot question God. It marks the moment when the man ceases to reason about God's justice and question it, and pleads that the memory of his sin be drowned in Christ's blood and the tears of repentance. In both cases, the use of the exclamation is psychologically justified, and is therefore dramatic.

Third, the idea is worked out in a series of contrasts, a device that, as we have seen, is often used to heighten interest. In the first four lines the lower creation is contrasted with man on the grounds of guilt—the mineral, vegetable, and animal kingdoms as distinguished from man. In the fifth and sixth lines the contrast is made on the grounds of the possession of reason. But these lines also imply a paradox: reason, which presumably is given man to raise him from the brute, is the source of his damnation, which even the brute cannot suffer. In the seventh and eighth lines there is the opposition of God's mercy and God's wrath. In the ninth line, human reason is contrasted with divine justice. In the tenth, eleventh, and twelfth lines, the climax, the method of argument is abandoned, and the man throws himself on the promise of redemption. But in the concluding couplet the whole poem is again summarized with a contrast: though some men, the poet says, have hoped for salvation by praying that God remember them, he himself, reflecting on his sinful state, hopes for salvation by a divine forgetfulness.

All of these devices for heightening the effect of the poem depend on the detailed working out of the idea, that is, on the relating of the logical structure to the psychological and emotional effect desired by the poet. (We can see that such devices are somewhat different from devices such as narrative incident, symbol, simile, and metaphor. This poem makes no use, in fact, of narrative incident to embody its theme, as does "Johnie Armstrong," and it seems peculiarly bare of simile and metaphor, which are so important in most poetry.) But there are still other ways in which the poet has heightened his statement of the idea. He does not give his contrast between man and the lower creation in general terms, but introduces the idea with concrete instances, "poisonous minerals," "that tree whose fruit threw death," "lecherous goats," and "serpents envious." By taking this approach he has put the reader's imagination to work; the objects named served to symbolize the idea to a certain extent. Though, as we have said, the poem is peculiarly bare of metaphor, the major metaphor in the poem is very violent and powerful. It seems that the poet, feeling the effectiveness of such a device, has reserved it for his climax, introducing it to focus the idea just stated. The image of the blood of Christ and the tears of the penitent combining to make a flood is very bold, and especially bold in contrast with the more direct method characteristic of the octave.

Let us return now to consider the versification. We may scan the poem as follows:

> If poi | sonous min | erals, | and if | that tree
> Whose fruit | threw death | on else | immor | tal us,
> If lech | erous goats, | if ser | pents en | vious

Cannot | be damned, | Alas! | why should | I be?
Why should | intent | or rea | son, born | in me,
Make sins, | else e | qual, in | me more | heinous?
And mer | cy be | ing eas | y, and glo | rious
To God, | in his | stern wrath | why threat | ens he?
But who | am I | that dare | dispute | with thee,
O God? | O! of | thine on | ly wor | thy blood
And my | tears, make | a heav | enly Le | thean flood,
And drown | in it | my sin's | black mem | ory;
That thou | remem | ber them, | some claim | as debt,
I think | it mer | cy, if | thou wilt | forget.

The poem opens with a calm, logical tone; that is, not with a burst of feeling or excitement, but with the conditional "if," which sets up a logical expectation. The meter of the first four feet of the first line is, appropriately, regular,* and the unaccented syllables are very light and at about the same level. But with the last foot of the first line,

that tree,

we have a sudden emphasis with the accentuation of *that*.

In the first two feet of the second line we find the same kind of emphasis, and in addition, the three forced pauses between *whose* and *fruit, fruit* and *threw,* and *threw* and *death*. In other words, the realization of the terrible event in the Garden is supported by the heavy retardation of rhythm and the general cacophony. However, as the thought turns from the terror of the Fall to the wistful "on else immortal us," the meter slips into an easy regularity, with the light syllables very light and even. We have, as it were, a tension and a release, a retardation and a flow.

In the third line the thin, tight texture and the hissing ejective *s*'s associate with the serpent (see comment on "No More Be Grieved," p. 166). The clipped meter of the line is changed

* We may say that the second foot, -sonous min-, is an anapaest, but it is a very light one, readily slurred or absorbed.

to the spondaic, retarded rhythm of line 4. We may glance particularly at the last two feet:

why should I be?

Here rhetorical consideration would accent *why* and *I,* but meter would accent *should* and *be.* Since *be* is a rhyme word, it must have an accent, and we cannot resolve the matter by a trochee. This tension and uncertainty in the accentuation points up the agonized question on which the quatrain concludes.

With the beginning of the second quatrain there is a return to the calm, logical tone, and to a regular meter, but with line 6, as the urgency of the problem begins to return, the spondaic distortions again appear. We may notice also how the meter "spreads" and emphasizes *heinous,* the meter forcing an accent on the normally unaccented second syllable (see the discussion of the word *consecrate* in "Rose Aylmer," p. 143). The first three feet of the next line are regular; then with the last two feet we get a strong, lifting effect. The anapaest

-y, and glo-

cuts across the units of phrasing,* the word *glorious* is spread to receive two metrical accents, and the last phrase runs over the end of the line to fulfill itself in the first foot of the next line. Then the triumphant thrust of the phrase "and glorious / To God," is broken, as it were, against the heavy, spondaic passage

in his stern wrath why threatens he?

The first line of the sestet falls again into a regular movement, as the tension is resolved momentarily into the speaker's

* We may indicate the phrasing by the loops above the line, and the foot grouping by the loops below:

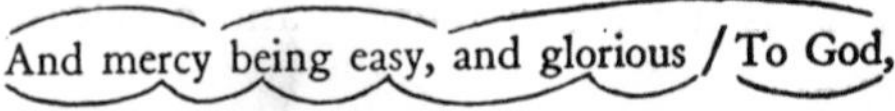
And mercy being easy, and glorious / To God,

The metrical pull has to re-establish itself by absorbing the *y* of *easy* and the pause at the end of the phrase, and the overcoming of this resistance increases the emphasis. (See the comment on the word *young* in line 7 of "Speech After Long Silence," p. 165.) We may notice, too, how the second foot, -ў bé-, is rhetorically almost absorbed into the third foot, and how this fact tends to emphasize further the word *glorious.*

resignation. This resignation, however, is interrupted by the cry,

// / //
O God? O!

with its massed accentuation, which falls away then into regularity. In the last four lines the regularity is interrupted only four times, with

// /
tears, make,

// /
black mem-,

// /
some claim,

and

// /
I think.

The logic of the emphasis is, in each instance, obvious. Throughout the passage, as the poem subsides to its conclusion in resignation to God's will, the meter is regular with an even level of accentuation.

We can see that in general, part of line against part of line, or line against line, the poem shows the principle of contrast between acceleration and retardation, lightness and weight, release and tension, and that the contrasts are associated with and emphasize the content. That is, the technical features of the poem help to dramatize the idea and give depth to the feeling.

Thou Art Indeed Just, Lord

Gerard Manley Hopkins [*1844–1889*]

Justus quidem tu es, Domine, si disputem tecum: verumtamen justa loquar ad te: Quare via impiorum prosperatur?

Thou art indeed just, Lord, if I contend
With thee; but, sir, so what I plead is just.
Why do sinners' ways prosper? And why must
Disappointment all I endeavor end?
Wert thou my enemy, O thou my friend,
How wouldst thou worse, I wonder, than thou dost
Defeat, thwart me? Oh, the sots and thralls of lust

Do in spare hours more thrive than I that spend,
Sir, life upon thy cause. See, banks and brakes
Now, leavèd how thick! lacèd they are again
With fretty chervil, look, and fresh wind shakes
Them; birds build—but not I build; no, but strain,
Time's eunuch, and not breed one work that wakes.
Mine, O thou lord of life, send my roots rain.

EXERCISE

1. This, like the previous poem, is a prayer—and a debate with God on the question of His justice. Summarize the debate in your own words. What is the place in the argument of the reference to the "banks and brakes"?

2. With reference to the discussion of the previous poem, write a short essay showing how the poet dramatizes his argument, with special attention to technical factors such as meter, rhythm, alliteration, and so on. How, for instance, is the rhythm of the last line related to the tone, and thus to the final meaning of the poem?

After Apple-Picking

Robert Frost [*1874–1963*]

My long two-pointed ladder's sticking through a tree
Toward heaven still,
And there's a barrel that I didn't fill
Beside it, and there may be two or three
Apples I didn't pick upon some bough.
But I am done with apple-picking now.
Essence of winter sleep is on the night,
The scent of apples: I am drowsing off.
I cannot rub the strangeness from my sight
I got from looking through a pane of glass
I skimmed this morning from the drinking trough
And held against the world of hoary grass.
It melted, and I let it fall and break.
But I was well
Upon my way to sleep before it fell,
And I could tell

What form my dreaming was about to take.
Magnified apples appear and disappear,
Stem end and blossom end,
And every fleck of russet showing clear.
My instep arch not only keeps the ache,
It keeps the pressure of a ladder-round.
I feel the ladder sway as the boughs bend.
And I keep hearing from the cellar bin
The rumbling sound
Of load on load of apples coming in.
For I have had too much
Of apple-picking: I am overtired
Of the great harvest I myself desired.
There were ten thousand thousand fruit to touch,
Cherish in hand, lift down, and not let fall.
For all
That struck the earth,
No matter if not bruised or spiked with stubble,
Went surely to the cider-apple heap
As of no worth.
One can see what will trouble
This sleep of mine, whatever sleep it is.
Were he not gone,
The woodchuck could say whether it's like his
Long sleep, as I describe its coming on,
Or just some human sleep.

As a realistic account of apple-picking in New England, this poem yields a great deal. The student may well feel that there is little to be gained by going beyond that reading. The poem is an admirable piece of description; the farmer who speaks the poem is simply "overtired" and turns away with a bit of whimsical humor and with an honest weariness to thoughts of sleep.

But as we have already found, a really fine piece of even "realistic" description—a piece of description that engages our feelings and stirs our imaginations—tends to generate symbolic overtones. Such a description is more than an account of physical objects: it suggests, if only vaguely, further experiences. All of this is true of "After Apple-Picking." Furthermore, a second glance at the poem reveals elements that cannot be readily accommodated to a merely realistic reading of the poem. The first of these elements obtrudes itself in line 7. Up to that point everything *may* be taken at the literal descriptive level.

With line 7 we are forced to consider nonrealistic readings. For one thing, and merely as a kind of preliminary, the word *essence* comes strangely into the poem. It is not the kind of everyday, ordinary word characteristic of the vocabulary of the previous part of the poem. We may have observed how sometimes in poetry the unusual word, unusual in the context if not absolutely, may be a signal, a sign-post.* But what of the word here? Here the word *essence* most readily brings in the notion of some sort of perfume, some sort of distillate; but it also involves the philosophical meaning of something permanent and eternal, of some necessary element or substance. The word *scent* (as contrasted with synonyms such as odor or smell) supports the first idea in *essence,* but the other meanings are there, too, with their philosophical weighting; and the assonance makes a further tie, suggestive and subtle. The scent of apples is a valuable perfume, as it were, but it is also to be associated in some significant way with the "winter sleep." Does the poet merely mean to say that the odor of apples, in a quite literal way, is a characteristic of the harvest season? It *is* a characteristic odor, but the word *essence* hints at something more fundamental.

We notice that a colon comes after the phrase "scent of apples" to introduce the statement, "I am drowsing off." The scent of apples, as it were, puts to sleep the harvester. The next line implies that this is scarcely a normal, literal sleep. The sleep, in fact, had begun that morning with a "strangeness" got from looking through the pane of ice. So somehow the scent of apples and the strangeness of the ice-view combine to produce the "winter sleep."

Then comes the dream. It is true that when we are over-

* In "Preludes," by T. S. Eliot (p. 112), we find a good example of this. In Part II, the word *masquerades* stands out in contrast to the very ordinary vocabulary of the preceding and surrounding parts of the poem. It stands out even more when regarded in its phrase—"the other masquerades / That time resumes," an arresting metaphor coming suddenly in a poem that thus far had presented no obviously metaphorical elements. And so in Part III with the metaphor involving the "sordid images" of which the woman's soul is "constituted." In the same section the word *vision* comes with a certain shock. And it, too, is a key word: we must understand the nature of the woman's "vision" in order to understand the poem.

tired we tend to repeat in dream the activity that has caused the fatigue, as when after driving all day one sees the road still coming at him. There is thus a realistic psychological basis for the nature of this dream, but at the same time we must remember that the dream had been previsioned that morning, and dreams that are literal in a literal world don't begin that way.

So even before we have got through the poem we are forewarned that it is not to be taken literally, even in the way that Frost's "Desert Places" (p. 104) can be taken literally. In that poem, for example, all the details are in their own right directly descriptive of nature; the snow falling into the dark field does become a kind of metaphorical rendering of the observer's loneliness in the world, but it also remains literal. But the details of "After Apple-Picking" are not like this: they are constantly implying a kind of fantasy.

To go back and take a fresh start with the poem, we see a set of contrasts gradually developing: the world of summer and the world of winter; the world of labor and the world of rest; the world of effort and the world of reward; the world of wakefulness and the world of sleep; the world of ordinary vision and the world distorted by the ice-view; the world of fact and the world of dream. And we understand that these various pairs are various aspects of a single contrast. But a contrast of what? A contrast of two views of experience, of the world in general, of life, if you will. In other words, we take a broad, simple, generalized view of apple-picking and harvest—the end of some human effort in the real world, which is followed by reward, rest, dream. To go one step further, we may say that the contrast is between the actual and the ideal. Now we can look back at the very beginning of the poem and see that what appeared to be but a casual, literal detail—the ladder sticking through a tree—initiates this line of meaning. The ladder is pointing "Toward heaven still." It points, not toward the sky or even the heavens, words that carry merely a literal meaning and in this context would merely say that the ladder was pointing upward; but toward *heaven,* the place of man's rewards, the home of his aspirations, the deposit of perfection and ideal values.

At this point it may be objected that to associate the dream in the poem with the ideal is a peculiar thing, for the dream seems to be a bad dream, a nightmare of the day's labor. But is the dream a nightmare? The poet, it is true, says that he has had too much of apple-picking and is "overtired." He knows that his sleep will be "troubled," and knows that the instep arch will keep the ache of the ladder-round. Over against these explicit statements, however, we must put the quality of the passage taken as a whole.

We start with the description of the apples:

> Magnified apples appear and disappear,
> Stem end and blossom end,
> And every fleck of russet showing clear.

The apples of reality had been a "good"; now in dream the apples become magnified. Furthermore, though the apples of reality had been a good, they had been a good in a practical sense; now in the dream they come as a good for contemplation—we see them bigger than life, every aspect, stem end and blossom end, every tiny fleck of russet. In the dream there is emancipation from the pressure of work; there can be appreciation of the object as object. Let us consider the words *russet* and *clear*. They are smuggling some kind of plus-value into the dream. *Russet* carries an agreeable, decorative, poetical flavor, and *clear* has all sorts of vague connotations of the desirable, opposed to the turgid, the murky, the dirty, the impure, the confused, and the like. Suppose we paraphrase the line:

> And every spot of brown now visible.

We have lost the plus-quality, the sense of the desirable in the apples.

To proceed with the passage, if the ache of the instep arch remains, there is also the line

> I feel the ladder sway as the boughs bend.

The experience described may be taken in itself as an agreeable one, and in addition the line is euphonius and delicately expressive. Notice how the swoop of the anapaest *as the boughs* is caught by the solid monosyllabic foot *bend,* and brought, as it were, safely to rest. Also notice that though the first three feet are regularly iambic,

> Ĭ féel | thĕ lád | dĕr swáy | ,

the phrase "the ladder" gives a kind of sweeping, then falling, movement across the iambic structure, a movement which, again, is brought to rest by an accented monosyllable, "sway." So the rhythmic structure of the line falls into two parts, each with a sweep brought to rest.

Then we have the sound of apples rumbling into the cellar bin. Is this part of a nightmare or of a good dream? We can say that the sound may "trouble" the sleep, but at the same time we must remember that the sound was the signal of the completion of labor, the accomplishing of the harvest. So it brings over into the dream the plus-value of reality. This is not to deny, necessarily, the negative aspect, the troubling effect. It is merely to affirm that both elements are present.

Immediately after the poet has said that he is overtired because there were "ten thousand thousand" fruit to handle, he uses the word *cherish.* This word, too, smuggles a plus-value into the dream. If the picking was labor, it was a loving labor, not a labor simply for practical reward. It is true that the word is applied to the work in the real world and not to the dream, but it appears in the context of the dream and colors the dream.

We may conclude, then, that though the dream does carry over the fatigue of the real world it also carries over its satisfactions in a magnified form, satisfactions now freed from the urgencies of practical effort—the apples may now be contemplated in their fullness of being. The ideal—if we have accepted the whole cluster of notions on one side of the contrast to amount to that—is not to be understood as something distinct from the actual, from man's literal, experience in the literal world. Rather, it is to be understood as a projection, a development, of the literal experience. When the poet picks his apples he gets his practical reward of apples and gets the satisfaction of a job well done, the fulfillment of his energies and ambitions. But the rest, the reward, the heaven, the dream that come after labor, all repeat, on a grander scale, the nature of the labor. This is not to be taken as a curse, but as a blessing. The dream, as we have seen, is not a nightmare.

We have not yet finished the poem. We still must account for the woodchuck. We notice that here the poet is still working with a contrast, the contrast between the woodchuck's sleep and "just some human sleep." The woodchuck's sleep will be dreamless and untroubled. The woodchuck is simply a part of the nature from which man is set apart. The woodchuck toils not, neither does he dream. Man does work and does dream. He is "troubled," but the trouble is exactly what makes him human and superior to the woodchuck. The word *just,* in the phrase "just some human sleep," gives a faintly ironical understatement to the notion of man's superiority, but this is merely whimsical, a way, not of denying the fact of man's superiority, but of avoiding the embarrassment of making a grandiose claim. It is appropriate that a poem which states the real as the necessary context for the ideal, should not end by making a grandiose claim; the whimsical understatement is a way of indicating a continuing awareness of the real as context of the ideal—of the natural as context of the human.

Some readers may be inclined to say that we have pushed matters too far. They are willing, perhaps, to admit that the poem is not to be taken with absolute literalness. They say that the poem is not merely about apple-picking, but is about life and death as imaged in a set of contrasts: summer-winter; labor-rest; ordinary view and the view seen through the pane of ice. They go on to say that the dream is an image for life-after-death, and indicates the kind of immortality the poet expects and/or wants. They support this notion by reference to the word *heaven* in the second line, and perhaps to the contrast between man and woodchuck (the woodchuck does not dream, that is, is not immortal).

This reading is still too literal. It takes the ideas of heaven and immortality at their face value, and does not comprehend the broad basic theme. It is true that *if* the poet did believe in immortality, he would by the logic of this poem want an immortality like the dream, and would recognize a continuity between this world and the next. It is conceivable, to be sure, that the poet does accept the idea of immortality, but there is no evidence in the poem that he does (nor, as a matter of fact, elsewhere in Frost's work). And even if the poet did accept the idea of immortality, that fact would not limit the theme; it would in itself be but *one application of the theme,* one illustration of it. All sorts of other applications of the basic idea which is the theme would still exist in relation to the human life of the here and now, a life involving both the real and the ideal.

What would be some of the other and more secular applications of the root-idea or fundamental attitude of the poem? The idea would apply to any ideal that man sets up for himself. An ideal to be valid must stem from the real world, and must not violate it or deny it. For instance, a certain theory of poetry, or of any of the other arts, is implied here. By this theory, poetry should develop from, and treat of, ordinary experience; it should reflect life and the needs and activities of life—it should present the apples magnified, but yet as apples. Or a theory of morality is implied: the ideal of conduct should not deny the human but should fulfill the human. Or a theory of labor and reward is there: reward and labor should not be distinct, the reward coming after, and distinct from, the labor; the reward should be in fulfillment through the labor.

These examples are intended merely to point us back into the poem, to the central impulse and root-idea of the poem. It is a root-idea that we can find developed in certain other poems by Frost, and lying behind many more. For instance, let us take the following one:

Mowing

There was never a sound beside the wood but one,
And that was my long scythe whispering to the ground.
What was it it whispered? I knew not well myself;
Perhaps it was something about the heat of the sun,
Something, perhaps, about the lack of sound—
And that was why it whispered and did not speak.
It was no dream of the gift of idle hours,
Or easy gold at the hand of fay or elf:
Anything more than the truth would have seemed too weak
To the earnest love that laid the swale in rows,
Not without feeble-pointed spikes of flowers
(Pale orchises), and scared a bright green snake.
The fact is the sweetest dream that labor knows.
My long scythe whispered and left the hay to make.

Here the line, "The fact is the sweetest dream that labor knows," might almost be taken as a kind of summing up of "After Apple-Picking." Or we can refer to the last stanza of "Two Tramps in Mud-Time" (p. 511) where "need" and "love," and "work" and "play" take the place of the contrast between "fact" and "dream":

> But yield who will to their separation,
> My object in living is to unite
> My avocation and my vocation
> As my two eyes make one in sight.
> Only where love and need are one,
> And the work is play for mortal stakes,
> Is the deed ever really done
> For Heaven and the future's sakes.

And the same theme appears in "Stopping by Woods on a Snowy Evening" (p. 218), "Come In" (p. 495), and "Birches" (p. 371).

We see here how one poem may help to interpret other poems by the same poet. We recognize a kind of continuity in the poet's work, the presence of a basic idea which can have various formulations. With Frost, however, we have more than the interrelations among the various poems. We have also some prose statements by the author. For instance, we can see the pertinence of the following passage to the discussion of the theme of "After Apple-Picking." Here Frost is comparing his own basic attitudes to those of E. A. Robinson:

> I am not the Platonist Robinson was. By Platonist I mean one who believes what we have here is an imperfect copy of what is in heaven. The woman you have is an imperfect copy of some woman in heaven or in somebody else's bed. Many of the world's greatest—maybe all of them—have been ranged on that romantic side. I am philosophically opposed to having one Iseult for my vocation and another for my avocation. . . . Let me not sound the least bit smug. I define a difference with proper humility. A truly gallant Platonist will remain a bachelor as Robinson did from unwillingness to reduce any woman to the condition of being used without being idealized.

To summarize Frost's attitude, we may try something like this: Man is set off from nature because he is capable of the "dream," because he is an ideal-creating being (the woodchuck has no dream). But man is also of nature, he fulfills himself in the world of labor and his ideals develop from the real world; he does not get his ideals from some Platonic realm of perfect "Ideas," but must create them from his experience and imagination.

EXERCISE

1. What is the tone of the poem? The poem, as we have seen, is very rich, and deals with very serious issues. Does the poem ever become oversolemn or pompously philosophical? How has the poet avoided this? What is the function of the whimsical reference to the woodchuck in this connection?

2. Return to the poem "Mowing" quoted above and try to see how the various details are related to the theme. That is, how does the line we have taken as summarizing the poem really develop from the poem?

3. What is the significance of the word *still* in the second line of "After Apple-Picking"?

4. Turn to "Stopping by Woods on a Snowy Evening" (p. 218) and "Come In" (p. 495) and compare the use of the little horse and the bird in those poems with that made of the woodchuck in "After Apple-Picking."

Birches

Robert Frost [*1874–1963*]

When I see birches bend to left and right
Across the lines of straighter darker trees,
I like to think some boy's been swinging them.
But swinging doesn't bend them down to stay.
Ice-storms do that. Often you must have seen them
Loaded with ice a sunny winter morning
After a rain. They click upon themselves
As the breeze rises, and turn many-colored
As the stir cracks and crazes their enamel.

Soon the sun's warmth makes them shed crystal shells
Shattering and avalanching on the snow-crust—
Such heaps of broken glass to sweep away
You'd think the inner dome of heaven had fallen.
They are dragged to the withered bracken by the load,
And they seem not to break; though once they are bowed
So low for long, they never right themselves:
You may see their trunks arching in the woods
Years afterwards, trailing their leaves on the ground
Like girls on hands and knees that throw their hair
Before them over their heads to dry in the sun.
But I was going to say when Truth broke in
With all her matter-of-fact about the ice-storm
I should prefer to have some boy bend them
As he went out and in to fetch the cows—
Some boy too far from town to learn baseball,
Whose only play was what he found himself,
Summer or winter, and could play alone.
One by one he subdued his father's trees
By riding them down over and over again
Until he took the stiffness out of them,
And not one but hung limp, not one was left
For him to conquer. He learned all there was
To learn about not launching out too soon
And so not carrying the tree away
Clear to the ground. He always kept his poise
To the top branches, climbing carefully
With the same pains you use to fill a cup
Up to the brim, and even above the brim.
Then he flung outward, feet first, with a swish,
Kicking his way down through the air to the ground.
So was I once myself a swinger of birches.
And so I dream of going back to be.
It's when I'm weary of considerations,
And life is too much like a pathless wood
Where your face burns and tickles with the cobwebs
Broken across it, and one eye is weeping
From a twig's having lashed across it open.
I'd like to get away from earth awhile
And then come back to it and begin over.
May no fate willfully misunderstand me
And half grant what I wish and snatch me away
Not to return. Earth's the right place for love:

I don't know where it's likely to go better.
I'd like to go by climbing a birch tree,
And climb black branches up a snow-white trunk
Toward heaven, till the tree could bear no more,
But dipped its top and set me down again.
That would be good both going and coming back.
One could do worse than be a swinger of birches.

EXERCISE

1. Does this poem have a developing structure? It begins with description (lines 1–20), then goes on to sketch the life of the boy who swings on the birches (lines 21–40); then it proceeds to make some comments on "life." What is the relation between the parts? What is the poem about?

2. Compare this poem with "After Apple-Picking" in theme and method. Are the first forty lines necessary to the statement that this poem makes? What do these lines do specifically?

3. Why has the poet had the word *toward* (line 56) printed in italic? In what senses does the speaker insist upon this word?

4. What variations of tone do we find in this poem? Does it contain humor, whimsy, serious comment?

5. Robert Frost has written (p. 524) that " 'Birches' is two fragments soldered together so long I have forgotten where the joint is." Can you locate the joint?

Dover Beach

Matthew Arnold [*1822–1888*]

The sea is calm tonight,
The tide is full, the moon lies fair
Upon the straits;—on the French coast the light
Gleams and is gone; the cliffs of England stand,
Glimmering and vast, out in the tranquil bay.
Come to the window, sweet is the night-air!
Only, from the long line of spray
Where the sea meets the moon-blanched land,
Listen! you hear the grating roar
Of pebbles which the waves draw back, and fling,
At their return, up the high strand,

Begin, and cease, and then again begin,
With tremulous cadence slow, and bring
The eternal note of sadness in.

Sophocles long ago
Heard it on the Aegean, and it brought
Into his mind the turbid ebb and flow
Of human misery; we
Find also in the sound a thought,
Hearing it by this distant northern sea.

The Sea of Faith
Was once, too, at the full, and round earth's shore
Lay like the folds of a bright girdle furled.
But now I only hear
Its melancholy, long, withdrawing roar,
Retreating, to the breath
Of the night-wind, down the vast edges drear
And naked shingles of the world.

Ah, love, let us be true
To one another! for the world, which seems
To lie before us like a land of dreams,
So various, so beautiful, so new,
Hath really neither joy, nor love, nor light,
Nor certitude, nor peace, nor help for pain;
And we are here as on a darkling plain
Swept with confused alarms of struggle and flight,
Where ignorant armies clash by night.

EXERCISE

1. To whom is the poem addressed? How may this question lead us to a comparison of "Dover Beach" with Auden's "Lay Your Sleeping Head, My Love" (p. 263) on the basis of theme and attitude? What relation in regard to theme do you find between "Dover Beach" and Eliot's "Preludes" (p. 112)? And Tate's "Last Days of Alice" (p. 307)? What differences strike you?

2. By using the last figure (lines 35–37) does the poet make an abrupt and unjustified shift in imagery? If not, how do you justify the figure?

3. The importance of the sea imagery in this poem is perfectly obvious. How important is it for the meaning of the poem that the scene be flooded with moonlight?

Church Going

Philip Larkin [1922–]

Once I am sure there's nothing going on
I step inside, letting the door thud shut.
Another church: matting, seats, and stone,
And little books; sprawlings of flowers, cut
For Sunday, brownish now; some brass and stuff
Up at the holy end; the small neat organ;
And a tense, musty, unignorable silence,
Brewed God knows how long. Hatless, I take off
My cycle-clips in awkward reverence,

Move forward, run my hand around the font.
From where I stand, the roof looks almost new—
Cleaned or restored? Someone would know: I don't.
Mounting the lectern, I peruse a few
Hectoring large-scale verses, and pronounce
"Here endeth" much more loudly than I'd meant.
The echoes snigger briefly. Back at the door
I sign the book, donate an Irish sixpence,
Reflect the place was not worth stopping for.

Yet stop I did: in fact I often do,
And always end much at a loss like this,
Wondering what to look for; wondering, too,
When churches fall completely out of use
What we shall turn them into, if we shall keep
A few cathedrals chronically on show,
Their parchment, plate, and pyx in locked cases,
And let the rest rent-free to rain and sheep.
Shall we avoid them as unlucky places?

Or, after dark, will dubious women come
To make their children touch a particular stone;
Pick simples for a cancer; or in some
Advised night see walking a dead one?

Power of some sort or other will go on
In games, in riddles, seemingly at random;
But superstition, like belief, must die,
And what remains when disbelief has gone?
Grass, weedy pavement, brambles, buttress, sky,

A shape less recognizable each week,
A purpose more obscure. I wonder who
Will be the last, the very last, to seek
This place for what it was; one of the crew
That tap and jot and know what rood-lofts were?
Some ruin-bibber, randy for antique,
Or Christmas-addict, counting on a whiff
Of gown-and-bands and organ-pipes and myrrh?
Or will he be my representative,

Bored, uninformed, knowing the ghostly silt
Dispersed, yet tending to this cross of ground
Through suburb scrub because it held unspilt
So long and equably what since is found
Only in separation—marriage, and birth,
And deaths, and thoughts of these—for whom was built
This special shell? For, though I've no idea
What this accoutred frowsty barn is worth,
It pleases me to stand in silence here;

A serious house on serious earth it is,
In whose blent air all our compulsions meet,
Are recognized, and robed as destinies.
And that much never can be obsolete,
Since someone will forever be surprising
A hunger in himself to be more serious,
And gravitating with it to this ground,
Which, he once heard, was proper to grow wise in,
If only that so many dead lie round.

EXERCISE

1. Why does the speaker enter this church?

2. What is the attitude of the speaker toward churches and religion? In this connection, consider the effect of the phrases "the holy end" and "a tense, musty, unignorable silence" in

the first stanza and "this special shell" and "this accoutred frowsty barn" in the sixth stanza.

3. What is the theme of this poem? Can you formulate it? Can you relate it to the theme of "Dover Beach"?

A Slumber Did My Spirit Seal

William Wordsworth [*1770–1850*]

A slumber did my spirit seal;
  I had no human fears—
She seemed a thing that could not feel
  The touch of earthly years.

No motion has she now, no force;
  She neither hears nor sees;
Rolled round in earth's diurnal course,
  With rocks, and stones, and trees.

EXERCISE

This poem has attracted a great deal of commentary and some divergent interpretations. Laura Riding and Robert Graves wrote, a good many years ago, that as "a prose fancy this poem is confused and illogical," and argued that if it were translated into a logical language such as French, "it would be no argument at all." They continued:

> The contrast between Lucy's once active evasion of the touch of earthly years and her present passive acquiescence in earth's diurnal course is the main argument. But from the prose view it may be facetiously pointed out that Lucy never in her most active days could have gone to counteract the daily rolling of the earth. The details are even more illogical than the main argument. Apparently what Wordsworth has in his mind is that 'I thought once that she was non-human in a spiritual sense, but now she is dead I find her non-human in the very opposite sense.' But all the words have got misplaced. 'Spirit' has got attached to Wordsworth when it should go with Lucy; 'no human' likewise. There is a false comparison made between 'A slumber did my spirit seal' and 'She neither hears nor

sees.' 'Trees' is an irrelevant climax to 'rocks and stones.' 'Thing' should not qualify the first Lucy but should be with the second Lucy among the rocks and stones. As a French poem it would run, more logically, something like this:

> A slumber sealed my *human fears*
> For her mortality:
> Methought *her spirit* could withstand
> The touch of earthly years.
>
> Yet now her spirit fails, she is
> Less sentient than a *tree,*
> Rolled round in earth's diurnal course
> With rocks and stones and *things.**

But Riding and Graves conceded that the poem has great beauty and a "supra-logical harmony," their justification of the illogical language being in effect that this illogicality mirrors "the inability of the mind to face the actual reality of death."

Other writers do not find the words of the poem "misplaced," but they do find in it apparent contradictions and elements in tensional opposition. Florence Marsh includes the poem among those that "exemplify Wordsworth's dual vision":

> In all these come elements of darkness. . . . But in all these poems the dark elements are as it were held in solution: light and life and love contain the darkness and solitude and death. Lucy has died but her death is a return to the great life of nature:
>
> No motion has she now, no force;
> She neither hears nor sees;
> Rolled round in earth's diurnal course,
> With rocks, and stones, and trees.
>
> The poet equates motion with life: the motionless girl has become part of the living motion of the earth, and the poignancy of the poem rises from the poet's awareness of death-within-life.†

* Laura Riding and Robert Graves: *A Pamphlet against Anthologies,* New York, 1928, pp. 128–129.

† Florence Marsh: *Wordsworth's Imagery,* New Haven, Conn., Yale University Press, 1952, pp. 55–56.

F. W. Bateson writes:

> The structural basis of the poem is clearly the contrast between the two verses. Verse one deals with the past (there are no less than four verbs in a past tense—*did, had, seem'd, could*). Lucy had been such a vital person that the possibility of her growing old or dying had not crossed Wordworth's mind. Verse two concerns the present (in addition to the *now* in the first line there are three main verbs in the present tense—*has, hears, sees*). Lucy is dead. The invulnerable Ariel-like creature is now as lifeless and immobile as stocks and stones. And the contrast is emphasized by the repetition of *earth:* Lucy, who had seemed immune from the passage of *earthly years,* must now submit to *earth's diurnal course.* So far from escaping the touch of years she is now undergoing a daily contact with the earth. The use of the solemn Latinism *diurnal,* the only three-syllable word in this mainly monosyllabic poem, completes the contrast. But the final impression the poem leaves is not of two contrasting moods, but of a single mood mounting to a climax in the pantheistic magnificence of the last two lines.*

Wordsworth's contemporary and friend, Samuel Coleridge, evidently found in the poem sublimity and gloom (or sublimity that had come out of gloom) for he wrote to a friend on April 6, 1799, that:

> Some months ago Wordsworth transmitted to me a most sublime Epitaph whether it had any reality, I cannot say. —Most probably, in some gloomier moment he had fancied the moment in which his Sister might die.

One of your editors has written of the poem:

> If a slumber has sealed the lover's spirit, a slumber, immersed in which he thought it impossible that his loved one could perish, so too a slumber has now definitely sealed *her* spirit: "No motion has she now, no force; / She neither hears nor sees." It is evident that it is her unnatural slumber that has waked him out of his. . . .
>
> Wordsworth . . . does not choose to exploit the contrast as such. Instead, he attempts to suggest something

* F. W. Bateson: *English Poetry, A Critical Introduction,* New York, Longmans, Green and Company, 1950, pp. 33–34.

of the lover's agonized shock at the loved one's present lack of motion—of his response to her utter and horrible inertness. And how shall he suggest this? He chooses to suggest it, not by saying that she lies as quiet as marble or as a lump of clay; on the contrary, he attempts to suggest it by imagining her in violent motion—violent, but imposed motion, the same motion indeed which the very stones share, whirled about as they are in earth's diurnal course. . . .

In the first stanza, the girl "could not feel / The touch of earthly years" because she seemed divine and immortal. But in the second stanza, now in her grave, she still does not "feel the touch of earthly years," for, like the rocks and stones, she feels nothing at all. It is true that Wordsworth does not repeat the verb "feels"; instead he writes "She neither *hears* nor *sees.*" But the contrast, though not commented upon directly by any device of verbal wit, is there nonetheless, and is bound to make itself felt in any sensitive reading of the poem. The statement of the first stanza has been literally realized in the second, but its meaning has been ironically reversed.*

1. Having considered these various comments, try to determine what, in your opinion, the poem means.

2. What is its tone?

3. What apparently contradictory elements (if any) occur in the poem? How are they reconciled, if in your opinion they are reconciled?

The Scoffers

William Blake [*1757–1827*]

Mock on, mock on, Voltaire, Rousseau,
  Mock on, mock on; 'tis all in vain;
You throw the sand against the wind
  And the wind blows it back again.

And every sand becomes a gem
  Reflected in the beams divine;

* Cleanth Brooks, in Morton D. Zabel, ed.: *Literary Opinion in America*, rev. ed., New York, Harper & Brothers, 1950, pp. 735–737.

Blown back, they blind the mocking eye,
  But still in Israel's paths they shine.

The atoms of Democritus
  And Newton's particles of light
Are sands upon the Red Sea shore,
  Where Israel's tents do shine so bright.

EXERCISE

The speaker begins abruptly by addressing two of the Scoffers, Voltaire and Rousseau. (It does not matter, in so far as the merit of the poem is concerned, whether or not we regard the historical Voltaire and Rousseau—or for that matter, Newton and Democritus—as really scoffers against the things of the spirit. The important matter is that Blake should have felt them to be so and should have been able to make poetry out of his indignation against them.) He taunts the Scoffers with the futility of their actions and uses a vivid figure with which to make his point: they are throwing sand against the wind. Such would be the action of a madman: though endlessly repeated, it is performed in vain.

The second stanza gives a further extension of meaning (though the development of the idea is made in terms of the development of the figure). "To throw dust into a person's eyes" is a proverbial image for an attempt at deception. Blake freshens and sharpens the conventional figure by having the wind blow the sand back into the eyes of the would-be deceivers. Blake makes further extensions of the meaning by stating that every "sand" (that is, grain of sand) becomes a gem, and by making the momentarily puzzling statement that the grains of sand shine in *Israel's* path.

The third stanza develops and extends the reference to Israel, by an allusion to Israel's journey out of Egyptian bondage to the Promised Land.

1. Is Blake's use of imagery, in your opinion, strained and forced? Or is it successful?

2. Democritus is alluded to as the founder of the atomic theory in ancient times, and Newton as an exponent of the theory in more modern times. What is the connection, if any,

between the atoms (particles of matter), the particles of light, and the grains of sand? Is there sufficient consistency of imagery?

3. Attempt to state the theme of this poem. Does the presentation of it gain by the use of vivid images? Does it lose in clarity by being presented through images?

London

William Blake [1757–1827]

I wander through each chartered street,
Near where the chartered Thames does flow
And mark in very face I meet
Marks of weakness, marks of woe.

In every cry of every man,
In every infant's cry of fear,
In every voice; in every ban,
The mind-forged manacles I hear:

How the chimney-sweeper's cry
Every blackening church appalls,
And the hapless soldier's sigh
Runs in blood down palace-walls.

But most, through midnight streets I hear
How the youthful harlot's curse
Blasts the new-born infant's tear,
And blights with plagues the marriage-hearse.

EXERCISE

1. What is the meaning of *chartered* in lines 1 and 2? What does the poet gain by repeating *mark* in lines 3 and 4? Does it have the effect of childish repetition? Or what?

2. In the eighteenth century, children were employed as chimney-sweepers. Does this help account for the fact that the chimney-sweeper's cry appalls the church?

3. The speaker says that he hears the "mind-forged

manacles" in every cry. In what sense do the various cries mentioned come under this description? Does the youthful harlot's voice serve as a climax to these cries? How?

4. Comment upon the words *blackening* and *appalls* in line 10. What do they mean literally or primarily? What further meanings do they take on in this context? Comment upon *youthful* and *curse* in line 14.

Brahma

Ralph Waldo Emerson [*1803–1882*]

If the red slayer think he slays,
  Or if the slain think he is slain,
They know not well the subtle ways
  I keep, and pass, and turn again.

Far or forgot to me is near;
  Shadow and sunlight are the same;
The vanished gods to me appear;
  And one to me are shame and fame.

They reckon ill who leave me out;
  When me they fly, I am the wings;
I am the doubter and the doubt,
  And I the hymn the Brahmin sings.

The strong gods pine for my abode,
  And pine in vain the sacred Seven;
But thou, meek lover of the good!
  Find me, and turn thy back on heaven.

EXERCISE

Brahma, in philosophic Hinduism, is the impersonal supreme being, the primal source and the ultimate goal of all that exists.

1. Does the poem give vitality and power to this concept?

2. Does the poem state meaningless contradictions or meaningful paradoxes?

The Miracle

Walter de la Mare [1873–1956]

Who beckons the green ivy up
  Its solitary tower of stone?
What spirit lures the bindweed's cup
        Unfaltering on?
Calls even the starry lichen to climb
By agelong inches endless Time?

Who bids the hollyhock uplift
  Her rod of fast-sealed buds on high;
Fling wide her petals—silent, swift,
        Lovely to the sky?
Since as she kindled, so she will fade,
Flower above flower in squalor laid.

Ever the heavy billow rears
  All its sea-length in green, hushed wall;
But totters as the shore it nears,
        Foams to its fall;
Where was its mark? on what vain quest
Rose that great water from its rest?

So creeps ambition on; so climb
  Man's vaunting thoughts. He, set on high,
Forgets his birth, small space, brief time,
        That he shall die;
Dreams blindly in his stagnant air;
Consumes his strength, strips himself bare;

Rejects delight, ease, pleasure, hope,
  Seeking in vain, but seeking yet,
Past earthly promise, earthly scope,
        On one aim set:
As if, like Chaucer's child, he thought
All but "O Alma!" nought.

EXERCISE

1. What does the poet gain by linking man's ambition with the force that exerts itself in lichen and plant and wave? Does

he suggest that "Man's vaunting thoughts" are really akin to some blind irrational force?

2. How do the previous images qualify and inform the description of man in stanza four? For example, "Dreams blindly" would apply to the ivy and the hollyhocks. What are other instances?

3. What is the speaker's attitude toward the progress of the ivy or that of the bindweed? What is his attitude toward man? One of mockery, pity, or what?

4. Lines 29–30 refer to Chaucer's "Prioress' Tale." In that story, the little clergeon sings his hymn to the Virgin, "O Alma Redemptoris," in spite of threats, and, miraculously, even after his throat has been cut. How does this comparison qualify what the poet has to say about man's ambition? How does it contrast with (or perhaps support) the images drawn from the blind motion of the billow or of the blind life-force in plants?

5. Compare the theme of this poem with that of the second of the "Songs" by Yeats (p. 403).

The Force That through the Green Fuse

Dylan Thomas [*1914–1953*]

The force that through the green fuse drives the flower
Drives my green age; that blast the roots of trees
Is my destroyer.
And I am dumb to tell the crooked rose
My youth is bent by the same wintry fever.

The force that drives the water through the rocks
Drives my red blood; that dries the mouthing streams
Turns mine to wax.
And I am dumb to mouth unto my veins
How at the mountain spring the same mouth sucks.

The hand that whirls the water in the pool
Stirs the quicksand; that ropes the blowing wind
Hauls my shroud sail.

And I am dumb to tell the hanging man
How of my clay is made the hangman's lime.

The lips of time leech to the fountain head;
Love drips and gathers, but the fallen blood
Shall calm her sores.
And I am dumb to tell a weather's wind
How time has ticked a heaven round the stars.

And I am dumb to tell the lover's tomb
How at my sheet goes the same crooked worm.

EXERCISE

1. Compare and contrast the theme of this poem with that of "The Miracle."

2. What is the speaker's attitude toward his kinship with plant and water and wind? Does he exult in the kinship? Or commiserate, as with fellow victims? Or what? Compare and contrast the tone of this poem with that of "The Miracle."

3. How do the last two lines sum up the poem? How do they bear upon the tone of the poem?

The Love Song of J. Alfred Prufrock

T. S. Eliot [*1888–*]

S'io credesse che mia risposta fosse
A persona che mai tornasse al mondo,
Questa fiamma staria senza piu scosse.
Ma perciocche giammai di questo fondo
Non torno vivo alcun, s'i'odo il vero,
Senza tema d'infamia ti rispondo.

Let us go then, you and I,
When the evening is spread out against the sky
Like a patient etherized upon a table;
Let us go, through certain half-deserted streets,
The muttering retreats
Of restless nights in one-night cheap hotels
And sawdust restaurants with oyster-shells:
Streets that follow like a tedious argument

Of insidious intent
To lead you to an overwhelming question. . . .
Oh, do not ask, "What is it?"
Let us go and make our visit.

In the room the women come and go
Talking of Michelangelo.

The yellow fog that rubs its back upon the windowpanes,
The yellow smoke that rubs its muzzle on the windowpanes
Licked its tongue into the corners of the evening,
Lingered upon the pools that stand in drains,
Let fall upon its back the soot that falls from chimneys,
Slipped by the terrace, made a sudden leap,
And seeing that it was a soft October night,
Curled once about the house, and fell asleep.

And indeed there will be time
For the yellow smoke that slides along the street,
Rubbing its back upon the windowpanes;
There will be time, there will be time
To prepare a face to meet the faces that you meet;
There will be time to murder and create,
And time for all the works and days of hands
That lift and drop a question on your plate;
Time for you and time for me,
And time yet for a hundred indecisions,
And for a hundred visions and revisions,
Before the taking of a toast and tea.

In the room the women come and go
Talking of Michelangelo.

And indeed there will be time
To wonder, "Do I dare?" and, "Do I dare?"
Time to turn back and descend the stair,
With a bald spot in the middle of my hair—
(They will say: "How his hair is growing thin!")
My morning coat, my collar mounting firmly to the chin,
My necktie rich and modest, but asserted by a simple pin—
(They will say: "But how his arms and legs are thin!")
Do I dare
Disturb the universe?

In a minute there is time
For decisions and revisions which a minute will reverse.

For I have known them all already, known them all:
Have known the evenings, mornings, afternoons,
I have measured out my life with coffee spoons;
I know the voices dying with a dying fall
Beneath the music from a farther room.
  So how should I presume?

And I have known the eyes already, known them all—
The eyes that fix you in a formulated phrase,
And when I am formulated, sprawling on a pin,
When I am pinned and wriggling on the wall,
Then how should I begin
To spit out all the butt-ends of my days and ways?
  And how should I presume?

And I have known the arms already, known them all—
Arms that are braceleted and white and bare
(But in the lamplight, downed with light brown hair!)
Is it perfume from a dress
That makes me so digress?
Arms that lie along a table, or wrap about a shawl.
  And should I then presume?
  And how should I begin?

. . . .

Shall I say, I have gone at dusk through narrow streets
And watched the smoke that rises from the pipes
Of lonely men in shirt-sleeves, leaning out of windows? . . .

I should have been a pair of ragged claws
Scuttling across the floors of silent seas.

. . . .

And the afternoon, the evening, sleeps so peacefully!
Smoothed by long fingers,
Asleep . . . tired . . . or it malingers,
Stretched on the floor, here beside you and me.
Should I, after tea and cakes and ices,
Have the strength to force the moment to its crisis?
But though I have wept and fasted, wept and prayed,
Though I have seen my head (grown slightly bald) brought
    in upon a platter,

I am no prophet—and here's no great matter;
I have seen the moment of my greatness flicker,
And I have seen the eternal Footman hold my coat, and snicker,
And in short, I was afraid.

And would it have been worth it, after all,
After the cups, the marmalade, the tea,
Among the porcelain, among some talk of you and me,
Would it have been worth while,
To have bitten off the matter with a smile,
To have squeezed the universe into a ball
To roll it toward some overwhelming question,
To say: "I am Lazarus, come from the dead,
Come back to tell you all, I shall tell you all"—
If one, settling a pillow by her head,
  Should say: "That is not what I meant at all;
  That is not it, at all."

And would it have been worth it, after all,
Would it have been worth while,
After the sunsets and the dooryards and the sprinkled streets,
After the novels, after the teacups, after the skirts that trail along the floor—
And this, and so much more?—
It is impossible to say just what I mean!
But as if a magic lantern threw the nerves in patterns on a screen:
Would it have been worth while
If one, settling a pillow or throwing off a shawl,
And turning toward the window, should say:
  "That is not it at all,
  That is not what I meant, at all."

. . .

No! I am not Prince Hamlet, nor was meant to be;
Am an attendant lord, one that will do
To swell a progress, start a scene or two,
Advise the prince; no doubt, an easy tool,
Deferential, glad to be of use,
Politic, cautious, and meticulous;
Full of high sentence, but a bit obtuse;
At times, indeed, almost ridiculous—
Almost, at times, the Fool.

I grow old . . . I grow old . . .
I shall wear the bottoms of my trousers rolled.

Shall I part my hair behind? Do I dare to eat a peach?
I shall wear white flannel trousers, and walk upon the beach.
I have heard the mermaids singing, each to each.

I do not think that they will sing to me.

I have seen them riding seaward on the waves
Combing the white hair of the waves blown back
When the wind blows the water white and black.

We have lingered in the chambers of the sea
By sea-girls wreathed with seaweed red and brown
Till human voices wake us, and we drown.

This poem is a dramatic monologue. As in Tennyson's "Ulysses" (p. 59), a person utters a speech that implies his story and reveals his character. The implication of the story is fairly clear in the poem by Tennyson and the revelation is fairly simple, but the reader must depend to some extent upon his imagination to fill in what is unsaid. In "The Love Song of J. Alfred Prufrock" the reader must assume even more responsibility for filling in the unsaid. For one thing, the events are not as fully indicated in Eliot's poem as in Tennyson's, but for another and more important thing, the continuity is not as clear. In "Ulysses" the transitions are not strictly logical. One thing suggests another in the flow of consciousness. But the transitions in Prufrock's utterance are more violent, at first glance less justifiable. But can we make sense of them? Is the poem a mere jumble?

It is no mere jumble, for even a superficial reading yields a general impression of Prufrock. He is a middle-aged man, somewhat over-sensitive and timid, yearning and procrastinating, fearful that life has passed him by and yet somehow resigned to the fact, very much a creature of his world of drawing rooms and yet feeling a vague dissatisfaction with that world. But only a closer inspection will give us the full significance of many details in the poem and permit us to realize the implications of the whole poem. To make this inspection, let us take up points in their order.

Who is the "you" of the poem? It is presumably the generalized reader. But in this poem the "you" is something more—it is the person to whom Prufrock wishes to make his revelation, to tell his secret. In the end we shall return to this question.

The time is evening, when the "you" is invited to make the visit, and this evening world becomes more and more important as the poem proceeds. It is a world of neither night nor day. Twilight is the atmosphere of the poem. It is an evening "Like a patient etherized upon a table," and with this image the twilight world becomes also the world of twilight in another way, the realm between life and death. Here, too, enters the notion of a sick world, the atmosphere of the operating room: the quiet is not that of natural sleep—it is an ominous hush.

To reach Prufrock's proper world, the "you" must pass through a slum section of sinister streets. The suggested walk through the slum points up the triviality of the conversation of the women in the effete drawing room to which we come. This is not to say that the subject of the women's conversation is trivial. Michelangelo was a man of violent personality, an artist of epic grandeur, and furthermore a typical figure of the great creative period of the Renaissance. But he has nothing to do with Prufrock's world and the bored women who turn his art into chit-chat.

With lines 15 to 22 we find more of the twilight atmosphere of the poem. But there is some development here, for the settling down of the smoke and fog tends to emphasize the isolation of the drawing room from the outside world. In addition, the image of the housecat falling asleep accords with the relaxed, aimless quality of Prufrock's world.

In the next section (lines 23–34) two new motifs enter the poem, the motif of time and that of appearance-and-reality. For the first, there will be time for some great, as yet unnamed, decision to settle the "overwhelming question"—for the "visions and revisions." The word *vision* here is important, for it implies the possibility of some fundamental insight, a flash of truth, a glimpse of beauty. Mystics, saint, seers, poets have "visions." But this word is played off against *revision,* with its implication of the second thought, the calculated change, etc. For the second motif of this section, we see that Prufrock prepares a mask for the world. He cannot face the world directly, there is a need for disguise.

What this need is, does not yet emerge, but in the next section (lines 37–48) we see that the disguise is prompted by fear of the mocking, inimical eyes of the world that will avidly note all defects and failings. And here, too, the time motif changes its emphasis. In the section before, there was enough time to allow for postponement of vital decision, but now mixed with that idea is the idea of the closing in of time, of age. With this sense of the closing in of time, and with the fear, does Prufrock dare disturb the universe with the significant question?

The next three sections (lines 49–69) further explain why Prufrock may not disturb the universe. First, he himself belongs to that world, and therefore it would be a presumption for him to criticize it. On what grounds could he, the perfect product of that world, enervated by its sense of fatuity, offer a judgment against it? Second, he fears the world, and again the inimical eyes appear. This fear would prevent him from changing his "days and ways."

The last of these three sections (lines 62–69) has the same outline, as it were, as the other two: I have known this world, and so on, therefore, how should I presume? But the content is new, the arms and the perfume, and cannot be accounted for as merely details of the Prufrock world. Now, not a woman, but women enter significantly. Prufrock is attracted by the sight of the bare arms, by the whiff of perfume, but in the midst of the lines recording the romantic attraction, we find the more realistic observation put as a parenthesis:

> But in the lamplight, downed with light brown hair!

Is this a mere observation, or does it indicate something about Prufrock? The fact that the observation of the "real" arms is put in contrast with the "romantic" arms, modifies the attraction: against the attraction there is a hint of revulsion, a hint of neurotic repudiation of the real, the physical. In the face of this situation, how should Prufrock "begin"?

After a brief digression (lines 70–74), we return to the drawing room and the etherized, peaceful twilight world in which Prufrock does not have the strength to force the "crisis," the overwhelming question. The motif that dominates the section is the time motif, the sense of physical decay and impending death, the sense of there being, not too much time, but not enough time. In this sense of time having run out Prufrock's agony now seems of no account; it has led to nothing. He admits that he is no prophet, no announcer of a new dispensation like John the Baptist. And in the reference to John the Baptist we catch also an allusion to the love story, for the prophet's death was demanded by Salome because he had rejected her love: Prufrock, too, has rejected love, but not because he is a prophet with a burning message and faith. He is merely a product of his world, where even Death is a kind of footman who holds the coat and snickers at the slightly ridiculous guest. Even Prufrock's death will lack dignity and meaning.

In the two sections from line 87 to line 110 Prufrock asks would it have been worth it, even if he had forced the crisis. But what would the crisis have been? It seems to involve the love story, it involves some understanding with a woman. We have an allusion to Marvell's love poem "To His Coy Mistress" (p. 308) in the line "To have squeezed the universe into a ball." Marvell's lovers would squeeze up their strength and sweetness into a supreme moment, but with Prufrock it is the universe which is to be rolled toward the "overwhelming question." In other words, with Prufrock it is not merely the personal relationship, but the meaning of the world, of life, that is involved. But the two are to be somehow related: the personal relationship cannot be significant if life is without significance.

Prufrock, if he had been able to force the crisis, would have seemed, he feels, like Lazarus come from the dead. Let us examine what is implied in the allusion. There are two characters by this name in the Bible. One is the beggar (*Luke,* 16) who lay at the rich man's gate, and the other is the brother of Mary and Martha who died and was raised by Jesus (*John,* 11). When the first Lazarus died he was carried by angels to Abraham's bosom, while the rich man was sent to hell. The rich man, seeing Lazarus happy, asked that Lazarus be sent to give him water. When Abraham replied that this was impossible, the rich man asked that at least Lazarus be sent to warn the rich man's five brothers so that they might not come to hell for their lack of charity. Abraham replied that the brothers already had the prophets.

> And he [the rich man] said, Nay, father Abraham: but if one went unto them from the dead, they will repent.
>
> And he [Abraham] said unto him, If they hear not Moses and the prophets, neither will they be persuaded, though one rose from the dead.

So both references involve a return from the dead, and we may say that elements of both are suggested by the allusion. To return from the dead would be for Prufrock to awaken from his meaningless existence. To tell all, as related to the raising of Lazarus by Jesus, would be to tell what it is like to be dead, to report the horror. In relation to the other Lazarus story, to tell all would mean to utter the warning to repentance. The story of the beggar Lazarus seems to have a little more weight in the allusion than the story of the other Lazarus. The warning from Prufrock, like that given to the rich men by the beggar Lazarus, would not be heeded by the lady of the drawing room; she simply would not understand what Prufrock was talking about if he should raise the "overwhelming question." (Neither of the Biblical stories gives an exact parallel to Prufrock's situation, for in the one from the Gospel of John the importance of the risen Lazarus to the living is not stressed, and in the one from the Gospel of Luke, the dead man, unlike Prufrock, is called back from bliss to the world. But the general import of the allusion is clear, and that is what matters.)

With the realization that even if he had had the strength to raise the question the lady would not have understood him, Prufrock is struck again by his own inadequacy. He is not Prince Hamlet (lines 111–120). Hamlet suffered doubt and despair. Hamlet brought an "overwhelming question" to Ophelia, who could not understand what he meant. Hamlet postponed decisive action. But there the parallel ends. Hamlet struggled grandly and passionately with his problem. The world he confronted was evil and violent, it was not twilit and relaxed. The play *Hamlet,* like the work of Michelangelo, belongs to a great creative period in history, and the mere reference evokes that world in contrast to Prufrock's world. Prufrock, with sad self-irony, sees all this, and knows that if he corresponds to any character in the play it is to the sententious, empty, old Polonius, the sycophantic Rosenkranz, or the silly, foppish Osric. Perhaps—though there is no fool in *Hamlet*—to the fool, that stock character of many Elizabethan tragedies.

So with line 121 we see Prufrock resigned to his role, resigned to the fact that he will never raise the overwhelming question, resigned to the fact of age which has overtaken his postponements. With this reference to the motif of time, we see him as an aging man on the beach wistfully watching the girls, who have no attention to spare for him. Suddenly this scene is transformed into a vision of beauty and vitality, in contrast to the world Prufrock has inhabited. The girls become mermaids, as it were, riding triumphantly and effortlessly seaward into their natural creative element. (We may notice how this refers also to the sea of the ragged claws: the brute vitality and the vision of beauty are both aspects of the sea, the life-source.)

The concluding reference to the mermaids (lines 129–31) gives us a kind of odd reversion to Prufrock's original situation: he has "lingered," not in the drawing-room surrounded by the women talking of Michelangelo, but in the "chambers of the sea," surrounded by "sea-girls." But such an experience can occur only in dream: "human voices wake us. . . ." And to wake is to return to the human world—is to suffocate and die: ". . . and we drown."

The concluding image thus summarizes brilliantly Prufrock's character and his plight: he can immerse himself in the life-giving sea only in dream, and even in that dream, it is essentially his passive, negative self that is projected: *he* does not ride "seaward on the waves"; he lingers in the "chambers" —he is wreathed by the "sea-girls." Yet, though he cannot live in the sea, or in a romantic dream of the sea, his desiccated "human" world suffocates him. He is a fish out of water indeed.

Is this poem merely a character sketch, the ironical self-revelation of a neurotic "case"? Or does the poem carry more? And if it does carry more, how are we to get at it? For one thing, we notice the sudden use of "we" in the last three lines of the poem. Prufrock has generalized the situation; not only himself but others are in the same predicament. Further, much is made of Prufrock's world—it is a meaningless world of half-lights and shadows, the world of an ether dream, and it is set in another world, the defeated world of the slum. But there is another indication that a generalized application is involved. The epigraph with which Eliot introduces the poem, from Dante's *Divine Comedy,* is part of a speech by Guido da Montefeltro, who is one of the damned in the Inferno. He speaks from his flame: "If I believed that my answer were to someone who might ever go back to the world, this flame would shake no more.* But since, if I hear truth, no one ever returned alive from this pit, I respond to you without fear of infamy." Guido thinks that Dante, to whom the words are addressed, is damned too; therefore, since Dante cannot go back to the world to report it, Guido does not mind telling his own story, exposing his infamy. So the epigraph is but a way of saying that Prufrock is like Guido, the damned man who speaks from his flame; but he speaks to the "you" of the poem—the reader—only because he takes the reader to be damned too, to belong to the same world and to share the same disease. It is the disease of loss of conviction, of loss of faith in the meaning of life, of loss of creativity of all kinds, of feeble purpose, of neurotic self-absorption. So the poem, in the end, is not about poor Prufrock. He is merely a symbol for a general disease, the same disease that Matthew Arnold has written about in "Dover Beach" (p. 373).

"Prufrock," we have suggested, is an ironical poem. It is ironical that Prufrock should expose himself. There is an irony in that he can see his predicament but cannot act to remedy it. There is an irony in his self-deprecation. He cannot claim too much, even for his despair: he is not Prince Hamlet. Irony is an awareness of the limits of response, an understating of response, a refusal to make exaggerations. Sentimentality, as we have said, is the exaggeration of response. This sounds as if irony were a kind of automatic salvation from sentimentality, but things are not that easy and simple. Irony can be-

* In the circle in the Inferno reserved for counselors of fraud and deceit, each of the damned is closed within a great flame, and when the damned speaks the voice issues from the tip of the flame, which thereupon shakes and wavers like a tongue.

come a mere mannerism, a mere mechanical juggling of opposites and contrasts. To judge the acceptable limits of response for any situation we must come back, on the one hand, to our own common-sense experience of the world, and on the other hand, to the context in the poem or other literary work that we are discussing. When King Lear and Cordelia are reunited, the effect is not sentimental because of the background of experience: Lear's remorse and his new attitude toward the world are merely finding here an appropriate expression. Marvell's "Definition of Love" (p. 295), though it makes very elaborate claims for the love celebrated, is not sentimental. The tone is, as we have indicated on p. 298, calm and reasoned. Large, direct, simple statements, not in the least "ironical" as we commonly use that term, may constitute fine poetry which avoids every trace of sentimentality. But in such instances we shall always find that these direct statements develop out of implied or presented contexts which justify them. There is no rule of thumb in such matters. Each instance must be studied independently.

As for "Prufrock," first, the irony is in keeping with the character. Prufrock is intelligent; he does see around and beyond himself; he sees his own failure in a perspective. Furthermore, Eliot the poet, as distinguished from the dramatic character in the poem, wants to make the point that the modern damnation is not a grand damnation: Prufrock is not to be taken too seriously, he is comic as well as tragic. It is easy to be self-pitying and over-serious about one's damnation, and Eliot would deprive the modern "you" of that satisfaction.

There are many shades of irony, and sometimes the direct statement or presentation that is meant to be taken with full seriousness may be accompanied by some irony, perhaps the merest flicker, to indicate that the poet, in making his statement, is still aware of other possible attitudes toward the subject. Or the weight may be shifted heavily toward the negative aspect of the statement, so that we feel it merely as a bitter, sardonic jest. Between these extremes, there are all sorts of intermediate shades, shadings as complex and various as those in Campion's "Blame Not My Cheeks" (p. 256), Ransom's "Winter Remembered" (p. 260), Hardy's "Channel Firing" (p. 190), Frost's "After Apple-Picking" (p. 362), or Robinson's

"Mr. Flood's Party" (p. 213). Irony, in skillful hands, is a very subtle and delicate instrument. It is not to be taken as indicating merely the negative and destructive attitudes, but as an indication of an awareness of the complication and depth of experience.

One last question may be glanced at, that raised by the literary allusions in the poem. If we do not get the allusions, we miss things more or less important to the whole poem. But has the poet a right to expect this knowledge on the part of the reader? Perhaps the best way to answer this question is, for the moment, to look at what has been the practice of poets. For centuries we find that poets, or at least a great many of them, have used literary, historical, and mythological allusions. They have felt themselves to belong to a certain broad cultural group in which certain things were common property. They felt that their society had a certain available inheritance. This is not to say that every reader would get every allusion but merely to say that certain kinds of references were available and significant. For instance, Milton's "Lycidas" (p. 417), as well as his epics, uses many allusions. So does Blake's "Scoffers" (p. 380). Housman's poetry, though seemingly so simple, is frequently packed with echoes of other literature, as, for example, in "The Immortal Part" (facing p. 539); if we miss them, the effect is poorer.

When we come to read traditional literature, we usually find that all the allusions have been cleared up for us, that generations of editors and scholars have prepared the texts and given us notes and comments. The fact that the poet originally used allusions therefore does not disturb us. We have been accustomed to it from school days. We tend, however, to take a different attitude when we confront a poem, like "Prufrock," by a contemporary poet. We feel that we ought to get it more easily and more immediately. If we do not have already at our disposal the necessary information, we are inclined to think that the poet is willful or perverse or proud of his learning. It is perfectly true that poets sometimes are willful and perverse and proud of their learning. But can we, on the other hand, take our own ignorance at any given moment to be the norm of poetry? If we are not willing to make that rather conceited assumption, then it is our responsibility to try to remedy our ignorance. The critics and scholars are there to help us. Then we can try to see if the allusions in a particular poem are really functional, if they really do something for the poem.

In "Prufrock," for instance, is the reference to Michelangelo a perverse parade of learning? We may not know much about him, but if we find out, we may be inclined to agree that by this reference Eliot has accomplished something not possible otherwise: he has quickly and dramatically introduced a significant contrast into the poem. Or with Lazarus he has implied a group of ideas immediately relevant but also useful in establishing a long perspective on the lady who does not understand: she is suddenly equated with the rich brothers who would not listen to Moses and the prophets. Furthermore, we may agree that the allusions are "in character" with the man Prufrock. He is a cultivated man, and one of the implied ironies is that he has lived only in the secondhand life of the past and not in the present on his own account. He sees himself in contrast with the force and creativity of the past.

We cannot, then, lay down any fixed rule for the permissible number or difficulty of allusions. There are many kinds of poetry in this respect, ranging from folk ballads or the songs of Robert Burns to "The Waste Land," by T. S. Eliot (p. 448), in which allusion is made into a system. We can only try to see if the allusions in any particular poem really accomplish something for the poem and are not willful. And here we must remind ourselves that the reading of any poetry requires some preparation. We must be ready for it. All our life and education is the preparation we bring to the poem which we can understand and appreciate today. If today we can read Shakespeare with pleasure, we can do so only because we have educated ourselves to it. A poem does not exist in isolation. It exists in history, and we can appreciate it only in so far as we are acquainted with the relevant history—the world that brought it to being and the world to which it refers.

EXERCISE

1. What is the relevance of the allusion to the "lonely men in shirt-sleeves" in lines 70–72? How are they like Prufrock? How unlike him? Contrast his loneliness with theirs.

2. The "ragged claws" (see lines 73–74) might be taken to suggest the very embodiment of blind, brute appetite, the opposite end of the scale from the over-refined Prufrock. Why does Prufrock say that he "should have been" such a creature? What does the wish reflect?

3. Can you justify the title of this poem? In what sense, if any, is it a "love song"?

The March into Virginia

Ending in the First Manassas
(July 1861)

Herman Melville [*1819–1891*]

Did all the lets and bars appear
  To every just or larger end,
Whence should come the trust and cheer?
  Youth must its ignorant impulse lend—
Age finds place in the rear.
  All wars are boyish, and are fought by boys,
The champions and enthusiasts of the state:
  Turbid ardors and vain joys
    Not barrenly abate—
  Stimulants to the power mature,
    Preparatives of fate.

Who here forecasteth the event?
What heart but spurns at precedent
And warnings of the wise,
Contemned foreclosures of surprise?
The banners play, the bugles call,
The air is blue and prodigal.
  No berrying party, pleasure-wooed,
No picnic party in the May,
Ever went less loth than they
  Into that leafy neighborhood.
In Bacchic glee they file toward Fate,
Moloch's uninitiate;
Expectancy, and glad surmise
Of battle's unknown mysteries.

All they feel is this: 'tis glory,
A rapture sharp, though transitory,
Yet lasting in belaureled story.
So they gaily go to fight,
Chatting left and laughing right.

But some who this blithe mood present,
  As on in lightsome files they fare,
Shall die experienced ere three days are spent—
  Perish, enlightened by the volleyed glare;
Or shame survive, and, like to adamant,
  The throe of Second Manassas share.

EXERCISE

1. What is the quality of irony in this poem? The speaker is not mocking the young soldiers, though he sees through their callowness. What, precisely, is his attitude toward them?

2. What shifts of tone occur in the poem? How are they indicated?

3. Note the change in rhythm in the third stanza. What effect does it have on the tone?

4. In line 34, the word *enlightened* has a complex significance. It might, in fact, be taken as the key word of the poem. One meaning is, of course, that the enemy's volley instructs the untried soldiers. How does it instruct them? But what other meaning do you find? Why, for example, does Melville use the word *glare* and not merely say that the volley "enlightens"? What is the dramatic effect of this other meaning?

5. What weight does the poet place upon *Second* Manassas? How does this last line relate to the subtitle of the poem?

6. What does this poem "say" about war? About soldiers? About the human being in crisis?

Losses

Randall Jarrell [1914–   ]

It was not dying: everybody died.
It was not dying: we had died before
In the routine crashes—and our fields

Called up the papers, wrote home to our folks,
And the rates rose, all because of us.
We died on the wrong page of the almanac,
Scattered on mountains fifty miles away;
Diving on haystacks, fighting with a friend,
We blazed up on the lines we never saw.
We died like ants or pets or foreigners.
(When we left high school nothing else had died
For us to figure we had died like.)

In our new planes, with our new crews, we bombed
The ranges by the desert or the shore,
Fired at towed targets, waited for our scores—
And turned into replacements and woke up
One morning, over England, operational.
It wasn't different: but if we died
It was not an accident but a mistake
(But an easy one for anyone to make).
We read our mail and counted up our missions—
In bombers named for girls, we burned
The cities we had learned about in school—
Till our lives wore out; our bodies lay among
The people we had killed and never seen.
When we lasted long enough they gave us medals;
When we died they said, "Our casualties were low."
They said, "Here are the maps"; we burned the cities.

It was not dying—no, not ever dying;
But the night I died I dreamed that I was dead,
And the cities said to me: "Why are you dying?
We are satisfied, if you are; but why did I die?"

EXERCISE

1. What is the purpose of the references to school (line 11 and line 23)?

2. What is meant by "the people we had killed and never seen" (line 25)? Is the speaker insisting upon the *abstractness* of modern war? Are there other suggestions of this sort in the poem?

3. What is the poem "about"? In trying to determine the answer to this question, consider again the descriptive details in the poem and, most of all, the tone of the poem.

Two Songs from a Play

William Butler Yeats [1865–1939]

I

I saw a staring virgin stand
Where holy Dionysus died,
And tear the heart out of his side,
And lay the heart upon her hand
And bear that beating heart away;
And then did all the Muses sing
Of Magnus Annus at the spring,
As though God's death were but a play.

Another Troy must rise and set,
Another lineage feed the crow,
Another Argo's painted prow
Drive to a flashier bauble yet.
The Roman Empire stood appalled:
It dropped the reins of peace and war
When that fierce virgin and her Star
Out of the fabulous darkness called.

II

In pity for man's darkening thought
He walked that room and issued thence
In Galilean turbulence;
The Babylonian starlight brought
A fabulous, formless darkness in;
Odor of blood when Christ was slain
Made all Platonic tolerance vain
And vain all Doric discipline.

Everything that man esteems
Endures a moment or a day.
Love's pleasure drives his love away,
The painter's brush consumes his dreams;
The herald's cry, the soldier's tread
Exhaust his glory and his might:
Whatever flames upon the night
Man's own resinous heart has fed.

Though these poems, two of Yeats's most famous ones, form the prologue and epilogue of a play, they are not integral parts of that play. Their obscurity, in so far as they are obscure poems, is not occasioned by their having been removed from the play.

Most readers would, in fact, admit to finding a certain obscurity in these poems. There are, however, really two types of obscurity involved. One type has been touched on in various connections in the discussion of previous poems, especially Blake's "The Scoffers" (p. 380), and Eliot's "The Love Song of J. Alfred Prufrock" (p. 386). This type of obscurity comes from the poet's allusions to history, literature, and so on. If the reader does not have the knowledge which the poet expects from his audience, he may miss part, or all, of the meaning. The reader of the present poems, for example, must be able to grasp the references to Dionysus, Magnus Annus, Troy, the Argo, the Roman Empire, Galilee, Babylon, Plato, and the Dorians. Information of this sort may be said to belong to the common heritage of our civilization, and a poet who makes such general references assumes that he is addressing readers of a certain degree of education. No one reader, of course, possesses a complete body of information of this sort, but he knows that the information is available to him for the interpretation of any particular poem.

But a second type of obscurity in these poems seems to derive from the poet's own private symbolism. Why, for example, "Babylonian starlight" (line 20)? The reader senses that it probably has to mean something more than "the starlight in Babylon," and yet dictionaries and encyclopedias will give him little direct help on this point. Does a poet have the right to use references and symbols that are not, as it were, in the public domain? If the poet insists upon using a private system of symbols, will he not render his work impenetrably obscure?

This is a difficult topic, all the more so since Yeats did have something of a private system of symbols which he set forth in *A Vision,* a book printed privately in 1925, and published in revised form in 1938. Yet to some extent every poet finds his own symbols or tends to modify the traditional symbols to his own use. How far does he have a right to go in doing this?

Where does one draw the line? At this point, our best procedure will probably be to discuss the "Two Songs" with as much help as we can get from *A Vision.* Then, with the "Two Songs" as an example, we may attempt a few comments on the general problem.

The "Two Songs from a Play," though separate poems, may be taken to have certain definite connections and to exhibit a certain progression. For one thing, they both deal with the moment of transition from the classical civilization to the Christian. In the first poem, the poet represents the birth of Christ, not only as marking a date in history, but as offering a new principle that was to change the nature of all human activity. But though emphasizing the contrast between the two civilizations ("The Roman Empire stood appalled"), the poet establishes, paradoxically, the continuity between them. The Virgin tears the heart from the slain Dionysus. (According to the rites of the Dionysiac cult, those who tasted sacramentally of the flesh of Dionysus might live again.) With her child (the "Star," which we may take as expressing the same principle as Dionysus) she then utters her challenge to the older civilization. The poet implies further that one cycle (according to *A Vision,* of roughly two thousand years) is merely ended and another is begun. The Great Year, the period in which twelve such cycles run their course, begins, according to Yeats's system, approximately at the birth of Christ. But this new cycle, the poet implies, will merely recapitulate that which has preceded it: it too will have Troys that rise to power and fall, races of heroes whose bodies feed the crows, and Argonauts who search for a Golden Fleece.

It is worth noting that a reader unacquainted with Yeats's special symbols and his special way of treating them might infer from the poem much of the foregoing account. He might even manage lines 15–16, taking "Star" to be a vague poetic epithet for child (or to be the Star of Bethlehem), and the "fabulous darkness," the night through which the Star of Bethlehem shone.

As a matter of fact, we can find almost all the imagery of the first "Song," including the "Star," in a passage which Yeats wrote in another connection. The poet, contemplating the positions of the heavenly bodies as they were at the birth of Christ, comments as follows:

> Three hundred years, two degrees of the Great Year, would but correspond to two days of the Sun's annual journey, and his transition from Pisces to Aries had for generations been associated with the ceremonial death and resurrection of Dionysus. Near that transition the women wailed him, and night showed the full moon separating from the constellation Virgo, with the star in the wheat-sheaf, or in the child, for in the old maps she is represented carrying now one now the other.*

Moreover, in another passage of the same work (p. 190), Yeats mentions the fact that a Roman philosopher of the fourth century described Christianity as "a fabulous formless darkness" which blotted out "every beautiful thing." To the reasonable, ordered thought of the Greco-Roman civilization this new religion seemed to be a superstitious, irrational belief inimical to all clarity and good order and to all its achievements:

> Meanwhile the irrational force that would create confusion and uproar as with the cry "The Babe, the Babe, is born"—the women speaking unknown tongues, the barbers and weavers expounding Divine revelation with all the vulgarity of their servitude, the tables that move or resound with raps—still but creates a negligible sect.†

This points the paradox of the antagonism and continuity of the two cycles. Furthermore, it helps explain why the Virgin, usually portrayed as meek, appears here as a fierce, pitiless force at which the Roman Empire stands appalled.

In dealing with the first "Song," we have already stated that Yeats believes in a cyclic theory of history. He has a particular set of symbols for describing the stages of these cycles through which human events move. The beginning of such a cycle he compares, in his system of symbols, to the new moon, or the dark of the moon; the height of the civilization of such a cycle he compares to the full moon; and the various phases of the moon as it waxes from new to full, or wanes from full

* *A Vision,* London, Werner Laurie, Ltd., 1938, p. 156.

† *A Vision,* pp. 188–189.

back to new, he uses to symbolize the stages in the development and decay of a civilization. Thus, the moment of transition from the classical to the Christian civilization he compares to the dark of the moon; and when the moon is dark one sees only the starlight. But why does he call it "Babylonian starlight"?

First, the Babylonians, from remote antiquity, have been associated with the study of the stars. Second, Yeats conceives of the motive power for the new Christian cycle as coming from Asia Minor, where, of course, Babylon had been situated. Yeats conceives of Christ as representing a "primary" force; by "primary" he means objective as opposed to subjective, physical as opposed to intellectual and rational, democratic as opposed to aristocratic. All of these "primary" attributes are associated with the dark of the moon as opposed to the full moon, which symbolizes the intellectual, the rational, the individual, the ordered. Moreover, Yeats associates the East with the "primary" and the West with its opposite, which he calls the "antithetical." Thus the lines

> The Babylonian starlight brought
> A fabulous, formless darkness in

indicate the impingement of a "primary" elemental force coming in from the East to put a close to the ordered, rational "antithetical" cycle of Greek civilization. Further, the two lines suggest a very powerful concrete image—a dark, mysterious cloud boiling up out of the ancient East to obscure all the distinctions that the rational Western mind had made.

We must not understand these opposed aspects, "primary" and "antithetical," to be absolute. They represent an emphasis in the temper of a civilization—not attitudes complete in themselves. The Greeks, for instance, had not been unaware of the supernatural and irrational aspect of life, but the temper of the Greek or Western mind had emphasized the search for rational explanations and systematic ordering, and the gradual development of Greek philosophy up through Aristotle was in the direction of rational explanation.

But the "odor of blood"—blood is another symbol Yeats uses in many of his poems for the "primary" force—renders vain the achievements of the "antithetical" civilization as represented here by Platonic tolerance and Doric discipline. Yeats, then, has used here three different symbols of the general "primary" force: first, "Babylonian starlight," as the symbol which indicates the history and the basic continuity of the force; second, the "fabulous, formless darkness" as the force as it appeared to men of the antithetical civilization; and third, blood as symbolizing the violent fact of the transition itself.

The last stanza of the second song seems to abandon the consideration of the particular matters involved in the first stanza of the second song, and, indeed, the matters involved in the whole of the first song. It makes a statement about the relation of a man to his various activities—love, art, politics, war. But we must assume that the content of this last stanza is determined by the content of the three preceding stanzas. The problem here is to define the particular nature of the relationship involved.

After presenting, in terms of his symbols, the recurrent cycles of history, the poet sums up by saying that

> Everything that man esteems
> Endures a moment or a day.

But the emphasis here is not merely upon the pathos of the transience of human achievements. Their very meaning, the last stanza implies, lies in the fact that they express man's deepest nature; that in expressing this nature, man's achievements fulfill his creative impulse in the act of consuming it.

Instead of the static idea of the vanity of all human glory—the fall of the mighty, the feebleness of man's might—the poem expresses a dynamic idea, an idea of development and fulfillment in this process. Most of all, we are to see the varied and constant pageant of man's life, either primary or antithetical in emphasis, as springing from man's own creative and imaginative force. This ties back to the idea of the repetition of the cycles as given in the first song—

> Another Troy must rise and set,
> Another lineage feed the crow.

The whole idea is brought to a climactic summary in the last figure which the poet uses, the figure of man's "resinous heart" feeding the flame.

The "Two Songs," as we have seen, are enriched by a full acquaintance with Yeats's system of symbols. But before we leap to conclusions about the general problem of the poet's right to make up his own symbolism or to the specific problem of the relation of Yeats's poetry to his *Vision,* several comments are in order. In the first place, we should point out that the reader who had never seen *A Vision* might, by a careful reading of a large part of Yeats's poetry, come to an adequate understanding of his symbols. In this view, *A Vision* can be regarded primarily as a special kind of dictionary—a compendium of materials which may be found at large elsewhere in the body of his poetry. In the second place, whether *A Vision* is or is not to be regarded as a book of philosophy or a book on the meaning of history, our use of it in this analysis has been to throw light upon the meanings of the symbols employed in "Two Songs." Understanding of the poems does not demand our literal belief in Yeats's philosophy or in his view of history. The "Songs" must justify themselves in their own right and the symbols they employ must be brought to life within the context in which they are used: they cannot be validated by an appeal to their "truth" in *A Vision* or elsewhere.

To sum up: the general problem we have raised is an aspect of the relation between a single poem and the complete body of the poet's work. It is a problem by no means confined to Yeats. It could be argued, for example, that any one of Keats's odes requires, for full appreciation, a knowledge of the rest of Keats's poetry. There is an approach to the body of a poet's works as well as to single examples of it.

Shine, Perishing Republic

Robinson Jeffers [*1887–1961*]

While this America settles in the mold of its vulgarity, heavily
  thickening to empire,
And protest, only a bubble in the molten mass, pops and sighs
  out, and the mass hardens,

I sadly smiling remember that the flower fades to make fruit,
  the fruit rots to make earth.

Out of the mother; and through the spring exultances, ripeness and decadence; and home to the mother.

You make haste on decay: not blameworthy; life is good, be it stubbornly long or suddenly
A mortal splendor: meteors are not needed less than mountains: shine, perishing republic.

But for my children, I would rather have them keep their distance from the thickening center; corruption
Never has been compulsory, when the cities lie at the monster's feet there are left the mountains.

And boys, be in nothing so moderate as in love of man, a clever servant, insufferable master.
There is the trap that catches noblest spirits, that caught—they say—God, when he walked on earth.

EXERCISE

1. Does this poet hate America? Is he trying to admonish his country? What does he mean by asking it to "shine"? Is he saying that America's course of action is "not blameworthy" (line 5)? Does he love the "perishing republic"?

2. To whom are the last two lines addressed? How do these lines relate to the first four stanzas of the poem?

3. Compare and contrast the theme of this poem with that of Yeats's "Two Songs."

4. What theory of history is implied in this poem?

The Return

John Peale Bishop [*1892–1944*]

Night and we heard heavy and cadenced hoofbeats
Of troops departing: the last cohorts left
By the North Gate. That night some listened late
Leaning their eyelids toward Septentrion.

Morning flared and the young tore down the trophies
And warring ornaments: arches were strong
And in the sun but stone; no longer conquests
Circled our columns; all our state was down

In fragments. In the dust, old men with tufted
Eyebrows whiter than sunbaked faces gulped
As it fell. But they no more than we remembered
The old sea-fights, the soldiers' names and sculptors'.

We did not know the end was coming: nor why
It came; only that long before the end
Were many wanted to die. Then vultures starved
And sailed more slowly in the sky.

We still had taxes. Salt was high. The soldiers
Gone. Now there was much drinking and lewd
Houses all night loud with riot. But only
For a time. Soon the taverns had no roofs.

Strangely it was the young, the almost boys,
Who first abandoned hope; the old still lived
A little, at last a little lived in eyes.
It was the young whose child did not survive.

Some slept beneath the simulacra, until
The gods' faces froze. Then was fear.
Some had response in dreams, but morning restored
Interrogation. Then O then, O ruins!

Temples of Neptune invaded by the sea
And dolphins streaked like streams sportive
As sunlight rode and over the rushing floors
The sea unfurled and what was blue raced silver.

EXERCISE

1. In this poem a Roman setting is suggested. But is the poem an account of the breakdown of Roman civilization? Or has the poet sought to give the poem a more general and wider reference? If so, how has he done this?

2. Investigate the details which the poet has chosen to give. On what principle have they been selected?

3. Why did the poet in line 29 write "Temples of Neptune" rather than, say, "Temples of Jupiter" or "Temples of Mars"? What is the meaning of this last stanza? Does it serve as a climactic summary of the poem?

4. Compare the theme of this poem with that of Yeats's "Two Songs" and that of Jeffers' "Shine, Perishing Republic."

Kubla Khan

Samuel Taylor Coleridge [*1772–1834*]

In Xanadu did Kubla Khan
  A stately pleasure-dome decree:
Where Alph, the sacred river, ran
Through caverns measureless to man
  Down to a sunless sea.
So twice five miles of fertile ground
With walls and towers were girdled round:
And here were gardens bright with sinuous rills,
Where blossomed many an incense-bearing tree,
And here were forests ancient as the hills,
Enfolding sunny spots of greenery.

But oh! that deep romantic chasm which slanted
Down the green hill athwart a cedarn cover!
A savage place! as holy and enchanted
As e'er beneath a waning moon was haunted
By woman wailing for her demon-lover!
And from this chasm, with ceaseless turmoil seething,
As if this earth in fast thick pants were breathing,
A mighty fountain momently was forced,
Amid whose swift half-intermitted burst
Huge fragments vaulted like rebounding hail,
Or chaffy grain beneath the thresher's flail:
And 'mid these dancing rocks at once and ever
It flung up momently the sacred river.
Five miles meandering with a mazy motion
Through wood and dale the sacred river ran,
Then reached the caverns measureless to man,
And sank in tumult to a lifeless ocean:
And 'mid this tumult Kubla heard from far
Ancestral voices prophesying war!
    The shadow of the dome of pleasure
    Floated midway on the waves;
    Where was heard the mingled measure
    From the fountain and the caves.
It was a miracle of rare device,
A sunny pleasure-dome with caves of ice!

A damsel with a dulcimer
In a vision once I saw:
It was an Abyssinian maid,
And on her dulcimer she played,
Singing of Mount Abora.
Could I revive within me
Her symphony and song,
To such a deep delight 't would win me,
That with music loud and long,
I would build that dome in air,
That sunny dome! those caves of ice!
And all who heard should see them there,
And all should cry, Beware! Beware!
His flashing eyes, his floating hair!
Weave a circle round him thrice,
And close your eyes with holy dread,
For he on honey-dew hath fed,
And drunk the milk of Paradise.

"Kubla Khan" begins with a piece of "history." * The first portion of the poem—thirty-five lines—is in the third person and the past tense. Somebody did something specific—decreed the erection of a pleasure dome. But most of the thirty-five lines are concerned not with the building, whatever kind of building it was, but with its location. As for the work of the building itself, very little is said. Kubla Khan decreed the pleasure dome; its shadow "Floated midway on the waves"; and it was a "miracle of rare device" since, though it was "sunny," it contained "caves of ice."

We have a great deal of material on the setting of the pleasure dome: the relation of the dome to the sacred river Alph and the caverns into which it disappears, the size of the tract of fertile ground that Kubla had walled as an immense garden, the kinds of trees, and so on. But most of all, the description deals with the sacred river with special reference to the chasm from which the river issued, the fountain hurling up the huge fragments, and the disappearance of the river into the "caverns measureless to man." It is as if the setting were more important than the pleasure dome itself. In any case, we

* For background of this poem, see How Poems Come About. For fuller discussion, see E. Schneider: *Coleridge, Opium, and Kubla Khan*, University of Chicago Press, 1953; M. H. Abrams: *The Milk of Paradise*, Harvard, 1934.

are bound to say that this work of art is not set down just anywhere in nature but has been very carefully accommodated to its natural setting. It crowns nature.

The place is special: it is dominated by the sacred river; it is carefully walled off and set apart, a kind of earthly paradise, walled off like Milton's paradise. The whole may be properly described as a garden—exactly in the sense that Milton's was a garden though it, too, contained "forests ancient as the hills."

One of the curious grammatical problems in the poem is the opening of line 12: "But oh! that deep romantic chasm which slanted. . . ." What is the force of "But"? Does it mean: *But how unlike the rest of the garden was the chasm?* Or: *In what sharp contrast to the enfolded sunny spots of greenery was that awesome chasm?* At any rate, the "But Oh!" signals a shift in mood, from sunlight to shadow, or from sunlight to moonlight: "As e'er beneath a waning moon was haunted. . . ." Milton made the hill leading up to his Garden "savage," and this place too is savage. It is also holy and enchanted, and the appropriateness of the spot as one in which a woman might wail for her demon lover connects the place with the darker aspects of the supernatural. The more sunlit and paradisiacal aspects of its sacred character have been emphasized in the first eleven lines. The description of the chasm completes the picture of a place which we should today call *numinous.* It is sacred in all the senses of that word—not merely the divine but including the demonic—in short, the numinous as primitive man apprehends it.

The river Alph participates in this quality. If it waters the blossoming garden of the incense-bearing trees and sparkles in the sun, it is also violent and darkly mysterious. The river is associated with both past and future. In its tempestuous descent Kubla can hear the voices of the past ("ancestral voices") predicting the future ("prophesying war").

The pleasure dome as a thing of art, then, is imposed upon a very special portion of nature. It is located very preciselv in the enclosed tract. Its shadow is reflected in the waves of the river at a point midway between the bursting forth of the river and its disappearance—at a point, at least, where the sound of the source fountain and of the waterfall into the abyss can both be heard as a "mingled measure."

The dome is a work of art imposed upon a particular nature; it dominates that nature; but it also incorporates some of the polarities of nature. The sunny dome imitates the heavens, but it imitates the earth as well with its ice caves. Its holding together in one artifact such extremes is referred to as miraculous:

> It was a miracle of rare device,
> A sunny pleasure-dome with caves of ice.

The dome is not said to be a precarious thing, but there is a hint that the good fortune of its builder is precarious. The dome is a dome built for the Khan's pleasure and repose, but if the prophecy is to be believed, he faces war. The walled garden reminds one of an earthly paradise, but forebodings of bloodshed and destruction are to be heard within it.

There is one further thing worthy of remark: nothing is told of the fabrication of the rare device. As the tale is told, there is a hint that the Khan had merely to decree the dome and miraculously it was in place. At any rate, the artisans are not mentioned. No one is mentioned except the Khan who spoke the fiat, and he is not the modern lonely and specialized artist but ruler and warrior and executive. The man of vision—the artist who projects the dome—is here also the man of power.

To sum up: in the first thirty-five lines of this poem we are given a "history" out of the remote past which, though related directly and simply as something that happened, is in every way different from the modern world. In this relation a man of power (not the modern alienated artist) decrees a work of art which is no mere fabrication but is miraculous and which is set down in a tract of nature that is not the emptied and deprived nature of modern man but is rich, mysterious, and numinous.

Some scholars regard the poem as a fragment, and the last eighteen lines of it as a kind of postscript. But one can argue that the break between the two parts is a meaningful break and that what is said in the last eighteen lines actually completes the poem, rendering it a whole. The first line of this postscript, "A damsel with a dulcimer," may seem to be one more detail of the earthly paradise within the Khan's domains, but the next line disabuses us and even comes as a shock. The narration has been abruptly broken off. A new topic has been introduced, and for the first time an "I" has been introduced into the poem. If the first section of the poem might have been read from a book or presented in a dream or sketched in reverie, suddenly we now have a person speaking: "I once saw a damsel with a dulcimer in a vision." We have an "I" and we also have a dream or vision for the first time in the poem. If the earthly paradise within the Khan's domain has the quality of vision or dream, it has been presented at least as factual truth. Now we have the "I" saying that he has had a vision.

There are continuities, of course. The damsel is out of the same vision of an earthly paradise. She is from a far-away land, playing a music of unutterable sweetness calculated to inspire one to recreate the Khan's paradise.

The "I" of this poem will not, of course, build the dome as Kubla did. He will build it with music. But the conditions he sets for his creativity are curiously roundabout. He does not say that if he could only dream of Kubla Khan's pleasure dome, out of the intensity of dream vision, he would build it for his listeners. He does not even say that if he could recover the music of the damsel in the vision, he could build it. Rather, if he could revive in himself the music of the maid in the vision, it would so stir him to joy, that he would become truly creative and could himself produce a musical recreation of the Khan's pleasure dome.

Several things would seem to follow. First, the building of an imaginative picture must come out of the joyous creativity of the artist; that is, the artist cannot simply imitate; he must in his joyful creativity build anew and through his own music the thing that is visioned. He cannot simply take over someone else's vision or someone else's music. (This makes good esthetic sense, of course.) Second, if the speaker could indeed recover the vision and build the dome for us, he would pass beyond the bounds of poetry as we know it and become himself a numinous thing—a creature to be held in awe and dread as one who had indeed been in paradise and tasted its milk and honey-dew. Poetry reaches beyond itself and aspires to vision so intense that the poet becomes seer and prophet, the teller of truth. In proportion as the poet succeeds, he becomes the man set apart from his fellows, to be viewed, perhaps, with superstitious dread.

In saying "I would build that dome in air," the speaker

challenges comparison with the Khan. He says in effect: I will build what Kubla built. But his mode of building sets him at the other extreme from the great Khan. He becomes not emperor and ruler, but the man cut off from his fellows by a magic circle and of whom all cry, "Beware, beware." If the shudder of awe and the warnings whispered by those listening to his song are a compliment and a testimony to his power, they also mark his exile and his isolation. To recover the joy excited by the revived visionary music would involve its penalties as well as its triumph. This, he seems to say, is the plight of the poet in the modern world where man's capacities and talents are so divided and specialized that he loses his full humanity.

EXERCISE

1. This poem has been often praised for its use of suggestion and evocation. Would you agree? In this connection, consider lines 14–16 and lines 37–42.

2. What is the important function of the imagery in this poem? To stimulate the imagination? To build up the magical atmosphere? To define the theme? Consider the measureless "caverns," "the forests ancient as the hills," the "sunny spots of greenery," and the "waning moon." What about the description of the "sacred river"?

3. "Mount Abora" (line 41) seems to be reminiscent of "Mount *Amara*" in Milton's *Paradise Lost* (Book IV, line 281). Read Milton's description of the Garden of Eden (Book IV, lines 173–287) and compare it with the description found in this poem. Does the Milton passage throw light upon "Kubla Khan"? Does a knowledge of it add depth to "Kubla Khan"?

Lycidas

John Milton [*1608–1674*]

Yet once more, O ye Laurels, and once more,
Ye Myrtles brown, with Ivy never sere,
I come to pluck your berries harsh and crude,
And with forced fingers rude
Shatter your leaves before the mellowing year.

Bitter constraint and sad occasion dear
Compels me to disturb your season due;
For Lycidas is dead, dead ere his prime,
Young Lycidas, and hath not left his peer.
Who would not sing for Lycidas? he knew
Himself to sing, and build the lofty rhyme.
He must not float upon his wat'ry bier
Unwept, and welter to the parching wind,
Without the meed of some melodious tear.
  Begin, then, Sisters of the Sacred Well
That from beneath the seat of Jove doth spring,
Begin, and somewhat loudly sweep the string.
Hence with denial vain and coy excuse:
So may some gentle Muse
With lucky words favor my destined urn,
And, as he passes, turn,
And bid fair peace be to my sable shroud!
For we were nursed upon the self-same hill,
Fed the same flocks, by fountain, shade, and rill;
  Together both, ere the high lawns appeared
Under the opening eyelids of the Morn,
We drove a-field, and both together heard
What time the gray-fly winds her sultry horn,
Battening our flocks with the fresh dews of night,
Oft till the star that rose at evening bright
Towards Heaven's descent had sloped his westering wheel.
Meanwhile the rural ditties were not mute,
Tempered to the oaten flute,
Rough Satyrs danced, and Fauns with cloven heel
From the glad sound would not be absent long;
And old Damætas loved to hear our song.
  But, O the heavy change, now thou art gone,
Now thou art gone, and never must return!
Thee, Shepherd, thee the woods and desert caves,
With wild thyme and the gadding vine o'ergrown,
And all their echoes mourn.
The willows, and the hazel copses green,
Shall now no more be seen
Fanning their joyous leaves to thy soft lays.
As killing as the canker to the rose,
Or taint-worm to the weanling herds that graze,
Or frost to flowers, that their gay wardrobe wear
When first the white thorn blows;
Such, Lycidas, thy loss to shepherd's ear.

Where were ye, Nymphs, when the remorseless deep
Closed o'er the head of your loved Lycidas?
For neither were ye playing on the steep
Where your old bards, the famous Druids, lie,
Nor yet on the shaggy top of Mona high,
Nor yet where Deva spreads her wizard stream.
Ay me! I fondly dream!
"Had ye been there"—for what could that have done?
What could the Muse heself that Orpheus bore,
The Muse herself, for her enchanting son,
Whom universal Nature did lament,
When, by the rout that made the hideous roar,
His gory visage down the stream was sent,
Down the swift Hebrus to the Lesbian shore?
Alas! what boots it with uncessant care
To tend the homely, slighted, shepherd's trade,
And strictly meditate the thankless Muse?
Were it not better done, as others use,
To sport with Amaryllis in the shade,
Or with the tangles of Neæra's hair?
Fame is the spur that the clear spirit doth raise
(That last infirmity of noble mind)
To scorn delights and live laborious days;
But the fair guerdon when we hope to find,
And think to burst out into sudden blaze,
Comes the blind Fury with the abhorrèd shears,
And slits the thin-spun life. "But not the praise,"
Phœbus replied, and touched my trembling ears:
"Fame is no plant that grows on mortal soil,
Nor in the glistering foil
Set off to the world, nor in broad Rumor lies,
But lives and spreads aloft by those pure eyes
And perfect witness of all-judging Jove;
As he pronounces lastly on each deed,
Of so much fame in Heav'n expect thy meed."
O fountain Arethuse, and thou honored flood,
Smooth-sliding Mincius, crowned with vocal reeds,
That strain I heard was of a higher mood:
But now my oat proceeds,
And listens to the Herald of the Sea,
That came in Neptune's plea.
He asked the waves, and asked the felon winds,
What hard mishap hath doomed this gentle swain?
And questioned every gust of rugged wings

That blows from off each beakèd promontory:
They knew not of his story;
And sage Hippotadés their answer brings,
That not a blast was from his dungeon strayed:
The air was calm, and on the level brine
Sleek Panopé with all her sisters played.
It was that fatal and perfidious bark,
Built in the eclipse, and rigged with curses dark,
That sunk so low that sacred head of thine.
  Next, Camus, reverend sire, went footing slow,
His mantle hairy, and his bonnet sedge,
Inwrought with figures dim, and on the edge
Like to that sanguine flower inscribed with woe.
"Ah! who hath reft," quoth he, "my dearest pledge?"
Last came, and last did go,
The pilot of the Galilean lake;
Two massy keys he bore of metals twain
(The golden opes, the iron shuts amain).
He shook his mitered locks, and stern bespake:—
"How well could I have spared for thee, young Swain,
Enow of such, as for their bellies' sake,
Creep, and intrude, and climb into the fold!
Of other care they little reckoning make
Than how to scramble at the shearers' feast,
And shove away the worthy bidden guest.
Blind mouths! that scarce themselves know how to hold
A sheep-hook, or have learned aught else the least
That to the faithful herdsman's art belongs!
What recks it them? What need they? they are sped;
And, when they list, their lean and flashy songs
Grate on their scrannel pipes of wretched straw;
The hungry sheep look up, and are not fed,
But, swollen with wind and the rank mist they draw,
Rot inwardly, and foul contagion spread;
Besides what the grim wolf with privy paw
Daily devours apace, and nothing said;
But that two-handed engine at the door
Stands ready to smite once, and smite no more."
  Return, Alphéus; the dread voice is past
That shrunk thy streams; return, Sicilian Muse,
And call the vales, and bid them hither cast
Their bells and flowerets of a thousand hues.
Ye valleys low, where the mild whispers use
Of shades, and wanton winds, and gushing brooks,

On whose fresh lap the swart star sparely looks,
Throw hither all your quaint enameled eyes,
That on the green turf suck the honied showers,
And purple all the ground with vernal flowers.
Bring the rathe primrose that forsaken dies,
The tufted crow-toe, and pale jessamine,
The white pink, and the pansy freaked with jet,
The glowing violet,
The musk-rose, and the well-attired woodbine,
With cowslips wan that hang the pensive head,
And every flower that sad embroidery wears;
Bid Amaranthus all his beauty shed,
And daffadillies fill their cups with tears,
To strew the laureate hearse where Lycid lies.
For so, to interpose a little ease,
Let our frail thoughts dally with false surmise,
Ay me! whilst thee the shores and sounding seas
Wash far away, where'er thy bones are hurled;
Whether beyond the stormy Hebrides,
Where thou, perhaps, under the whelming tide
Visit'st the bottom of the monstrous world;
Or whether thou, to our moist vows denied,
Sleep'st by the fable of Bellerus old,
Where the great Vision of the guarded mount
Looks toward Namancos and Bayona's hold:
Look homeward, angel, now, and melt with ruth;
And, O ye Dolphins, waft the hapless youth.
  Weep no more, woeful shepherds, weep no more,
For Lycidas, your sorrow, is not dead,
Sunk though he be beneath the watery floor:
So sinks the day-star in the ocean bed
And yet anon repairs his drooping head,
And tricks his beams, and with new-spangled ore
Flames in the forehead of the morning sky:
So Lycidas sunk low, but mounted high,
Through the dear might of Him that walked the waves,
Where, other groves and other streams along,
With nectar pure his oozy locks he laves,
And hears the unexpressive nuptial song,
In the blest kingdoms meek of Joy and Love.
There entertain him all the Saints above,
In solemn troops, and sweet societies,
That sing, and singing in their glory move,
And wipe the tears forever from his eyes.

Now, Lycidas, the shepherds weep no more;
Henceforth thou art the Genius of the shore,
In thy large recompense, and shalt be good
To all that wander in that perilous flood.

Thus sang the uncouth swain to the oaks and rills,
While the still Morn went out with sandals gray;
He touched the tender stops of various quills,
With eager thought warbling his Doric lay:
And now the sun had stretched out all the hills,
And now was dropped into the western bay.
At last he rose, and twitched his mantle blue:
Tomorrow to fresh woods and pastures new.

EXERCISE

1. This is a pastoral elegy written at the death of one of Milton's friends, Edward King, a young scholar who was drowned in the Irish Sea. At this time Milton was a relatively young man already engaged in his pursuit of literary fame. Is the poem a mere compliment to King and a mere expression of grief at his death? What is the real theme of the poem? How is the theme related to the fact of the death of King? What is the relation of the apparently irrelevant passages (line 64 to line 84, line 103 to line 131) to the theme?

2. Dr. Samuel Johnson criticized this poem adversely in the following terms:

> One of the poems on which much praise has been bestowed is *Lycidas* of which the diction is harsh, the rhymes uncertain, and the numbers unpleasing. What beauty there is we must therefore seek in the sentiments and images. It is not to be considered as the effusion of real passion; for passion runs not after remote allusions and obscure opinions. Passion plucks no berries from the myrtle and ivy, nor calls upon Arethuse and Mincius, nor tells of rough *satyrs* and *fauns with cloven heel*. Where there is leisure for fiction there is little grief.
>
> In this poem there is no nature, for there is no truth; there is no art, for there is nothing new. Its form is that of a pastoral, easy, vulgar, and therefore disgusting; whatever images it can supply are long ago exhausted, and its inherent improbability always forces dissatisfaction on the

mind. When Cowley [a poet who was the contemporary of Milton] tells of Hervey, that they studied together, it is easy to suppose how much he must miss the companion of his labors, and the partner of his discoveries; but what image of tenderness can be excited by these lines?—

> We drove a-field, and both together heard
> What time the gray-fly winds her sultry horn,
> Batt'ning our flocks with the fresh dews of night.

We know that they never drove a-field, and that they had no flocks to batten; and though it be allowed that the representation may be allegorical, the true meaning is so uncertain and remote that it is never sought because it cannot be known when found. . . . He who thus grieves will excite no sympathy; he who thus praises will confer no honor.

(From "John Milton," in *Lives of the English Poets*)

Dr. Johnson, to sum up, attacks the poem for awkward technique and for insincerity. What do you make of these two charges?

In regard to the first, scan lines 1–4 and 64–84, and comment on the rhythm, verse texture, alliteration, consonance, and other technical factors.

3. In regard to the second charge, is the pastoral convention *necessarily* more artificial than the fiction indulged in by Yeats that his loved one is a "daughter of the swan" (p. 335)? What do you mean by "insincerity" in poetry?

Note, further, that the speaker of the poem acknowledges the difficulty in maintaining a pastoral note. Apollo was one of the high gods, and his pronouncement is acknowledged as a strain of "higher mood" as the speaker tries to resume the humbler pastoral note. After St. Peter's scathing comment on the unworthy shepherd, the speaker calls back the Sicilian muse (the muse of pastoral poetry) as if she had been frightened away. Do these admissions weaken the poem, or strengthen it? How do they bear on the charge by Dr. Johnson that the pastoral was by Milton's time a worn-out and artificial form?

4. Discuss the shifts in tone of this poem. How are they marked? What do they indicate about the narrative element in the poem? What do the last eight lines do for the tone as a

whole? (Note that we have a third-person ending, though the poem begins in the first person, with the swain speaking. Can you justify this lack of symmetry?)

5. Dr. Johnson objected to the mixture of pagan and Christian elements in this poem. Can you justify it? Is there evidence that the poet mixed them consciously and for a purpose?

6. Note the water imagery. Why is there so much of it? Does it develop into a symbolism?

7. What is the significance of allusion in "Lycidas"? Do you see any difference between the use here and that in Yeats's "Two Songs" (p. 403) and Eliot's "Prufrock" (p. 386)?

8. For an interpretation of "Lycidas," see E. M. W. Tillyard's *Milton* (New York, The Macmillan Company, 1930, pp. 80–85). What bearing does this interpretation have on the whole question of sincerity and convention?

Ode to a Nightingale

John Keats [*1795–1821*]

My heart aches, and a drowsy numbness pains
  My sense, as though of hemlock I had drunk,
Or emptied some dull opiate to the drains
  One minute past, and Lethe-wards had sunk:
'Tis not through envy of thy happy lot,
  But being too happy in thine happiness,—
    That thou, light-wingèd Dryad of the trees,
        In some melodious plot
  Of beechen green, and shadows numberless,
    Singest of summer in full-throated ease.

O for a draught of vintage! that hath been
  Cooled a long age in the deep-delvèd earth,
Tasting of Flora and the country-green,
  Dance, and Provençal song, and sunburnt mirth!
O for a beaker full of the warm South,
  Full of the true, the blushful Hippocrene,
    With beaded bubbles winking at the brim,
        And purple-stainèd mouth;
  That I might drink, and leave the world unseen,
    And with thee fade away into the forest dim:

Fade far away, dissolve, and quite forget
  What thou among the leaves hast never known,
The weariness, the fever, and the fret
  Here, where men sit and hear each other groan;
Where palsy shakes a few, sad, last gray hairs,
  Where youth grows pale, and specter-thin, and dies;
    Where but to think is to be full of sorrow
      And leaden-eyed despairs,
  Where Beauty cannot keep her lustrous eyes,
    Or new Love pine at them beyond tomorrow.

Away! away! for I will fly to thee,
  Not charioted by Bacchus and his pards,
But on the viewless wings of Poesy,
  Though the dull brain perplexes and retards:
Already with thee! tender is the night,
  And haply the Queen-Moon is on her throne,
    Clustered around by all her starry Fays;
      But here there is no light,
  Save what from heaven is with the breezes blown
    Through verdurous glooms and winding mossy ways.

I cannot see what flowers are at my feet,
  Nor what soft incense hangs upon the boughs,
But, in embalmèd darkness, guess each sweet
  Wherewith the seasonable month endows
The grass, the thicket, and the fruit-tree wild;
  White hawthorn, and the pastoral eglantine;
  Fast-fading violets covered up in leaves;
      And mid-May's eldest child,
  The coming musk-rose, full of dewy wine,
    The murmurous haunt of flies on summer eves.

Darkling I listen; and, for many a time
  I have been half in love with easeful Death,
Called him soft names in many a musèd rhyme,
  To take into the air my quiet breath;
Now more than ever seems it rich to die,
  To cease upon the midnight with no pain,
    While thou art pouring forth thy soul abroad
      In such an ecstasy!
  Still wouldst thou sing, and I have ears in vain—
    To thy high requiem become a sod.

Thou wast not born for death, immortal Bird!
  No hungry generations tread thee down;
The voice I hear this passing night was heard
  In ancient days by emperor and clown:
Perhaps the self-same song that found a path
  Through the sad heart of Ruth, when, sick for home,
    She stood in tears amid the alien corn;
        The same that oft-times hath
  Charmed magic casements, opening on the foam
    Of perilous seas, in faery lands forlorn.

Forlorn! the very word is like a bell
  To toll me back from thee to my sole self!
Adieu! the fancy cannot cheat so well
  As she is famed to do, deceiving elf.
Adieu! adieu! thy plaintive anthem fades
  Past the near meadows, over the still stream,
        Up the hill-side; and now 'tis buried deep
        In the next valley-glades:
Was it a vision, or a waking dream?
Fled is that music:—Do I wake or sleep?

In this poem the world of mankind and the world of the nightingale stand over against each other. The listener in the human world responds to the song of the nightingale and, caught up into reverie, yearns to find his way into the world in which the bird sings "of summer in full-throated ease." What the world of the nightingale means to the listener is conveyed in great part through the imagery of the poem. It is a world of richness and vitality, of deep sensuousness, of natural beauty and fertility, but it is not grossly sensuous; it appeals to the imagination and has its own ideality.

Invoking the help of wine and then of poetry, the speaker aspires to attain the nightingale's felicity. But the very description of the wine makes it not so much a passport to the world of the nightingale as a vintage belonging to that world. Indeed the transition from wine to poetry is perfectly smooth, for the wine as realized in the second stanza turns into poetry —a poetic evocation of the spirit of wine.

The images are lovingly elaborated, and the slowed movement of the images resembles the slowed movement of meditative trance or reverie. The reverie carries the listener deep into the "embalmèd darkness" out of which the bird is singing and deep into a communion in which he can make his peace even with death. But the meditative trance cannot last. With the very first word of the eighth stanza, the reverie is broken. The word "forlorn" occurs to the listener as the adjective describing the remote and magical world evoked by the nightingale's song—"in faery lands forlorn." But the listener suddenly realizes that *forlorn* applies only too accurately to himself. The effect is that of an abrupt stumbling. With the new and chilling meaning of "forlorn," the song of the nightingale itself alters: what had a moment before been an ecstatic "high requiem" becomes a "plaintive anthem." The song becomes fainter: what had had power to make the sorrowing man "fade . . . away" from a harsh and bitter world, now itself "fades" (line 75) and the speaker is left alone in the silence.

"Ode to a Nightingale" is a very rich poem. It contains some complications which we must not gloss over if we are to appreciate the depth and significance of the issues engaged. One of these complications has to do with the close connection between pleasure and pain; another, with that between life and death.

The song of the nightingale has a curious double effect. It makes the listener's heart "ache," but makes it ache, as he is to say in line 6, from "being too happy in thine happiness." The song also acts as an opiate, making the listener feel drowsy and benumbed. Opiates are used to deaden pain, and in a sense the song of the bird does give the man momentary surcease from his unhappiness, oppressed as he is with the "weariness, the fever, and the fret" of the world of humanity.

The student will have to decide whether there is confusion here in this first stanza or an admirable condensation. The initial effect of a heavy opiate, though it leads to an escape from pain in drowsy forgetfulness—"Lethe-wards"—may indeed be painfully numbing. (He who drank of the waters of the river Lethe forgot the sadness of life.) The drowsiness also looks forward to the sense of tranced reverie which is the mood of most of the poem. In that mood the listener does try very hard to immerse himself in the happiness of the bird, projecting himself imaginatively into the world that the bird seems to inhabit.

With the listener's attempt to find his way into the world of the nightingale, we encounter the second complication, that in which death and life change relationship. The nightingale's song makes him yearn to escape from a world overshadowed by death—"where youth grows pale . . . and dies," "Where but to think is to be full of sorrow." Yet when he has approached closest to the nightingale's world, the highest rapture that he can conceive of is to die—"To cease upon the midnight with no pain." * The world of the nightingale is, as we shall see, not a world untouched by death—natural processes involve death—but one in which death is not a negative and blighting thing. But at this point the most useful thing to ask ourselves is, "What is it that bars the speaker from entering the world of the nightingale?" He tells us himself: it is the "dull brain" that "perplexes and retards." The opiate, the draught of vintage for which he had earlier called, and the free play of the imagination ("the viewless wings of Poesy")—all have this in common: they release one from the tyranny of the "dull brain." The brain insists upon clarity and logical order; it is an order that must be "dissolved" if the speaker is to escape into, and merge himself with, the richer world for which he longs.

But the word which the speaker uses to describe this process is "fade." His entry into this world of the nightingale is a fading into the rich darkness out of which the nightingale sings. We associate darkness with death, but this darkness is instinct with the most intense life. How is the darkness stressed—and thus defined? The nightingale sings in a plot of "shadows numberless" (line 9); the speaker would leave the world "unseen" (line 19) and join the bird in "the forest dim" (line 20); he would "fade far away"—would "dissolve" (line 21); and when he feels that he is actually with the nightingale, he is in a place of "verdurous glooms" (line 40).

The stress upon a darkness in which clear relations are blotted out continues through the fifth stanza. Having attained to the bird's dark covert, he "cannot see." Though the

* It would be a superficial reading that would make the issue between a painless and an agonizing death. The speaker is saying much more than that he would like to die if he could only be sure that his death would be without pain.

passage abounds in sensuous detail and appeals so powerfully to all the senses, most of the images of sight are *fancied* by the speaker. He does not actually see the Queen-Moon or the stars. He "guess[es]" at what flowers are at his feet. He has found his way into a warm "embalmèd darkness." The last adjective means primarily "filled with incense," "sweet with balm," but it must also have suggested death—in Keats's day as well as in ours. In finding his way imaginatively into the dark covert, the speaker has approached death. He has wished to fade far away, "dissolve, and quite forget"; but the final dissolution and the ultimate forgetting is death. True, death here is apprehended in a quite different fashion from the death depicted in the third stanza. Here the balm is the natural perfume of growing flowers and the gloom is "verdurous," with suggestions of rich organic growth. But the fading has been complete—he is completely encompassed with darkness.

It is worth remarking that Keats has described the flowery covert with full honesty. If his primary emphasis is on fertility and growth, he accepts the fact that death and change have their place here too: the violets, for instance, are thought of as "fast-fading." But the atmosphere of this world of nature is very different from that of the human world haunted by death, where "men sit and hear each other groan." The world of nature is a world of cyclic change (the "seasonable month," "the coming musk-rose") and consequently can seem fresh and immortal, like the bird whose song seems to be its spirit.

Let us suggest that the poem is not only about man's world as contrasted with the world of nature, or death and deathlessness, but also about alienation and wholeness. It is man's necessary alienation from nature that invests death with its special horror. To "dissolve"—to "fade"—into the warm darkness is to merge into the eternal pattern of nature. In such a communion, death itself becomes something positive—a flowering, a fulfillment.*

* Keats has stressed this association very cunningly in the sixth stanza. The men of the ancient world thought that at death a man breathed out his soul with his last breath. In the seventh stanza, the nightingale is "pouring forth" its "soul"; and at this high moment, the man who is listening in the darkness thinks it would be "rich to die." The most intense expression of life (the nightingale's ecstatic song) invites the human listener to pour forth his soul (breathe his last breath).

The bird lacks man's self-consciousness. It is not alienated from nature, but wholly merged in nature. Such considerations suggest the sense in which the nightingale is "immortal." The bird shares in the immortality of nature which, harmonious with itself, remains, through all its myriad changes, unwearied and beautiful. We need not suppose that the speaker, even in his tranced reverie, thinks of this bird—this particular biological mechanism of flesh and bone and feathers—as deathless, any more than he thinks of the "fast-fading violets" and the "coming musk-rose" as unwithering. Keats makes perfectly clear the sense in which the nightingale is immortal: it is in harmony with its world—not, as man is, in competition with his ("No hungry generations tread thee down," line 62); and the bird cannot conceive of its separation from the world which it expresses and of which it is a part ("Thou wast not born for death," line 61). Man knows that he was born to die, knows "The weariness, the fever, and the fret" of the world of mortality, knows in short "What thou among the leaves hast never known" (line 22); and this knowledge overshadows man's life and all his songs.

Such knowledge overshadows the Ode and gives it its special poignancy. With the word "forlorn," the speaker's attempt to enter the world of the nightingale collapses. The music which almost succeeded in making him "fade far away" now itself "fades / Past the near meadows" (lines 75–76) and in a moment is "buried deep / In the next valley-glades" (lines 77–78). The word "buried" conveys in this context a view of death very different from that conjured up by "embalmed darkness" in the fifth stanza. The poem has come full circle. The speaker, like the knight in Keats's "La Belle Dame sans Merci" is left alone "On the cold hill's side."

EXERCISE

1. The imagery of the second stanza is justly celebrated for its evocative power. What is evoked? Can you justify the use here of "Flora," "Provençal," and "Hippocrene"? Can wine be said to taste of *dance* and *song*? Note that the poet does not say that the wine *gives* the drinker a "purple-stained mouth"

but seems to say that the wine itself *has* such a mouth. Discuss the use of language which is being made here.

2. Discuss lines 38–40. What does the poet gain by suggesting that light can be blown about by the breezes? What would a literal statement of this phenomenon be?

3. For the story of Ruth, see the *Book of Ruth* in the Bible. Why does the phrase "alien corn" come with special poignancy? Why would either "alien trees" or "alien hills" be less effective?

4. What kind of world is suggested by lines 69–70? Some of the adjectives, like "perilous," "faery," and "forlorn," seem vague and indefinite; but note that the scene is precisely visualized. Discuss the special use of imagery that is being made in this passage.

5. Justify "Do I wake or sleep?" as the proper conclusion for the poem. How is this question related to the rest of the eighth stanza and to the rest of the whole poem?

Ode on a Grecian Urn

John Keats [*1795–1821*]

Thou still unravished bride of quietness,
Thou foster-child of silence and slow time,
Sylvan historian, who canst thus express
A flowery tale more sweetly than our rime:
What leaf-fringed legend haunts about thy shape
Of deities or mortals, or of both,
In Tempe or the dales of Arcady?
What men or gods are these? What maidens loth?
What mad pursuit? What struggle to escape?
What pipes and timbrels? What wild ecstasy?

Heard melodies are sweet, but those unheard
Are sweeter; therefore, ye soft pipes, play on;
Not to the sensual ear, but, more endeared,
Pipe to the spirit ditties of no tone:
Fair youth, beneath the trees, thou canst not leave
Thy song, nor ever can those trees be bare;
Bold Lover, never, never canst thou kiss,

Though winning near the goal—yet, do not grieve;
She cannot fade, though thou hast not thy bliss,
Forever wilt thou love, and she be fair!

Ah, happy, happy boughs! That cannot shed
Your leaves, nor ever bid the Spring adieu:
And, happy melodist, unwearièd,
Forever piping songs forever new;
More happy love! more happy, happy love!
Forever warm and still to be enjoy'd,
Forever panting, and forever young;
All breathing human passion far above,
That leaves a heart high-sorrowful and cloyed,
A burning forehead, and a parching tongue.

Who are these coming to the sacrifice?
To what green altar, O mysterious priest,
Lead'st thou that heifer lowing at the skies,
And all her silken flanks with garlands drest?
What little town by river or sea shore,
Or mountain-built with peaceful citadel,
Is emptied of this folk, this pious morn?
And, little town, thy streets for evermore
Will silent be; and not a soul to tell
Why thou are desolate, can e'er return.

O Attic shape! Fair Attitude! with brede
Of marble men and maidens overwrought,
With forest branches and the trodden weed;
Thou, silent form, dost tease us out of thought
As doth eternity: Cold Pastoral!
When old age shall this generation waste,
Thou shalt remain, in midst of other woe
Than ours, a friend to man, to whom thou sayst,
Beauty is Truth,—Truth Beauty,—that is all
Ye know on earth, and all ye need to know.*

* In lines 49–50, the editors follow the punctuation of four extant manuscripts of the poem made by Keats's friends, "all unquestionably not far removed from the original, and all [of which] agree." See Alvin Whitley, "The Message of the Grecian Urn," *Keats-Shelley Memorial Bulletin,* V (1953), pp. 2–3.

EXERCISE

1. In what sense is the urn a "sylvan historian" (line 3)? What are some of the "flowery tales" that it expresses to the observer?

2. How is the paradox of the speaking urn—the urn that can express tales "more sweetly than our rime"—related to some of the other paradoxes in the poem (for example, the unheard pipes that play ditties)?

3. The ideal life expressed in the scenes wrought upon the urn avoids the disappointments of actual life. Has the poet played fair in presenting these scenes as being in a sense lifeless and cold? Is the ironic counterpoise maintained in the poem?

4. What is the force of the phrase "Cold Pastoral" (line 45)? How does it gather up and summarize the relation of the ideal to the actual?

5. Is the famous concluding passage (lines 49–50) insisted upon as a philosophic generalization in its own right? Or is it to be regarded as a dramatic utterance spoken by the urn? The poet has said that the urn "tease[s] us out of thought / As doth eternity." The timeless ideal world of the urn is as enigmatic as eternity. It bewilders our time-ridden human minds: it teases us. Are the last two lines a teasing utterance or not? What is their truth? Do the preceding forty-eight lines serve to define it?

VII

Poems for Study

FOREWORD

This section consists of a group of poems presented without any critical apparatus or discussion. There is a certain virtue—a dramatic impact—in letting the student confront poems in their "wild" state, unhobbled and ungentled by the manipulations of an editor. This direct confrontation is, of course, the way things ordinarily happen—as they happen when somebody pulls a book off a shelf or opens a magazine. But even then one does not read the poem without reference to one's previous experience. One reads the poem with meaning only if one is ready to read it. This section, we may say, offers the student an opportunity to test his readiness.

Most of the poems in previous sections of this book have been drawn from poetry of the past, but the poems here are modern, if we may be allowed to stretch the term to include Gerard Manley Hopkins. The choice of modern poems, moreover, works towards an immediate confrontation. Though some of the poems here are famous and have already generated a large body of scholarship and criticism, they do come out of, and refer to, the world the student himself inhabits. It is to be clearly understood, however, that this selection, even with the addition of other modern poems elsewhere in this book, does not pretend to give a survey of modern poetry. Some of the finest examples are omitted. But we do hope that a number of modern techniques and themes are represented.

The arrangement of the poems in this section is not haphazard and random. We have tried to set up some natural groupings—for example, the first five poems may be regarded as elegies, or again, "The Waste Land" and the half dozen or more pieces following have to do with values and lack of values in the modern world. Such groupings are not to be thought of as rigid categories. They are, rather, fluid and shifting, arrangements made for convenience. A poem now in one constellation might, with a change of perspective, be transferred to another. For example, the last section of "In Memory of W. B. Yeats," by Auden, which now appears among the elegies, might very well be put after "The Waste Land," among the pieces dealing with the modern world. Every good poem is a dense and vital thing, and therefore involves more than one interest and offers more than one suggestive aspect. Our hope is simply that alignments and contrasts here indicated will provide the student with useful leads into the individual poems.

Upon a Dying Lady

William Butler Yeats [1865–1939]

I. *Her Courtesy*

With the old kindness, the old distinguished grace,
She lies, her lovely piteous head amid dull red hair
Propped upon pillows, rouge on the pallor of her face.
She would not have us sad because she is lying there,
And when she meets our gaze her eyes are laughter-lit,
Her speech a wicked tale that we may vie with her,
Matching our broken-hearted wit against her wit,
Thinking of saints and of Petronius Arbiter.

II. *Certain Artists Bring Her Dolls and Drawings*

Bring where our Beauty lies
A new modeled doll, or drawing,

With a friend's or an enemy's
Features, or maybe showing
Her features when a tress
Of dull red hair was flowing
Over some silken dress
Cut in the Turkish fashion,
Or, it may be, like a boy's.
We have given the world our passion,
We have naught for death but toys.

III. *She Turns the Dolls' Faces to the Wall*

Because to-day is some religious festival
They had a priest say Mass, and even the Japanese,
Heel up and weight on toe, must face the wall
—Pedant in passion, learned in old courtesies,
Vehement and witty she had seemed—; the Venetian lady
Who had seemed to glide to some intrigue in her red shoes,
Her domino, her panniered skirt copied from Longhi;
The meditative critic; all are on their toes,
Even our Beauty with her Turkish trousers on.
Because the priest must have like every dog his day
Or keep us all awake with baying at the moon,
We and our dolls being but the world were best away.

IV. *The End of Day*

She is playing like a child
And penance is the play,
Fantastical and wild
Because the end of day
Shows her that some one soon
Will come from the house, and say—
Though play is but half done—
"Come in and leave the play."

V. *Her Race*

She has not grown uncivil
As narrow natures would
And called the pleasures evil
Happier days thought good;
She knows herself a woman,
No red and white of a face,

Or rank, raised from a common
Unreckonable race;
And how should her heart fail her
Or sickness break her will
With her dead brother's valor
For an example still?

VI. *Her Courage*

When her soul flies to the predestined dancing-place
(I have no speech but symbol, the pagan speech I made
Amid the dreams of youth) let her come face to face,
Amid that first astonishment, with Grania's shade,
All but the terrors of the woodland flight forgot
That made her Diarmuid dear, and some old cardinal
Pacing with half-closed eyelids in a sunny spot
Who had murmured of Giorgione at his latest breath—
Aye, and Achilles, Timor, Babar, Barhaim, all
Who have lived in joy and laughed into the face of Death.

VII. *Her Friends Bring Her a Christmas Tree*

Pardon, great enemy,
Without an angry thought
We've carried in our tree,
And here and there have bought
Till all the boughs are gay,
And she may look from the bed
On pretty things that may
Please a fantastic head.
Give her a little grace,
What if a laughing eye
Have looked into your face?
It is about to die.

In Memory of W. B. Yeats

W. H. Auden [1907–   ]

I

He disappeared in the dead of winter:
The brooks were frozen, the airports almost deserted,
And snow disfigured the public statues;

The mercury sank in the mouth of the dying day.
O all the instruments agree
The day of his death was a dark cold day.

Far from his illness
The wolves ran on through the evergreen forests,
The peasant river was untempted by the fashionable quays;
By mourning tongues
The death of the poet was kept from his poems.

But for him it was his last afternoon as himself,
An afternoon of nurses and rumors;
The provinces of his body revolted,
The squares of his mind were empty,
Silence invaded the suburbs,
The current of his feeling failed: he became his admirers.

Now he is scattered among a hundred cities
And wholly given over to unfamiliar affections;
To find his happiness in another kind of wood
And be punished under a foreign code of conscience.
The words of a dead man
Are modified in the guts of the living.

But in the importance and noise of tomorrow
When the brokers are roaring like beasts on the floor of the Bourse,
And the poor have the sufferings to which they are fairly accustomed,
And each in the cell of himself is almost convinced of his freedom;
A few thousand will think of this day
As one thinks of a day when one did something slightly unusual.
O all the instruments agree
The day of his death was a dark cold day.

II

You were silly like us: your gift survived it all;
The parish of rich women, physical decay,
Yourself; mad Ireland hurt you into poetry.
Now Ireland has her madness and her weather still,
For poetry makes nothing happen: it survives

In the valley of its saying where executives
Would never want to tamper; it flows south
From ranches of isolation and the busy griefs,
Raw towns that we believe and die in; it survives,
A way of happening, a mouth.

III

Earth, receive an honored guest;
William Yeats is laid to rest:
Let the Irish vessel lie
Emptied of its poetry.

Time that is intolerant
Of the brave and innocent,
And indifferent in a week
To a beautiful physique,

Worships language and forgives
Everyone by whom it lives;
Pardons cowardice, conceit,
Lays its honors at their feet.

Time that with this strange excuse
Pardoned Kipling and his views,
And will pardon Paul Claudel,
Pardons him for writing well.

In the nightmare of the dark
All the dogs of Europe bark,
And the living nations wait,
Each sequestered in its hate;

Intellectual disgrace
Stares from every human face,
And the seas of pity lie
Locked and frozen in each eye.

Follow, poet, follow right
To the bottom of the night,
With your unconstraining voice
Still persuade us to rejoice;

With the farming of a verse
Make a vineyard of the curse,

Sing of human unsuccess
In a rapture of distress;

In the deserts of the heart
Let the healing fountain start,
In the prison of his days
Teach the free man how to praise.

Praise for an Urn

Hart Crane [*1899–1932*]

It was a kind and northern face
That mingled in such exile guise
The everlasting eyes of Pierrot
And, of Gargantua, the laughter.

His thoughts, delivered to me
From the white coverlet and pillow,
I see now, were inheritances—
Delicate riders of the storm.

The slant moon on the slanting hill
Once moved us toward presentiments
Of what the dead keep, living still,
And such assessments of the soul

As, perched in the crematory lobby,
The insistent clock commented on,
Touching as well upon our praise
Of glories proper to the time.

Still, having in mind gold hair,
I cannot see that broken brow
And miss the dry sound of bees
Stretching across a lucid space.

Scatter these well-meant idioms
Into the smoky spring that fills
The suburbs, where they will be lost.
They are no trophies of the sun.

The Quaker Graveyard in Nantucket

(For *Warren Winslow,* Dead at Sea)

Robert Lowell [*1917–*]

Let man have dominion over the fishes of the sea and the fowls of the air and the beasts and the whole earth, and every creeping creature that moveth upon the earth.

I

A brackish reach of shoal off Madaket,—
The sea was still breaking violently and night
Had steamed into our North Atlantic Fleet,
When the drowned sailor clutched the drag-net. Light
Flashed from his matted head and marble feet,
He grappled at the net
With the coiled, hurdling muscles of his thighs:
The corpse was bloodless, a botch of reds and whites,
Its open, staring eyes
Were lusterless dead-lights
Or cabin-windows on a stranded hulk
Heavy with sand. We weight the body, close
Its eyes and heave it seaward whence it came,
Where the heel-headed dogfish barks its nose
On Ahab's void and forehead; and the name
Is blocked in yellow chalk.
Sailors, who pitch this portent at the sea
Where dreadnaughts shall confess
Its hell-bent deity,
When you are powerless
To sand-bag this Atlantic bulwark, faced
By the earth-shaker, green, unwearied, chaste
In his steel scales: ask for no Orphean lute
To pluck life back. The guns of the steeled fleet
Recoil and then repeat
The hoarse salute.

II

Whenever winds are moving and their breath
Heaves at the roped-in bulwarks of this pier,
The terns and sea-gulls tremble at your death

In these home waters. Sailor, can you hear
The Pequod's sea wings, beating landward, fall
Headlong and break on our Atlantic wall
Off 'Sconset, where the yawing S-boats splash
The bellbuoy, with ballooning spinnakers,
As the entangled, screeching mainsheet clears
The blocks: off Madaket, where lubbers lash
The heavy surf and throw their long lead squids
For blue-fish? Sea-gulls blink their heavy lids
Seaward. The winds' wings beat upon the stones,
Cousin, and scream for you and the claws rush
At the sea's throat and wring it in the slush
Of this old Quaker graveyard where the bones
Cry out in the long night for the hurt beast
Bobbing by Ahab's whaleboats in the East.

III

All you recovered from Poseidon died
With you, my cousin, and the harrowed brine
Is fruitless on the blue beard of the god,
Stretching beyond us to the castles in Spain,
Nantucket's westward haven. To Cape Cod
Guns, cradled on the tide,
Blast the eelgrass about a waterclock
Of bilge and backwash, roil the salt and sand
Lashing earth's scaffold, rock
Our warships in the hand
Of the great God, where time's contrition blues
Whatever it was these Quaker sailors lost
In the mad scramble of their lives. They died
When time was open-eyed,
Wooden and childish; only bones abide
There, in the nowhere, where their boats were tossed
Sky-high, where mariners had fabled news
Of IS, the whited monster. What it cost
Them is their secret. In the monster's slick
I see the Quakers drown and hear their cry:
"If God himself had not been on our side,
If God himself had not been on our side,
When the Atlantic rose against us, why
Then it had swallowed us up quick."

IV

This is the end of the whaleroad and the whale
Who spewed Nantucket bones on the thrashed swell
And stirred the troubled waters to whirlpools
To send the Pequod packing off to hell:
This is the end of them, three-quarters fools,
Snatching at straws to sail
Seaward and seaward on the turntail whale,
Spouting out blood and water as it rolls,
Sick as a dog to these Atlantic shoals:
Clamavimus, O depths. Let the sea-gulls wail

For water, for the deep where the high tide
Mutters to its hurt self, mutters and ebbs.
Waves wallow in their wash, go out and out,
Leave only the death-rattle of the crabs,
The beach increasing, its enormous snout
Sucking the ocean's side.
This is the end of running on the waves;
We are poured out like water. Who will dance
The mast-lashed master of Leviathans
Up from this field of Quakers in their unstoned graves?

V

When the whale's viscera go and the roll
Of its corruption orerruns this world
Beyond tree-swept Nantucket and Woods Hole
And Martha's Vineyard, Sailor, will your sword
Whistle and fall and sink into the fat?
In the great ash-pit of Jehoshaphat
The bones cry for the blood of the white whale,
The fat flukes arch and whack about its ears,
The death-lance churns into the sanctuary, tears
The gun-blue swingle, heaving like a flail,
And hacks the coiling life out: it works and drags
And rips the sperm-whale's midriff into rags,
Gobbets of blubber spill to wind and weather,
Sailor, and gulls go round the stoven timbers
Where the morning stars sing out together
And thunder shakes the white surf and dismembers
The red flag hammered in the mast-head. Hide,
Our steel, Jonas Messias, in Thy side.

VI

Our Lady of Walsingham

There once the penitents took off their shoes
And then walked barefoot the remaining mile;
And the small trees, a stream and hedgerows file
Slowly along the munching English lane,
Like cows to the old shrine, until you lose
Track of your dragging pain.
The stream flows down under the druid tree,
Shiloah's whirlpool gurgle and make glad
The castle of God. Sailor, you were glad
And whistled Sion by that stream. But see:

Our Lady, too small for her canopy,
Sits near the altar. There's no comeliness
At all or charm in that expressionless
Face with its heavy eyelids. As before,
This face, for centuries a memory,
Non est species, neque decor,
Expressionless, expresses God: it goes
Past castled Sion. She knows what God knows,
Not Calvary's Cross nor crib at Bethlehem
Now, and the world shall come to Walsingham.

VII

The empty winds are creaking and the oak
Splatters and splatters on the cenotaph,
The boughs are trembling and a gaff
Bobs on the untimely stroke
Of the greased wash exploding on a shoal-bell
In the old mouth of the Atlantic. It's well;
Atlantic, you are fouled with the blue sailors,
Sea-monsters, upward angel, downward fish:
Unmarried and corroding, spare of flesh
Mart once of supercilious, wing'd clippers,
Atlantic, where your bell-trap guts its spoil
You could cut the brackish winds with a knife
Here in Nantucket, and cast up the time
When the Lord God formed man from the sea's slime
And breathed into his face the breath of life,
And blue-lung'd combers lumbered to the kill.
The Lord survives the rainbow of His will.

Christmas Eve in Whitneyville, 1955

to my father

Donald Hall [*1928–*]

December, and the closing of the year;
The momentary carolers complete
Their Christmas Eves, and quickly disappear
Into their houses on each lighted street.

Each car is put away in each garage;
Each husband home from work, to celebrate,
Has closed his house around him like a cage,
And wedged the tree until the tree stood straight.

Tonight you lie in Whitneyville again,
Near where you lived, and near the woods or farms
Which Eli Whitney settled with the men
Who worked at mass-producing firearms.

The main-street, which was nothing after all
Except a school, a stable, and two stores,
Was improvised and individual,
Picking its way alone, until the wars.

Now Whitneyville is like the other places,
Ranch-houses stretching flat beyond the square,
Same stores and movie, same composite faces
Speaking the language of the public air.

Old buildings loiter by the cemetery.
When you were twelve, they dressed you up in black
With five companions from the class, to carry
The body of a friend. Now you are back,

Beside him, but a man of fifty-two.
Talk to the boy. Tell him about the years
When Whitneyville quadrupled, and how you
And all his friends went on to make careers,

Had cars as long as hayricks, flew in planes,
And took vacation trips across the sea.

Like millionaires. Tell him how yearly gains,
Profit and volume built the company.

"The things you had to miss," you said last week,
"Or thought you had to, take your breath away."
You propped yourself on pillows, where your cheek
Was hollow, stubbled lightly with new gray.

This love is jail; another sets us free.
Tonight the houses and their noise distort
The thin rewards of solidarity.
The houses lean together for support.

The noises fail. Now lights go on upstairs.
The men and women are undressing now
To go to sleep. They put their clothes on chairs
To take them up again. I think of how,

Across America, when midnight comes,
They lie together and are quieted,
To sleep as children sleep, who suck their thumbs,
Cramped in the narrow rumple of each bed.

They will not have unpleasant thoughts tonight.
They make their houses jails, and they will take
No risk of freedom for the appetite,
Or knowledge of it, when they are awake.

The lights go out and it is Christmas Day.
The stones are white, the grass is black and deep;
I will go back and leave you here to stay,
While the dark houses harden into sleep.

My Father Moved through Dooms of Love

E. E. Cummings [*1894–1962*]

my father moved through dooms of love
through sames of am through haves of give,
singing each morning out of each night
my father moved through depths of height

this motionless forgetful where
turned at his glance to shining here;

that if (so timid air is firm)
under his eyes would stir and squirm

newly as from unburied which
floats the first who, his april touch
drove sleeping selves to swarm their fates
woke dreamers to their ghostly roots

and should some why completely weep
my father's fingers brought her sleep:
vainly no smallest voice might cry
for he could feel the mountains grow.

Lifting the valleys of the sea
my father moved through griefs of joy;
praising a forehead called the moon
singing desire into begin

joy was his song and joy so pure
a heart of star by him could steer
and pure so now and now so yes
the wrists of twilight would rejoice

keen as midsummer's keen beyond
conceiving mind of sun will stand,
so strictly (over utmost him
so hugely) stood my father's dream

his flesh was flesh his blood was blood:
no hungry man but wished him food;
No cripple wouldn't creep one mile
uphill to only see him smile.

Scorning the pomp of must and shall
my father moved through dooms of feel;
his anger was as right as rain
his pity was as green as grain

septembering arms of year extend
less humbly wealth to foe and friend
than he to foolish and to wise
offered immeasurable is

proudly and (by octobering flame
beckoned) as earth will downward climb,

so naked for immortal work
his shoulders marched against the dark

his sorrow was as true as bread:
no liar looked him in the head;
if every friend became his foe
he'd laugh and build a world with snow.

My father moved through theys of we,
singing each new leaf out of each tree
(and every child was sure that spring
danced when she heard my father sing)

then let men kill which cannot share,
let blood and flesh be mud and mire,
scheming imagine, passion willed,
freedom a drug that's bought and sold

giving to steal and cruel kind,
a heart to fear, to doubt a mind,
to differ a disease of same,
conform the pinnacle of am

though dull were all we taste as bright,
bitter all utterly things sweet,
maggoty minus and dumb death
all we inherit, all bequeath

and nothing quite so least as truth
—i say though hate were why men breathe—
because my father lived his soul
love is the whole and more than all

The Waste Land

T. S. Eliot [*1888–*]

"Nam Sibyllam quiden Cumis ego ipse oculis meis vidi in ampulla pendere, et cum illi pueri dicerent: Σίβυλλα τι θέλεις; respondebat illa: ἀποθανεῖν θέλω."

I. *The Burial of the Dead*

April is the cruelest month, breeding
Lilacs out of the dead land, mixing
Memory and desire, stirring

Dull roots with spring rain.
Winter kept us warm, covering
Earth in forgetful snow, feeding
A little life with dried tubers.
Summer surprised us, coming over the Starnbergersee
With a shower of rain; we stopped in the colonnade,
And went on in sunlight, into the Hofgarten,
And drank coffee, and talked for an hour.
Bin gar keine Russin, stamm' aus Litauen, echt deutsch.
And when we were children, staying at the archduke's,
My cousin's, he took me out on a sled,
And I was frightened. He said, Marie,
Marie, hold on tight. And down we went.
In the mountains, there you feel free.
I read, much of the night, and go south in the winter.

What are the roots that clutch, what branches grow
Out of this stony rubbish? Son of man,
You cannot say, or guess, for you know only
A heap of broken images, where the sun beats,
And the dead tree gives no shelter, the cricket no relief,
And the dry stone no sound of water. Only
There is shadow under this red rock,
(Come in under the shadow of this red rock),
And I will show you something different from either
Your shadow at morning striding behind you
Or your shadow at evening rising to meet you;
I will show you fear in a handful of dust.
Frisch weht der Wind
Der Heimat zu
Mein Irisch Kind,
Wo weilest du?
"You gave me hyacinths first a year ago;
"They called me the hyacinth girl."
—Yet when we came back, late, from the hyacinth garden,
Your arms full, and your hair wet, I could not
Speak, and my eyes failed, I was neither
Living nor dead, and I knew nothing,
Looking into the heart of light, the silence.
Oed' und leer das Meer.

Madame Sosostris, famous clairvoyante,
Had a bad cold, nevertheless
Is known to be the wisest woman in Europe,

With a wicked pack of cards. Here, said she,
Is your card, the drowned Phoenician Sailor,
(Those are pearls that were his eyes. Look!)
Here is Belladonna, the Lady of the Rocks,
The lady of situations.
Here is the man with three staves, and here the Wheel,
And here is the one-eyed merchant, and this card,
Which is blank, is something he carries on his back,
Which I am forbidden to see. I do not find
The Hanged Man. Fear death by water.
I see crowds of people, walking around in a ring.
Thank you. If you see dear Mrs. Equitone,
Tell her I bring the horoscope myself:
One must be so careful these days.

Unreal City,
Under the brown fog of a winter dawn,
A crowd flowed over London Bridge, so many,
I had not thought death had undone so many.
Sighs, short and infrequent, were exhaled,
And each man fixed his eyes before his feet.
Flowed up the hill and down King William Street,
To where Saint Mary Woolnoth kept the hours
With a dead sound on the final stroke of nine.
There I saw one I knew, and stopped him, crying: "Stetson!
"You who were with me in the ships at Mylae!
"That corpse you planted last year in your garden,
"Has it begun to sprout? Will it bloom this year?
"Or has the sudden frost disturbed its bed?
"Oh keep the Dog far hence, that's friend to men,
"Or with his nails he'll dig it up again!
"You! hypocrite lecteur!—mon semblable,—mon frère!"

II. *A Game of Chess*

The chair she sat in, like a burnished throne,
Glowed on the marble, where the glass
Held up by standards wrought with fruited vines
From which a golden Cupidon peeped out
(Another hid his eyes behind his wing)
Doubled the flames of sevenbranched candelabra
Reflecting light upon the table as
The glitter of her jewels rose to meet it,
From satin cases poured in rich profusion;

In vials of ivory and colored glass
Unstoppered, lurked her strange synthetic perfumes,
Unguent, powdered, or liquid—troubled, confused
And drowned the sense in odors; stirred by the air
That freshened from the window, these ascended
In fattening the prolonged candle-flames,
Flung their smoke into the laquearia,
Stirring the pattern on the coffered ceiling.
Huge sea-wood fed with copper
Burned green and orange, framed by the colored stone,
In which sad light a carvèd dolphin swam.
Above the antique mantel was displayed
As though a window gave upon the sylvan scene
The change of Philomel, by the barbarous king
So rudely forced; yet there the nightingale
Filled all the desert with inviolable voice
And still she cried, and still the world pursues,
"Jug Jug" to dirty ears.
And other withered stumps of time
Were told upon the walls; staring forms
Leaned out, leaning, hushing the room enclosed.
Footsteps shuffled on the stair.
Under the firelight, under the brush, her hair
Spread out in fiery points
Glowed into words, then would be savagely still.

"My nerves are bad tonight. Yes, bad. Stay with me.
"Speak to me. Why do you never speak. Speak.
  "What are you thinking of? What thinking? What?
"I never know what you are thinking. Think."

I think we are in rats' alley
Where the dead men lost their bones.

"What is that noise?"
            The wind under the door.

"What is that noise now? What is the wind doing?"
            Nothing again nothing.
                              "Do
"You know nothing? Do you see nothing? Do you remember
"Nothing?"

I remember
Those are pearls that were his eyes.
"Are you alive or not? Is there nothing in your head?"
But
O O O O that Shakespeherian Rag—
It's so elegant
So intelligent
"What shall I do now? What shall I do?"
"I shall rush out as I am, and walk the street
"With my hair down, so. What shall we do tomorrow?
"What shall we ever do?"
The hot water at ten.
And if it rains, a closed car at four.
And we shall play a game of chess,
Pressing lidless eyes and waiting for a knock upon the door.

When Lil's husband got demobbed, I said—
I didn't mince my words, I said to her myself,
HURRY UP PLEASE ITS TIME
Now Albert's coming back, make yourself a bit smart.
He'll want to know what you done with that money he gave you
To get yourself some teeth. He did, I was there.
You have them all out, Lil, and get a nice set,
He said, I swear, I can't bear to look at you.
And no more can't I, I said, and think of poor Albert,
He's been in the army four years, he wants a good time,
And if you don't give it him, there's others will, I said.
Oh is there, she said. Something o'that, I said.
Then I'll know who to thank, she said, and give me a straight look.
HURRY UP PLEASE ITS TIME
If you don't like it you can get on with it, I said.
Others can pick and choose if you can't.
But if Albert makes off, it won't be for lack of telling.
You ought to be ashamed, I said, to look so antique.
(And her only thirty-one.)
I can't help it, she said, pulling a long face,
It's them pills I took, to bring it off, she said.
(She's had five already, and nearly died of young George.)
The chemist said it would be all right, but I've never been the same.
You *are* a proper fool, I said.
Well, if Albert won't leave you alone, there it is, I said,

What you get married for if you don't want children?
HURRY UP PLEASE ITS TIME
Well, that Sunday Albert was home, they had a hot gammon,
And they asked me in to dinner, to get the beauty of it hot—
HURRY UP PLEASE ITS TIME
HURRY UP PLEASE ITS TIME
Goonight Bill. Goonight Lou. Goonight May. Goonight.
Ta ta. Goonight. Goonight.
Good night, ladies, good night, sweet ladies, good night, good night.

III. *The Fire Sermon*

The river's tent is broken: the last fingers of leaf
Clutch and sink into the wet bank. The wind
Crosses the brown land, unheard. The nymphs are departed.
Sweet Thames, run softly, till I end my song.
The river bears no empty bottles, sandwich papers,
Silk handkerchiefs, cardboard boxes, cigarette ends
Or other testimony of summer nights. The nymphs are departed.
And their friends, the loitering heirs of city directors;
Departed, have left no addresses.
By the waters of Leman I sat down and wept . . .
Sweet Thames, run softly till I end my song,
Sweet Thames, run softly, for I speak not loud or long.
But at my back in a cold blast I hear
The rattle of the bones, and chuckle spread from ear to ear.
A rat crept softly through the vegetation
Dragging its slimy belly on the bank
While I was fishing in the dull canal
On a winter evening round behind the gashouse
Musing upon the king my brother's wreck
And on the king my father's death before him.
White bodies naked on the low damp ground
And bones cast in a little low dry garret,
Rattled by the rat's foot only, year to year.
But at my back from time to time I hear
The sound of horns and motors, which shall bring
Sweeney to Mrs. Porter in the spring.
O the moon shone bright on Mrs. Porter
And on her daughter
They wash their feet in soda water
Et O ces voix d'enfants, chantant dans la coupole!

Twit twit twit
Jug jug jug jug jug jug
So rudely forc'd.
Tereu

Unreal City
Under the brown fog of a winter noon
Mr. Eugenides, the Smyrna merchant
Unshaven, with a pocket full of currants
C. i. f. London: documents at sight,
Asked me in demotic French
To luncheon at the Cannon Street Hotel
Followed by a weekend at the Metropole.

At the violet hour, when the eyes and back
Turn upward from the desk, when the human engine waits
Like a taxi throbbing waiting,
I Tiresias, though blind, throbbing between two lives,
Old man with wrinkled female breasts, can see
At the violet hour, the evening hour that strives
Homeward, and brings the sailor home from sea,
The typist home at teatime, clears her breakfast, lights
Her stove, and lays out food in tins.
Out of the window perilously spread
Her drying combinations touched by the sun's last rays,
On the divan are piled (at night her bed)
Stockings, slippers, camisoles, and stays.
I Tiresias, old man with wrinkled dugs
Perceived the scene, and foretold the rest—
I too awaited the expected guest.
He, the young man carbuncular, arrives,
A small house agent's clerk, with one bold stare,
One of the low on whom assurance sits
As a silk hat on a Bradford millionaire.
The time is now propitious, as he guesses,
The meal is ended, she is bored and tired,
Endeavors to engage her in caresses
Which still are unreproved, if undesired.
Flushed and decided, he assaults at once;
Exploring hands encounter no defense;
His vanity requires no response,
And makes a welcome of indifference.
(And I Tiresias have foresuffered all
Enacted on this same divan or bed;

I who have sat by Thebes below the wall
And walked among the lowest of the dead.)
Bestows one final patronizing kiss,
And gropes his way, finding the stairs unlit . . .

She turns and looks a moment in the glass,
Hardly aware of her departed lover;
Her brain allows one half-formed thought to pass:
"Well now that's done: and I'm glad it's over."
When lovely woman stoops to folly and
Paces about her room again, alone,
She smooths her hair with automatic hand,
And puts a record on the gramophone.

"This music crept by me upon the waters"
And along the Strand, up Queen Victoria Street.
O City city, I can sometimes hear
Beside a public bar in Lower Thames Street,
The pleasant whining of a mandolin
And a clatter and a chatter from within
Where fishmen lounge at noon: where the walls
Of Magnus Martyr hold
Inexplicable splendor of Ionian white and gold.

The river sweats
Oil and tar
The barges drift
With the turning tide
Red sails
Wide
To leeward, swing on the heavy spar.
The barges wash
Drifting logs
Down Greenwich reach
Past the Isle of Dogs.
Weialala leia
Wallala leialala

Elizabeth and Leicester
Beating oars
The stern was formed
A gilded shell
Red and gold
The brisk swell

Rippled both shores
Southwest wind
Carried down stream
The peal of bells
White towers
            Weialala leia
            Wallala Leialala

"Trams and dusty trees.
Highbury bore me. Richmond and Kew
Undid me. By Richmond I raised my knees
Supine on the floor of a narrow canoe."

"My feet are at Moorgate, and my heart
Under my feet. After the event
He wept. He promised 'a new start.'
I made no comment. What should I resent?"

"On Margate Sands.
I can connect
Nothing with nothing
The broken fingernails of dirty hands.
My people humble people who expect
Nothing."
            la la

To Carthage then I came
Burning burning burning burning
O Lord Thou pluckest me out
O Lord Thou pluckest

burning

IV. *Death by Water*

Phlebas the Phoenician, a fortnight dead,
Forgot the cry of gulls, and the deep sea swell
And the profit and loss.
                        A current under sea
Picked his bones in whispers. As he rose and fell
He passed the stages of his age and youth
Entering the whirlpool.
                        Gentile or Jew

O you who turn the wheel and look to windward,
Consider Phlebas, who was once handsome and tall as you.

V. *What the Thunder Said*

After the torchlight red on sweaty faces
After the frosty silence in the gardens
After the agony in stony places
The shouting and the crying
Prison and palace and reverberation
Of thunder of spring over distant mountains
He who was living is now dead
We who were living are now dying
With a little patience

Here is no water but only rock
Rock and no water and the sandy road
The road winding above among the mountains
Which are mountains of rock without water
If there were water we should stop and drink
Amongst the rock one cannot stop or think
Sweat is dry and feet are in the sand
If there were only water amongst the rock
Dead mountain mouth of carious teeth that cannot spit
Here one can neither stand nor lie nor sit
There is not even silence in the mountains
But dry sterile thunder without rain
There is not even solitude in the mountains
But red sullen faces sneer and snarl
From doors of mudcracked houses
If there were water
And no rock
If there were rock
And also water
And water
A spring
A pool among the rock
If there were the sound of water only
Not the cicada
And dry grass singing
But sound of water over a rock
Where the hermit-thrush sings in the pine trees
Drip drop drip drop drop drop drop
But there is no water

Who is the third who walks always beside you?
When I count, there are only you and I together
But when I look ahead up the white road
There is always another one walking beside you
Gliding wrapped in a brown mantle, hooded
I do not know whether a man or a woman
—But who is that on the other side of you?

What is that sound high in the air
Murmur of maternal lamentation
Who are those hooded hordes swarming
Over endless plains, stumbling in cracked earth
Ringed by the flat horizon only
What is the city over the mountains
Cracks and reforms and bursts in the violet air
Falling towers
Jerusalem Athens Alexandria
Vienna London
Unreal

A woman drew her long black hair out tight
And fiddled whisper music on those strings
And bats with baby faces in the violet light
Whistled, and beat their wings
And crawled head downward down a blackened wall
And upside down in air were towers
Tolling reminiscent bells, that kept the hours
And voices singing out of empty cisterns and exhausted wells.

In this decayed hole among the mountains
In the faint moonlight, the grass is singing
Over the tumbled graves, about the chapel
There is the empty chapel, only the wind's home.
It has no windows, and the door swings,
Dry bones can harm no one.
Only a cock stood on the rooftree
Co co rico co co rico
In a flash of lightning. Then a damp gust
Bringing rain

Ganga was sunken, and the limp leaves
Waited for rain, while the black clouds
Gathered far distant, over Himavant.
The jungle crouched, humped in silence.

Then spoke the thunder
DA
Datta: what have we given?
My friend, blood shaking my heart
The awful daring of a moment's surrender
Which an age of prudence can never retract
By this, and this only, we have existed
Which is not to be found in our obituaries
Or in memories draped by the beneficent spider
Or under seals broken by the lean solicitor
In our empty arms
DA
Dayadhvam: I have heard the key
Turn in the door once and turn once only
We think of the key, each in his prison
Thinking of the key, each confirms a prison
Only at nightfall, ethereal rumors
Revive for a moment a broken Coriolanus
DA
Damyata: The boat responded
Gaily, to the hand expert with sail and oar
The sea was calm, your heart would have responded
Gaily, when invited, beating obedient
To controlling hands

I sat upon the shore
Fishing, with the arid plain behind me
Shall I at least set my lands in order?
London Bridge is falling down falling down falling down
Poi s'ascose nel foco che gli affina
Quando fiam uti chelidon—O swallow swallow
Le Prince d'Aquitaine à la tour abolie
These fragments I have shored against my ruins
Why then Ile fit you. Hieronymo's mad againe.
Datta. Dayadhvam. Damyata.
Shantih shantih shantih

T. S. Eliot's Notes on "The Waste Land"

Not only the title, but the plan and a good deal of the incidental symbolism of the poem were suggested by Miss Jessie L. Weston's book on the Grail legend: *From Ritual to Romance* (Cambridge). Indeed, so deeply am I indebted, Miss Weston's book will elucidate the difficulties of the poem much better than my notes can do; and I recommend it (apart from the great interest of the book itself) to any who think such elucidation of the poem worth the trouble. To another work of anthropology I am indebted in general, one which has influenced our generation profoundly; I mean *The Golden Bough;* I have used especially the two volumes *Adonis, Attis, Osiris.* Anyone who is acquainted with these works will immediately recognize in the poem certain references to vegetation ceremonies.

I. THE BURIAL OF THE DEAD

Line 20. Cf. Ezekiel II, i.

23. Cf. Ecclesiastes XII, v.

31. V. Tristan und Isolde, I, verses 5–8.

42. Id. III, verse 24.

46. I am not familiar with the exact constitution of the Tarot pack of cards, from which I have obviously departed to suit my own convenience. The Hanged Man, a member of the traditional pack, fits my purpose in two ways: because he is associated in my mind with the Hanged God of Frazer, and because I associate him with the hooded figure in the passage of the disciples to Emmaus in Part V. The Phoenician Sailor and the Merchant appear later; also the "crowds of people," and Death by Water is executed in Part IV. The Man with Three Staves (an authentic member of the Tarot pack) I associate, quite arbitrarily, with the Fisher King himself.

60. Cf. Baudelaire:

"Fourmillante cité, cité pleine de rêves,
"Où le spectre en plein jour raccroche le passant."

63. Cf. Inferno III, 55–57:

"si lunga tratta
di gente, ch'io non avrei mai creduto
che morte tanta n'avesse disfatta."

64. Cf. Inferno IV, 25–27:

"Quivi, secondo che per ascoltare,
"non avea pianto, ma' che di sospiri,
"che l'aura eterna facevan tremare."

68. A phenomenon which I have often noticed.

74. Cf. the Dirge in Webster's *White Devil.*

76. V. Baudelaire, Preface to *Fleurs du Mal.*

II. A GAME OF CHESS

77. Cf. *Antony and Cleopatra,* II, ii, l. 190.

92. Laquearia. V. *Aeneid,* I, 726:

dependent lychni laquearibus aureis incensi, et noctem flammis funalia vincunt.

98. Sylvan scene. V. Milton, *Paradise Lost,* IV, 140.

99. V. Ovid, *Metamorphoses,* VI, Philomela.

100. Cf. Part III, l. 204.

115. Cf. Part III, l. 195.

118. Cf. Webster: "Is the wind in that door still?"

126. Cf. Part I, ll. 37, 48.

138. Cf. the game of chess in Middleton's *Women beware Women.*

III. THE FIRE SERMON

176. V. Spenser, *Prothalamion.*

192. Cf. *The Tempest,* I, ii.

196. Cf. Marvell, *To His Coy Mistress.*

197. Cf. Day, *Parliament of Bees:*

"When of the sudden, listening, you shall hear,
"A noise of horns and hunting, which shall bring
"Actaeon to Diana in the spring,
"Where all shall see her naked skin . . ."

199. I do not know the origin of the ballad from which these lines are taken: it was reported to me from Sydney, Australia.

202. V. Verlaine, *Parsifal.*

210. The currants were quoted at a price "carriage and insurance free to London"; and the Bill of Lading etc. were to be handed to the buyer upon payment of the sight draft.

218. Tiresias, although a mere spectator and not indeed a "character," is yet the most important personage in the poem, uniting all the rest. Just as the one-eyed merchant, seller of currants, melts into the Phoenician Sailor, and the latter is not wholly distinct from Ferdinand Prince of Naples, so all the women are one woman, and the two sexes meet in Tiresias. What Tiresias *sees,* in fact, is the substance of the poem. The whole passage from Ovid is of great anthropological interest:

'. . . Cum Iunone iocos et maior vestra profecto est

Quam, quae contingit maribus,' dixisse, 'voluptas.'
Illa negat; placuit quae sit sententia docti
Quaerere Tiresiae: venus huic erat utraque nota.
Nam duo magnorum viridi coeuntia silva
Corpora serpentum baculi violaverat ictu
Deque viro factus, mirabile, femina septem
Egerat autumnos; octavo rursus eosdem
Videt et 'est vestrae si tanta potentia plagae,'
Dixit 'ut auctoris sortem in contraria mutet,
Nunc quoque vos feriam!' percussis anguibus isdem
Forma prior rediit genetivaque venit imago.
Arbiter hic igitur sumptus de lite iocosa
Dicta Iovis firmat; gravius Saturnia iusto
Nec pro materia fertur doluisse suique
Iudicis aeterna damnavit lumina nocte,
At pater omnipotens (neque enim licet inrita cuiquam
Facta dei fecisse deo) pro lumine adempto
Scire futura dedit poenamque levavit honore.

221. This may not appear as exact as Sappho's lines, but I had in mind the "longshore" or "dory" fisherman, who returns at nightfall.

253. V. Goldsmith, the song of *The Vicar of Wakefield.*

257. V. *The Tempest,* as above.

264. The interior of St. Magnus Martyr is to my mind one of the finest among Wren's interiors. See *The Proposed Demolition of Nineteen City Churches* (P. S. King & Son, Ltd.).

266. The Song of the (three) Thames-daughters begins here. From line 292 to 306 inclusive they speak in turn. V. *Götterdämmerung* III, i: the Rhine-daughters.

279. V. Froude, *Elizabeth,* Vol. I, ch. iv, letter of De Quadra to Philip of Spain:

"In the afternoon we were in a barge, watching the games on the river. (The queen) was alone with Lord Robert and myself on the poop, when they began to talk nonsense, and went so far that Lord Robert at last said, as I was on the spot there was no reason why they should not be married if the queen pleased."

293. Cf. *Purgatorio,* V, 133:

"Ricorditi di me, che son la Pia;
"Siena mi fe', disfecemi Maremma."

307. V. St. Augustine's *Confessions:* "to Carthage then

I came, where a cauldron of unholy loves sang all about mine ears."

308. The complete text of the Buddha's Fire Sermon (which corresponds in importance to the Sermon on the Mount) from which these words are taken, will be found translated in the late Henry Clarke Warren's *Buddhism in Translation* (Harvard Oriental Series). Mr. Warren was one of the great pioneers of Buddhist studies in the Occident.

309. From St. Augustine's *Confessions* again. The collocation of these two representatives of eastern and western asceticism, as the culmination of this part of the poem, is not an accident.

V. WHAT THE THUNDER SAID

In the first part of Part V three themes are employed: the journey to Emmaus, the approach to the Chapel Perilous (see Miss Weston's book) and the present decay of eastern Europe.

357. This is *Turdus aonalaschkae pallasii,* the hermit-thrush which I have heard in Quebec County. Chapman says (*Handbook of Birds of Eastern North America*) "it is most at home in secluded woodland and thickety retreats. . . . Its notes are not remarkable for variety or volume, but in purity and sweetness of tone and exquisite modulation they are unequalled." Its "water-dripping song" is justly celebrated.

360. The following lines were stimulated by the account of one of the Antarctic expeditions (I forget which, but I think one of Shackleton's): it was related that the party of explorers, at the extremity of their strength, had the constant delusion that there was *one more member* than could actually be counted.

366–76. Cf. Hermann Hesse, *Blick ins Chaos:* "Schon ist halb Europa, schon ist zumindest der halbe Osten Europas auf dem Wege zum Chaos, fährt betrunken im heiligen Wahn am Abgrund entlang und singt dazu, singt betrunken und hymnisch wie Dmitri Karamasoff sang. Ueber diese Lieder lacht der Bürger beleidigt, der Heilige und Seher hört sie mit Tränen."

401. "Datta, dayadhvam, damyata" (Give, sympathize, control). The fable of the meaning of the Thunder is found in the *Brihadaranyaka—Upanishad,* 5, 1. A trans-

lation is found in Deussen's *Sechzig Upanishads des Veda,* p. 489.

407. Cf. Webster, *The White Devil,* V, vi:

"... they'll remarry
Ere the worm pierce your winding-sheet, ere the spider
Make a thin curtain for your epitaphs."

411. Cf. *Inferno,* XXXIII, 46:

"ed io sentii chiavar l'uscio di sotto
all'orribile torre."

Also F. H. Bradley, *Appearance and Reality,* p. 346. "My external sensations are no less private to myself than are my thoughts or my feelings. In either case my experience falls within my own circle, a circle closed on the outside; and, with all its elements alike, every sphere is opaque to the others which surround it. . . . In brief, regarded as an existence which appears in a soul, the whole world for each is peculiar and private to that soul."

424. V. Weston: *From Ritual to Romance;* chapter on the Fisher King.

427. V. *Purgatorio,* XXVI, 148.

" 'Ara vos prec per aquella valor
'que vos guida al som le l'escalina,
'sovegna vos a temps de ma dolor.'
Poi s'ascose nel foco che gli affina."

428. V. *Pervigilium Veneris.* Cf. Philomela in Parts II and III.

429. V. Gerard de Nerval, Sonnet *El Desdichado.*

431. V. Kyd's *Spanish Tragedy.*

433. Shantih. Repeated as here, a formal ending to an Upanishad. "The Peace which passeth understanding" is our equivalent to this word.

The Second Coming

William Butler Yeats [*1865–1939*]

Turning and turning in the widening gyre
The falcon cannot hear the falconer;
Things fall apart; the center cannot hold;
Mere anarchy is loosed upon the world,
The blood-dimmed tide is loosed, and everywhere
The ceremony of innocence is drowned;
The best lack all conviction, while the worst
Are full of passionate intensity.

Surely some revelation is at hand;
Surely the Second Coming is at hand.
The Second Coming! Hardly are those words out
When a vast image out of *Spiritus Mundi*
Troubles my sight: somewhere in sands of the desert
A shape with lion body and the head of a man,
A gaze blank and pitiless as the sun,
Is moving its slow thighs, while all about it
Reel shadows of the indignant desert birds.
The darkness drops again; but now I know
That twenty centuries of stony sleep
Were vexed to nightmare by a rocking cradle,
And what rough beast, its hour come round at last,
Slouches towards Bethlemen to be born?

Ode to the Confederate Dead

Allen Tate [*1899–*]

Row after row with strict impunity
The headstones yield their names to the element,
The wind whirrs without recollection;
In the riven troughs the splayed leaves
Pile up, of nature the casual sacrament
To the seasonal eternity of death;
Then driven by the fierce scrutiny
Of heaven to their election in the vast breath,
They sough the rumor of mortality.

Autumn is desolation in the plot
Of a thousand acres where these memories grow
From the inexhaustible bodies that are not
Dead, but feed the grass row after rich row.
Think of the autumns that have come and gone!—
Ambitious November with the humors of the year,
With a particular zeal for every slab,
Staining the uncomfortable angels that rot
On the slabs, a wing chipped here, an arm there:
The brute curiosity of an angel's stare
Turns you, like them, to stone,
Transforms the heaving air
Till plunged to a heavier world below
You shift your sea-space blindly
Heaving, turning like the blind crab.

Dazed by the wind, only the wind
The leaves flying, plunge

You know who have waited by the wall
The twilight certainty of an animal,
Those midnight restitutions of the blood
You know—the immitigable pines, the smoky frieze
Of the sky, the sudden call: you know the rage,
The cold pool left by the mounting flood,
Of muted Zeno and Parmenides.
You who have waited for the angry resolution
Of those desires that should be yours tomorrow,
You know the unimportant shrift of death
And praise the vision
And praise the arrogant circumstance
Of those who fall
Rank upon rank, hurried beyond decision—
Here by the sagging gate, stopped by the wall.

Seeing, seeing only the leaves
Flying, plunge and expire

Turn your eyes to the immoderate past,
Turn to the inscrutable infantry rising
Demons out of the earth—they will not last.
Stonewall, Stonewall, and the sunken fields of hemp,
Shiloh, Antietam, Malvern Hill, Bull Run.
Lost in that orient of the thick-and-fast
You will curse the setting sun.

Cursing only the leaves crying
Like an old man in a storm

You hear the shout, the crazy hemlocks point
With troubled fingers to the silence which
Smothers you, a mummy, in time.

The hound bitch
Toothless and dying, in a musty cellar
Hears the wind only.

Now that the salt of their blood
Stiffens the saltier oblivion of the sea,
Seals the malignant purity of the flood,
What shall we who count our days and bow

Our heads with a commemorial woe
In the ribboned coats of grim felicity,
What shall we say of the bones, unclean,
Whose verdurous anonymity will grow?
The ragged arms, the ragged heads and eyes
Lost in these acres of the ínsane green?
The gray lean spiders come, they come and go;
In a tangle of willows without light
The singular screech-owl's tight
Invisible lyric seeds the mind
With the furious murmur of their chivalry.

We shall say only the leaves
Flying, plunge and expire

We shall say only the leaves whispering
In the improbable mist of nightfall
That flies on multiple wing:
Night is the beginning and the end
And in between the ends of distraction
Waits mute speculation, the patient curse
That stones the eyes, or like the jaguar leaps
For his own image in a jungle pool, his victim.
What shall we say who have knowledge
Carried to the heart? Shall we take the act
To the grave? Shall we, more hopeful, set up the grave
In the house? The ravenous grave?

Leave now
The shut gate and the decomposing wall:
The gentle serpent, green in the mulberry bush,
Riots with his tongue through the hush—
Sentinel of the grave who counts us all!

Frescoes for Mr. Rockefeller's City

Archibald MacLeish [*1892–*]

1. *Landscape as a Nude*

She lies on her left side her flank golden:
Her hair is burned black with the strong sun:
The scent of her hair is of rain in the dust on her shoulders:
She has brown breasts and the mouth of no other country:

Ah she is beautiful here in the sun where she lies:
She is not like the soft girls naked in vineyards
Nor the soft naked girls of the English islands
Where the rain comes in with the surf on an east wind:

Hers is the west wind and the sunlight: the west
Wind is the long clean wind of the continents—
The wind turning with earth: the wind descending
Steadily out of the evening and following on:

The wind here where she lies is west: the trees
Oak ironwood cottonwood hickory: standing in
Great groves they roll on the wind as the sea would:
The grasses of Iowa Illinois Indiana.

Run with the plunge of the wind as a wave tumbling:

Under her knees there is no green lawn of the Florentines:
Under her dusty knees is the corn stubble:
Her belly is flecked with the flickering light of the corn:

She lies on her left side her flank golden:
Her hair is burned black with the strong sun:
The scent of her hair is of dust and of smoke on her
shoulders:
She has brown breasts and the mouth of no other country:

II. *Wildwest*

There were none of my blood in this battle:
There were Minneconjous: Sans Arcs: Brules:
Many nations of Sioux: they were few men galloping:

This would have been in the long days in June:
They were galloping well deployed under the plum-trees:
They were driving riderless horses: themselves they were
few:

Crazy Horse had done it with few numbers:
Crazy Horse was small for a Lakota:
He was riding always alone thinking of something:

He was standing alone by the picket lines by the ropes:
He was young then: he was thirty when he died:
Unless there were children to talk he took no notice:

When the soldiers came for him there on the other side
On the Greasy Grass in the villages we were shouting
"Hoka Hey! Crazy Horse will be riding!"

They fought in the water: horses and men were drowning:
They rode on the butte: dust settled in sunlight:
Hoka Hey! they lay on the bloody ground:

No one could tell of the dead which man was Custer . . .
That was the end of his luck: by that river:
The soldiers beat him at Slim Buttes once:

They beat him at Willow Creek when the snow lifted:
The last time they beat him was the Tongue:
He had only the meat he had made and of that little:

Do you ask why he should fight? It was his country:
My God should he not fight? It was his:
But after the Tongue there were no herds to be hunting:

He cut the knots of the tails and he led them in:
He cried out "I am Crazy Horse! Do not touch me!"
There were many soldiers between and the gun glinting. . . .

And a Mister Josiah Perham of Maine had much of the
land Mister Perham was building the Northern Pacific
railroad that is Mister Perham was saying at lunch that

forty say fifty millions of acres in gift and
government grant outright ought to be worth a
wide price on the Board at two-fifty and

later a Mister Cooke had relieved Mister Perham and
later a Mister Morgan relieved Mister Cooke:
Mister Morgan converted at prices current:

It was all prices to them: they never looked at it:
why should they look at the land: they were Empire Builders:
it was all in the bid and the asked and the ink on their books . . .

When Crazy Horse was there by the Black Hills
His heart would be big with the love he had for that country
And all the game he had seen and the mares he had ridden

And how it went out from you wide and clean in the sunlight

III. *Burying Ground by the Ties*

Ayee! Ai! This is heavy earth on our shoulders:
There were none of us born to be buried in this earth:
Niggers we were Portuguese Magyars Polacks:

We were born to another look of the sky certainly:
Now we lie here in the river pastures:
We lie in the mowings under the thick turf:

We hear the earth and the all-day rasp of the grasshoppers.
It was we laid the steel on this land from ocean to ocean:
It was we (if you know) put the U. P. through the passes

Bringing her down into Laramie full load
Eighteen mile on the granite anticlinal
Forty-three foot to the mile and the grade holding:

It was we did it: hunkies of our kind:
It was we dug the caved-in holes for the cold water:
It was we built the gully spurs and the freight sidings:

Who would do it but we and the Irishmen bossing us?
It was all foreign-born men there were in this country:
It was Scotsmen Englishmen Chinese Squareheads Austrians. . . .

Ayee! but there's weight to the earth under it:
Not for this did we come out—to be lying here
Nameless under the ties in the clay cuts:

There's nothing good in the world but the rich will buy it:
Everything sticks to the grease of a gold note—
Even a continent—even a new sky!

Do not pity us much for the strange grass over us:
We laid the steel to the stone stock of these mountains:
The place of our graves is marked by the telegraph poles!

It was not to lie in the bottoms we came out
And the trains going over us here in the dry hollows. . . .

IV. *Oil Painting of the Artist as the Artist*

The plump Mr. Pl'f is washing his hands of America:
The plump Mr. Pl'f is in ochre with such hair:

America is in blue-black-grey-green-sandcolor:
America is a continent—many lands:

The plump Mr. Pl'f is washing his hands of America:
He is pictured at Pau on the *place* and his eyes glaring:

He thinks of himself as an exile from all this:
As an émigré from his own time into history—

(History being an empty house without owners
A practical man may get in by the privy stones—

The dead are excellent hosts: they have no objections—
And once in he can nail the knob on the next one

Living the life of a classic in bad air with
Himself for the Past and his face in the glass for Posterity)

The Cinquecento is nothing at all like Nome
Or Natchez or Wounded Knee or the Shenandoah:

Your vulgarity Tennessee: your violence Texas:
The rocks under your fields Ohio Connecticut:

Your clay Missouri your clay: you have driven him out:
You have shadowed his life Appalachians purple mountains:

There is much too much of your flowing Mississippi:
He prefers a tidier stream with a terrace for trippers and

Cypresses mentioned in Horace or Henry James:
He prefers a country where everything carries the name of a

Countess or real king or an actual palace or
Something in Prose and the stock prices all in Italian:

There is more shade for an artist under a fig
Than under the whole damn range (he finds) of the Big
  Horns.

v. *Empire Builders*

The Museum Attendant:

This is *The Making of America in Five Panels:*

This is Mister Harriman making America:
Mister-Harriman-is-buying-the-Union-Pacific-at-Seventy:
The Sante Fe is shining on his hair:

This is Commodore Vanderbilt making America:
Mister-Vanderbilt-is-eliminating-the-short-interest-in-Hudson:
Observe the carving on the rocking chair:

This is J. P. Morgan making America:
(The Tennessee Coal is behind to the left of the Steel Company:)
Those in mauve are braces he is wearing:

This is Mister Mellon making America:
Mister-Mellon-is-represented-as-a-symbolical-figure-in-aluminum-
Strewing-bank-stocks-on-a-burnished-stair:

This is the Bruce is the Barton making America:
Mister-Barton-is-selling-us-Doctor's-Deliciousest-Dentifrice:
This is he in beige with the canary:

You have just beheld the Makers making America:
This is *The Making of America in Five Panels:*
America lies to the west-southwest of the Switch-Tower:
There is nothing to see of America but land:

The Original Document
under the Panel Paint:

"To Thos. Jefferson Esq. his obd't serv't
M. Lewis: captain: detached:
Sir:
Having in mind your repeated commands in this matter:
And the worst half of it done and the streams mapped:

And we here on the back of this beach beholding the
Other ocean—two years gone and the cold

Breaking with rain for the third spring since St. Louis:
The crows at the fishbones on the frozen dunes:

The first cranes going over from south north:
And the river down by a mark of the pole since the morning:

And time near to return, and a ship (Spanish)
Lying in for the salmon: and fearing chance or the

Drought or the Sioux should deprive you of these discoveries—
Therefore we send by sea in this writing:

Above the
Platte there were long plains and a clay country:
Rim of the sky far off: grass under it:

Dung for the cook fires by the sulphur licks:
After that there were low hills and the sycamores:

And we poled up by the Great Bend in the skiffs:
The honey bees left us after the Osage River:

The wind was west in the evenings and no dew and the
Morning Star larger and whiter than usual—

The winter rattling in the brittle haws:
The second year there was sage and the quail calling:

All that valley is good land by the river:
Three thousand miles and the clay cliffs and

Rue and beargrass by the water banks
And many birds and the brant going over and tracks of

Bear elk wolves marten: the buffalo
Numberless so that the cloud of their dust covers them:

The antelope fording the fall creeks: and the mountains and
Grazing lands and the meadow lands and the ground

Sweet and open and well-drained:
We advise you to
Settle troops at the forks and to issue licenses:

Many men will have living on these lands:
There is wealth in the earth for them all and the wood standing

And wild birds on the water where they sleep:
There is stone in the hills for the towns of a great people . . ."

You have just beheld the Makers making America:

They screwed her scrawny and gaunt with their seven-year panics:
They bought her back on their mortgages old-whore-cheap:
They fattened their bonds at her breasts till the thin blood ran from them:

Men have forgotten how full clear and deep
The Yellowstone moved on the gravel and grass grew
When the land lay waiting for her westward people!

VI. *Background with Revolutionaries*

And the corn singing Millennium!
Lenin! Millennium! Lennium!

When they're shunting the cars on the Katy a mile off
When they're shunting the cars when they're shunting the cars on the Katy
You can hear the clank of the couplings riding away

Also Comrade Devine who writes of America
Most instructively having in 'Seventy-four
Crossed to the Hoboken side on the Barclay Street Ferry

She sits on a settle in the State of North Dakota
O she sits on a settle in the State of North Dakota
She can hear the engines whistle over Iowa and Idaho

Also Comrade Edward Remington Ridge
Who has prayed God since the April of 'Seventeen
To replace in his life his lost (M.E.) religion.

And The New York Daily Worker *goes a'blowing over Arkansas*

The New York Daily Worker *goes a'blowing over Arkansas*
The grasses let it go along the Ozarks over Arkansas

Even Comrade Grenadine Grilt who has tried since
August tenth for something to feel about strongly in
Verses—his personal passions having tired

I can tell my land by the jays in the apple-trees
Tell my land by the jays in the apple-trees
I can tell my people by the blue-jays in the apple-trees

Aindt you read in d'books you are all brudders?
D' glassic historic objective broves you are brudders!
You and d'Wops and d'Chinks you are all brudders!
Havend't you got it d' same ideology? Havend't you?

When it's yesterday in Oregon it's one A M in Maine
And she slides: and the day slides: and it runs: runs over us:
And the bells strike twelve strike twelve strike twelve
In Marblehead in Buffalo and Cheyenne in Cherokee
Yesterday runs on the states like a crow's shadow

For Marx has said to us Workers what do you need?
And Stalin has said to us Starvers what do you need?
You need the Dialectical Materialism!

She's a tough land under the corn mister:
She has changed the bone in the cheeks of many races:
She has winced the eyes of the soft Slavs with her sun on them:
She has tried the fat from the round rumps of Italians:
Even the voice of the English has gone dry
And hard on the tongue and alive in the throat speaking:

She's a tough land under the oak-trees mister:
It may be she can change the word in the book
As she changes the bone of a man's head in his children:
It may be that the earth and the men remain. . . .

There is too much sun on the lids of my eyes to be listening

Lee in the Mountains

1865–1870

Donald Davidson [*1893–*]

Walking into the shadows, walking alone
Where the sun falls through the ruined boughs of locusts
Up to the president's office . . .
Hearing the voices
Whisper, *Hush, it is General Lee!* And strangely
Hearing my own voice say, *Good morning, boys.*
(Don't get up. You are early. It is long
Before the bell. You will have long to wait
On these cold steps. . . .)
The young have time to wait.
But soldiers' faces under their tossing flags
Lift no more by any road or field,
And I am spent with old wars and new sorrow.
Walking the rocky path, where steps decay
And the paint cracks and grass eats on the stone.
It is not General Lee, young men only . . .
It is Robert Lee in a dark civilian suit who walks,
An outlaw fumbling for the latch, a voice
Commanding in a dream where no flag flies.

My father's house is taken and his hearth
Left to the candle-drippings where the ashes
Whirl at a chimney-breath on the cold stone.
I can hardly remember my father's look, I cannot
Answer his voice as he calls farewell in the misty
Mounting where riders gather at gates.
He was old then—I was a child—his hand
Held out for mine, some daybreak snatched away,
And he rode out, a broken man. Now let
His lone grave keep, surer than cypress roots,
The vow I made beside him. God too late
Unseals to certain eyes the drift
Of time and the hopes of men and a sacred cause.
The fortune of the Lees goes with the land
Whose sons will keep it still. My mother
Told me much. She sat among the candles,
Fingering the *Memoirs,* now so long unread.

And as my pen moves on across the page
Her voice comes back, a murmuring distillation
Of old Virginia times now faint and gone,
The hurt of all that was and cannot be.

Why did my father write? I know he saw
History clutched as a wraith out of blowing mist
Where tongues are loud, and a glut of little souls
Laps at the too much blood and the burning house.
He would have his say, but I shall not have mine.
What I do is only a son's devoir
To a lost father. Let him only speak.
The rest must pass to men who never knew
(But on a written page) the strike of armies,
And never heard the long Confederate cry
Charge through the muzzling smoke or saw the bright
Eyes of the beardless boys go up to death.
It is Robert Lee who writes with his father's hand—
The rest must go unsaid and the lips be locked.
If all were told, as it cannot be told—
If all the dread opinion of the heart
Now could speak, now in the shame and torment
Lashing the bound and trampled States—

If a word were said, as it cannot be said—

I see clear waters run in Virginia's Valley
And in the house the weeping of young women
Rises no more. The waves of grain begin.
The Shenandoah is golden with new grain.
The Blue Ridge, crowned with a haze of light,
Thunders no more. The horse is at plow. The rifle
Returns to the chimney crotch and the hunter's hand.
And nothing else than this? Was it for this
That on an April day we stacked our arms
Obedient to a soldier's trust? To lie
Ground by heels of little men,
Forever maimed, defeated, lost, impugned?
And was I then betrayed? Did I betray?

If it were said, as still it might be said—
If it were said, and a word should run like fire,
Like living fire into the roots of grass,
The sunken flag would kindle on wild hills,

The brooding hearts would waken, and the dream
Stir like a crippled phantom under the pines,
And this torn earth would quicken into shouting
Beneath the feet of ragged bands—
                                        The pen
Turns to the waiting page, the sword
Bows to the rust that cankers and the silence.

Among these boys whose eyes lift up to mine
Within gray walls where droning wasps repeat
A hollow reveillé, I still must face,
Day after day, the courier with his summons
Once more to surrender, now to surrender all.
Without arms or men I stand, but with knowledge only
I face what long I saw, before others knew,
When Pickett's men streamed back, and I heard the tangled
Cry of the Wilderness wounded, bloody with doom.

The mountains, once I said, in the little room
At Richmond, by the huddled fire, but still
The President shook his head. The mountains wait,
I said, in the long beat and rattle of siege
At cratered Petersburg. Too late
We sought the mountains and those people came.
And Lee is in mountains now, beyond Appomattox,
Listening long for voices that never will speak
Again; hearing the hoofbeats come and go and fade
Without a stop, without a brown hand lifting
The tent-flap, or a bugle call at dawn,
Or ever on the long white road the flag
Of Jackson's quick brigades. I am alone,
Trapped, consenting, taken at last in mountains.

It is not the bugle now, or the long roll beating.
The simple stroke of a chapel bell forbids
The hurtling dream, recalls the lonely mind.
Young men, the God of your fathers is a just
And merciful God Who in this blood once shed
On your green altars measures out all days,
And measures out the grace
Whereby alone we live;
And in His might He waits,
Brooding within the certitude of time,
To bring this lost forsaken valor

And the fierce faith undying
And the love quenchless
To flower among the hills to which we cleave,
To fruit upon the mountains whither we flee,
Never forsaking, never denying
His children and His children's children forever
Unto all generations of the faithful heart.

On the Move

Thom Gunn [*1929–*]

"Man, you gotta Go."

The blue jay scuffling in the bushes follows
Some hidden purpose, and the gust of birds
That spurts across the field, the wheeling swallows,
Have nested in the trees and undergrowth.
Seeking their instinct, or their poise, or both,
One moves with an uncertain violence
Under the dust thrown by a baffled sense
Or the dull thunder of approximate words.

On motorcycles, up the road, they come:
Small, black, as flies hanging in heat, the Boys,
Until the distance throws them forth, their hum
Bulges to thunder held by calf and thigh,
In goggles, donned impersonality,
In gleaming jackets trophied with the dust,
They strap in doubt—by hiding it, robust—
And almost hear a meaning in their noise.

Exact conclusion of their hardiness
Has no shape yet, but from known whereabouts
They ride, direction where the tires press.
They scare a flight of birds across the field:
Much that is natural, to the will must yield.
Men manufacture both machine and soul,
And use what they imperfectly control
To dare a future from the taken routes.

It is a part solution, after all.
One is not necessarily discord

On earth; or damned because, half animal,
One lacks direct instinct, because one wakes
Afloat on movement that divides and breaks.
One joins the movement in a valueless world,
Choosing it, till, both hurler and the hurled,
One moves as well, always toward, toward.

A minute holds them, who have come to go:
The self-defined, astride the created will
They burst away; the towns they travel through
Are home for neither bird nor holiness,
For birds and saints complete their purposes.
At worst, one is in motion; and at best,
Reaching no absolute, in which to rest,
One is always nearer by not keeping still.

Hugh Selwyn Mauberley (Life and Contacts) I–V

Ezra Pound [*1885–*]

E. P. Ode Pour l'Election de Son Sepulchre

For three years, out of key with his time,
He strove to resuscitate the dead art
Of poetry; to maintain "the sublime"
In the old sense. Wrong from the start—

No, hardly, but seeing he had been born
In a half savage country, out of date;
Bent resolutely on wringing lilies from the acorn;
Capaneus; trout for factitious bait;

Ἴδμεν γάρ τοι πάνθ', ὅσ' ἐνὶ τροίῃ
Caught in the unstopped ear;
Giving the rocks small lee-way
The chopped seas held him, therefore, that year.

His true Penelope was Flaubert,
He fished by obstinate isles;
Observed the elegance of Circe's hair
Rather than the mottoes on sun-dials.

Unaffected by "the march of events,"
He passed from men's memory in *l'an trentiesme*
De son eage; the case presents
No adjunct to the Muses' diadem.

II

The age demanded an image
Of its accelerated grimace,
Something for the modern stage,
Not, at any rate, an Attic grace;

Not, not certainly, the obscure reveries
Of the inward gaze;
Better mendacities
Than the classics in paraphrase!

The "age demanded" chiefly a mould in plaster,
Made with no loss of time,
A prose kinema, not, not assuredly, alabaster
Or the "sculpture" of rhyme.

III

The tea-rose tea-gown, etc.
Supplants the mousseline of Cos,
The pianola "replaces"
Sappho's barbitos.

Christ follows Dionysus,
Phallic and ambrosial
Made way for macerations;
Caliban casts out Ariel.

All things are a flowing,
Sage Heracleitus says;
But a tawdry cheapness
Shall outlast our days.

Even the Christian beauty
Defects—after Samothrace;
We see τὸ καλόν
Decreed in the market place.

Faun's flesh is not to us,
Nor the saint's vision.
We have the press for wafer;
Franchise for circumcision.

All men, in law, are equals.
Free of Pisistratus,
We choose a knave or an eunuch
To rule over us.

O bright Apollo,
τίν' ἄνδρα, τίν' ἥρωα, τίνα θεόν,
What god, man, or hero
Shall I place a tin wreath upon!

IV

These fought in any case,
and some believing,
pro domo, in any case . . .
Some quick to arm,
some for adventure,
some from fear of weakness,
some from fear of censure,
some for love of slaughter, in imagination,
learning later . . .
some in fear, learning love of slaughter;

Died some, pro patria, non "dulce" non "et decor" . . .
walked eye-deep in hell
believing in old men's lies, then unbelieving
came home, home to a lie,
home to many deceits,
home to old lies and new infamy;
usury age-old and age-thick
and liars in public places.

Daring as never before, wastage as never before.
Young blood and high blood,
fair cheeks, and fine bodies;

fortitude as never before,

frankness as never before,
disillusions as never told in the old days,
hysterias, trench confessions,
laughter out of dead bellies.

V

There died a myriad,
And of the best, among them

For an old bitch gone in the teeth,
For a botched civilization,

Charm, smiling at the good mouth,
Quick eyes gone under earth's lid,

For two gross of broken statues,
For a few thousand battered books.

O Where Are You Going?

W. H. Auden [1907–]

"O where are you going?" said reader to rider,
"That valley is fatal when furnaces burn,
Yonder's the midden whose odors will madden,
That gap is the grave where the tall return."

"O do you imagine," said fearer to farer,
"That dusk will delay on your path to the pass,
Your diligent looking discover the lacking
Your footsteps feel from granite to grass?"

"O what was that bird," said horror to hearer,
"Did you see that shape in the twisted trees?
Behind you swiftly the figure comes softly,
The spot on your skin is a shocking disease?"

"Out of this house"—said rider to reader,
"Yours never will"—said farer to fearer,
"They're looking for you"—said hearer to horror,
As he left them there, as he left them there.

Just a Smack at Auden

William Empson [1906–]

Waiting for the end, boys, waiting for the end.
What is there to be or do?
What's become of me or you?
Are we kind or are we true?
Sitting two and two, boys, waiting for the end.

Shall I build a tower, boys, knowing it will rend
Crack upon the hour, boys, waiting for the end?
Shall I pluck a flower, boys, shall I save or spend?
All turns sour, boys, waiting for the end.

Shall I send a wire, boys? Where is there to send?
All are under fire, boys, waiting for the end.
Shall I turn a sire, boys? Shall I choose a friend?
The fat is in the pyre, boys, waiting for the end.

Shall I make it clear, boys, for all to apprehend,
Those that will not hear, boys, waiting for the end,
Knowing it is near, boys, trying to pretend,
Sitting in cold fear, boys, waiting for the end?

Shall we send a cable, boys, accurately penned,
Knowing we are able, boys, waiting for the end,
Via the Tower of Babel, boys? Christ will not ascend,
He's hiding in his stable, boys, waiting for the end.

Shall we blow a bubble, boys, glittering to distend,
Hiding from our trouble, boys, waiting for the end?
When you build on rubble, boys, Nature will append
Double and re-double, boys, waiting for the end.

Shall we make a tale, boys, that things are sure to mend,
Playing bluff and hale, boys, waiting for the end?
It will be born stale, boys, stinking to offend,
Dying ere it fail, boys, waiting for the end.

Shall we go all wild, boys, waste and make them lend,
Playing at the child, boys, waiting for the end?
It has all been filed, boys, history has a trend,
Each of us enisled, boys, waiting for the end.

What was said by Marx, boys, what did he perpend?
No good being sparks, boys, waiting for the end.
Treason of the clerks, boys, curtains that descend,
Lights becoming darks, boys, waiting for the end.

Waiting for the end, boys, waiting for the end.
Not a chance of blend, boys, things have got to tend.
Think of those who vend, boys, think of how we wend,
Waiting for the end, boys, waiting for the end.

Journey of the Magi

T. S. Eliot [*1888–*]

"A cold coming we had of it,
Just the worst time of the year
For a journey, and such a long journey:
The ways deep and the weather sharp,
The very dead of winter."
And the camels galled, sore-footed, refractory,
Lying down in the melting snow,
There were times we regretted
The summer palaces on slopes, the terraces,
And the silken girls bringing sherbet.
Then the camel men cursing and grumbling
And running away, and wanting their liquor and women,
And the night-fires going out, and the lack of shelters,
And the cities hostile and the towns unfriendly
And the villages dirty and charging high prices:
A hard time we had of it.
At the end we preferred to travel all night,
Sleeping in snatches,
With the voices singing in our ears, saying
That this was all folly.

Then at dawn we came down to a temperate valley,
Wet, below the snow line, smelling of vegetation;
With a running stream and a water-mill beating the darkness,
And three trees on the low sky,
And an old white horse galloped away in the meadow.
Then we came to a tavern with vine-leaves over the lintel,
Six hands at an open door dicing for pieces of silver,
And feet kicking the empty wine-skins.
But there was no information, and so we continued
And arrived at evening, not a moment too soon
Finding the place; it was (you may say) satisfactory.

All this was a long time ago, I remember,
And I would do it again, but set down
This set down
This: were we led all that way for
Birth or Death? There was a Birth, certainly,

We had evidence and no doubt. I had seen birth and death,
But had thought they were different; this Birth was
Hard and bitter agony for us, like Death, our death.
We returned to our places, these Kingdoms,
But no longer at ease here, in the old dispensation,
With an alien people clutching their gods.
I should be glad of another death.

NOTE: The first lines of the poem are taken from a sermon preached by Lancelot Andrews (1555–1626) on Christmas Day, 1622. The relevant passage reads as follows:

> It was no summer progress. A cold coming they had of it at this time of the year, just the worst time of the year to take a journey, and specially a long journey in. The ways deep, the weather sharp, the days short, the sun farthest off, *in solstitio brumali,* the very dead of winter.

Twelfth Night

John Peale Bishop [*1892–1944*]

All night I thought on those wise men who took
A midnight leave of towers and came peering
Pyramidally down to the dark guards
And stared apart, each with a mad, hid look
Twitching his mummied beard
while the night swords
Conferred and chains fell and the unwieldy bar
Slid and swung back
then wandered out to name
The living demon of an unnamed star.

All night I followed them and came at last
On a low hutch propped in an alleyway
And stretched aside
while one by one they passed
Those stilted mages mitred in stiff blue
Under the sagging beams and through the stalls.

Following, through stench and misty fug I saw
And nothing were clearer in the scrupulous day
The rigid drooping of their ancient palls

Burnish with light, where on a toss of straw
Swaddled in rags, to their abashment, lay
Not the pedantic god whose name they knew
But a small child petulant with cries.

With courtesies unperturbed and slow
They laid their gifts down, unburnt scents and gold:
But gray evasions shamed their skeptic eyes
And the starved hands were suddenly boned with cold
As plucking their gorgeous skirts they shook to go.

The Windhover:

To Christ Our Lord

Gerard Manley Hopkins [*1844–1889*]

I caught this morning morning's minion, king-
  dom of daylight's dauphin, dapple-dawn-drawn Falcon, in his riding
  Of the rolling level underneath him steady air, and striding
High there, how he rung upon the rein of a wimpling wing
In his ecstasy! then off, off forth on swing,
  As a skate's heel sweeps smooth on a bow-bend: the hurl and gliding
  Rebuffed the big wind. My heart in hiding
Stirred for a bird,—the achieve of, the mastery of the thing!
Brute beauty and valor and act, oh, air, pride, plume, here
  Buckle! AND the fire that breaks from thee then, a billion
Times told lovelier, more dangerous, Oh my chevalier!

  No wonder of it; shéer plód makes plow down sillion
Shine, and blue-bleak embers, ah my dear,
  Fall, gall themselves, and gash gold-vermilion.

The Owl

Edward Thomas [*1878–1917*]

Down hill I came, hungry, and yet not starved;
Cold, yet had heat within me that was proof
Against the North wind; tired, yet so that rest
Had seemed the sweetest thing under a roof.

Then at the inn I had food, fire, and rest,
Knowing how hungry, cold, and tired was I.
All of the night was quite barred out except
An owl's cry, a most melancholy cry

Shaken out long and clear upon the hill,
No merry note, nor cause of merriment,
But one telling me plain what I escaped
And others could not, that night, as in I went.

And salted was my food, and my repose,
Salted and sobered, too, by the bird's voice
Speaking for all who lay under the stars.
Soldiers and poor, unable to rejoice.

The Heron

Vernon Watkins [1906–]

The cloud-backed heron will not move:
He stares into the stream.
He stands unfaltering while the gulls
And oyster-catchers scream.
He does not hear, he cannot see
The great white horses of the sea,
But fixes eyes on stillness
Below their flying team.

How long will he remain, how long
Have the gray woods been green?
The sky and the reflected sky,
Their glass he has not seen,
But silent as a speck of sand
Interpreting the sea and land,
His fall pulls down the fabric
Of all that windy scene.

Sailing with clouds and woods behind,
Pausing in leisured flight,
He stepped, alighting on a stone,
Dropped from the stars of night.
He stood there unconcerned with day,

Deaf to the tumult of the bay,
Watching a stone in water,
A fish's hidden light.

Sharp rocks drive back the breaking waves,
Confusing sea with air.
Bundles of spray blown mountain-high
Have left the shingle bare.
A shipwrecked anchor wedged by rocks,
Loosed by the thundering equinox,
Divides the herded waters,
The stallion and his mare.

Yet no distraction breaks the watch
Of that time-killing bird.
He stands unmoving on the stone;
Since dawn he has not stirred.
Calamity about him cries,
But he has fixed his golden eyes
On water's crooked tablet,
On light's reflected word.

At the Slackening of the Tide

James Wright [*1927–*]

Today I saw a woman wrapped in rags
Leaping along the beach to curse the sea.
Her child lay floating in the oil, away
From oarlock, gunwale, and the blades of oars.
The skinny lifeguard, raging at the sky,
Vomited sea, and fainted on the sand.

The cold simplicity of evening falls
Dead on my mind.
And underneath the piles the water
Leaps up, leaps up, and sags down slowly, farther
Than seagulls disembodied in the drag
Of oil and foam.

Plucking among the oyster shells a man
Stares at the sea, that stretches on its side.
Now far along the beach, a hungry dog

Announces everything I knew before:
Obliterate naiads weeping underground,
Where Homer's tongue thickens with human howls.

I would do anything to drag myself
Out of this place:
Root up a seaweed from the water,
To stuff it in my mouth, or deafen me,
Free me from all the force of human speech;
Go drown, almost.

Warm in the pleasure of the dawn I came
To sing my song
And look for mollusks in the shallows,
The whorl and coil that pretty up the earth,
While far below us, flaring in the dark,
The stars go out.

What did I do to kill my time today,
After the woman ranted in the cold,
The mellow sea, the sound blown dark as wine?
After the lifeguard rose up from the waves
Like a sea-lizard with the scales washed off?
Sit there, admiring sunlight on a shell?

Abstract with terror of the shell, I stared
Over the waters where
God brooded for the living all one day.
Lonely for weeping, starved for a sound of mourning,
I bowed my head, and heard the sea far off
Washing its hands.

Little Exercise

Elizabeth Bishop [*1911–*]

Think of the storm roaming the sky uneasily
like a dog looking for a place to sleep in,
listen to it growling.

Think how they must look now, the mangrove keys
lying out there unresponsive to the lightning
in dark, coarse-fibered families,

where occasionally a heron may undo his head,
shake up his feathers, make an uncertain comment
when the surrounding water shines.

Think of the boulevard and the little palm trees
all stuck in rows, suddenly revealed
as fistfuls of limp fish-skeletons.

It is raining there. The boulevard
and its broken sidewalks with weeds in every crack,
are relieved to be wet, the sea to be freshened.

Now the storm goes away again in a series
of small, badly lit battle-scenes,
each in "Another part of the field."

Think of someone sleeping in the bottom of a row-boat
tied to a mangrove root or the pile of a bridge;
think of him as uninjured, barely disturbed.

The Open Sea

William Meredith [*1919–*]

We say the sea is lonely; better say
Ourselves are lonesome creatures whom the sea
Gives neither yes nor no for company.

Oh, there are people, all right, settled in the sea;
It is as populous as Maine today,
But no one who will give you the time of day.

A man who asks there of his family
Or a friend or teacher gets a cold reply
Or finds him dead against that vast majority.

Nor does it signify that people who stay
Very long, bereaved or not, at the edge of the sea
Hear the drowned folk call: that is mere fancy,

They are speechless. And the famous noise of sea
Which a poet has beautifully told us in our day
Is hardly a sound to speak comfort to the lonely.

Although not yet a man given to prayer, I pray
For each creature lost since the start at sea,
And give thanks it was not I, nor yet one close to me.

A Grave

Marianne Moore [*1887–*]

Man looking into the sea
taking the view from those who have
as much right to it as you have to it yourself,
it is human nature to stand in the middle of a thing,
but you cannot stand in the middle of this;
the sea has nothing to give but a well excavated grave.
The firs stand in a procession, each with an emerald turkey-foot at the top,
reserved as their contours, saying nothing;
repression, however, is not the most obvious characteristic of the sea;
the sea is a collector, quick to return a rapacious look.
There are others besides you who have worn that look—
Whose expression is no longer a protest; the fish no longer investigate them
for their bones have not lasted:
men lower nets, unconscious of the fact that they are desecrating a grave,
and row quickly away—the blades of the oars
moving together like the feet of water-spiders as if there were no such thing as death.
The wrinkles progress among themselves in a phalanx—beautiful under networks of foam,
and fade breathlessly while the sea rustles in and out of the seaweed;
the birds swim through the air at top speed, emitting catcalls as heretofore—
the tortoise-shell scourges about the feet of the cliffs, in motion beneath them;
and the ocean, under the pulsation of lighthouses and noise of bell-buoys,
advances as usual, looking as if it were not that ocean in which dropped things are bound to sink—
into which if they turn and twist, it is neither with volition nor consciousness.

Rainy Summer

Ruth Pitter [1897–   ]

Remember, though we cannot write it, the delicate dream.
Though the wheat be cankered, the woodbine and wild rose
Drink, and exhale in perfume their pensive being:
The lily's life prolonged plays on to an extreme
And elegiac poignancy; the bee goes
Solitary with subdued hum in the green, beyond our seeing.

We are spirits, though, the dream denied, we are also ghosts.
We repose in our secret place, in the rainy air,
By the small fire, the dim window, in the ancient house;
Kind to the past, and thoughtful of our hosts,
Shadows of those now beyond thought and care,
Phantoms that the silence engenders, the flames arouse.

Those we have never seen, and those we shall see no more,
Haunting the tender gloom and the wan light,
Are there, as the secret bird is there, is betrayed
By the leaf that moved when she slipped from her twig by the door,
As the mouse unseen is perceived by her gliding shade,
As the silent owl is known by the wind of her flight.

Thus poor, forgotten, in a summer without sun,
In a decaying house, an unvisited place,
We remember the delicate dream, the voice of the clay;
Recalling the body before the life was begun,
Stealing through blood and bone with bodiless grace
In the elfish night and green cool gloom of the day.

Grapes Making

Léonie Adams [1899–   ]

Noon sun beats down the leaf; the noon
Of summer burns along the vine
And thins the leaf with burning air,
Till from the underleaf is fanned,

And down the woven vine, the light.
Still the pleached leaves drop layer on layer
To wind the sun on either hand,
And echoes of the light are bound,
And hushed the blazing cheek of light,
The hurry of the breathless noon,
And from the thicket of the vine
The grape has pressed into its round.

The grape has pressed into its round,
And swings, aloof chill green, clean won
Of light, between the sky and ground;
Those hid, soft-flashing lamps yet blind,
Which yield an apprehended sun.
Fresh triumph in a courteous kind,
Having more ways to be, and years,
And easy, countless treasuries,
You whose all-told is still no sum,
Like a rich heart, well-said in sighs,
The careless autumn mornings come,
The grapes drop glimmering to the shears.

Now shady sod at heel piles deep,
An overarching shade, the vine
Across the fall of noon is flung;
And here beneath the leaves is cast
A light to color noonday sleep,
While cool, bemused the grape is swung
Beneath the eyelids of the vine;
And deepening like a tender thought
Green moves along the leaf, and bright
The leaf above, and leaf has caught,
And emerald pierces day, and last
The faint leaf vanishes to light.

A Summer Commentary

Yvor Winters [*1900–*]

When I was young, with sharper sense,
The farthest insect cry I heard
Could stay me; through the trees, intense,
I watched the hunter and the bird.

Where is the meaning that I found?
Or was it but a state of mind,
Some old penumbra of the ground,
In which to be but not to find?

Now summer grasses, brown with heat,
Have crowded sweetness through the air;
The very roadside dust is sweet;
Even the unshadowed earth is fair.

The soft voice of the nesting dove,
And the dove in soft erratic flight
Like a rapid hand within a glove,
Caress the silence and the light.

Amid the rubble, the fallen fruit,
Fermenting in its rich decay,
Smears brandy on the trampling boot
And sends it sweeter on its way.

Come In

Robert Frost [*1874–1963*]

As I came to the edge of the woods,
Thrush music—hark!
Now if it was dusk outside,
Inside it was dark.

Too dark in the woods for a bird
By sleight of wing
To better its perch for the night,
Though it still could sing.

The last of the light of the sun
That had died in the west
Still lived for one song more
In a thrush's breast.

Far in the pillared dark
Thrush music went—
Almost like a call to come in
To the dark and lament.

But no, I was out for stars:
I would not come in.
I meant not even if asked,
And I hadn't been.

To Juan at the Winter Solstice

Robert Graves [*1895–*]

There is one story and one story only
That will prove worth your telling,
Whether as learned bard or gifted child;
To it all lines or lesser gauds belong
That startle with their shining
Such common stories as they stray into.

Is it of trees you tell, their months and virtues,
Of strange beasts that beset you,
Of birds that croak at you the Triple will?
Or of the Zodiac and how slow it turns
Below the Boreal Crown,
Prison of all true kings that ever reigned?

Water to water, ark again to ark,
From woman back to woman:
So each new victim treads unfalteringly
The never altered circuit of his fate,
Bringing twelve peers as witness
Both to his starry rise and starry fall.

Or is it of the Virgin's silver beauty,
All fish below the thighs?
She in her left hand bears a leafy quince;
When with her right she crooks a finger, smiling,
How may the King hold back?
Royally then he barters life for love.

Or of the undying snake from chaos hatched,
Whose coils contain the ocean,
Into whose chops with naked sword he springs,
Then in black water, tangled by the reeds,
Battles three days and nights,
To be spewed up beside her scalloped shore?

Much snow is falling, winds roar hollowly,
The owl hoots from the elder,
Fear in your heart cries to the loving-cup:
Sorrow to sorrow as the sparks fly upward.
The log groans and confesses
There is one story and one story only.

Dwell on her graciousness, dwell on her smiling,
Do not forget what flowers
The great boar trampled down in ivy time.
Her brow was creamy as the long ninth wave,
Her sea-blue eyes were wild.
But nothing promised that is not performed.

Bavarian Gentians

D. H. Lawrence [1885–1930]

Not every man has gentians in his house
In soft September, at slow, sad Michaelmas.

Bavarian gentians, tall and dark
Darkening the day-time torch-like with the smoking blueness of Pluto's gloom,
Ribbed hellish flowers erect, with their blaze of darkness spread blue
Blown into points, by the heavy white draught of the day.

Torch-flowers of the blue-smoking darkness, Pluto's dark-blue blaze
Black lamps from the halls of Dio, smoking dark blue
Giving off darkness, blue darkness, upon Demeter's yellow-pale day

Reach me a gentian, give me a torch!
Let me guide myself with the blue, forked torch of a flower
Down the darker and darker stairs, where blue is darkened on blueness
Down the way Persephone goes, just now, in first-frosted September
To the sightless realm where darkness is married to dark
And Persephone herself is but a voice, as a bride
A gloom invisible enfolded in the deeper dark

Of the arms of Pluto as he ravishes her once again
And pierces her once more with his passion of the utter dark.
Among the splendor of black-blue torches, shedding fathomless
  darkness on the nuptials.

Give me a flower on a tall stem, and three dark flames,
For I will go to the wedding, and be wedding-guest
At the marriage of the living dark.

Low Barometer

Robert Bridges [*1844–1930*]

The south-wind strengthens to a gale,
Across the moon the clouds fly fast,
The house is smitten as with a flail,
The chimney shudders to the blast.

On such a night, when Air has loosed
Its guardian grasp on blood and brain,
Old terrors then of god or ghost
Creep from their caves to life again;

And Reason kens he herits in
A haunted house. Tenants unknown
Assert their squalid lease of sin
With earlier title than his own.

Unbodied presences, the pack'd
Pollution and remorse of Time,
Slipp'd from oblivion reënact
The horrors of unhouseld crime.

Some men would quell the thing with prayer
Whose sightless footsteps pad the floor,
Whose fearful trespass mounts the stair
Or bursts the lock'd forbidden door.

Some have seen corpses long interr'd
Escape from hallowing control,
Pale charnel forms—nay ev'n have heard
The shrilling of a troubled soul,

That wanders till the dawn hath cross'd
The dolorous dark, or Earth hath wound
Closer her storm-spredd cloke, and thrust
The baleful phantoms under ground.

Counting the Mad

Donald Justice [1925–]

This one was put in a jacket,
This one was sent home,
This one was given bread and meat
But would eat none,
And this one cried No No No No
All day long

This one looked at the window
As though it were a wall,
This one saw things that were not there,
This one things that were,
And this one cried No No No No
All day long.

This one thought himself a bird,
This one a dog,
And this one thought himself a man,
An ordinary man,
And cried and cried No No No No
All day long.

The Heavy Bear Who Goes with Me

Delmore Schwartz [1913–]

"the withness of the body"—WHITEHEAD

The heavy bear who goes with me,
A manifold honey to smear his face,
Clumsy and lumbering here and there,
The central ton of every place,
The hungry beating brutish one
In love with candy, anger, and sleep,

Crazy factotum, dishevelling all,
Climbs the building, kicks the football,
Boxes his brother in the hate-ridden city.

Breathing at my side, that heavy animal,
That heavy bear who sleeps with me,
Howls in his sleep for a world of sugar,
A sweetness intimate as the water's clasp,
Howls in his sleep because the tight-rope
Trembles and shows the darkness beneath.
—The strutting show-off is terrified,
Dressed in his dress-suit, bulging his pants,
Trembles to think that his quivering meat
Must finally wince to nothing at all.

That inescapable animal walks with me,
Has followed me since the black womb held,
Moves where I move, distorting my gesture,
A caricature, a swollen shadow,
A stupid clown of the spirit's motive,
Perplexes and affronts with his own darkness,
The secret life of belly and bone,
Opaque, too near, my private, yet unknown,
Stretches to embrace the very dear
With whom I would walk without him near,
Touches her grossly, although a word
Would bare my heart and make me clear,
Stumbles, flounders, and strives to be fed
Dragging me with him in his mouthing care.
Amid the hundred million of his kind,
The scrimmage of appetite everywhere.

The Minute

Karl Shapiro [*1913–*]

The office building treads the marble dark,
The mother-clock with wide and golden dial
Suffers and glows. Now is the hour of birth
Of the tremulous egg. Now is the time of correction.
O midnight, zero of eternity,
Soon on a million bureaus of the city
Will lie the new-born minute.

The new-born minute on the bureau lies,
Scratching the glass with infant kick, cutting
With diamond cry the crystal and expanse
Of timelessness. This pretty tick of death
Etches its name upon the air. I turn
Titanically in distant sleep, expelling
From my lungs the bitter gas of life.

The loathsome minute grows in length and strength,
Bending its spring to forge an iron hour
That rusts from link to link, the last one bright,
The late one dead. Between the shining works
Range the clean angels, studying that tick
Like a strange dirt, but will not pick it up.
Nor move it gingerly out of harm's way.

An angel is stabbed and is carried aloft howling,
For devils have gathered on a ruby jewel
Like red mites on a berry; others arrive
To tend the points with oil and smooth the heat.
See how their vicious faces, lit with sweat,
Worship the train of wheels; see how they pull
The tape-worm Time from nothing into thing.

I with my distant heart lie wide awake
Smiling at that Swiss-perfect engine room
Driven by tiny evils. Knowing no harm
Even of gongs that loom and move in towers,
And hands as high as iron masts, I sleep,
At which sad sign the angels in a flock
Rise and sweep past me, spinning threads of fear.

The Cottage Hospital

John Betjeman [*1906–*]

At the end of a long-walled garden
  in a red provincial town,
A brick path led to a mulberry
  scanty grass at its feet.
I lay under blackening branches
  where the mulberry leaves hung down
Sheltering ruby fruit globes

from a Sunday-tea-time heat.
Apple and plum espaliers
basked upon bricks of brown;
The air was swimming with insects,
and children played in the street.

Out of this bright intentness
into the mulberry shade
Musca domestica (housefly)
swung from the August light
Slap into slithery rigging
by the waiting spider made
Which spun the lithe elastic
till the fly was shrouded tight.
Down came the hairy talons
and horrible poison blade
And none of the garden noticed
that fizzing, hopeless fight.

Say in what Cottage Hospital
whose pale green walls resound
With the tap upon polished parquet
of inflexible nurses' feet
Shall I myself be lying
when they range the screens around?
And say shall I groan in dying,
as I twist the sweaty sheet?
Or gasp for breath uncrying,
as I feel my senses drown'd
While the air is swimming with insects
and children play in the street?

The Gallows

Edward Thomas [*1878–1917*]

There was a weasel lived in the sun
With all his family,
Till a keeper shot him with his gun
And hung him up on a tree,
Where he swings in the wind and rain,
In the sun and in the snow,
Without pleasure, without pain,
On the dead oak tree bough.

There was a crow who was no sleeper,
But a thief and a murderer
Till a very late hour; and this keeper
Made him one of the things that were,
To hang and flap in rain and wind
In the sun and in the snow.
There are no more sins to be sinned
On the dead oak tree bough.

There was a magpie, too,
Had a long tongue and a long tail;
He could both talk and do—
But what did that avail?
He, too, flaps in the wind and rain
Alongside weasel and crow,
Without pleasure, without pain,
On the dead oak tree bough.

And many other beasts
And birds, skin, bone, and feather,
Have been taken from their feasts
And hung up there together.
To swing and have endless leisure
In the sun and in the snow,
Without pain, without pleasure,
On the dead oak tree bough.

The Groundhog

Richard Eberhart [*1904–*]

In June, amid the golden fields,
I saw a groundhog lying dead.
Dead lay he; my senses shook,
And mind outshot our naked frailty.
There lowly in the vigorous summer
His form began its senseless change,
And made my senses waver dim
Seeing nature ferocious in him.
Inspecting close his maggots' might
And seething cauldron of his being,
Half with loathing, half with a strange love,
I poked him with an angry stick.
The fever arose, became a flame

And Vigor circumscribed the skies,
Immense energy in the sun,
And through my frame a sunless trembling.
My stick had done nor good nor harm.
Then stood I silent in the day
Watching the object, as before;
And kept my reverence for knowledge
Trying for control, to be still,
To quell the passion of the blood;
Until I had bent down on my knees
Praying for joy in the sight of decay.
And so I left; and I returned
In Autumn strict of eye, to see
The sap gone out of the groundhog,
But the bony sodden hulk remained.
But the year had lost its meaning,
And in intellectual chains
I lost both love and loathing,
Mured up in the wall of wisdom.
Another summer took the fields again
Massive and burning, full of life,
But when I chanced upon the spot
There was only a little hair left,
And bones bleaching in the sunlight
Beautiful as architecture;
I watched them like a geometer,
And cut a walking stick from a birch.
It has been three years, now.
There is no sign of the groundhog.
I stood there in the whirling summer,
My hand capped a withered heart,
And thought of China and of Greece,
Of Alexander in his tent;
Of Montaigne in his tower,
Of Saint Theresa in her wild lament.

Sailing to Byzantium

William Butler Yeats [*1865–1939*]

That is no country for old men. The young
In one another's arms, birds in the trees
—Those dying generations—at their song,
The salmon-falls, the mackerel-crowded seas,

Fish, flesh, or fowl, commend all summer long
Whatever is begotten, born, and dies.
Caught in that sensual music all neglect
Monuments of unaging intellect.

An aged man is but a paltry thing,
A tattered coat upon a stick, unless
Soul clap its hands and sing, and louder sing
For every tatter in its mortal dress,
Nor is there singing school but studying
Monuments of its own magnificence;
And therefore I have sailed the seas and come
To the holy city of Byzantium.

O sages standing in God's holy fire
As in the gold mosaic of a wall,
Come from the holy fire, perne in a gyre,
And be the singing-masters of my soul.
Consume my heart away; sick with desire
And fastened to a dying animal
It knows not what it is; and gather me
Into the artifice of eternity.

Once out of nature I shall never take
My bodily form from any natural thing,
But such a form as Grecian goldsmiths make
Of hammered gold and gold enameling
To keep a drowsy Emperor awake;
Or set upon a golden bough to sing
To lords and ladies of Byzantium
Of what is past, or passing, or to come.

Peter Quince at the Clavier

Wallace Stevens [*1879–1955*]

I

Just as my fingers on these keys
Make music, so the self-same sounds
On my spirit make a music too.

Music is feeling, then, not sound;
And thus it is that what I feel,
Here in this room, desiring you,

Thinking of your blue-shadowed silk,
Is music. It is like the strain
Waked in the elders by Susanna:

Of a green evening, clear and warm,
She bathed in her still garden, while
The red-eyed elders, watching, felt

The basses of their being throb
In witching chords, and their thin blood
Pulse pizzicati of Hosanna.

II

In the green evening, clear and warm,
Susanna lay.
She searched
The touch of springs,
And found
Concealed imaginings.
She sighed
For so much melody.

Upon the bank she stood
In the cool
Of spent emotions.
She felt, among the leaves,
The dew
Of old devotions.

She walked upon the grass,
Still quavering.
The winds were like her maids,
On timid feet,
Fetching her woven scarves,
Yet wavering.

A breath upon her hand
Muted the night.
She turned—
A cymbal clashed,
And roaring horns.

III

Soon, with a noise like tambourines,
Came her attendant Byzantines.

They wondered why Susanna cried
Against the elders by her side:

And as they whispered, the refrain
Was like a willow swept by rain.

Anon their lamps' uplifted flame
Revealed Susanna and her shame.

And then the simpering Byzantines
Fled, with a noise like tambourines.

IV

Beauty is momentary in the mind—
The fitful tracing of a portal;
But in the flesh it is immortal.

The body dies; the body's beauty lives.
So evenings die, in their green going,
A wave, interminably flowing.

So gardens die, their meek breath scenting
The cowl of Winter, done repenting.
So maidens die to the auroral
Celebration of a maiden's choral.

Susanna's music touched the bawdy strings
Of those white elders; but, escaping,
Left only Death's ironic scraping.
Now in its immortality, it plays
On the clear viol of her memory,
And makes a constant sacrament of praise.

From *Canto LXXXI*

Ezra Pound [1885–   ]

What thou lovest well remains,
                    the rest is dross
What thou lov'st well shall not be reft from thee
What thou lov'st well is thy true heritage
Whose world, or mine or theirs
                    or is it of none?

First came the seen, then thus the palpable
        Elysium, though it were in the halls of hell,
What thou lovest well is thy true heritage

The ant's a centaur in his dragon world.
Pull down thy vanity, it is not man
Made courage, or made order, or made grace,
        Pull down thy vanity, I say pull down.
Learn of the green world what can be thy place
In scaled invention or true artistry,
Pull down thy vanity,
                Paquin pull down!
The green casque has outdone your elegance.

"Master thyself, then others shall thee beare"
        Pull down thy vanity
Thou art a beaten dog beneath the hail,
A swollen magpie in a fitful sun,
Half black half white
Nor knowst'ou wing from tail
Pull down thy vanity
                How mean thy hates
Fostered in falsity,
                Pull down thy vanity,
Rathe to destroy, niggard in charity,
Pull down thy vanity,
                I say pull down.

But to have done instead of not doing
                this is not vanity.

In Distrust of Merits

Marianne Moore [*1887–*]

Strengthened to live, strengthened to die for
  medals and positioned victories?
They're fighting, fighting, fighting the blind
  man who thinks he sees,—
who cannot see that the enslaver is
enslaved; the hater, harmed. O shining O
        firm star, O tumultuous
          ocean lashed till small things go
        as they will, the mountainous
          wave makes us who look, know

depth. Lost at sea before they fought! O
  star of David, star of Bethlehem,
O black imperial lion
  of the Lord—emblem
of a risen world—be joined at last, be
joined. There is hate's crown beneath which all is
    death; there's love's without which none
      is king; the blessed deeds bless
    the halo. As contagion
      of sickness makes sickness,

contagion of trust can make trust. They're
  fighting in deserts and caves, one by
one, in battalions and squadrons;
  they're fighting that I
may yet recover from the disease, *my*
self; some have it lightly, some will die. "Man's
    wolf to man?" And we devour
      ourselves? The enemy could not
    have made a greater breach in our
      defenses. One pilot-

ing a blind man can escape him, but
  Job disheartened by false comfort knew,
that nothing is so defeating
  as a blind man who
can see. O alive who are dead, who are
proud not to see, O small dust of the earth
    that walks so arrogantly,
      trust begets power and faith is
    an affectionate thing. We
      vow, we make this promise

to the fighting—it's a promise—"We'll
  never hate black, white, red, yellow, Jew,
Gentile, Untouchable." We are
  not competent to
make our vows. With set jaw they are fighting,
fighting, fighting,—some we love whom we know,
    some we love but know not—that
      hearts may feel and not be numb.
    It cures me; or am I what
      I can't believe in? Some

in snow, some on crags, some in quicksands,
little by little, much by much, they
are fighting fighting fighting that where
there was death there may
be life. "When a man is prey to anger,
he is moved by outside things; when he holds
his ground in patience patience
patience, that is action or
beauty," the soldier's defense
and hardest armor for

the fight. The world's an orphans' home. Shall
we never have peace without sorrow?
without pleas of the dying for
help that won't come? O
quiet form upon the dust, I cannot
look and yet I must. If these great patient
dyings—all these agonies
and woundbearings and blood shed–
can teach us how to live, these
dyings were not wasted.

Hate-hardened heart, O heart of iron,
iron is iron till it is rust.
There never was a war that was
not inward; I must
fight till I have conquered in myself what
causes war, but I would not believe it.
I inwardly did nothing.
O Iscariotlike crime!
Beauty is everlasting
and dust is for a time.

The Visitant

Theodore Roethke [*1908–1963*]

1

A cloud moved close. The bulk of the wind shifted.
A tree swayed overwater.
A voice said:
Stay. Stay by the slip-ooze. Stay.

Dearest tree, I said, may I rest here?
A ripple made a soft reply.
I waited, alert as a dog.
The leech clinging to a stone waited;
And the crab, the quiet breather.

2

Slow, slow as a fish she came,
Slow as a fish coming forward,
Swaying in a long wave;
Her skirts not touching a leaf,
Her white arms reaching towards me.

She came without sound,
Without brushing the wet stones,
In the soft dark of early evening,
She came,
The wind in her hair,
The moon beginning.

3

I woke in the first of morning.
Staring at a tree, I felt the pulse of a stone.
Where's she now, I kept saying.
Where's she now, the mountain's downy girl?

But the bright day had no answer.
A wind stirred in a web of appleworms;
The tree, the close willow, swayed.

Two Tramps in Mud Time

Robert Frost [*1874–1963*]

Out of the mud two strangers came
And caught me splitting wood in the yard.
And one of them put me off my aim
By hailing cheerily "Hit them hard!"
I knew pretty well why he dropped behind
And let the other go on a way.
I knew pretty well what he had in mind:
He wanted to take my job for pay.

Good blocks of beech it was I split,
As large around as the chopping block;
And every piece I squarely hit
Fell splinterless as a cloven rock.
The blows that a life of self-control
Spares to strike for the common good
That day, giving a loose to my soul,
I spent on the unimportant wood.

The sun was warm but the wind was chill.
You know how it is with an April day
When the sun is out and the wind is still,
You're one month on in the middle of May.
But if you so much as dare to speak,
A cloud comes over the sunlit arch,
A wind comes off a frozen peak,
And you're two months back in the middle of March.

A bluebird comes tenderly up to alight
And fronts the wind to unruffle a plume
His song so pitched as not to excite
A single flower as yet to bloom.
It is snowing a flake: and he half knew
Winter was only playing possum.
Except in color he isn't blue,
But he wouldn't advise a thing to blossom.

The water for which we may have to look
In summertime with a witching-wand,
In every wheelrut's now a brook,
In every print of a hoof a pond.
Be glad of water, but don't forget
The lurking frost in the earth beneath
That will steal forth after the sun is set
And show on the water its crystal teeth.
The time when most I loved my task
These two must make me love it more
By coming with what they came to ask.
You'd think I never had felt before
The weight of an ax-head poised aloft,
The grip on earth of outspread feet.
The life of muscles rocking soft
And smooth and moist in vernal heat.

Out of the woods two hulking tramps
(From sleeping God knows where last night,
But not long since in the lumber camps).
They thought all chopping was theirs of right.
Men of the woods and lumberjacks,
They judged me by their appropriate tool.
Except as a fellow handled an ax,
They had no way of knowing a fool.

Nothing on either side was said.
They knew they had but to stay their stay
And all their logic would fill my head:
As that I had no right to play
With what was another man's work for gain.
My right might be love but theirs was need.
And where the two exist in twain
Theirs was the better right—agreed.

But yield who will to their separation,
My object in living is to unite
My avocation and my vocation
As my two eyes make one in sight.
Only where love and need are one,
And the work is play for mortal stakes,
Is the deed ever really done
For Heaven and the future's sakes.

VIII

How Poems Come About: Intention and Meaning

Why are we, or why should we be, interested in how poems come about? A historian or biographer might be intensely interested in the materials that got into a poem—the personal experiences or observations of the poet, or ideas current in his time. Or a psychologist might equally well be interested in the mental process of creation that gave us the poem. But the historian or psychologist, strictly as historian or psychologist, would not be interested in the quality of the poem. For his interests, the bad poem might be as useful as the good poem. But our present concern is different from that of the historian or psychologist. We are primarily interested in the nature of the poem and its quality.

If the poem itself is our primary interest, we may say that there is no good reason why we should investigate the origins of the poem, and that a knowledge of the materials that went into the poem or of the process by which it came to be, cannot change the nature of the poem itself. Many people take the view that we have no proper concern with the private lives of writers even if the lives do provide material for the work. Wordsworth says in a letter to James Gray, a friend of Robert Burns:

> Our business is with their books,—to understand and to enjoy them. And, of poets more especially, it is true—that, if their works be good, they contain within themselves all that is necessary to their being comprehended and relished.

And Charles Lamb was shocked when he saw the manuscript of Milton's "Lycidas," as he reports in his essay "Oxford in the Vacation":

> I had thought of the Lycidas as a full-grown beauty—as springing up with all its parts absolute—till, in an evil hour, I was shown the original copy of it, together with the other minor poems of the author, in the library of Trinity, kept like some treasure to be proud of. I wish they had thrown them in the Cam, or sent them after the latter Cantos of Spenser, into the Irish Channel. How it staggered me to see the fine things in their ore! interlined, corrected! as if their words were mortal, alterable, displaceable at pleasure! as if they might have been otherwise, and just as good! as if inspiration were made up of parts, and these fluctuating, successive, indifferent! I will never go into the workshop of any great artist again.

In one sense, Wordsworth is right. We must not confuse information about the life of a poet, or his time, or his materials, with the poem itself. For the reader of poetry Lamb is right. What is important is the poem itself and not the psychological process whereby it was created. But in another sense both Wordsworth and Lamb are wrong. What we can learn about the origin of a poem may, if we do not confuse origin and poem, enlarge our understanding and deepen our appreciation.*

* This gain in understanding and appreciation is not merely, in fact not primarily, of the poem whose development we can trace because early drafts or information about the poet's experience have been preserved to us. It is, rather, a gain in our understanding and appreciation of poetry in general; when we learn about the materials of poetry and about the poetic process, we also learn something about the nature of poetry. The value of this study of biographical and textual material is to be distinguished sharply, however, from the value of certain historical information which is necessary for the understanding of particular literary works from another age or another culture. For example, we can presum-

In thinking of the origin of a poem we may distinguish two general aspects of the question: first, the *materials* of the poem, and second, the *process* whereby the poem is made.

The materials of a poem are various. We can, for instance, say that language itself is a material of poetry. It is one of the things the poet shapes and uses. We have to know something of the language a poet is using before we can appreciate his poem—before we can see how the poem came to be. This applies not only to poems in foreign languages but also to poems in our own tongue. The English of one time is not like the English of another. Words are born and die, and to make matters more complicated, the same word may change its meaning from one period to another. Furthermore, the poet himself may twist and wrench the language he uses so that words get new meanings.

To take another example, we may regard literary convention as a material for poetry. When Campion came to write "Blame Not My Cheeks" (p. 256), he used as one of the elements in his poem the Petrarchan convention of the lover who is abject and self-pitying before the cruel lady who despises him. Actually in the course of the poem this convention is brought into contrast with other attitudes, and the almost whimsical irony of the last line, which yet remains serious, is anything but Petrarchan. But the convention provides the starting point. The same is true of the convention of the pastoral elegy in Milton's "Lycidas." Milton is simply using this conventional fiction which had persisted from classical times. It is a material which he adapts in his own way.

Or let us consider the ideas that are available at a given time. Those, too, are materials. Tennyson uses a foreshadowing of the theory of evolution in his *In Memoriam,* and Whitman expresses certain notions of democracy. But it is nonsense to read "Sir Patrick Spence" as a statement of modern democratic ideas, for that poem came out of a feudal society. A poet may, of course, do something original with the ideas available to him. But his ideas are conditioned by his time.

So far we have been speaking of some of the materials of

ably understand *Hamlet* without knowing Shakespeare's private life or the steps in the composition of the play, but we cannot understand the play unless we know something of the heroic tradition that revenge is honorable.

poetry that are generally available in a period: the language, the literary conventions, the ideas. But the personal experiences of the poet are also materials. This is not to say that a poet simply reports his personal experiences. Because Shakespeare wrote a play about Macbeth, who killed a king and stole a throne, we do not have to assume that Shakespeare ever committed murder or robbery. Sometimes, very often in fact, the events in a poem are fictitious, are products of imagination. But the imagination is not entirely free; it is conditioned, too, by the experience of the poet. It is true, as Robert Frost says, that the poet needs only samples for the imagination to work on, but it does not work in a vacuum.

The relation between the actual work of a poet and his personal experiences may be a very delicate and tenuous one, but sometimes we find a very close correlation between the actual events and the poetry. Dorothy Wordsworth, the sister of the poet, records in her journal for April 15, 1802, the episode that gave the material for his poem on the daffodils entitled "I Wandered Lonely as a Cloud" (p. 550):

> It was a threatening, misty morning, but mild. . . . The wind was furious, and we thought we must have returned. We first rested in the large boat-house, then under a furze bush opposite Mr. Clarkson's. Saw the plow going in the field. The wind seized our breath. The Lake was rough. There was a boat by itself floating in the middle of the bay below Water Millock. . . . When we were in the woods beyond Gowbarrow Park we saw a few daffodils close to the water-side. We fancied that the lake had floated the seeds ashore, and that the little colony had so sprung up. But as we went along there were more and yet more; and at last, under the boughs of the trees, we saw that there was a long belt of them along the shore, about the breadth of a country turnpike road. I never saw daffodils so beautiful. They grew among the mossy stones about and about them; some rested their heads upon these stones as on a pillow for weariness; and the rest tossed and reeled and danced, and seemed as if they verily laughed with the wind, that blew upon them over the lake; they looked so gay, ever glancing, ever changing. This wind blew directly over the lake to them. There was here and there a little knot, and a few stragglers a few

> yards higher up; but they were so few as not to disturb the simplicity, unity, and life of that one busy highway.

It is true that in his poem Wordsworth does more than merely report the scene, but the scene is vividly there, a piece of material from his experience. And we are fairly safe in concluding that when he came to write the poem two years after the event, in 1804, the interpretation he gives the original event—the notion that experience grows in the imagination and the notion of the sympathetic relation between man and nature—is drawn also from personal experience. The real scene had really flashed upon his inward eye. That is, the whole poem, event and interpretation, presumably come as a presentation of real experience, *preceding* the act of composition.

To take another instance, we have an account by William Butler Yeats of a visit to a dying friend, the sister of the artist Aubrey Beardsley, who himself had died young and courageously:

> She was propped up on pillows with her cheeks I think a little rouged and looking very beautiful. Beside her an Xmas tree with little toys containing sweets, which she gave us. . . . I will keep the little toy she gave me and I dare say she knew that. On a table near were four dolls dressed like people out of her brother's drawings. . . . Ricketts had made them, modeling the faces and sewing the clothes. They must have taken him days. She had all her great lady airs and asked after my work and health as if they were the most important things in the world to her. "A palmist told me," she said, "that when I was forty-two my life would take a turn for the better and now I shall spend my forty-second year in heaven," and then emphatically pretending we were incredulous. "O yes, I shall go to heaven. Papists do." . . . Then she began telling improper stories and inciting us (there were two men besides myself) to do the like. At moments she shook with laughter. . . . I lay awake most of the night with a poem in my head. I cannot overstate her strange charm—the pathetic gaiety—It was her brother but her brother was not I think lovable, only astonishing and intrepid.*

* Quoted by A. Norman Jeffares: *W. B. Yeats: Man and Poet,* New Haven, Yale University Press, 1949, p. 166.

If we compare this with the poems on the same dying lady (p. 435), we find that most of the details and attitudes had already been present in the prose account, either explicitly or implicitly.

In the journal of Dorothy Wordsworth and the letter of Yeats, we have accounts of personal experiences that later become the material of poetry. In these instances, the relation between the experience and the poem is close. We have the impression that the poet had the experience and then did his thinking about its significance before he entered upon composition, before he had the impulse to make a poem.

We may, of course, be wrong about this. Wordsworth may have begun to turn around in his mind the idea of a poem on the daffodils even as he looked marveling at them. But what is important is that the first simple experience is interpreted, is turned about and about, until it gets a meaning for the poet and until he finds words that develop the meaning.

It may be objected here that the thinking about the original experience is also *material,* that it is as much material as the sight of the daffodils, and that it is certainly to be regarded as material if the poet did his thinking and interpreting *before* he actually began the process of composition. Then the question arises as to what we mean by the process of composition. Does it begin when the poet first takes pen in hand, or when, without necessarily intending a poem, he begins to think about the material and try to interpret it?

But does it really matter which view we take? The important thing is to see some line of connection between the experience and the poem which in its finished form interprets the experience.

All poems, however, do not start directly from a personal experience of the poet. A poet may actually start from a general idea—a theme—and seek episodes and images to embody it. For example, Coleridge apparently intended to write a poem about guilt and atonement, and actually began a prose-poem on Cain, long before he struck on the story of the Ancient Mariner to embody his ideas. And Milton, too, was casting about for a story to embody his ideas on guilt and atonement before he settled on *Paradise Lost.* In the manuscript of Milton's minor poems, preserved in the library of Trinity

College at Cambridge University, there are notes toward a drama on the Deluge as well as a drama on the Fall of Man. Or a poem may start from a story, an episode, or a situation heard about or read. It strikes the poet as interesting, and he begins to try to make a poem of that material, even before he is clear as to why it interests him or what it means to him. Or it may start with a casual phrase that pops into the poet's head or is picked up somewhere; or an image of some kind or a comparison may fire his imagination.

However the process may start, what is its nature?

At first glance, the accounts we have of the process seem contradictory and confusing. Some poets work very slowly and carefully. Some work by fits and starts, trusting to the suggestion of the moment. Some poems have been dreamed up in an instant. Some have required years of thought. There is Poe's famous account, in "The Philosophy of Composition," of the creation of "The Raven." After arguing that a poem must make its effect immediately, in a limited time, Poe says:

> Holding in view these considerations, as well as that degree of excitement which I deemed not above the popular, while not below the critical, taste, I reached at once what I conceived the proper *length* for my intended poem—a length of about one hundred lines. It is, in fact, a hundred and eight.
>
> My next thought concerned the choice of an impression, or effect, to be conveyed: and here I may as well observe that, throughout the construction, I kept steadily in view the design of rendering the work *universally* appreciable. . . . That pleasure which is at once the most intense, the most elevating, and the most pure, is, I believe, found in the contemplation of the beautiful. When, indeed, men speak of Beauty, they mean, precisely, not a quality, as is supposed, but an effect. . . . Now I designate Beauty as the province of the poem, merely because it is an obvious rule of Art that effects should be made to spring from direct causes. . . .
>
> Regarding, then, Beauty as my province, my next question referred to the *tone* of its highest manifestation—and all experience has shown that this tone is one of *sadness*. . . . Melancholy is thus the most legitimate of all the poetical tones. . . .

> The length, the province, and the tone, being thus determined, I betook myself to ordinary induction with the view of obtaining some artistic piquancy which might serve me as a key-note in the construction of the poem—some pivot upon which the whole structure might turn. In carefully thinking over all the usual artistic effects . . . I did not fail to perceive immediately that no one had been so universally employed as that of the *refrain.*

Poe continues in this fashion, as systematically as though working out a theorem in geometry. The refrain must be a single word, it must close each stanza, it must be sonorous, it must be melancholy, for that is the already determined tone. So he selects the word *nevermore,* as logically as a mechanic picks up the proper monkey-wrench.

Over against this systematic approach of Poe (which seems almost too systematic to be true) we can put the account given by Coleridge of the composition of "Kubla Khan."

> In the summer of the year 1797, the author, then in ill health, had retired to a lonely farmhouse between Porlock and Linton, on the Exmoor confines of Somerset and Devonshire. In consequence of a slight indisposition, an anodyne had been prescribed, from the effects of which he fell asleep in his chair at the moment that he was reading the following sentence, or words of the same substance, in *Purchas's Pilgrimage:* "Here the Khan Kubla commanded a palace to be built, and a stately garden thereunto. And thus ten miles of fertile ground were inclosed with a wall." The author continued for about three hours in a profound sleep, at least of the external senses, during which time he has the most vivid confidence, that he could not have composed less than from two to three hundred lines; if that indeed can be called composition in which all the images rose up before him as *things,* with a parallel production of the correspondent expressions, without any sensation or consciousness of effort. On awaking he appeared to himself to have a distinct recollection of the whole, and taking his pen, ink, and paper, instantly and eagerly wrote down the lines that are here preserved. At this moment he was unfortunately called out by a person on business from Porlock, and detained by him above an hour, and on his return to his room, found, to his no small surprise and mortification, that though he still retained some vague

> and dim recollection of the general purport of the vision, yet, with the exception of some eight or ten scattered lines and images, all the rest has passed away like the images on the surface of a stream into which a stone has been cast, but, alas! without the after restoration of the latter.

In between these two extremes there are all sorts of ways of composition. Though Shakespeare never, as far as we know, dreamed up a poem, he apparently did compose with great speed and fluency, and did little revision. Dryden, too, came to have more and more readiness so that, as he says, the thoughts outran the pen. The French poet Bonnard * records that when he composed, all the words seemed to crowd in at the same time so that he had the impression of having a thousand voices. But one part of the same poem may be composed in almost a flash and another part may require long and tedious effort. A. E. Housman provides us with such a poem. He tells us, in *The Name and Nature of Poetry,* how he was accustomed to compose on his afternoon walk, when he was a little drowsy from lunch and beer and his mind was relaxed and free for the movement of association. Under these circumstances, sometimes stanzas, or even whole poems, would come almost in a flash, sometimes merely the germs of poems which had to be developed later. He tells us, for example, that of the poem given below two stanzas came immediately while he was walking along, that another stanza came that same afternoon during tea time, but that another took a year and went through thirteen versions. Unfortunately, Housman did not specify the stanzas, but one critic † has argued that the first and second stanzas must have come spontaneously on the walk, for they make a finished thought, and that the last most probably came at tea time, separate from the first two. Then the problem was to get something that would carry over from the second to the fourth stanza to give balance to the repetition and return of the poem.

I hoed and trenched and weeded,
And took the flowers to fair:

* N. Kostyleff: *Le Mécanisme Cérébral de la Pensée,* Paris, Librairie Félix Alcan, 1914, p. 187.

† Donald A. Stauffer, *Poets at Work,* New York, Harcourt, Brace and Company, 1948, pp. 42–43.

I brought them home unheeded;
  The hue was not the wear.

So up and down I sow them
  For lads like me to find,
When I shall lie below them,
  A dead man out of mind.

Some seed the birds devour,
  And some the season mars,
But here and there will flower
  The solitary stars,

And fields will yearly bear them
  As light-leaved spring comes on,
And luckless lads will wear them
  When I am dead and gone.

Robert Frost says that many of his best poems came spontaneously, without effort:

> I won't deny I have worried quite a number of my poems into existence. But my sneaking preference remains for the ones I carried through like the stroke of a racquet, club, or headsman's ax. It is only under pressure from friends that I can consent to come out into the open and expose myself in a weakness so sacred and in the present trend of criticism so damaging. When I look into myself for the agony I am supposed to lay claim to as an artist it has to be over the poems that went wrong and came to grief without coming to an end; and they made me less miserable than I deserved when I discovered that though lost they were not entirely lost: I could and did quite freely quote lines and phrases of them from memory. I never wrote a poem for practice: I am always extended for the best yet. But what I failed with I learned to charge up to practice after the fact. Now if I had only treasured my first drafts along with my baby shoes to bear me out in all this I should be more comfortably off in a world of suspicion. My word will be more or less taken for it that I played certain poems through without fumbling a sentence: such as for example November Days, The Mountain, After Apple-Picking, The Wood-Pile, Desert Places, The Gift Outright, The Lovely Shall Be Choosers, Directive. With what pleasure I remember their tractability.

> They have been the experience I couldn't help returning for more of—I trust I may say without seeming to put on inspired airs.*

As Housman spontaneously caught little or much of a poem on his walks, so Hart Crane † tried to evoke the creative process by drink and jazz music, which might hypnotically start trains of verbal association; and so Schiller is reported to have kept a rotting apple in his desk because he found the odor stimulating. And many poets have had little tricks and habits which seem to make the process easier, more automatic, more like Coleridge's dream, ways to reach what Katherine Anne Porter has called "that undistracted center of being where the will does not intrude and the sense of passing time is lost, or has no power over the imagination.‡

What are we to make of all this? Is there one kind of poetry

* From a letter to Charles Madison, February 26, 1950. The letter continues: "Then for a small chaser of the low-down under the head perhaps of curiosa I might confess the trade secret that I wrote the third line of the last stanza of Stopping by Woods in such a way as to call for another stanza when I didn't want another stanza and didn't have another stanza in me, but with great presence of mind and a sense of what a good boy I was I instantly struck the line out and made my exit with a repeat end. I left the Ingenuities of Debt lying round nameless for forty years because I couldn't find a fourth line for it to suit me. A friend, a famous poet, saw it in 1913 and wasn't so much disturbed by my bad fourth line as he was by the word "terrelation" further on. The same famous poet did persuade me to omit a line or two from the Death of the Hired Man and wanted me to omit the lines Home is the place where when you have to go there they have to take you in. The last three lines of Nothing Gold Can Stay were once entirely different. A lady in Rochester, N. Y., has, I think, the earlier version. I haven't. Birches is two fragments soldered together so long ago I have forgotten where the joint is."

† See "The Roaring Boy," in Malcolm Cowley: *Exile's Return,* New York, Viking Press, 1941.

‡ "Notes on Writing," in *New Directions* 1940, James Loughlin, ed., Norfolk, Conn., New Directions. And here is Charlie Chaplin's account of how he provokes the unconscious: "There's no use just sitting down and waiting for an inspiration, though. You've got to play along. The main thing you've got to do is preserve your vitality. A couple of days of complete rest and solitude helps. Not seeing anybody. I even conserve my emotions. 'I'm not going to get excited about anybody or anything,' I say, 'until I get this gag worked out.' I go along that way, living a quiet and righteous life, and then I stay out late one night, and have a couple of drinks—perhaps all night—and the next morning the reserve pours out. But you've got to have the reserve. Dissipation is no use except as a release. You've been damming it up inside of you, and all of a sudden you say: 'Oh, here it is!' And then you go to work." (From Max Eastman· *Heroes I Have Known,* New York, Simon and Schuster, 1942, p. 177.)

that comes from calculation and another kind that comes from inspiration?

Perhaps the best way to approach the question is to ask how the composition of poetry compares with other kinds of creative activity, for instance, the discovery of a scientific principle. We find parallels here to the poetic activity. Some scientific discoveries have been made as the result of elaborate calculation, but some have been dreamed up as was "Kubla Khan."

The great German chemist Kekulé quite literally dreamed up his two most important discoveries, dealing with the structure of the molecule. He describes his discovery of the structure of benzene, which came to him one night as he sat at his desk trying to write a section of a text book on chemistry. "But it did not go well; my spirit was with other things. I turned my chair to the fireplace and sank into a half-sleep. Again the atoms flitted before my eyes." The atoms took the pattern of rings:

> Long rows, variously, more closely, united; all in movement, wriggling and turning like snakes. And see, what was that? One of the snakes seized its own tail and the image whirled scornfully before my eyes. As though from a flash of lightning I awoke; this time again I occupied the rest of the night in working out the consequences of the hypothesis.*

There is the account, too, of William Oughtred, the seventeenth-century mathematician who introduced the multiplication and proportion signs, as given in Aubrey's *Brief Lives*:

> He has told Bishop Ward, and Mr. Elias Ashmole . . . that on this spott of ground (or leaning against this Oake, or that ashe) the Solution of such or such a Probleme came into my head, as if infused by a Divine Genius, after I had thought on it without Successe for a yeare, two, or three.†

* Quoted by John R. Baker: *The Scientific Life,* New York, The Macmillan Company, 1943, p. 14.

† Henry D. Smyth, an important physicist, says: ". . . the outstanding mathematicians quite frequently are able to guess at the truth of a theorem. Their problem is then to fill in the proof by a series of logical steps. . . . Thus we have a paradox in the method of science. The research man may often think and work like an artist but he has to talk like a bookkeeper, in terms of precise facts, figures, and logical sequences of thought." (Address at Amherst College, March 23, 1950.)

The German scientist von Helmholtz almost made a method of getting solutions for his problems from the intuitive flash. Kekulé even went so far as to say to his fellow-scientists: "Let us learn to dream, gentlemen; then perhaps we shall find the truth."

Are we prepared to say that there is a difference between scientific discoveries arrived at by calculation and those dreamed up in a flash? No, we judge them in exactly the same way, by the same standards. The fact that in one instance the scientist had the conscious intention of getting the solution and in the other instance did not have it does not affect the solution.

But people ask: "If poets sometimes write poems in such a crazy way, how can we know what the poet intended? Isn't any interpretation we put on it just what we personally happen to make of the poem?"

But what does the word *intend* mean in such a connection?

It is true that sometimes the poet has a pretty clear idea of what he wants his poem to be. He may be able to state a theme and describe the sort of atmosphere or feeling he wants the whole thing to have. But even in such circumstances, is the process of creation analogous to that of building a house by a blueprint? An architect intends a certain kind of house and he can predict it down to the last nail. The carpenter simply follows the blueprint. But at the best the poet cannot envisage the poem as the architect can envisage the house; and in so far as the poet can envisage the poem, he cannot transfer it into words in a mechanical fashion corresponding to the builder's work on the house. As he begins to work with the poem he is never simply following a plan; he is also exploring the possibilities of imagination and language. Until the poem is actually written down to the last word, the poet cannot be sure *exactly* what it will mean—for we know that the meaning of a poem is fuller than the paraphrasable idea, that the rhythms, the verbal texture, the associations of words, the atmosphere, all the elements, enter into the meaning.

Sometimes, as we have said above, the poet may not have a very clear idea, perhaps not any idea, to start with. He may start with a personal experience as yet uninterpreted, a general, vague feeling, an episode, a metaphor, a phrase—anything that comes along to excite the imagination. Then as he composes, he moves toward his idea—toward his general conception of the poem. At the same time that he is trying to envisage the poem as a whole, he is trying to relate the individual items to that whole. He cannot assemble them in a merely arbitrary fashion; they must bear some relation to each other. So he develops his sense of the whole, the anticipation of the finished poem, as he works with the parts, and moves from one part to another. Then, as the sense of the whole develops, it modifies the process by which the poet selects and relates the parts, the words, images, rhythms, local ideas, events, etc. As the sense of the poem develops, as the idea becomes clearer, the poet may have to go back and change his beginnings, revise them or drop them entirely. It is a process in which one thing leads to another, then to a whole, and the whole leads back to single things. It is an infinitely complicated process of establishing interrelations.*

We can trace something of this process in certain passages of Shakespeare. When Shakespeare came to compose a particular passage in one of his plays, he had some notion of the relations of the characters and of the over-all business of the scene, but the local composition often seems to move by a fairly free process of association and suggestion.† In the fol-

* One of the best accounts of the creative process, of the way in which the parts become related to each other and to an envisaged whole, is in Mozart's description: "My ideas come as they will, I don't know how, all in a stream. If I like them I keep them in my head, and people say that I often hum them over to myself. Well, if I can hold on to them, they begin to join on to one another, as if they were bits that a pastry cook should joint together in his pantry. And now my soul gets heated, and if nothing disturbs me the piece grows larger and brighter until, however long it is, it is all finished at once in my mind, so that I can see it at a glance, as if it were a pretty picture or a pleasing person. Then I don't hear the notes one after another, as they are hereafter to be played, but it is as if in my fancy they were all at once. And that *is* a revel (*das ist nun ein Schmaus*). While I'm inventing, it all seems to me like a fine vivid dream; but that hearing it all at once (when the invention is done), that's the best. What I have once so heard I forget not again, and perhaps this is the best gift that God has granted me." (Quoted by Josiah Royce: *The Spirit of Modern Philosophy,* Boston, Houghton Mifflin Company, 1920, p. 457.)

† The examples here are drawn from E. E. Kellett's "Some Notes on a Feature of Shakespeare's Style" in *Suggestions,* Cambridge, Cambridge University Press, 1923, pp. 57–78.

lowing passage from *Henry V,* the oration of Henry V to his army before the battle of Agincourt, the italicized words indicate the links of thoughts: how a word used in one connection prompts its use in another connection and suggests a new idea:

> We few, we happy few, we band of *brothers:*
> For he to-day that sheds his blood with me
> Shall be *my brother;* be he ne'er so vile,
> This day shall *gentle* his *condition:*
> And *gentlemen* in England now abed
> Shall think themselves accurst they were not here,
> And hold their *manhoods* cheap whiles any speaks
> That fought with us upon St. Crispin's Day.

Again, let us take the speech of Antony, in *Antony and Cleopatra,* when he sees his followers deserting him for Octavius Caesar:

> The hearts
> That *spanieled* me at heels, to whom I gave
> Their wishes, do *discandy, melt* their *sweets,*
> On *blossoming* Caesar; and this *pine* is *barked*
> That overtopped them all.

The word *discandy* combines the notions of melting and of sweetness; *spanieled* leads to *barked,* but in another sense than that of a dog barking; *barked* leads to *pine* (perhaps with some notion of languishing away or losing strength also leading to the word), and to *blossoming* (though this pine is barked and dies, another, i.e., Caesar, is blossoming).

Here, in a limited way, by verbal suggestion, we can see something of the process that sometimes works more generally.

In these instances, however, the drift is established by the dramatic situation. There is a predetermined direction, more or less general, for the development of a passage. But what of poems that, like "Kubla Khan," spring fully formed, or almost fully formed, without any predetermining intention? Can they be said to express a poet's meaning?

They can be said to embody meaning in exactly the same way as any other poem: by the relations among the various elements that constitute the poem. The scientific discoveries of Kekulé or Oughtred are to be judged as any other scientific theories are judged. In the same way, it is the nature of the poem that counts.

But, granting this, it may still be asked how the dreamed-up poem, the poem that comes by a kind of inspiration, is related to the poet himself. Is the poem that is dreamed up irrelevant to the kind of man the poet is? Can it be said to express him? Or are we to regard it, as the ancients sometimes did, as the words of a god coming through the mouth of a man? Or as a kind of accident? Does it just happen, and might it equally well happen to somebody else?

It is the last question that gives us our clue. Only poets dream up poems, and only scientists dream up scientific discoveries. That is, the thing dreamed up is the product of the kind of mind and the kind of training possessed by the dreamer. As Louis Pasteur said: "Chance favors only the prepared spirits." So with inspiration: it only comes to those who are ready for it. Coleridge could dream up "Kubla Khan" because he had thought long and deeply about poetry, because his mind was stocked with certain materials, images and rhythms and ideas. Kekulé could dream up the benzene ring because he had devoted years of conscious and rigorously logical effort to the study of chemistry. The effortlessness was the result of long effort.*

To sum up this last matter, we may turn to Wordsworth's famous Preface to the second edition (1800) of the *Lyrical Ballads,* the volume of poems that he and Coleridge published together. He says that his poems will be distinguished by a "worthy *purpose,*" and *purpose* we can interpret as theme, meaning, or idea. He continues:

> Not that I always began to write with a distinct purpose formally conceived: but habits of meditation have, I trust, so prompted and regulated my feelings, that my descriptions of such objects as strongly excite those feelings, will be found to carry along with them a *purpose.* If this opinion be erroneous, I can have little right to the name of a

* The relation of "Kubla Khan" to the background of Coleridge's reading and experience is investigated by John Livingston Lowes: *The Road to Xanadu,* Boston, Houghton Mifflin. 1927.

> Poet. For all good poetry is the spontaneous overflow of powerful feelings: and though this be true, Poems to which any value can be attached were never produced on any variety of subjects but by a man who, being possessed of more than usual organic sensibility, had also thought long and deeply.

We find a parallel to Wordsworth's account of how ideas get into poetry, or may get into poetry, in a letter from T. S. Eliot concerning an essay on the themes of one of his poems:

> I think that this kind of analysis is perfectly justified so long as it does not profess to be a reconstruction of the author's method of writing. Reading your essay made me feel, for instance, that I had been a great deal more ingenious than I had been aware of, because the conscious problems with which one is concerned in the actual writing are more those of a quasi musical nature, in the arrangement of metric and pattern, than of a conscious exposition of ideas.*

What is important here for our purpose is that Wordsworth takes the most spontaneous poem, which might have begun in a burst of feeling and with no preconceived notion of its "purpose" or meaning, to be the fruit of his serious thinking at some earlier time. He took the poem to represent him, and accepted the full responsibility for it. The "objects" that excited the feelings carried along with them the "purpose" without the poet's conscious concern with the purpose. And Eliot, also, emphasizes the poet's conscious concern with the immediate problems of the poem, with the problems of the medium, rather than with the ideas as such. But if the unconscious is, as Coleridge says, the genius in the man of genius, it is still far from independent of the conscious; both the conscious and the unconscious are of the same man.

For better or for worse, the poet is responsible for his poem. He can always reject any ideas, images, phrases, etc., that come into his head. He cannot guarantee to himself that the right thing for his poem will come along out of his unconscious, but he can certainly refrain from putting the wrong one down on paper. As the poem grows during the process of composi-

* Letter to Cleanth Brooks, March 15, 1937.

tion, as he more clearly senses the kind of poem it is to be, he can more consciously criticize and reject elements that are not adequate or coherent, or do not express him. Some years ago a young scholar who greatly admired Housman's work wrote to the poet and asked him how he managed always to select the right word. Housman replied that he didn't bother about trying to get the right word, he simply bothered about getting rid of the wrong one.* That is, the conscious activity was critical, and the unconscious was productive. But the conscious activity is extremely important. It lays down, as it were, the limits for the activity of the unconscious. And in the end, if a poet feels that a poem doesn't represent him, that it does violence to his ideas, etc., he can always burn the poem instead of publishing it. His veto is absolute.

All this is not to say that the process of rejection and revision is carried on at a fully conscious level, that the poet gives himself the reasons for every rejection he makes. He may simply "feel" that the line isn't right, that the image does not fulfill the idea, that the rhythm is awkward. The rejection, that is, may be spontaneous, too. On the other hand, the poet may be fully aware of the issues, and may argue out each step with himself. But it doesn't matter which line he pursues. His act finally represents him. And if the poem is a good poem we can say that the act, whether the poet consciously reasoned about it or not, is a reasonable act.

Here is Randall Jarrell's account of how "The Woman at the Washington Zoo" came to be:

> Late in the summer of 1956 my wife and I moved to Washington. We lived with two daughters, a cat, and a dog, in Chevy Chase; every day I would drive to work through Rock Creek Park, past the zoo. I worked across the street from the Capitol, at the Library of Congress. I knew Washington fairly well, but had never lived there; I had been in the army, but except for that had never worked for the government.
>
> Some of the new and some of the old things there—I was often reminded of the army—had a good deal of effect on me: after a few weeks I began to write a poem. I have most of what I wrote, though the first page is gone; the earliest lines are

* Letter to Arnold Stein, August 22, 1935.

any color
My print, that has clung to its old colors
Through many washings; this dull null
Navy I wear to work, and wear from work, and so
~~And so to bed~~ To bed
With no complaint, no comment—neither from my chief,
nor
The Deputy Chief Assistant, ~~from~~ his chief,
Nor nor
~~From~~ Congressmen, ~~from~~ their constituents—
~~thin~~
Only I complain; this ~~poor~~ worn serviceable . . .

The woman talking is a near relation of women I was seeing there in Washington—some at close range, at the Library—and a distant relation of women I had written about before, in "The End of the Rainbow" and "Cinderella" and "Seele im Raum." She is a kind of aging machine-part. I wrote, as they say in suits, "acting as next friend"; I had for her the sympathy of an aging machine-part. (If I was also something else, that was just personal; and she also was something else.) I felt that one of these hundreds of thousands of government clerks might feel all her dresses one dress, a faded navy blue print, and that dress her body. This work- or life-uniform of hers excites neither complaint, nor comment, nor the mechanically protective *No comment* of the civil servant; excites them neither from her "chief," the Deputy Chief Assistant, nor from his, nor from any being on any level of that many-leveled machine: all the system is silent, except for her own cry, which goes unnoticed just as she herself goes unnoticed. (I had met a Deputy Chief Assistant, who saw nothing remarkable in the title.) The woman's days seem to her the going-up-to-work and coming-down-from-work of a worker; each ends in *And so to bed,* the diarist's conclusive unvarying entry in the daybook of his life.

These abruptly opening lines are full of duplications and echoes, like what they describe. And they have about them a familiar wrongness—lie under the curse of all beginnings: either there is too much of something or it is not yet there. The lines break off with *this worn serviceable*—the words can apply either to her dress or to her body, but anything so obviously suitable to the dress must be intended for the body. *Body that no sunlight dyes, no hand suffuses,* the page written the next day goes on; then after a space there is *Dome-shadowed, with-*

ering among columns, / Wavy upon the pools of fountains, small beside statues . . . No sun colors, no hand suffuses with its touch, this used, still-useful body. It is subdued to the element it works in: is shadowed by the domes, grows old and small and dry among the columns, of the buildings of the capital; becomes a reflection, its material identity lost, upon the pools of the fountains of the capital; is dwarfed beside the statues of the capital—as, year by year, it passes among the public places of this city of space and trees and light, city sinking beneath the weight of its marble, city of graded voteless workers.

The word *small,* as it joins the reflections in the pools, the trips to the public places, brings the poem to its real place and subject—to its title, even: next there is *small and shining,* then (with the mark beside it that means *use, don't lose*) *small, far-off, shining in the eyes of animals;* the woman ends at the zoo, looking so intently into its cages that she sees her own reflection in *the eyes of animals, these wild ones trapped / As I am trapped but not, themselves, the trap* . . . The lines have written above them, now, *The Woman at the Washington Zoo.*

The next page has the title and twelve lines:

This print, that has kept the memory of color
Alive through many cleanings; this dull null
Navy I wear to work, and wear from work, and so
To bed (with no complaints, no comment: neither from my
chief,
The Deputy Chief Assistant, nor her chief,
Nor his, nor Congressmen, nor their constituents
~~wan~~
—Only I complain); this ~~plain,~~ worn, serviceable
sunlight
Body that no ~~sunset~~ dyes, no hand suffuses
But, dome-shadowed, withering among columns,
Wavy beneath fountains—small, far-off, shining
~~wild~~
In the eyes of animals, these beings trapped
As I am trapped but not, themselves, the trap . . .

Written underneath this, in the rapid ugly disorganized handwriting of most of the pages, is *bars of my body burst blood breath breathing—lives aging but without knowledge of age / Waiting in their safe prisons for death, knowing not of death;* immediately this is changed into two lines, *Aging, but without knowledge of their age, / Kept safe here, knowing not of death, for death*—and out at the side, scrawled heavily, is: *O bars of my own body, open, open!* She recognizes herself in the animals—and recognizes herself, also, in the cages.

Written across the top of this page is *2nd and 3rd alphabet.* Streets in Washington run through a one-syllable, a two-syllable, and a three-syllable (Albemarle, Brandywine, Chesapeake . . .) alphabet, so that people say to you, "Let's see, that's in the second alphabet, isn't it?" It made me think of Kronecker's, "God made the integers, all else is the work of man"; but I felt that it was right for Washington to have alphabets of its own—made up the title of a detective story, *Murder in the Second Alphabet.* The alphabets were a piece of Washington that should have fitted into the poem, but didn't; but the zoo was a whole group of pieces, a little Washington, into which the poem itself fitted.

Rock Creek Park, with its miles of heavily wooded hills and valleys, its rocky stream, is like some National Forest dropped into Washington by mistake. Many of the animals of the zoo are in unroofed cages back in its ravines. My wife and I had often visited the zoo, and now that we were living in Washington we went to it a great deal. We had made friends with a lynx that was very like our cat that had died the spring before, at the age of sixteen. We would feed the lynx pieces of liver or scraps of chicken and turkey; we fed liver, sometimes, to two enormous white timber wolves that lived at the end of one ravine. Eager for the meat, they would stand up against the bars on their hind legs, taller than a man, and stare into our eyes; they reminded me of Akela, white with age, in the *Jungle Books,* and of the wolves who fawn at the man Mowgli's brown feet in *In the Rukh.* In one of the buildings of the zoo there was a lioness with two big cubs; when the keeper came she would come over, purring her bass purr, to rub her head against the bars—almost as our lynx would rub his head against the turkey-skin, in rapture, before he finally gulped it down. In the lions' building there were two black leopards; when you got close to them you saw they had not lost the spots of the ordinary leopards—were the ordinary leopards, but spotted black on black, dingy somehow.

On the way to the wolves one went by a big unroofed cage of foxes curled up asleep; on the concrete floor of the enclosure there would be scattered two or three white rats—stiff, quite untouched—that the foxes had left. (The wolves left their meat, too—big slabs of horse-meat, glazing, covered with flies.) Twice when I came to the foxes' cage there was a turkey-buzzard that had come down for the rats; startled at me, he flapped up heavily, with a rat dangling underneath. (There are usually vultures circling over the zoo; nearby, at the tennis courts of the Sheraton-Park, I used to see vultures perched on the tower of WTTG, above the court on which Defense Secretary McElroy was playing doubles—so that I would say to myself, like Peer Gynt: "Nature is witty.") As a child, coming around the bend of a country road, I had often seen a turkey-buzzard, with its black wings and naked red head, flap heavily up from the mashed body of a skunk or possum or rabbit.

A good deal of this writes itself on the next page, almost too rapidly for line-endings or punctuation: *to be and never know I am when the vulture buzzard comes for the white rat that the foxes left May he take off his black wings, the red flesh of his head, and step to me as man—a man at whose brown feet the white wolves fawn—to whose hand of power / The lioness stalks, leaving her cubs playing / and rubs her head along the bars as he strokes it.* Along the side of the page, between these lines, two or three words to a line, is written *the animals who are trapped but are not themselves the trap black leopards spots, light and darkened, hidden except to the close eyes of love, in their life-long darkness, so I in decent black, navy blue.*

As soon as the zoo appeared, all the things of the poem settled into it and were at home there; now it begins to be plain that all the things of the poem come out of, and are divided between, color and colorlessness. Colored women and colored animals and colored cloth—all that the woman sees as her own opposite—come into the poem to begin it. Beside the typed lines are many hurried phrases, most of them crossed out: *red and yellow as October maples rosy, blood seen through flesh in summer colors wild and easy natural leaf-yellow cloud-rose leopard-yellow, cloth from another planet the leopards look back at their wearers, hue for hue the women look back at the leopard.* And on the back of the vulture's page there is a flight of ideas, almost a daydream, coming out of these last phrases: *we have never mistaken you for the others among the legations one of a different architecture women, saris of a different color envoy impassive clear bullet-proof glass lips, through the clear glass of a rose sedan color of blood you too are represented on this earth . . .*

One often sees on the streets of Washington—fairly often sees at the zoo—what seem beings of a different species: women from the embassies of India and Pakistan, their sallow skin and black hair leopardlike, their yellow or rose or green saris exactly like the robes of Greek statues, before the statues had lost their color. I was used to saying in a serious voice, about the sun red over the horizon, the moon white over the ocean: "It's like another planet"; partly because of this joke, the saris seemed to me cloth from another planet. After I had worked a little longer, the poem began as it begins now:

> The saris go by me from the embassies.
>
> Cloth from the moon. Cloth from another planet.
> They look back at the leopard like the leopard.
>
> And I . . . This print of mine, that has kept its color
> Alive through so many cleanings; this dull null
> Navy I wear to work, and wear from work, and so
> To my bed, so to my grave, with no
> Complaints, no comment: neither from my chief,
> The Deputy Chief Assistant, nor his chief—
> Only I complain; this serviceable
> Body that no sunlight dyes, no hand suffuses
> But, dome-shadowed, withering among columns,
> Wavy beneath fountains—small, far-off, shining
> In the eyes of animals, these beings trapped
> As I am trapped but not, themselves, the trap,
> Aging, but without knowledge of their age,
> Kept safe here, knowing not of death, for death
> —Oh, bars of my own body, open, open!

It is almost as if, once all the materials of the poem were there, the middle and end of the poem made themselves, as the beginning had just made itself. After the imperative *open, open!* there is a space, and the middle of the poem begins evenly—since her despair is beyond expression—in a statement of accomplished fact: *The world goes by my cage and never sees me.* Inside the mechanical official cage of her life, her body, she lives invisibly; no one feeds this animal, reads out its name, pokes a stick through the bars at it—the cage is empty. She feels that she is even worse off than the other animals of the zoo: they are still wild animals—since they do not know how to change into domesticated animals, beings that are their own cages—and they are surrounded by a world that does not know how to surrender them, still thinks them part of itself. This natural world comes through or over the bars of the cages, on its continual visits to those within: to those who are not machine-parts, convicts behind the bars of their penitentiary, but wild animals—the free beasts come to their imprisoned brothers and never know that they are not also free. Written on the back of one page, crossed out, is *Come still, you free;* on the next page this becomes

The world goes by my cage and never sees me.
And there come not to me, as come to these,
The wild ~~ones~~ beasts, sparrows pecking the llamas' grain,
Pigeons ~~fluttering to~~ settling on the bears' bread, turkey-buzzards
~~Coming with grace first, then with horror~~ ~~Vulture seizing~~
Tearing the meat the flies have clouded . . .

In saying mournfully that the wild animals do not come to her as they come to the animals of the zoo, she is wishing for their human equivalent to come to her. But she is right in believing that she has become her own cage—she has changed so much, in her manless, childless, fleshless existence, that her longing wish has inside it an increasing repugnance and horror: the innocent sparrows *pecking* the llamas' grain become larger in the pigeons *settling on* (not *fluttering to*) the bears' bread; and these grow larger and larger, come (with grace first, far off in the sky, but at last with horror) as turkey-buzzards seizing, no, *tearing* the meat the flies have clouded. She herself is that stale left-over flesh, nauseating just as what comes to it is horrible and nauseating. The series *pecking, settling on,* and *tearing* has inside it a sexual metaphor: the stale flesh that no one would have is taken at last by the turkey-buzzard with his naked red head and dangling wattles.

Her own life is so terrible to her that, to change, she is willing to accept even this, changing it as best she can. She says: *Vulture* (it is a euphemism that gives him distance and solemnity), *when you come for the white rat that the foxes left* (to her the rat is so plainly herself that she does not need to say so; the small, white, untouched thing is more accurately what she is than was the clouded meat—but, also, it is euphemistic, more nearly bearable), *take off the red helmet of your head* (the bestiality, the obscene sexuality of the flesh-eating death-bird is really—she hopes or pretends or desperately is sure—merely external, *clothes,* an intentionally-frightening war-garment like a Greek or Roman helmet), *the black wings that have shadowed me* (she feels that their inhuman colorless darkness has always, like the domes of the inhuman city, shadowed her; the wings are like a black parody of the wings the Swan Brothers wear in the fairy tale, just as the whole costume is like that of the Frog Prince or the other beast-princes of the stories) *and step* (as a human being, not fly as an animal) *to me as* (what you really are under the disguising clothing of red flesh and black feathers) *man*—not the machine-part, the domesticated animal that is its own cage, but man as he was first, still must be, is: the animals' natural lord,

> The wild brother at whose feet the white wolves fawn,
> To whose hand of power the great lioness
> Stalks, purring . . .

And she ends the poem when she says to him:

> You know what I was,
> You see what I am: change me, change me!

Here is the whole poem:

The Woman at the Washington Zoo

The saris go by me from the embassies.

Cloth from the moon. Cloth from another planet.
They look back at the leopard like the leopard.

And I . . . This print of mine, that has kept its color
Alive through so many cleanings; this dull null
Navy I wear to work, and wear from work, and so
To my bed, so to my grave, with no
Complaints, no comment: neither from my chief,
The Deputy Chief Assistant, nor his chief—
Only I complain; this serviceable
Body that no sunlight dyes, no hand suffuses
But, dome-shadowed, withering among columns,
Wavy beneath fountains—small, far-off, shining
In the eyes of animals, these beings trapped
As I am trapped but not, themselves, the trap,
Aging, but without knowledge of their age,
Kept safe here, knowing not of death, for death
—Oh, bars of my own body, open, open!

The world goes by my cage and never sees me.
And there come not to me, as come to these,
The wild beasts, sparrows pecking the llamas' grain,
Pigeons settling on the bears' bread, buzzards
Tearing the meat the flies have clouded . . .
Vulture,
When you come for the white rat that the foxes left,
Take off the red helmet of your head, the black
Wings that have shadowed me, and step to me as man,
The wild brother at whose feet the white wolves fawn,
To whose hand of power the great lioness
Stalks, purring . . .
You know what I was,
You see what I am: change me, change me!

Let us take an example from A. E. Housman (see insert following). Here the poet has left no record of his reasoning. We must, then, try to reconstruct the stages by which the poet moved from his original idea to the finished poem. Our poem is "The Immortal Part," by Housman. In its finished form the poem has forty-four lines, but the version given here is much shorter and is very early. It is clearly not the first version, however; on the manuscript we can see erasures beneath the first visible text. Let us try to reconstruct the stages of the poem.

First we notice that the manuscript has a title, "The Immortal Part." Very rarely does Housman give a title to a poem, and so we can hazard that the title was the start of the poem, that the germ is the ironical idea that the bones are the immortal part of man.

The first line has been erased, but as far as we can now tell it ran

Every —— night and day.

And was followed by

(2) I hear my bones within me say
(3) "Another eve another morn

The next line, (4), intended to rhyme with (3), had two versions, both of which are erased, but we can make out that the second version ended with *born*. But the stanza was unsatisfactory. For one thing, "Every —— night and day" is a rather flat line. And for another thing, it doesn't seem to be enough preparation for line (2). Furthermore, the sharp, succinct effect of what the bones say would be weakened by the addition of another line, and the line ending in *born* was, in all likelihood, but a descriptive elaboration. So Housman began again on the right margin, lines (2a) and (3a). The erasure here leaves little legible, but line (2a) seems to end with *betray*. We may guess that Housman was with his new rhyme trying to get a new preparation for line (2). In any case, this couplet did not work out. So Housman came back to lines (2) and (3), and by changing *eve* and *morn* in line (3) to *night* and *day,* got the sharp, epigrammatic couplet to embody his key idea, where before the idea had been split between the last line of one couplet and the first of another. So we have what, except for punctuation, is the final version:

I hear my bones within me say
"Another night another day,

The next line (5) came fairly well:

When shall this slough of flesh be cast,

But line (6) caused more trouble. Under the erasure we see something that looks like:

This flame —— be past.

And above the erasure the word *life,* which seems to have been a revision of the rejected line, perhaps something like, "flame of life." Another try gives us:

This dust of thought be laid at last.

But the word *thought* is not satisfactory to Housman, probably because it does not somehow associate with *flesh,* the key word of the above line. So he cancels *thought* and substitutes *life* (suggested perhaps by the revision of the earlier version of the same line), a word that pairs more readily with *flesh.* Neither line is now in its final form, but the poet, as we shall see, probably did not touch them again until he had worked out his last stanza.

Now we face a question. We see that the next two lines on the manuscript, (7) and (8), though in their final form, are not in their final place Did Housman jot them down here, as they

The Immortal Part

When I meet the morning beam
Or lay me down at night to dream,
I hear my bones within me say,
"Another night, another day.

"When shall this slough of sense be cast,
This dust of thoughts be laid at last,
The man of flesh and soul be slain
And the man of bone remain?

"This tongue that talks, these lungs that shout,
These thews that hustle us about,
This brain that fills the skull with schemes,
And its humming hive of dreams,—

"These to-day are proud in power
And lord it in their little hour:
The immortal bones obey control
Of dying flesh and dying soul.

" 'Tis long till eve and morn are gone:
Slow the endless night comes on,
And late to fulness grows the birth
That shall last as long as earth.

"Wanderers eastward, wanderers west,
Know you why you cannot rest?
'Tis that every mother's son
Travails with a skeleton.

"Lie down in the bed of dust;
Bear the fruit that bear you must;
Bring the eternal seed to light,
And morn is all the same as night.

"Rest you so from trouble sore,
Fear the heat o' the sun no more,
Nor the snowing winter wild,
Now you labor not with child.

"Empty vessel, garment cast,
We that wore you long shall last.
—Another night, another day."
So my bones within me say.

Therefore they shall do my will
To-day while I am master still,
And flesh and soul, now both are strong,
Shall hale the sullen slaves along,

Before this fire of sense decay,
This smoke of thought blow clean away,
And leave with ancient night alone
The steadfast and enduring bone.

came into his mind, realizing that they were to be placed later, or did he first think of them as coming after line (6) and leading up to line (11)? Under any circumstances, lines (7) and (8) could not lead up to lines (9) and (10).

So far in the poem, Housman is thinking in couplets, not in stanzas, and he is not establishing a very clear progression from one couplet to the next. It is true that we do get a progression from lines (2–3) to lines (5–6), but otherwise what we seem to find are germinal bits, points of focus, pegs on which the poem is to be hung as it develops.

In the next four lines, however, Housman composes a rounded stanza, one that is clearly intended to end the speech of the bones. In line (11) he repeats the night-day motif, which starts the speech of the bones, but after he has struck on the phrase "endless night" in the next line, he comes back and changes *nights* to *morn* and *days* to *eve,* to avoid repetition. But this stanza is not to survive.

After the speech of the bones, the turn of the poem comes, the consequence of the speech:

(15) Therefore I shall have my will
(16) Today while I am master still,
(17) And flesh and soul, now both are strong,
(18) Shall lug the sullen slaves along,

The form of statement in line (15) throws the emphasis off the bones, the key word; and so "I shall have my will" is altered to "they shall do my will." And in the last line of the stanza *lug* becomes *haul,* which, in the final version, becomes *hale.*

The first change in line (18) may be argued like this: the word *lug* sets up too positive an alliteration on *l* in the line, and a nonfunctional forced pause between *shall* and *lug*. Housman uses alliteration very freely but rather discreetly. As for the forced pause, the general notion of the line is that flesh and soul get their will done effortlessly, masterfully, and freely, and the impediment of the pause destroys this impression. Furthermore, the word *lug* means carrying an absolutely dead weight—and that is not what a man does to his bones, which are active, or what a master does to his slaves. So Housman tries *haul.* This does avoid the forced pause and the obvious alliteration; the *l* sound is not initial and is lightly absorbed into the texture of the line. Also the word doesn't imply as much dead weight as *lug,* it is not quite as chunky a word, as it were. But it still fails on this general score: the bones are still passive. But sometime between this version and the last, Housman strikes on *hale,* an easy sound association from *haul.* The new word fulfills all the requirements indicated above, and brings, besides, a new element. The *a*-sound in *hale* provides an assonantal binder with the *a*-sound in *slaves,* and emphasizes the flow and unity of the line, but discreetly.

This brings us to the last stanza. In line (19) the first version "these fires of flesh" becomes "this fire of sense," and in line (20) "smoke of soul" becomes "smoke of thoughts." But it seems unlikely that these changes were made until Housman had written the last two lines. We might argue in this way: Line (21) with "ancient night" is really an echo of line (12). Then in line (22) Housman first put down "immortal and enduring," the word *immortal* coming almost automatically from the title, which, as we have said, probably contained the germ of the poem. But the word didn't suit. Perhaps it is too closely associated with *soul,* used above, carrying some notion of lightness, of delicacy, of an aspiring quality, of a continuity in life. So *senseless* comes next. This try indicates something of Housman's objection to *immortal.* The new word covers part of the objection, but it does not retain the idea of permanence in *immortal.* Then he finds what he in the manuscript spells as "stedfast." This word avoids the objections to *immortal* and yet carries the idea of permanence, but permanence by solidity, by weight, by massive indestructibility, with the faint hint of some sort of moral victory in its permanence. We may notice, too, that *enduring* carries a sort of double meaning, mere durability as its primary sense and a capacity for surviving suffering as its secondary sense. But to return to *steadfast,* the word introduces a new rhythm, a *spondaic effect* (*Note on Versification*) that adds appropriately to the solidity and heaviness of the line, and to the final stoical temper of the poem.

It is the revision of this last line, further, that may react on the poem to instigate other revision. Perhaps the try at *senseless* for *immortal* suggested *sense* for *flesh* in line (19): if the bones are "senseless," then the flesh is "senseful," and the contrast between flesh and bone becomes more precise. But once having struck on *sense* in (19), Housman cannot let *soul* stand in the next line. In traditional psychology, the aspects of consciousness to be associated are sensation and thought, and thought was supposed to derive from sensation; so the "fire of sense," which, by the way, is a good image for man's appetite for the immediate experience of the world, leads to the "smoke of thought," the evanescent, useless thing that comes from man's experience.

Of course, Housman may have arrived at the sense-thought notion before he wrote the last line. He may have simply objected to *soul* because it did carry the idea of immortality, and he wished to imply that the only immortality was in the bone. Thus, having rejected *soul* he would have to start on a new train of thinking; and then he may have picked up the rejected *thought* of line (6). But in any case, having set up the last stanza, he went back at some point, as we know from the final version, and changed the *flesh* in line (5) to *sense,* and the *life* in line (6) back to *thoughts.* It is even possible that the version of line (6) as we have it in the manuscript was not written at all until after the last stanza, that Housman came back and erased his earlier line (6) which may very well have had *soul* in it to pair with *flesh* above, and then got his "dust of thought" idea and changed *thought* to *life* on a bad hunch that he later had to revoke. The precise order of events here is not what is important. What is important is a kind of relation among them.

To sum up, we may say that Housman probably struck on the idea of man's bones as being his immortal part. That gave the germ of the poem, and the title. Next he struck on the idea that the bones would speak in pitying protest against their enslavement to flesh. After jotting down several almost unrelated couplets, which served as notes, as it were for the speech of the bones, Housman worked seriously at what was to be the climax of his poem, the response to the bones. Even in this first manuscript these last two stanzas, with the exception of one word in line (18), come out in final form. This much may have come on a walk and at an hour at tea time, but the actual time involved here is not very significant. It *is* significant that we have here the germ of a poem, the development of its plan (introduction, speech of bones, reply), the establishing of its theme and tonality. What the poet had to do later was to get a satisfactory introduction to the speech of the bones, and then fill in the speech. This meant finding a principle of continuity for the speech, and, in fact, the splitting of the one stanza (lines 11–14) already set up in this section. The process may have required a long time, but the control by which it would take place already existed.

Let us take another example, from another poet, the second stanza of Keats's "Ode to Autumn" (p. 109). In the original draft it began:

> Who hath not seen thee? for thy haunts are many
> Sometimes whoever seeks for thee may find

Keats, according to one critic,* sees that *many* is going to be a difficult rhyme, and so starts over again, "feeling also no doubt a kind of thin abruptness in the half-line question, and a certain feebleness both of sound and sense in *for thee.*" Almost immediately, for the manuscript shows signs of haste, Keats composes the first four lines of the stanza:

> Who hath not seen thee oft amid thy stores?
> Sometimes whoever seeks abroad may find
> Thee sitting careless on a granary floor
> Thy hair soft lifted by the winnowing wing

Then Keats strikes off the final *s* of *stores* to make his rhyme with *floor,* and changes *wing* to *wind.*

Ridley continues the analysis:

> However, whatever small points there may have been in the first four lines, they were soon and easily solved. Now the real troubles begin.
>
> husky
> While bright the Sun slants through the / barn;
> Or sound asleep in a half reaped field
> Dosed with read poppies; while thy reeping hook
> Spares form Some slumbrous
>
> At this point the lines, which have clearly been going from bad to worse, have petered out altogether, and no

* M. R. Ridley: *Keats' Craftsmanship,* Oxford, Clarendon Press, 1933, pp. 285–287.

rhyme for *field* is in sight anyway. The next stage is some minor tinkering. The line about the sun, and the next line, are deleted altogether, and the second rewritten as

on on a half reap'd furrow sound asleep

(i.e., intending not to delete the *Or* and to write *on* once only), then *Some slumbrous* is deleted, and under it written

minutes while wam slumpers creep

So that now he has in front of him

~~husky~~
~~While bright the Sun slants through the~~ barn
on on a half reap'd furrow sound asleep
~~Or sound asleep in a half reaped field~~
Dosed with read poppies; while thy reeping hook
Spares form ~~Some slumbrous~~
minutes while wam slumpers creep

That has at least achieved a rhyme; but if the line about the sun is to disappear altogether the rhyme is in the wrong place; none of it is very satisfactory; and the *eep* sound has got out of hand. So Keats cancels the whole passage with some vigorous cross-hatching, and begins all over again, using the rewritten sixth line as the fifth, and improving the old seventh for use as the new sixth.

Or on a half reap'd furrow sound asleep
Dos'd with the fume of poppies, while thy hook
Spares for ~~one~~some slumbrous minutes the next swath;

So far, so good; and as any troubles about a rhyme for the unpromising *swath* are still four lines off he goes on his way rejoicing:

And sometimes like a gleans thost dost keep
Steady thy laden head across the brook
Or by a Cyder-press with patent look
Thou . . .

Well, and now what about the swath, waiting four lines above for its rhyme. But the Cyder-press is going as well as can be, so for the moment confound the swath, and finish

watchest the last oozing hours by hours

and now go back and get the rhyme, even if we have to sacrifice in the process the idea of the tenacious *slumpers* which has hung onto existence through two corrections.

> Spares the next swath and all its twined flowers;

The copy in the Woodhouse letter omits to notice the cancellation of the *s* of *stores;* corrects some spellings, but writes *Stready* for *Steady;* does some punctuating; reads *a brook* for *the brook,* and *Dased* for *Dos'd,* either an easy misreading of a word so written that it might be either, or a deliberate alteration; and greatly accentuates the opiate *z* sound of the last line by reading *oozings* for *oozing.**

EXERCISE:

1. Below are three versions of Housman's "To an Athlete Dying Young." Version A is very early, but Version B is approaching the finished form, which appears below. Study both versions in comparison with the finished poem. On the basis of this evidence write an account of the development of the poem. Try to define the reasons for the changes in text.

(To an Athlete Dying Young: no title on manuscript)

VERSION A.

```
                               your
(1)  The day you won ~~the~~ town the race
                                 through
(2)        We chaired you ~~in~~ the market place,
        ————~~folk~~
(3)  ——————————stood cheering by,                xxxxxxxxxxxxxxx
     And home                                    xxxxxxxxxxxxxxx
(4)  ~~Home~~ we brought you shoulder-high.           xxxxxxxxxxxxxxx
(5)        So——————————————fade   (5a)——————————————betrayed (?)
                ~~feet (?)~~                So set, before its echoes fade,
(6)        ——————~~race,~~ sill of shade,   (6a) ~~Set foot upon~~ the sill of shade
                         low                The fleet foot on
(7)  And hold to the ~~dark~~ lintel up
(8)  The still defended challenge cup.
(9)                                 Wise lad, to steal betimes away
```

* For instructive accounts of methods of creation, in science as well as the arts, see Brewster Ghiselin: *The Creative Process,* Berkeley, Calif. University of California Press, 1952.

(10) From fields where victory will not stay
xxxxxxxxxx xxx

(11) A garland briefer than a girl's A garland briefer than a————

(12) ~~xxxxxxxx~~xxxxx ————————that night has shut

(13) ————see your record cut
that young

(14) And round your early laurelled head

(15) Will throng to gaze the strengthless dead
find unwithered on

(16) And ~~yet unfaded round~~ its curls

(17) ~~The xx~~ The garland briefer than a girl's.

(18) Of runners whom renown outran
~~Or~~

(19) And the name died before the man

VERSION B.

time

(1) The ~~day~~ you won your town the race

(2) We chaired you through the market place;

(3) Man and boy stood cheering by,

(4) And home we brought you shoulder-high.

(5) Today, the road all runners come,

(6) Shoulder-high we bring you home,

(7) And set you at your threshold down,

(8) Townsman of a stiller town.

Well done,

(9) Wise lad, to slip betimes away Smart lad,
glory

(10) From fields where ~~victory~~ will not stay.

(11) ~~And glory for the runner braids~~ And early though the laurel grows
lasts no ~~longer~~ better a

(12) ~~A chaplet briefer than a maid's~~ It withers sooner than ~~the~~ rose.
The man cloudy

(13) ~~He~~ whose eye the night has shut Eyes the shady night has shut
~~Will never~~

(14) ~~Never sees his record cut~~ ~~never see the record cut~~
sounds no worse than

(15) And silence ~~is the same~~ as cheers
~~his~~

(16) After earth has stopped the ears.
~~have~~ ~~swelled,~~

(17) ~~And~~ Now you will not ~~join~~ the throng swell No fear you now should join the throng

stayed spell

(18) Of lads that lived a ~~day~~ too long,

(19) Runners whom renown outran

(20) And the name died before the man.
(21) So set before its echoes fade,
(22) The fleet foot on the sill of shade,
(23) And hold to the low lintel up
(24) The still defended challenge-cup

~~that your~~
(25) And round ~~that~~ early-laurelled head
(26) Will flock to gaze the strengthless dead
(27) And find unwithered on its curls
(28) The garland briefer than a girl's
Eyes the cloudy
(29) ~~Now the eye that~~ night has shut
(30) Will never see the record cut,
(31) And silence sounds no worse than cheers
After
(32) ~~Now that~~ earth has stopped the ears.
(33) Cannot see the record cut
Now you'll never
(34) ~~xxxxxxxxx~~ swell the rout
(35) Of lads that wore their honours out.

To an Athlete Dying Young

The time you won your town the race
We chaired you through the market-place;
Man and boy stood cheering by,
And home we brought you shoulder-high.

Today, the road all runners come,
Shoulder-high we bring you home,
And set you at your threshold down,
Townsman of a stiller town.

Smart lad, to slip betimes away
From fields where glory does not stay
And early though the laurel grows
It withers quicker than the rose.

Eyes the shady night has shut
Cannot see the record cut,
And silence sounds no worse than cheers
After earth has stopped the ears:

Now you will not swell the rout
Of lads that wore their honors out,
Runners whom renown outran
And the name died before the man.

So set, before its echoes fade,
The fleet foot on the sill of shade,
And hold to the low lintel up
The still-defended challenge-cup.

And round that early-laureled head
Will flock to gaze the strengthless dead,
And find unwithered on its curls
The garland briefer than a girl's.

2. Below is a section rejected by Yeats for his "Upon a Dying Lady." Study it carefully and compare it with the sections which he published (p. 435). What grounds can you give for his rejection of this? Are there elements here better developed in the poem as we finally have it?

Although she has turned away
The pretty waxen faces
And hid their silk and laces
For mass was said today
She has not begun denying
Now that she is dying
The pleasures she loved well
The strong milk of her mother
The valor of her brother
Are in her body still
She will not die weeping
May God be with her sleeping.*

3. On page 517 we have quoted a passage from Dorothy Wordsworth's journal in which she describes the incident on which the following poem is presumably based. Note that in the poem Wordsworth makes the speaker of the poem say that he had been wandering alone. What, do you think, led him to do this? What other changes do you observe in Wordsworth's treatment of the material of the poem?

* Quoted in A. Norman Jeffares: *W. B. Yeats: Man and Poet,* New Haven, Conn., Yale University Press, 1949, pp. 166–167.

I Wandered Lonely as a Cloud

William Wordsworth [*1770–1850*]

I wandered lonely as a cloud
That floats on high o'er vales and hills,
When all at once I saw a crowd,
A host of golden daffodils;
Beside the lake, beneath the trees,
Fluttering and dancing in the breeze.

Continuous as the stars that shine
And twinkle on the milky way,
They stretched in never-ending line
Along the margin of a bay:
Ten thousand saw I at a glance,
Tossing their heads in sprightly dance.

The waves beside them danced, but they
Outdid the sparkling waves in glee:—
A poet could not but be gay
In such a jocund company:
I gazed—and gazed—but little thought
What wealth the show to me had brought.

For oft when on my couch I lie
In vacant or in pensive mood,
They flash upon that inward eye
Which is the bliss of solitude,
And then my heart with pleasure fills,
And dances with the daffodils.

Glossary

abstract, abstraction Abstractions are qualities and characteristics isolated as pure ideas. (The word is derived from the Latin *abstractus,* which means literally "drawn away from": thus an abstraction is a quality or idea considered apart from the thing or situation in which it inheres. *Sweetness, whiteness, roughness* are abstract, but *sugar* is concrete: *concrete* is derived from the Latin *concretus* which means "grown together.") The fundamental method of literature is to present a subject concretely—not abstractly. It depends, therefore, rather heavily upon implication rather than upon explicit statement. For instance, a novel or a play tells a particular story of particular people and does not merely give general comments on human nature. It presents individual human beings and presents them in action (p. 34). Poetry, even more than other literary forms, makes use of particular images and incidents for presenting its ideas (pp. 38–39).

alexandrine A line consisting of six feet. See Note on Versification, p. 562.

allegory See **imagery.**

alliteration See Note on Versification, p. 565.

allusion A reference to some event, person, or place of literary or historical significance. For example, Keats in his "Ode to a Nightingale" alludes to Bacchus, to Provence, to an incident related in the Book of Ruth in the Bible, and so on.

ambiguity Multiplicity of meaning. In expository prose, ambiguity is a defect, for what is wanted is one clear, unequivocal meaning. An ambiguous statement is one which is doubtful or obscure. A better term for poetic ambiguity is *richness.* See pp. 249, 258, 259–60.

anapaest A metrical foot consisting of two unaccented syllables followed by an accented syllable. See Note on Versification, p. 562.

anticlimactic, anticlimax Characterized by a flatness and falling off in intensity. See **climax.**

assonance See Note on Versification, p. 565.

atmosphere This term is obviously a metaphor in itself. It refers to the general pervasive feeling which may be said to condition the treatment of the subject of any literary work. It is a mistake to connect atmosphere exclusively with the setting or background, even though the setting usually does contribute heavily to the establishing of the atmosphere of a particular piece. Rhythm and imagery, for instance, may also contribute to the establishing of the atmosphere (pp. 33, 40, 228–31, 237).

attitude The author's way of regarding his materials, especially as it reflects his understanding and interpretation of them. See the Foreword to Section IV, pp. 181–85.

ballad A song that tells a story. (1) Folk ballad (pp. 28, 32, 38). (2) Literary ballad (pp. 28, 50, 52, 69).

ballad stanza See Note on Versification, p. 566.

blank verse See Note on Versification, p. 567.

cacophony Harshness or dissonance. See Note on Versification, p. 564.

caesura The main pause within a line of verse. See p. 139 and Note on Versification, p. 564.

cliché This term is really a metaphor, for in French a *cliché* is a stereotype plate. It is applied to any expression which has lost all freshness and vitality because of continued use—that is, an expression which has become trite (pp. 92, 223–25, 236, 253, 257, 301–02).

climax, climactic The peak of interest or intensity (pp. 44, 356).

closed couplet See Note on Versification, p. 566.

concentration An effect of compactness and intensity. In addition to what has already been said on this topic (pp. 75, 76), it may be pointed out that the concentration characteristic of poetry is a result of its highly organized form. This concentration does not depend on logical succinctness. Rather, it depends on the functional relationships existing among a number of complex factors—rhythm, imagery, theme, and so on. See also pp. 259–60, 527–28.

concrete See **abstract.**

connotation See **denotation.**

consonance See Note on Versification, p. 565.

convention, conventional Techniques and modes of treatment that are accepted by common agreement. For example, there are the conventions of the *pastoral* (which see) or the conventions that govern verse. But though conventions are necessary, the term *conventional* is frequently used in an adverse sense to indicate a merely dead and mechanical reliance upon past models. See **form** and pp. 222, 253, 256, 516.

couplet Two consecutive lines of verse rhyming together. See Note on Versification, p. 566.

dactyl A metrical foot consisting of an accented syllable followed by two unaccented syllables. See Note on Versification, p. 562.

denotation The denotation of a word is its specific signification. For instance, the denotation of the word *hound* is "one of a class of carnivorous mammals (*Canis familiaris*) of the family *Canidae,* and so on." But the word also has a large number of **connotations,** or implied meanings and associations. The connotations of a word may vary considerably from person to person and from context to context. For instance, in the discussion of the poem "The Three Ravens" (pp. 44–45), it is pointed out that the hounds symbolize fidelity. That is, certain connotations of the word *hound* are emphasized in the poem. But the word also has other connotations which, in another context, might appear. For instance, the word *hound* can be used as an insult. (For another discussion of connotation, see p. 106.)

diction Diction is simply the choice of words in poetry or in any other form of discourse. Critics sometimes refer to **poetic diction** as if certain words were especially poetic without regard to context. But the choice of words in any given poem must be determined by the needs of that specific case in terms of the whole context (pp. 92, 106, 143, 188, 194).

dimeter A line consisting of two feet. See Note on Versification, p. 562.

double rhyme See Note on Versification, pp. 565–66.

drama, dramatic In earlier discussions frequent reference has been made to the means by which a poet may dramatize his theme. This term is, of course, metaphorical. It must not be taken to mean that a given poem represents in any detail the structure and circumstance of a play except in the sense which has been discussed (pp. 20, 84–86, 355–61). But the fact that a drama presents its materials concretely and through action justifies the use of the term, for poetry tends to present its themes in the same manner, not abstractly. See **abstract.**

elegy The term is used loosely for any poem of subjective and meditative nature, but more specially for a poem of grief, such as "Lycidas" (p. 417).

end-stopped lines See Note on Versification, p. 564.

enjambment See **run-on** and **end-stop** under Note on Versification, p. 564.

epic A long narrative poem dealing with persons of heroic proportions and actions of great significance. The general type includes poems as different as Homer's *Iliad,* Spenser's *Faerie Queene,* and Milton's *Paradise Lost.* The *mock epic,* or the *mock heroic* poem, adopts for ironical or comic purposes the manner of the true epic. It presents trivial materials in a grandiose style. See "A City Shower," p. 200, or "The Maimed Debauchee," p. 205.

euphony Agreeableness of sound. See Note on Versification, p. 564.

exposition The process of giving the information necessary for the understanding of an action (p. 32).

feminine ending See Note on Versification, p. 562.

feminine rhyme See Note on Versification, p. 565.

figurative language See **image.**

focus This term is metaphorical. Just as a burning glass concentrates and unifies the rays of the sun, so a poet may, by various means, concentrate and unify various elements of a poem. This concentration may be accomplished in many different ways. For instance, the farewell spoken by the youngest brother in "The Wife of Usher's Well" may be said to provide a focus for the poem (pp. 40–41).

foot See Note on Versification, p. 562.

form This term is used in various senses. Usually when people use the term they mean **metrical form** or **stanza form** (see Note on Versification, pp. 566–67). But since metrical form, or stanza form, describes an organization of the rhythm of a poem, and since rhythm is only one element contributing to the poetic effect, it is obvious that the consideration of the form of a poem must, finally, involve the discussion of the organization of other elements in relation to the total effect. In "Lord Randal," for example, both the sequence of questions and answers and the use of refrain build toward the effect in the last stanza (pp. 47–49). In the same way, the use of imagery contributes to the forming of a poem. For example, one may consider the functional interrelations among the images in "The Definition of Love" (pp. 296–99) or in "After Great Pain" (pp. 328–29). In brief, the form of a poem is the organization of the material (rhythm, imagery, idea, etc.) for the creation of the total effect. Though the poet must finally work out a form for each particular poem, this does not mean that he may not make use of elements of form handed down from other poets—elements such as metrical patterns, symbols, and ways of relating images to a theme, etc. Such elements, when their use has become fixed and recognized, are called **conventions.** For instance, the sonnet in respect to its stanza pattern is a conventional form; or the pastoral elegy, such as "Lycidas," is a conventional form in regard to the "fictions" and symbols it employs in treating the subject of bereavement. A poet may properly make use of conventional patterns of all sorts, but, in so far as he is successful, he must relate the conventional elements to the total form of the individual poem. But the term *conventional* is sometimes used in an adverse sense to indicate that the poet has merely imitated his models and has failed to adapt the conventional elements to the general form of the individual poem (pp. 223–25, 253).

free verse See pp. 172–80 and Note on Versification, p. 568.

heptameter A line consisting of seven feet. See Note on Versification, p. 562.

heroic couplet Two consecutive lines of iambic pentameter rhyming together. See Note on Versification, p. 566.

hexameter A line consisting of six feet. See Note on Versification, p. 562.

iamb A metrical foot consisting of an unaccented syllable followed by an accented syllable. See Note on Versification, p. 562.

image, imagery The representation in poetry of any sense experience is called imagery. Imagery does not consist merely of "mental pictures," but may make an appeal to any of the senses. Poetry characteristically appeals continually to the senses; this is another way of saying that poetry is concrete. But frequently the poet does not use imagery merely in an obviously descriptive fashion; the poet characteristically makes his statements and conveys his ideas through comparisons, that is, through what is called **figurative language.** The most common types of figurative language are **simile** and **metaphor.** The first is usually defined as a stated comparison (generally announced by *like* or *as*); the second as an implied comparison (in which the two things compared are identified with each other). The following comparison is a simile:

This city now doth like a garment wear
The beauty of the morning. . . .

The following comparison is a metaphor:

So the soul, that drop, that ray
Of the clear fountain of eternal day. . . .

We must emphasize, however, that comparison is merely the *method* of metaphor; the function is to arrive at, and communicate, insight (pp. 40–41, 77–78, 83–85, 89–90, 92–93, 268–79, 286–87, 290–93). The particular ways in which imagery functions are too numerous to be dealt with summarily here; indeed, every poem involves imagery in some respect, and in this book two sections (Section II and Section V) have been devoted to studying a number of special instances. Even in so brief a statement as this, however, one fact should be insisted upon: *The function of imagery in poetry is never that of mere illustration.* Closely related to the metaphorical process is the process by which a poet creates or makes use of a **symbol.** The symbol may be regarded as a metaphor from which the first term has been omitted. For example,

Queen rose of the rosebud garden of girls

is a metaphor, but if the poet simply refers to the rose in order to suggest the qualities of love which he is treating, and does not indicate the metaphorical framework, he has turned the rose into a symbol. We use the term *metaphor* when we are emphasizing the metaphorical transfer: for example, the girl is a rose—that is, the qualities of the rose are transferred to the girl. We use the term *symbol* when we are thinking of the object or action as standing for something else. Symbols, then, are "signs" pointing to meanings. Certain symbols are conventional, that is, arbitrary, and we agree upon what they are to signify. For instance, the cross is by convention a symbol of the Christian religion and the flag is the symbol of a nation. The important use of symbol which the poet makes, however, is not a conventional one: he must frequently create his own symbols (pp. 17–18, 102, 404–09). The poems toward the end of Section II will indicate instances of objects which have been given symbolic force.

Allegory, also, is a development of the metaphorical process. Allegory is often defined as an extended metaphor, and, in regard to the matter of structure, this is an adequate description, for an allegory, strictly speaking, is a narrative in which the objects and persons are equated with meanings lying outside the narrative itself. For example, *The Pilgrim's Progress* is on the surface the story of the journey which one of the characters, Christian, makes from his home to the Heavenly City; but, as the name implies, Christian really stands for any Christian man, and the various adventures which befall him stand for the perils and temptation which beset any Christian man in his progress through life. But most allegories are much less obvious than this. Allegory is bad when the system of equivalents used seems to be mechanical and arbitrary, or when it seems to be confused (pp. 301–03).

Allegorical personages are frequently **personifications**, that is, abstract qualities treated in the narrative as though they were real persons. For instance, the Giant Despair in *The Pilgrim's Progress* is a personification. But the device of personification is not confined to formal allegory. "Elegy Written in a Country Churchyard" (p. 350) is not an allegory, yet in such a line as the following it employs personification:

Let not Ambition mock their useful toil. . . .

intensity It has been said previously (pp. 75–76) that intensity is a result of the highly organized form of poetry. This implies, not simply a loose emotionalism or a preoccupation with thrilling subject matter (pp. 12–14, 72–74), but a meaningful relationship among all the factors involved in a poem.

internal rhyme Rhyme occurring within a line unit. See Note on Versification, p. 566.

irony An ironical statement indicates a meaning contrary to the one it professes to give; an ironical event or situation is one in which there is a contrast between expectation and fulfillment or desert and reward. In the irony of both statement and event there is an element of contrast. Either form of irony, or both, may appear in a poem. For instance, the irony of situation appears in "Johnie Armstrong" (p. 33). But the irony of statement, and of tone and attitude, are more important for poetry. The successful management of ironical effects is one of the most difficult problems of a poet. In actual speech, gesture, tone of voice, and expression all serve to indicate an ironical intention, but poetry must indicate an ironical interpretation in other ways (pp. 181, 184).

There are many shades of irony and many functions which irony may perform. Certainly, the term is not to be limited to an obvious and heavy sarcasm. For instance, one may observe the different uses of irony in "Portrait" (pp. 185–87), "Channel Firing" (pp. 191–93), "A Litany" (pp. 251–55), "Ode to a Nightingale" (pp. 426–30), and "The Love Song of J. Alfred Prufrock" (pp. 390–99).

Obviously, irony, along with **understatement** (in which there is a discrepancy, great or small, between what is *actually* said and what *might* be said), is a device of indirection. That is, the poet does not present his meaning abstractly and explicitly, but depends on the reader's capacity to develop implications imaginatively.

lyric Originally a poem to be sung, but now much more loosely applied to any short poem of which the verse seems to be especially musical. In a more special sense, the term is applied to poems having a marked subjective element, for instance, "Tears, Idle Tears," by Tennyson (p. 317), "In Tenebris, I," by Hardy (p. 168), or "Rose Aylmer," by Landor (p. 141).

metaphor See **image.**

meter See Note on Versification, p. 562.

mock epic, mock heroic See **epic.**

monometer A line consisting of one foot. See Note on Versification, p. 562.

objective See **subjective.**

octave See Note on Versification, p. 567.

ode A rather extended poem, usually complicated in metrical and stanzaic form, dealing with a serious theme. Examples are Shelley's "Ode to the West Wind" (p. 115) and Keats's "Ode to a Nightingale" (p. 424).

onomatopoeia See Note on Versification, p. 565.

ottava rima See Note on Versification, p. 567.

paradox A statement which seems on the surface contradictory, but which involves an element of truth. Since there is an element of contrast between the form of the statement and its real implications, paradox is closely related to **irony** (pp. 296–99, 427–30).

pastoral A term loosely used in application to any sympathetic literary treatment of simple rural life. In this sense, "Lycidas" (p. 417) is a pastoral poem. But more specially used, the term applies to a poetry which is based on the conventions descended from the classic poetry of shepherd life. The persons involved are presented as shepherds, although, as in "Lycidas," they may be poets, scholars, and churchmen; and the subjects treated, such as ecclesiastical abuses (as in "Lycidas") may have no reference to rural life.

pentameter A line consisting of five feet. See Note on Versification, p. 562.

personification Representation of an idea or thing as a person. See **imagery.**

Petrarchan convention This convention stems from the love sonnets of the Italian poet Petrarch. His sonnets represented his mistress as more than humanly beautiful, but cold and disdainful, and himself as completely abased before her. The imagery is frequently elaborate and far-fetched (pp. 253, 256).

poetic diction See **diction.**

quantitative variation See pp. 148–49 and Note on Versification, p. 563.

quantity See Note on Versification, p. 563.

quatrain A stanza consisting of four lines. See Note on Versification, p. 566.

realism, realistic The term is used throughout this book with reference to the presentation of ordinary, easily observable details, which give an impression of fidelity to the facts of ordinary life (pp. 39, 200, 245–46). It is to be contrasted with *romantic,* which implies the remote, the exotic, the uncontrolled, and the exaggerated. The special senses in which such terms as *realistic, romantic,* and *classic* are used by many critics do not appear in this book.

rhetorical variation See pp. 136–39 and Note on Versification, p. 564.

rhyme, rhyme scheme See Note on Versification, pp. 565–66.

rhythmical movement A movement with recurrent beat or stress. See Note on Versification, p. 562.

rime royal See Note on Versification, p. 567.

romantic, romanticism See **realism.**

run-on line See Note on Versification, p. 564.

sentimentality Emotional response in excess of the occasion; emotional response not prepared for nor justified by the poem in question (pp. 223–25, 236–38, 247, 253, 296–99, 301–03). See also **sincerity.**

sestet See Note on Versification, p. 567.

simile See **imagery.**

sincerity This term is often used in two senses which are not clearly discriminated. The first sense refers to the poet's attitude, in his private life, toward a subject which he treats in a poem. This sense *may* have no reference to the critical judgment to be passed on a poem, for a poet may be thoroughly sincere in this personal sense and yet produce a very bad and sentimental piece of work (pp. 223–25, 240–42, 301–03). The second sense in which the term is used really refers to the degree of success which the poet has achieved in integrating the various elements of a poem. When one says that a poem is "sincere," one is actually saying, consciously or unconsciously, that it does not overreach itself, that it is not sentimental. Such a judgment is irrelevant to any biographical information concerning the poet.

slant rhyme See Note on Versification, p. 566.

sonnet See Note on Versification, p. 567.

Spenserian stanza See Note on Versification, p. 567.

spondee In classical metrics, a foot of two accented syllables. See Note on Versification, p. 563.

stanza See Note on Versification, p. 566.

stock response The general uncritical response made on conventional or habitual grounds to a situation, subject, phrase, or word. Advertisers frequently attempt to appeal to stock responses by arbitrarily associating a product with patriotism, mother love, and so on. The good poet tries to provide in his work the grounds for the responses he seeks from his audience, but the bad poet, like the writer of advertising copy, merely appeals to the already established attitudes, however crude or general they may be (pp. 223–25, 230–31).

structure In its fullest sense the structure of a poem may be said to be synonymous with the form, but in practice there is a tendency to use the term with special reference to the arrangement of, and the relationships among, episodes, statements, scenes, and details of action (p. 41), as contrasted with the arrangement of words, for which the term *style* is usually employed.

style This term is usually used with reference to the poet's manner of choosing, ordering, and arranging his words. But when one asks on what grounds certain words are chosen and ordered, one is raising, of course, the whole problem of form. Style, in its larger sense, is essentially the same thing as form (see **form** and **structure**).

subjective The ordinary terms used to denote the person who perceives or experiences a thing and the thing perceived or experienced, are *subject* and *object*. Of course, there is a sense in which all poetry is subjective, that is, it represents the response of a person, the poet, to an object or to a body of objects (p. 84). But we shall use the term at another level: we shall apply it to the "speaker" in the poem and his manner of presentation, and here we shall find widely differing degrees of subjectivity. One may properly say, for example, that the "Ode to a Nightingale" (p. 424) or "The Love Song of J. Alfred Prufrock" (p. 386) is highly subjective, and that "The Main-Deep" (p. 82) or "Pear Tree" (p. 86) is objective.

substitution See Note on Versification, p. 563.

symbol See **image.**

terza rima See Note on Versification, p. 566.

tetrameter A line consisting of four feet. See Note on Versification, p. 562.

thematic development The structure of a poem as related to the presentation of the theme.

theme The basic idea or attitude presented in a poem (pp. 8–12, 34, 46, 340–43).

tone See pp. 63, 91, 95, 105–07, 181–85.

trimeter A line consisting of three feet. See Note on Versification, p. 562.

triple rhyme See Note on Versification, p. 566.

trochee A metrical foot consisting of an accented syllable followed by an unaccented syllable. See Note on Versification, p. 562.

understatement Saying less than might be expected. See **irony.**

unity The unity of a poem, like that of any work of art, is a unity of final meaning. This does not imply simplicity (in the sense of poverty of idea or emotion) or merely logical congruity or sequence. Poetry that is *merely* simple (or which strikes the sensitive reader as "simplified") achieves its effect by eliminating all elements that might prove discordant; but all really good poetry attains its unity by establishing meaningful relationships among its apparently discordant elements. This is why critics sometimes say of a successful poem that it gives a sense of revelation, or gives a new insight. For—far from trimming our view of a subject down to a single, neatly ordered category—the poet ties together the items of ordinarily disordered experience into a new, and perhaps unsuspected, pattern. For example, there is the sort of imaginative unity which is analyzed in Coleridge's discussion of Shakespeare's *Venus and Adonis* (pp. 270–72). Poems like "Lycidas" (p. 417), "Among School Children" (p. 335), "Frescoes for Mr. Rockefeller's City" (p. 467), and "Ode to a Nightingale" (p. 424) offer examples of the unification of apparently discordant materials. Moreover, many poems, like some of the folk ballads or like "The Solitary Reaper" (p. 280), which are praised for their "fine simplicity," reveal, on examination, a very complicated structure underlying the effect of simplicity which they achieve. A student should be careful to make the distinction between poems that are *apparently* simple because the poet has unified his materials, and poems that are simple because the poet has avoided using all recalcitrant or difficult materials.

variation See Note on Versification, p. 564.

vers de société Light verse, usually occasional and complimentary, which deals in a witty and polished fashion with subjects that, on the surface at least, are not very serious (see p. 249). But there is no sharp line of demarcation between *vers de société* and serious poetry. For instance, "To His Coy Mistress" by Andrew Marvell (p. 308) opens with the tone and manner of *vers de société.*

verse This term is sometimes used to mean a single line of a poem. But the more usual and more important meaning of the term, and the one which will be discussed here, is that form of literary composition in which the rhythms are regularized and systematized. See Note on Versification.

verse texture The general relationship among the sounds in verse, of which euphony and cacophony are aspects. See Note on Versification, p. 564.

weak rhyme See Note on Versification, p. 566.

NOTE ON VERSIFICATION

All language, as has been pointed out, has the quality of rhythm (pp. 120–22). It has also been pointed out that there are varying degrees of formalization of rhythm and that between the clear extremes of ordinary prose and strict verse there are many intermediary types (pp. 120–21).

Meter, in English verse, is the systematization of rhythm in so far as this systematization is determined by the relationships between **accented,** or stressed, and **unaccented,** or unstressed, syllables. (This relationship between accented and unaccented syllables is a fundamental factor, but not the only factor, in determining the **rhythm.** Other factors involved—pause and emphasis conditioned by the length of syllables, consideration of sense, rhyme, and so on, which will be treated below—contribute to the total rhythmical effect.) The following set of terms is conventionally accepted to describe meter:

foot The metrical unit, a combination of one accented and one or more unaccented syllables. The following types of feet will describe most metrical situations which occur in English verse:

iamb An unaccented followed by an accented syllable (ăvóid).
anapaest Two unaccented syllables followed by an accented syllable (ĭntĕrvéne).
trochee One accented followed by one unaccented syllable (ónlў).
dactyl One accented syllable followed by two unaccented syllables (háppĭlў).

The **line** of verse is composed of one or more feet. The following names are used to denominate various line lengths:

monometer One foot
dimeter Two feet
trimeter Three feet
tetrameter Four feet
pentameter Five feet
hexameter Six feet (or **alexandrine**)
heptameter Seven feet

(Since a line is really a unit of attention, lines composed of more than six feet tend to break up into smaller units. Thus a heptameter line tends to break up into a tetrameter and a trimeter line.) There are two items involved in the metrical description of a line: the kind of foot and the number of feet. Thus, a line containing five iambic feet would be described as *iambic pentameter.* A line that ends with an extra unaccented syllable is said to have a *feminine ending.* (See pp. 131, 133.)

Even in a single poem a poet does not necessarily adhere to a single type of foot. For various reasons, he may make a **substitution** of one type of foot for another (p. 163). For instance, in the opening of the following line a trochaic foot has been substituted for an iambic foot:

Crowned from | some sin | gle herb | or tree

Thus far in discussing a scheme for indicating the scansion of verse, all accented syllables have been assumed to have equal value; and in an abstract schematic sense this is true. But obviously, in the rhythm as one actually experiences it in a particular line, accented syllables may be of very unequal emphasis (pp. 136–37). By the same token, unaccented syllables are not on the level as an abstract scheme would seem to indicate (p. 129*n*). Sometimes a syllable which, according to the abstract metrical pattern, would be unaccented, receives, because of rhetorical considerations, what appears to be an additional accent in its own right. For instance, consider the first foot of the following line:

Ah, what | avails | the scep | tred race (p. 141)

The syllable *Ah* may be said to receive a **secondary accent** (indicated as above). In considering the relationship between the two syllables of such a foot as *Ah, what,* some metrists describe the situation by saying that there is a **hovering effect,** or a **hovering accent** (indicated as follows: *Ah, what*). In this connection, see also p. 129*n*. A similar situation is created when by substitution, or by the use of an **imperfect foot** (a foot from which the unaccented syllable or syllables are missing,* indicated thus ∧), two regularly accented feet are thrown into juxtaposition (pp. 130, 160*n*). When a secondary accent occurs, or when two regular accents are forced together, there is said to exist a **spondaic movement.** (This term is derived from one of the feet in classical metrics, the **spondee,** which is composed of long syllables, for classical verse is founded on **quantity.** But the term is frequently used with reference to English verse, which is founded on accent, to describe any situation in which two accents appear in succession—either when the two accents are not in the same foot, or when one is a secondary accent.)

Though English metrics is founded on accent, the factor of quantity has an importance in determining the final rhythmical result of

* Such a defect may be **compensated** for in either or both of two ways. First, by the addition of an unaccented syllable elsewhere in the line, or second, by a pause before the accented syllable. As an example of the first:

Upon | the supreme | theme | of Art | and Song (p. 164)

[cont. on p. 564]

a piece of verse as actually experienced. But quantity never appears in systematic form; it works, merely, to condition and modify the rhythmical pattern defined by accent (pp. 148–49).

Another factor which influences the total rhythmical effect of a particular line is the location of pauses defined by sense units. Although the line may be abstractly considered as a metrical unit, it is obvious that the sense unit does not always coincide with the line unit. In practice, sense divisions—phrase, clause, sentence—often terminate within the line; and conversely, the end of a line unit may divide a sense unit. The pauses within the line, their number and their emphasis, are extremely important in determining the tempo of the rhythm. The main pause is called the **caesura,** but obviously there may be other pauses, which may be called **secondary pauses.** Variety, from line to line, in the location of the caesura and of secondary pauses is extremely important in versification. But mere variety is not the only consideration, for in good verse there is usually a connection between the handling of pauses and the rhetorical (and other) devices employed in the poem (pp. 136–39, 159). Just as sense units may divide a line, so the end of a line, conversely, may divide sense units. This interplay between sense units and metrical units becomes extremely important when considered, not in relation to a single line, but in relation to a group of lines. When the end of the line does not coincide with a normal speech pause of any kind, it is called **run-on;** it is an example of **enjambment.** When a line end does coincide with a normal pause, the line is said to be **end-stopped.**

But sound as well as sense may condition the rhythm of verse. For example, the presence of certain groups of consonants may create a **forced pause.** Such combinations, which cause a sense of strain in pronunciation and a slowing of rhythmical tempo, are said to be **cacophonous** (p. 149). Conversely, consonant combinations easily pronounced give a sense of ease and tend to speed up the rhythmical tempo. Such combinations are said to be **euphonious.** Euphonious effects are pleasant, but euphony in itself is never a primary objective of any good poem—that is, poetry, even lyrical poetry, is not *merely* "verbal music."

Of the second:

$_\wedge$Spéech | ăftĕr lóng | sílĕnce; | $_\wedge$ít | ĭs ríght (p. 164)

In the first instance, there is **compensation** for the imperfect foot *theme* by the preceding anapaest, *the supreme;* in the second, there is compensation for the imperfect foot *it* by the caesural pause. (The second example also shows how an imperfect foot, *Speech,* may be compensated for by a following anapaest, *after long.*)

Thus far we have spoken of relationships among consonants. The term euphony in its largest sense is used also to designate agreeable relationships among vowel sounds. Obviously, some vowels are closely related to each other; others are much more distantly related. For example, the vowel sounds *oh* and *ah* are formed far back in the voice chamber; the vowel sounds *ee* and *ay* far to the front. Obviously, a line dominated by closely related vowels gives—provided other factors support this effect—a sense of ease and fluency. Some lines may achieve a sense of vitality by the fact that the vowels in them are not closely related—involve shifts in position, which may be either violent or modulated. The combinations in this matter are, of course, infinite. One may be tempted to associate certain effects with certain vowels—an effect of heaviness with the sonority of the long back vowel sounds (*oh, ah, aw, oo*)—but this element is effective only in so far as it operates in conjunction with other factors.

Certain words have been developed, as a matter of fact, in imitation of the sounds which they designate. Words like *hiss* and *bang* are called **onomatopoeic** words. But the relation of sound to sense, in onomatopoeia, and the relation of mood to specific vowel sounds, are not fundamental factors in poetic effects (pp. 148–51).

Euphony, like cacophony, is to be considered in its functional relation to the total effect of a poem. This general relationship among the sounds in verse, of which cacophony, euphony, and onomatopoeia are aspects, is sometimes called **verse texture.** Other aspects of this relationship are **assonance, consonance,** and **alliteration.** Assonance may be defined as identity of vowel sounds, as in the words *scream* and *beach;* consonance as the identity of the pattern of consonants, as in the words *leaves* and *lives;* alliteration as the repetition of consonants, particularly initial consonants, as in the words *lovely* and *lullaby.* But assonance, consonance, and alliteration may also be considered as forms of **rhyme** because they involve degrees of identity of sound combinations. The term *rhyme,* however, is ordinarily used in the sense of **end rhyme,** which is the identity in the rhyming words of the accented *vowels* and of all consonants and vowels following. (This is sometimes called *rime suffisante* in distinction from *rime riche,* or identical rhyme, in which there is identity of the accented *syllables* of the words rhymed. For instance: *incline* and *decline.*) The forms of end rhyme may be classified as follows:

masculine rhyme The rhymed syllables are the last syllables of the words in question, as in *surmount* and *discount.*

feminine rhyme The rhymed syllables are followed by identical unaccented syllables, as in *delightful* and *frightful.* When only one unaccented syllable occurs after the accented syllable, there is an instance of **double rhyme,** as in the above example. When two unaccented syllables, identical in the rhymed words, follow the accented syllable, there is an instance of **triple rhyme.** For example: *delightfully* and *frightfully.*

weak rhyme The rhymed syllables are unstressed or only lightly stressed. For examples, see "In Distrust of Merits," p. 508.

internal rhyme Rhyme occurring within a line unit.

In addition to the above forms of rhyme there are approximate rhymes, sometimes called **slant rhymes.** For instance, *rover* and *lover,* or *steel* and *chill.* Such rhymes are not necessarily indications of a poet's carelessness, but may be used for various special effects. When the student discovers examples of slant rhyme, he should try to determine what the effect would have been with the emphasis of full rhyme. Many rhymes that now are apparently slant rhymes were, in the past, full rhymes; therefore, a student should try to determine the pronunciation used by the poet before passing judgment on a poem of the past.

Although there is a pleasure in rhyme itself, and rhyme may serve as a decoration to verse, the fundamental function of rhyme is that of a binder. It is this function which makes rhyme so important as a device of emphasis and as a means of defining a pattern of lines, or a **stanza.** Indeed, most stanzas involve not only a fixed pattern of lines, but also a pattern of rhymes, or a **rhyme scheme.** An unrhymed stanza is to be defined by the prevailing type of foot, the number of feet in each line, and the number of lines. That is, a poem might be written in iambic tetrameter quatrains. The definition of a rhymed stanza would add to such items the description of the rhyme scheme. For instance, the rhyme scheme of the envelope quatrain, in which the first and fourth lines and the second and third lines rhyme, would be described as follows: *abba.* The most ordinary stanzas and line patterns are these:

couplet (1) **tetrameter** couplet, sometimes called the octosyllabic couplet: iambic tetrameter, *aa.* (2) **heroic** couplet: iambic pentameter, *aa.* (A couplet is **closed** when the sense is completed within its compass.)

terza rima iambic pentameter **tercets** in **linked** rhyme: *aba-bcb-cdc,* etc.

quatrain (1) **ballad measure:** iambic, first and third lines tetrameter, second and fourth lines trimeter, with second and fourth lines rhyming. (This may be indicated as follows: iambic, 4,3,4,3, *xaxa.*) A very common variant of this pattern rhymes *abab.* (2) **envelope,** or **"In Memoriam"** quatrain: iambic tetrameter, *abba.*

(3) **"Rubaiyat"** quatrain: iambic pentameter, *aaxa.* (4) Several other types of quatrains are commonly used but have no specific names.

rime royal iambic pentameter, *ababbcc.*

ottava rima iambic pentameter, *abababcc.*

Spenserian stanza iambic pentameter, *ababbcbcc.* The last line is an alexandrine.

sonnet An iambic pentameter poem in fourteen lines. There are two general types: (1) **Italian** sonnet: iambic pentameter, *abbaabbacdecde.* The first eight lines, in which the general theme of the sonnet is usually presented, is called the **octave.** The last six lines, in which the poet presents the conclusion he has drawn from the theme, is called the **sestet.** Common variants on the rhyme scheme of the sestet are *cdeedc, cdedce.* (2) **Shakespearean** sonnet: iambic pentameter, *ababcdcdefefgg.* In its typical form this sonnet presents and develops its theme in the three quatrains, and states a conclusion in the couplet. But there are many variations of this method of handling the idea. For instance, the first two quatrains may be used as the octave of the Italian sonnet is used and the last quatrain and couplet as the sestet. (3) Irregular sonnets: in addition to various slight departures from the strict rhyme scheme of the Italian and Shakespearean sonnet, there occur rhyme schemes which are highly irregular.

Although **blank verse** is not a form of stanza it may be considered here. Blank verse is unrhymed iambic pentameter not broken into formal units. This is not to say that a poem written in blank verse (or for that matter, in other verse forms not employing the stanza) may not be broken up into **verse paragraphs,** which may be defined as large rhetorical units. "Lycidas" (p. 417) is divided into verse paragraphs.

The definitions given above present various elements of **versification** in an abstract and schematic form. In studying such definitions one should realize that they are merely terms conventionally accepted to describe certain verbal situations which occur in poetry and are not to be taken as "laws" for the making of poetry. When they are applied to the criticism of particular poems, it should be remembered that the degree of excellence achieved by any poet in his management of such technical factors is to be determined by answering the following question: *How has he adapted these technical factors to the other elements in the poem?*

We have given above in schematic form the conventions which apply to most modern English verse, a verse which is based on the patterned relationship between the number of syllables in a line and the disposition of accents. But there are two general types of verse represented in this book to which these conventions do not apply.

The first is **free verse.** Free verse, as the term implies, does not conform to any fixed pattern. This is not to say that none of the individual metrical situations previously discussed here may not appear, incidentally, in a free verse poem. But it is to say that such situations occur only incidentally. For a fuller discussion, see pp. 172–80.

The second of the two types of verse to which the conventions we have sketched earlier do not apply is the **old native meter,*** sometimes called **strong-stress meter.** This is a pattern derived originally from the Old English four-beat alliterative verse (pp. 154–55). In the modern survivals of this verse, the alliteration may or may not appear, but the verse is still usually characterized by four heavily accented syllables, and the line is often broken between the second and third accents by an emphatic caesura. For example:

> Sing a song of | six pence, || pocketful of | rye
> Four and twenty | blackbirds || baked within a | pie

In view of the amount of stress given to the first syllable of *twenty* and to the syllable *birds* (perhaps also to the second syllable of *within*), it might be more accurate to use secondary accents and scan the line as follows:

> Four and twenty | blackbirds || baked within a | pie

Observe that the feet in this line have as many as four syllables and as few as one. Indeed the foot used in this kind of verse has no fixed number of unaccented syllables to the foot. In the line just scanned, the foot *pie* has not even one unaccented syllable.

It must be conceded that some verse that reflects the old native meter can be scanned in terms of iambs and anapaests. For example, though the following lines from William Morris's poem "Love Is Enough" clearly reflect the old native meter, they can be described readily enough in terms of normal English meter:

> If thus | the king's glo | ry, || our gain | and salva | tion
> Must go | down the wind || amid gloom | and despair | ing.

But it would be hard to scan "Rocky Acres" (p. 103) in this fashion without a good deal of forcing. True, we can scan line 4 in fairly regular fashion:

> But voice | of cold | water | that runs | here and there

* See Jakob Schipper, *A History of English Versification,* Oxford, England: Oxford University Press, pp. 85–125.

But this scansion is awkward in that it gives us five rather than the four beats that are so prominent in most of the lines. And if we scan the line to give four beats, thus,

˘ / ˘ // / ˘ ˘ / // ˘ /
But voice | of cold wa | ter that runs | here and there

the heavy secondary accents in the second and fourth feet make these feet seem awkwardly forced, as though we were denying the actual spirit of the movement. But even so, line 4 is a fairly "regular" line. How would we scan the difficult line 23?

˘ / ˘ ˘ / ˘ / ˘ ˘ ˘ /
The first | land that rose | from Cha | os and the Flood

(We would need, by the way, a special name for the fourth foot: a foot consisting of three unaccented and one accented syllable is called a *paeon*.) Lines 1, 2 and 5 set problems even more difficult. On the whole, it would seem best to abandon the conventions of normal English verse and to scan "Rocky Acres" in terms of a pattern of four strong beats, with feet of a varying number of weak syllables.

Other poems in this text that reflect more or less strongly the old native meter are Hopkins's "The Windhover" (p. 487), Auden's "O Where Are You Going?" (p. 483), Empson's "Just a Smack at Auden" (p. 483), Auden's "Doom Is Dark" (p. 316), Eliot's "Journey of the Magi" * (p. 485), and parts of his *Waste Land* (p. 448). In some of the modern developments of the old native meter, there may be more or fewer than four beats to the line. Some of the poems just mentioned are rather easily scanned in terms of the conventional metrical pattern. Indeed in nearly all the recent developments of the old native meter, the poet has not used it for its own sake but has played it off against the conventional meter so as to gain a special tension and a special effect. As Monroe Beardsley and W. K. Wimsatt, Jr., put it:

> A wise and shifty modern poet [T. S. Eliot], always in search of rhythmical invention, writes a stanza containing in the middle such a line as:
>
> Her hair over her arms and her arms full of flowers,
>
> and at the end:
>
> Sometimes these cogitations still amaze
> The troubled midnight and the noon's repose.
>
> This is playing in and out of the metrical inheritance. Part V of *The Waste Land* begins:
>
> After the torchlight red on sweaty faces
> After the frosty silence in the gardens
> After the agony in stony places. . . .

* For this poem and the metric of Eliot's later poetry in general, see Helen Gardner, *The Art of T. S. Eliot,* London, 1949, pp. 19–35.

Coming after four parts of a poem written largely in strong-stress meter, these lines, with their marked swinging parallel of construction, will most likely be read at a fast walk as strong-stress meter, four stresses to the first, three each to the second and the third. But each is also a perfectly accurate pentameter line, each complicated in the same two traditional ways, the inverted beginning and the hypermetric ending. ("Whether 'tis nobler in the mind to suffer . . .")

It is probably not until about the time of Mr. Eliot and his friends that the free and subtle moving in and out and coalescing of strong-stress and syllable-stress meters in the same poem, the same stanza, begins to appear with any frequency. This is something remarkable in the history of metrics. But the understanding of it depends precisely upon the recognition of the few homely and sound, traditional and objective, principles of prosody. . . . Without recognition of the two distinct principles of strong-stress and of syllable-stress meter, it seems doubtful if anything at all precise or technical can be said about Mr. Eliot's peculiar rhythms and tensions.*

* PMLA, LXXIV (December, 1959), p. 598.

Index of Authors and Titles

[*Names of authors are in capital letters*]